T0358538

Routledge Revivals

The Primary Sector in Economic Development

It is a major problem for less developed countries to make their primary sectors sufficiently profitable in order to be able to build up their manufacturing and service sectors. This edited collection, first published in 1985, examines the nature of the primary sector and its role in economic development. Chapters consider problems of stagnation and income distribution in such countries as Chile and Brazil; trade in national primary products and exports in Africa and the Middle East; and reform and policies of development in countries such as Peru. An interesting volume with an international scope, this title will be of value to economics students with a particular interest in the role of the primary sector in developing economies.

The Primary Sector in Economic Development

Proceedings of the Seventh Arne Ryde
Symposium, Frostavallen, August 29-30 1983

Edited by
Mats Lundahl

Routledge
Taylor & Francis Group

First published in 1985
by Croom Helm Ltd

This edition first published in 2015 by Routledge
2 Park Square, Milton Park, Abingdon, Oxon, OX14 4RN
and by Routledge
711 Third Avenue, New York, NY 10017

Routledge is an imprint of the Taylor & Francis Group, an informa business

© 1985 Mats Lundahl

Publisher's Note
The publisher has gone to great lengths to ensure the quality of this reprint but
points out that some imperfections in the original copies may be apparent.

Disclaimer
The publisher has made every effort to trace copyright holders and welcomes
correspondence from those they have been unable to contact.

ISBN 13: 978-1-138-81887-3 (hbk)
ISBN 13: 978-1-315-74493-3 (ebk)

THE PRIMARY SECTOR IN ECONOMIC DEVELOPMENT

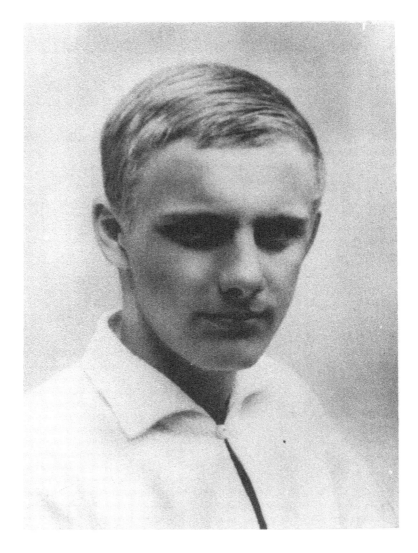

ARNE RYDE
8 DECEMBER 1944 — 1 APRIL 1968

THE ARNE RYDE FOUNDATION

Arne Ryde was an exceptionally promising young student on the doctorate programme at the Department of Economics at the University of Lund. He died after an automobile accident in 1968 when only 23 years old. In his memory his parents Valborg Ryde and pharmacist Sven Ryde created the Arne Ryde Foundation for the advancement of research at our Department. We are most grateful to them. The Foundation has made possible important activities to which our ordinary resources are not applicable.

In agreement with Valborg and Sven Ryde we have decided to use the means of the Foundation mainly to arrange a series of symposia, as a rule one every second year. Our intention is to alternate between pure theory and applications. The themes of our previous Arne Ryde Symposia have been: Economics of Information (1973), Econometric Methods (1975), The Theoretical Contributions of Knut Wicksell (1977), The Economic Theory of Institutions (1979), Social Insurance (1981) and Pharmaceutical Economics (1982).

Björn Thalberg

THE PRIMARY SECTOR IN ECONOMIC DEVELOPMENT

Proceedings of the Seventh Arne Ryde Symposium
Frostavallen, August 29–30, 1983

Edited by **MATS LUNDAHL**

CROOM HELM
London & Sydney

© 1985 Mats Lundahl
Croom Helm Ltd, Provident House, Burrell Row,
Beckenham, Kent BR3 1AT
Croom Helm Australia Pty Ltd, First Floor, 139 King Street,
Sydney, NSW 2001, Australia

British Library Cataloguing in Publication Data

Arne Ryde Symposium (*7th 1983: Frostavallen*)
  The primary sector in economic development:
  proceedings of the seventh Arne Ryde Symposium,
  Frostavallen, August 29–30, 1983.
  1. Natural resources—Developing countries
  2. Developing countries—Industries
  I. Title   II. Lundahl, Mats
  338′.09172′4   HC59.7

ISBN 0-7099-1697-3

Printed and bound in Great Britain
by Billing & Sons Limited, Worcester.

CONTENTS

Preface
Introduction *Mats Lundahl*   1

Part One: The Role of the Primary Sector   41

1. The Primary Sector: Composition and Functions *Markos
   J. Mamalakis*   43
2. The Role of the Primary Sector in African Development
   Ester Boserup   56
3. What Do Smallholders Do for a Living? Some Evidence
   from Kenya *Arne Bigsten*   66

Part Two: Problems of Stagnation and Income Distribution   85

4. The Effect of Population Growth on a Peasant Econ-
   omy: The Case of Bangladesh *Alia Ahmad*   87
5. Agricultural Stagnation in Chile, 1930–55: A Result of
   Factor Market Imperfections? *Mats Lundahl*   105
6. The Distribution of Income in Brazil and Its Dependence
   on International and Domestic Agricultural Policies *Per
   Lundborg*   131
7. Growth and Stagnation in the Malaysian Rubber Smallholder Industry *Christer Gunnarsson*   152

Part Three: Trade in Primary Products   179

8. The Impact of Primary Exports on the Ghanaian
   Economy: Linkages and Leakages from Mining and
   Cocoa 1956–69 *Edward Horesh and Susan Joekes*   181
9. Mineral-led Development: The Political Economy of
   Namibia *Bo Södersten*   206
10. Primary Exports, Manufacturing and Development
    Ronald Findlay   218
11. Dutch Disease in Developing Countries: Swallowing
    Bitter Medicine *Michael Roemer*   234
12. Migration and Emigrants' Remittances: Theory and
    Evidence from the Middle East *Frank Kirwan*   253

Contents

Part Four: Generating Change   271

13. Dynamic Aspects of Agricultural Policy: Intervention or
    Regulation? *Ian G. Simpson*   273
14. Peru — 20 Years of Agrarian Reform *Tom Alberts*   291
15. The Interaction of Research and Training in Agricultural
    Development *A. Steven Englander*   309

Part Five: The Socialist Experience   327

16. On the Socialisation of Labour in Rural Cooperation
    Stefan Hedlund   329
17. Agricultural Development in Tanzania 1961–82: Perfor-
    mance and Major Constraints *Benno J. Ndulu and
    Lucian A. Msambichaka*   352
18. Agriculture in the Transition to Socialism: The Case of
    South Vietnam *Melanie Beresford*   370

List of Contributors   396

Index   399

PREFACE

The present volume contains a selection of the papers presented at the Seventh Arne Ryde Symposium, on *The Primary Sector in Economic Development*, August 29–30, 1983, at Frostavallen, Sweden. The topic of the symposium was chosen against the background of the importance of agriculture and mineral resources in the development of the Third World. Among the fields of interest were the role played by the primary sector in the development process, the lagging primary sector as an obstacle to development and the generation of change and obstacles to change in the sector.

As head of the organising committee, my gratitude goes to all who made the present volume of proceedings possible. Above all, it goes to the Arne Ryde Foundation for the generous financial assistance both for the symposium and for the printing of the proceedings and to Åsa Weibull, who acted as administrative secretary and thus had to handle all the tedious and thankless work that the undersigned chose to ignore. Göte Hansson, Bo Södersten and Björn Thalberg supported me in the organising committee. Alan Harkess checked the English of various contributions. Agneta Kjellgren and Pia Åkerman typed a number of manuscripts and Agnetta Kretz drew the figures. Keith Persson photocopied all the papers for the symposium. Ronald Findlay provided generous assistance at various stages during the preparation of the proceedings and so did a number of referees who unfortunately will have to remain anonymous. Hopefully, the result, which is hereby communicated to the readers, stands in some reasonable proportion to all these efforts.

Mats Lundahl
Lund

INTRODUCTION

Mats Lundahl

The term 'primary production' or 'primary sector' appears to be a New Zealand contribution to the economic science. Allan Fisher traces its use back to a New Zealand Census Report from 1891 where 'agricultural, pastoral, mineral and other primary producers' appear in the occupational classification.[1] Ten years later, the term had made it across to Australia where, in a census, primary producers were defined as 'embracing all persons mainly engaged in the cultivation or acquisition of food products, and in obtaining other raw materials from natural sources', i.e. those engaged in agriculture and pastoral activities and in 'capture, etc., of wild animals and their produce, fisheries, forestry, water conservation and supply, mining and quarrying.'[2] From then on, however, it spread relatively slowly. Writing in 1939, Fisher states that the words 'primary' and 'secondary' production 'did not appear until quite recently in the writings of English economists',[3] while 'some American writers apparently still find then novel.'[4]

Today, the terms 'primary', 'secondary' and 'tertiary' are no longer novel to anybody working in the field of economics but constitute a universally accepted part of the profession's vocabulary, having gained acceptance not least through the writings of Allan Fisher[5] and Colin Clark.[6] Still, it must be admitted that the definition of 'primary' has not become fully standardised. The problem in this context is mining, which sometimes is included in the primary sector, sometimes not. Colin Clark, in his monumental work *The Conditions of Economic Progress*, offers the following discussion of what constitutes the primary sector:

> The first division is agriculture. With this we include all forms of grazing, including nomadic grazing; the business of obtaining meat and skins by hunting and trapping, in most parts of the world now only carried on a very small scale indeed; and the much more substantial business of fishing. It is also convenient to include forestry at this stage. Mining is a border-line case, which is sometimes included here, sometimes with manufacture, and which perhaps deserves a class to itself.

1

The common feature about all the above, of course, is that they all depend upon the direct and immediate utilisation of natural resources. By their nature, therefore, they can only be carried out at the point where the natural resources are — one of the most important considerations distinguishing them from manufacture.[7]

In the present volume we will not go into any terminological intricacies but simply include mining in the primary sector.

The Role of the Primary Sector

Several authors have observed that there is a tendency for the relative importance of the primary sector to fall as real income *per capita* rises, both in terms of output value and in terms of employment. This conjecture goes at least as far back as to William Petty who in 1691, wrote:

> . . . there is much more to be gained by *Manufacture* than by *Husbandry*; and by *Merchandise* than by *Manufacture*. . . We may take notice that as Trade and Curious Arts increase; so the Trade of Husbandry will decrease, or else the wages of Husbandmen must rise and consequently the Rents of Lands must fall.[8]

The modern version of this statement is above all due to Colin Clark:

> We may . . . observe that the data support the generalisation that a high proportion of the total labour force engaged in agriculture and associated forms of employment is only to be found in economically undeveloped communities, and that in an economically developed community there is almost invariably, through time, a tendency for this proportion to fall.[9]

In the growth process of advanced economies there has been a secular tendency for the share of the primary sector in total output to fall and for the share of the secondary sector to rise. However, the share of the tertiary sector does not display any systematic relationship with this process, with the exception of transport and communications whose shares have risen.[10]

Still it cannot be denied that during the past and (especially) present centuries, the role of services in the developed economies has been strongly enhanced and that the rising importance of services is intimately connected with the character of economic growth itself in these nations. According to R.M. Hartwell:

The result . . . of economic growth and industrialisation in the advanced economies was, ultimately, *the service revolution*: those economies with the highest *per capita* real incomes are today experiencing service revolutions comparable with the industrial revolutions of the eighteenth and nineteenth centuries. This new stage of development is the culmination of a long process of growth and structural change from which are emerging economies with fifty per cent or more of their employed population engaged in the production of non-tangible goods. . . The lesson of history is, undoubtedly, that what has already happened in the United States will happen elsewhere, and that the trend in employment towards the services in all developed and developing economies will finally result in a world-wide service revolution.[11]

The first paper in the present volume presents an objection to the customary division of economic activities into 'primary', 'secondary' and 'tertiary' as well as to the 'evolutionary' sequence that has just been sketched. In his 'sermon' on economic development, *Markos Mamalakis* begins by noting that development economics is frequently cast in a dualistic framework which leaves no room at all for service activities. On the other hand, the traditional threefold division is not a meaningful one either but only serves to create analytical confusion. The process of economic development never was one from primary to secondary and tertiary activities, but one from *embryonic rural* activities of *all* three kinds to *modern* rural *and* urban ones with a higher productivity, *and* where industrial and service activities at the same time increase their importance in relation to agriculture.

Mamalakis examines four different concepts of 'primary' sector (excluding mining). The first one of these treats 'primary' as synonymous with agricultural. This definition corresponds to a certain notion of 'surplus' labour, i.e. labour that cannot be fully employed in the primary sector, whose magnitude Mamalakis places in the order of 80 per cent of the rural labour force. The second definition is broader and includes all activities needed to produce and *deliver* agricultural goods to the final consumer. Thus, a number of service activities which traditionally are considered 'tertiary' enter the picture: storage, transport and trade. With this definition, the size of the labour surplus shrinks to something like 50 per cent. The third concept of the primary sector is even wider, since in addition to the foregoing it also includes the production of rural *industrial consumer goods*, i.e. industrial consumer goods produced in rural areas. The labour surplus in this case amounts to a mere 20 per cent. Finally, we have the most extensive of the four definitions, where not only rural industrial consumer goods' but also rural industrial *capital* goods' production are taken into account. 'Primary' corresponds to rural, and the labour surplus at most amounts to 10 per cent of the rural labour force.

These extended definitions of 'primary' sector have certain implications for the strategy of economic development. One of the most important goals of development must be to increase the productivity of all activities and among those of course also the rural ones. Much in the same way as Michael Lipton,[12] Mamalakis argues in favour of a correction of the bias against rural areas which permeates development planning in many countries and advocates the decentralisation of both political power and government services as necessary for transforming the countryside in the direction of higher productivity and a fuller, more multifaceted life.

Mamalakis also goes on to discuss income distribution problems and their relation to the problems of the primary sector and points to the failure of industrialisation to bring about a more egalitarian distribution. Here services also have a role to play, as one of the components in a package which also contains land reforms and higher relative prices of agricultural products. To reach the basic needs targets, an upgrading of services is needed, not only in urban areas but in rural districts as well. An end must be put to the various forms of discrimination of the countryside, and in this, according to Mamalakis, services have a catalytic role to play, since making services available to the rural population serves to break a number of urban monopolies, like education, as well as rural power concentrations, like the monopoly-monopsony nexus which characterises factor markets in many developing countries,[13] while at the same time it contributes to capital accumulation in the widest sense of the word, i.e. including the human capital component as well.[14]

Agriculture constitutes the most important part of the primary sector. Traditionally, agriculture has been given a fivefold role in the process of economic development.[15] Enough food has to be provided to meet the rise in demand as the population grows and real incomes increase when the non-agricultural sectors of the economy develop. Agriculture also has to provide the economy with foreign exchange, in particular at the early stages of development when the non-agrarian sectors are still relatively undeveloped. Thirdly, agriculture has to release labour to man the other sectors as these grow, and conversely, to provide work when other sectors cannot. The fourth role is that agriculture must contribute both to the formation of overhead capital in the economy and to investment in the other sectors of the economy if these are to be able to grow. Finally, it is the responsibility of agriculture to increase the cash incomes of the rural population, thereby stimulating the demand for non-agricultural goods and services.

Thus, the development of an economy calls not only for developing the non-agricultural sectors but for developing agriculture as well. Failing to pay attention to the latter sector may jeopardise the entire development process. There was a time in the history of development economics when the question was frequently posed whether industry or agriculture should be given priority.[16] However, after the balanced–unbalanced growth debate in the late 1950s and early 1960s,[17] a consensus gradually emerged that even though during shorter periods one sector could be allowed to leap ahead of the others, in the longer run some kind of overall balance would be needed in the economy if the speed of the development process was not to slow down.

In order words, agriculture should not be allowed to become a lagging sector, since this would also pose obstacles to the development of the rest of the economy. Should farmers, for example, prove unable to provide enough food, valuable foreign exchange which could have been used to increase the capital stock of the economy may have to be spent on food imports, or the price of food will rise. The latter will not only serve to feed inflation in countries where food occupies a large share of household budgets, but may also endanger the health and nutrition standard of the poorer segments of the population.

In the same way, if agricultural exports are insufficient to make for a steady inflow of foreign exchange, and no other export revenues are available, capital formation is likely to suffer, since most underdeveloped economies are too small from the domestic market point of view to allow for profitable production of investment goods. Agriculture has to serve as a 'quasi capital goods sector'.[18]

The third role of agriculture, as a provider of labour to the remainder of the economy, has been the one which has proved easiest to fulfil, given the relatively high rate of population growth in most underdeveloped countries. The problem has instead been that when the non-agricultural sectors have not grown fast enough agriculture has had to step in and act as a 'sink' from the employment point of view. An inadequately developed agricultural sector faces great difficulties in doing this without depressing *per capita* incomes excessively.

Nor is an inefficient agricultural sector where productivity is low likely to be able to save very much, and this in turn poses another problem for capital formation, unless recourse is made to forced savings via taxation of the sector or via turning the domestic terms of trade against agriculture. Both of these measures have been frequently practised. Coercion is, however, not a good way of mobilising savings if, in addition, the fifth and final role of agriculture is taken into account. If a domestic market for the products of, for example, manufacturing industry, is to be created, purchasing power from large population segments is needed. If the other sectors of the economy are not particularly well developed, the only group that can possibly provide this purchasing power is the agricultural population, assuming however, that this power is not taxed away.

Ester Boserup discusses some of the factors that have precluded African agriculture from successfully playing the five development roles which we have sketched above. She begins by offering yet another definition of the 'primary' sector. According to Boserup, a primary sector does not emerge until the economy has left the pure subsistence stage and begins to sell food or other goods. The notion of 'primary' is hence connected with the notion of 'surplus', above what is consumed by the producer families themselves.

In Africa, the primary sector often exports more or less its entire surplus while the secondary sector remains relatively undeveloped. The problem facing the African nations is that there are strong factors which tend to hamper the development of both primary and secondary production.

In a historical perspective, Africa is not unique in exporting most of what the primary sector produces without having developed any secondary sector. The same was true, for example, of the European countries a couple of centuries ago and of other non-European economies when they came into contact with Europe. The difference between Europe and the rest of the world lay rather in the fact that the European primary sectors were domestically owned whereas, elsewhere, foreign ownership played a very important role. These foreign interests repatriated large parts of their earnings instead of reinvesting and developing the secondary and tertiary sectors of the host countries, as they had done in Europe itself.

Africa stands out in one respect, as far as the relationship between the primary sector and the rest of the economy is concerned. The development of the secondary sector has often proceeded at a much slower pace than elsewhere, including Asia and Latin America. The density of the African population has been low, people are scattered over large areas, and infrastructural facilities are as a rule lacking. Railroads and roads have not been adequately developed and this in turn makes transport and exchange of all sorts of goods difficult. Thus, it has proved difficult to develop commercial food production, with the result that Africa has to import large amounts of food. Transport is expensive, unless the crop in question is one of high value in relation to its weight.

Other obstacles have militated against the development of the primary sector. The sex division of labour turns out to be a big problem. In Africa, the women cultivate the fields but at the same time they are responsible for a host of household duties. According to Boserup, as the population grows, the demand on their time increases. Faced with diminishing returns to labour, they have to devote an increasing amount of time to cultivation in order to feed their families. Consequently, they find it more difficult to produce a surplus which can be sold outside the household.

The development of commercially based food production is also hampered by the fact that modernisation efforts have by and large centred on non-food export crops. African food producers have also had to compete with low-priced food imports, which are frequently the result of subsidies to food producers in developed countries. Moreover these imports often enter Africa at overvalued exchange rates.

Boserup ends her paper by discussing the possibilities for developing the African primary sectors. In the long run, the African nations will want to industrialise, but this is hardly feasible unless the primary sector can produce enough to finance industrialisation. In order for this to be possible, food imports which eat into the scarce reserves of foreign exchange must be avoided. Cultivation practices can be intensified in regions where the population density is already high, and more lands can be brought into cultivation provided only that they can be reached. Infrastructural investments, not least in transport and communication facilities, are essential in order to open up peripheral areas. If this does not take place, rural people will continue to migrate to mining centres, plantations and other areas, which provide employment, and also give rise to food imports.

Arne Bigsten picks up one of Mamalakis' threads, namely that analysis conducted in the dual economy framework may be completely misleading. In the rural context, for example, this means that a smallholder family has many sources of income besides agriculture proper.

Bigsten analyses the composition and change of incomes of Kenyan smallholder families from the mid-1960s to the mid-1970s, which is a period when the Kenyan rural economy became increasingly monetised and diversified. He then finds that smallholder incomes may be divided into four different categories: farm income, wage income, transfers and non-agricultural operating surpluses. During the period under study, the smallholders of central Kenya saw their farm incomes increase, both absolutely and as a share of their total incomes. Wage incomes as well rose considerably in real terms although their share of the total fell. Transfers (from relatives outside the rural area) increased sufficiently fast to make for an increased share as well. The final category, surpluses from such activities as manufacturing and businesses of various kinds, suffered a declining share. However, this income category appears far too difficult to measure and far too heterogeneous to permit any meaningful conclusions to be drawn.

The diversification of incomes was present both in the mid-1960s and ten years later. According to Bigsten, this is to a large extent the result of the inherent risks of farming. Nevertheless, the farming component increased its relative importance over the decade, probably because it became progressively easier for the smallholders to go into lucrative cash crop production. As a result, the subsistence component of farm income fell. Presumably, smallholders first meet the subsistence needs of the family and thereafter expand in the direction of more cash crops.

Bigsten also carries out a disaggregation of his data, according to income classes. This disaggregation reveals that the share of farm incomes in the total increases with the size of incomes, i.e. it is the poorer families who most often have to rely on non-farm incomes. On the other hand, families with a large wage income component are as a rule found in the upper income brackets. This seems to be due to a tendency to move out of *agricultural* wage employment to take better-paid jobs outside whenever this possibility arises. The share of transfer incomes decreases with income size, which may indicate that rural–urban migration is concentrated in the poorer families.

Kenya's economic structure is in a process of change. This is also reflected in what takes place in rural areas. The farm household does not derive its income solely from agriculture but has also other important sources of income. Bigsten concludes that this has implications for development strategy. It is probably not by accident that the households that have good contacts with urban areas and labour markets are also those that do best in agriculture. Improvement of communications between country and town has an important role to play when it comes to speeding up the development process.

Problems of Stagnation and Income Distribution

As is well known, agricultural production easily stagnates in less developed economies. Agricultural stagnation may be due to several reasons. The reason which certainly most easily springs to mind is that of excessive population growth in relation to the growth of agricultural output. The Malthusian spectre is a more or less permanent guest in many areas of the Third World.[19]

However, population growth is not an unconditional evil.[20] It not only makes for more people to be fed but these same conditions also tend to lead to positive changes on the output side. More land is brought into cultivation, the length of the fallow period is shortened, more labour is used, capital equipment and crop mixes change and new, more efficient, technologies are introduced.[21] The net outcome of these two mutually counteracting forces is not given. Some countries have managed to increase agricultural output *per capita* in the face of heavy population growth. Others have failed to do so.

Alia Ahmad's contribution deals with the tension between the negative and positive effects of population growth. In this, she takes Ester Boserup's theory of population growth and agricultural change as her point of departure. Thomas Malthus, in his *Essay on the Principles of Population*, postulated that the cause–effect relationship between agricultural output and population growth went from the former to the latter. Boserup, in her widely read book, *The Conditions of Agricultural Growth*,[22] challenged the Malthusian view and instead advanced the idea that population growth should be considered as the exogenous variable which determines output.

Ahmad analyses how in the case of Bangladesh a high population growth has led to the stagnation of agricultural output *per capita*. Bangladesh has an agricultural economy which is highly labour-intensive. The typical farm is devoted to wet-rice production. Population growth rates have been high throughout the present century. As a result, more and more land has been put into cultivation and the agricultural practices have changed. With time, however, these efforts have proved insufficient to prevent the stagnation of agricultural production *per capita*.

One of the main reasons for this stagnation is that population growth has not only acted as a stimulus to increased output but it has simultaneously created *obstacles* to growth, since the growth of the population has taken place within a setting characterised by highly imperfect factor markets. In the land market, large landowners dominate the smaller ones who encounter difficulties in obtaining access to land. The labour market also operates in a dualistic fashion. According to Ahmad, the small farmers are not guided by opportunity cost principles in their allocation of labour time to farming while large scale farmers who use outside labour are motivated by these considerations. The latter find it difficult to obtain workers during the peak season, since the workers as a rule at that same time are farming their own plots and give priority to these, increasing the labour input as long as this adds to output while large farmers equalise wages and marginal value products of labour. As the population grows, the discrepancies in labour/land ratios that arise as a result of the difference in the modes of operation of large and small farmers are accentuated. By the same token, the inefficiency of Bangladesh agriculture tends to increase over time.

In addition, the rural credit market is segmented. Only large farmers have access to the former part of the market, while smallholders have to make do with informal credit at high effective interest rates.

Since the scope for substitution of capital for labour is limited in Bangladesh agriculture, the relative cheapness of capital has not resulted in investment in the large farm sector. Instead, cheap credit has been used to acquire more land, which in turn has enhanced the discrepancy between the land/labour ratios in large and small agriculture. This, in turn has stimulated the employment of share contracts. The landowners thereby obtain labour whereas the workers/sharecroppers make the landlords bear some of the risks inherent in agriculture and at the same time find a safe outlet for their family labour. However, sharecropping as such, in the case of Bangladesh, tends to be less efficient from the production point of view, than owner-cultivated areas.

In this way, population growth tends to exacerbate inefficiencies. This, in turn, has not been adequately offset by outside forces. The government has largely ignored the welfare of the rural population and private incentives have been stifled by the tax, subsidy, foreign exchange and credit policies pursued. An urban bias has been operating, with resources flowing from agriculture to urban occupations rather than vice versa. In those instances where the government has tried to stimulate agriculture, resources have been channelled towards the large-scale end of the sector rather than towards the small farmers.

It is not only in Bangladesh that rural factor markets are imperfect. This feature is notorious in many developing economies, not least in Latin America, where the heavy concentration of land in the hands of a tiny minority has led to imperfections in the other factor markets as well.[23] From economic theory we know that an economic system where perfect competition prevails in all product and factor markets will display efficiency in production and not lead to any waste in the allocation of production factors, whereas economies characterised by monopolies or monopsonies will not. In this way, production will be constrained when factor markets are imperfect.

The paper by *Mats Lundahl* deals with imperfections in factor markets as a possible cause of agricultural stagnation. Between 1930 and 1955 agricultural output *per capita* stagnated in Chile. Two different explanations have been advanced. The first one contends that agricultural stagnation was due to the change in economic policy which took place at the onset of the Depression, when, after several decades of an outward-oriented trade policy, Chile turned inwards and began a process of promoting industrialisation by means of import substitution. By favouring manufacturing at the expense of agriculture and by simultaneously importing food at subsidised prices, agriculture was squeezed into stagnation.

The second explanation is the one taken up by Lundahl. Rural factor markets in Chile during the period under consideration were highly imperfect. The land was concentrated in the hands of a minority of monopolistic landowners who by virtue of their control of the land also exercised monopsonistic control over the local labour markets. Their landed property and consequent political influence allowed them to obtain credit at low effective rates of interest. At the other end of the scale we find on the one hand, landless labourers and on the other small farmers, *minifundistas*, who have problems in obtaining access to land. Moreover they have to work for the monopsonistic landowners and are forced to obtain credit from the informal credit markets where loans can be obtained only at high effective interest. Such a system is inefficient in the sense that when different producers face different relative factor prices, less is produced than would otherwise have been possible given the technology and the factor endowments of the sector.

Lundahl traces developments in the land, labour and credit markets of rural Chile between 1930 and 1955 to find out whether the degree of monopolistic or monopsonistic control and other imperfections increased or decreased. He finds that the distribution of agricultural land was very uneven both at the beginning and at the end of the period. However, a slight decrease in inequality seems to have taken place. In the labour market there were very few changes. The budding labour movement had considerable problems in organising the rural workers, but at least it cannot be contended that the labour market was *more* imperfect in 1955 than in 1930. Finally the situation in the credit market is harder to examine, since data for informal credit are lacking, but the evidence concerning formal credit indicates that the market inequalities at the beginning of the period of investigation in the factor markets of rural Chile either remained largely unchanged or decreased slightly. Hence the explanation of agricultural stagnation which runs in terms of factor market imperfections does not seem correct. Lundahl concludes that the economic policies pursued by the Chilean governments probably go much further towards offering a satisfactory explanation of what took place.

Faulty economic policies often go a long way towards explaining agricultural stagnation in many developing countries. Even though the rate of population growth is not exceedingly high and the distribution of assets not excessively lopsided in agrarian districts, government economic policies frequently create negative incentives for agriculture with the result that this sector lags behind and is consequently unable to fulfil satisfactorily the five roles in the development process that were discussed earlier. Agriculture is over-taxed, both directly and via manipulation of the relative prices of food and industrial goods in favour of the urban population, to the detriment of the farmers. Overvalued exchange rates make exports of agricultural products less profitable. Credits are channelled to industry while agriculture suffers. Public investments, e.g. in infra-structure are concentrated in urban areas with the consequent neglect of the countryside. Rural areas are starved of education with the result that the most gifted among the rural youths leave for the cities.[24]

Third World agriculture does not suffer only from the effects of domestic policies, however. What happens in the industrialised nations affects them as well. 'Export pessimism' is no novelty in the discussion of the future of the Third World, but has for several decades constituted one of the fundamental arguments in favour of accelerated industrialisation of less developed countries.[25] The markets for agricultural products in the nations of North America and Western Europe have in the main been characterised by a high degree of protectionism which in turn has also had repercussions in those development countries whose exports would otherwise have competed favourably with domestic agricultural producers.[26]

Per Lundborg takes up a particular aspect of this problem, namely the extent to which in the case of Brazil the unequal distri-bution of incomes is a result of protectionistic measures in the United States and Western Europe.

Many researchers have dealt with income distribution in Brazil and its tendency to become more unequal during the 1960s and 1970s. However, the majority of these studies do not centre on the agricultural sector which, as Lundborg points out, is slightly surprising, since in countries like Brazil the poorer segments of the population include large rural groups. Thus, if we are to explain the development of the distribution of incomes in Brazil, an examina-tion of agriculture is called for.

Lundborg simulates the impact on the Brazilian income distribu-tion of different international and domestic policy changes for the 1960–68 period with the aid of a global, dynamic computable gen-eral equilibrium model. A basic run is carried out to account for the actual development, and the results of this basic run are in turn compared to what would have happened if either of the following four changes had taken place:

1. The EEC increased its wheat imports by 10 per cent in each period.

2. The EEC pursued the same policy as under (1) and in addition doubled imports of other cereals and rice in each period, while the United States simultaneously doubled taxes or cut subsidies to domestic grain producers by 50 per cent per time period.
3. The government support to Brazilian wheat producers (tariffs and subsidies) was doubled.
4. Government subsidies to Brazilian coffee producers were doubled.

What Lundborg finds is that changes in international policies would not have had much of an impact on income distribution in Brazil. The coordination of policies in the EEC and the United States, for example, leads to improved relative prices for agriculture, but the main beneficiaries are the richer rather than the poorer groups within the rural sector.

When it comes to domestic policies, the picture that emerges is somewhat divided. Increasing support to wheat producers has a different impact on the distribution of incomes depending on the criterion that is employed to measure this distribution, whereas increased support to coffee yields a more equal distribution of incomes.

Income distribution problems and government policies also constitute one of the themes in *Christer Gunnarsson's* contribution. Gunnarsson analyses the factors behind growth and stagnation in the Malaysian rubber smallholder sector. Since the late 1950s, the previously unknown tendency for growth in smallholder rubber production to generate inequalities in the distribution of incomes within the smallholder sector has begun to emerge.

Malaysian rubber production takes place in two different kinds of settings: large estates and peasant smallholdings. Production among smallholders began around the turn of the century. The 1910s and 1920s were decades of rapid growth whereas during the 1930s the colonial government restricted smallholder expansion. At the outbreak of World War II, some 40 per cent of the rubber acreage in Malaya consisted of smallholdings. The post-1957 period, in turn, has seen new growth in the sector.

Gunnarsson focuses on these two growth periods: the early one and its connection with the opening of trade, and the post-1957 period and the relationship of this period with government policies. For the early period, three different theories of international trade are tested. The first is dependency theory,[27] according to which the expansion of the capitalist system created underdevelopment in the colonies. The introduction of rubber was, according to this theory, forced upon the smallholders, who had few incentives to take up cash production voluntarily. Gunnarsson does not accept this view but instead argues that smallholder rubber production in Malaysia has been a result of voluntary decisions on the part of the peasants, while the colonial power, contrary to what the theory predicts, tried to limit rubber production to European-owned large estates. Besides, dependency theory fails to specify the mechanisms that made the Malayan peasants respond to incentives that were actually created by the market mechanism.

The second theory discussed by Gunnarsson is the neoclassical comparative cost doctrine. As it seems, the introduction of rubber was *not* a neoclassical process of reallocation of production along the production possibility frontier. Food production did not decline even though rubber production increased.

Instead Gunnarsson turns to the 'vent for surplus' theory.[28] This theory assumes that both land and labour are idle before trade is opened, due to the limitations of the domestic market. This, according to Gunnarsson, fits the Malaysian economy well. By sacrificing leisure, the peasants could use hitherto idle land to develop rubber production. The triggering event here was the establishment of British rule which ensured a demand for the export product and simultaneously provided the economy with import goods which gave an incentive to the peasants to begin cash crop production.

The second phase of expansion, after 1957, was due to completely different reasons. During the introductory phase, the complementarity of rubber with existing peasant crops had played a decisive role for growth. The second expansion, on the other hand, was largely a result of government policy, in particular when it came to introducing high-yielding varieties. This policy has affected the smallholder group unevenly. The group is not a homogeneous entity and the assistance given by the government in the substitution of high-yielding varieties for the traditional ones has favoured the larger and medium-sized among the smallholders, while the smallest units have not benefited to the same extent. In this way income equalities appear to have been created within the sector. This has particularly given rise to increasing poverty for the smallest producers.

Trade in Primary Products

The vast majority of developing countries are basically primary producers in the sense that the primary sector accounts for the largest share of both GDP and employment. A majority are also primary *exporters*.[29] This fact has frequently been a cause for worry. Thus, in his celebrated Wicksell lectures, Ragnar Nurkse observed that while international trade had been an 'engine for growth' for the primary producing countries during the nineteenth century, due to the expanding markets in the countries that were industrialising at the time, the twentieth century presented a much gloomier picture.[30] Shifts in the composition of manufacturing industry in the developed countries in the direction of a lower raw material content and increased use of synthetics, low income elasticities of demand for agricultural goods in combination with agricultural protectionism, for example, made it difficult for growth impulses in developed countries to be transmitted via trade. Gone were the days when the markets of the industrialised nations could lead to growth via staple product trade.[31] Instead, arguments were presented to show that the less developed countries could easily export away domestically generated growth impulses via secularly falling terms-of-trade[32] or that export incomes of primary producers would fluctuate heavily and thereby have a negative impact on the rate of economic growth.[33]

Some of the problems facing primary exporting countries are dealt with in the article by *Edward Horesh* and *Susan Joekes*. Horesh and Joekes examine the 'linkage' and 'leakage' effects of primary exports on a developing economy: the case of mining and cocoa in Ghana 1956–69. Neither of these two concepts is a clearcut operational one. The linkage approach was developed by Albert Hirschman in *The Strategy of Economic Development* where 'forward' and 'backward' linkages were defined in terms of the relation of a particular industry with other industries using this industry's outputs as inputs or delivering inputs to it.[34] Hirschman has subsequently attempted to generalise the linkage concept[35] and Horesh and Joekes use his notions of 'consumption' linkages — the spending of export revenues on consumer goods — and 'fiscal' linkages — taxation of exports where the proceeds are used for productive investment.

The idea of 'leakages' departs from the opposite idea, i.e. leakages prevent linkages from coming into play, e.g. when part of the export proceeds are repatriated abroad instead of being reinvested in the exporting country. To quantify potential linkages and leakages Horesh and Joekes derive functional distributions of incomes by making a distinction between incomes that are repatriated (out of profits and salaries of foreign employees), domestic profits and labour income and government income. While data problems make it difficult to establish any clear trends as far as leakages are concerned, it is shown that between 1956 and 1969, domestic wage incomes and profits fell in mining while the government's share rose steadily. By and large, the same trend could be established in cocoa production, with the tax share accruing to the government rising dramatically.

Thus, in the Ghanaian case there appears to have been a trade-off between potential fiscal and consumption linkages. The potential for the former rose, while that of the latter fell. With respect to fiscal linkages the mining and cocoa sectors proved to be of more or less equal magnitude, whereas the amount of leakages differed significantly between the two: 23 per cent against 3 per cent of net export proceeds. It would seem that there were few direct production linkages in any of the two sectors. Cocoa and mining products were both exported in an unrefined state and all the capital equipment needed in the mining sector was imported. Only in relation to cocoa farming did some minor backward linkages develop.

Altogether, Horesh and Joekes conclude that linkages from export-related activities were weak in Ghana during the period under consideration while the leakages from mining were quite substantial. The only potential linkages to develop were the fiscal ones, but unfortunately, the government did a poor job when it came to investing the tax proceeds productively.

Bo Södersten also deals with the theme of mineral exports, but from a different angle. He addresses himself to the question of what a newly independent mineral-rich economy may make of its minerals in its development effort. Basing himself on Mamalakis' ideas of 'mineral-led' development,[36] Södersten examines two concepts of rents which may accrue to mineral producers. The first is the traditional Ricardian rent which arises due to the existence of deposits of different qualities and which accrues to the owners of the mines where superior ores are exploited. The second is a short-period rent which is due to the fluctuations of the price around a 'normal' or trend value typical for minerals which may be captured by selling when the price is above the trend.

Södersten poses the question of how rents should be divided

between the state and the capital and labour employed in mining. His suggestion is that the mines should be run with a minimum of capital so that the total share going to this factor is also minimised. The share of labour is somewhat more difficult, since when Namibia gains independence from South Africa, there will most probably be a tendency among mine workers to press for high wages, because this group may easily come to constitute an elite within the labour force. Therefore Södersten underlines the importance of restraint on the part of the Namibian government when setting levels of wages in the mines.

The government must then deal with the question of how rents accruing to the state should be spent. Södersten recommends the creation of a specific development budget with earmarking of funds for industrial development and the institution of a norm for the division of government spending between current expenditure and development expenditure.

The subject of trade policy is also brought up. From the market point of view Namibia is far too small for any import substitution policy to work. An export push, based on minerals, is needed. The country's strong comparative advantage in mineral production should also allow Namibia to leave the customs union with South Africa, which has apparently not been particularly beneficial. Finally, Södersten makes some specific recommendations regarding industrial promotion, identifying suitable industries and pointing to fishing and agriculture as suitable bases for industrial expansion.

The perceived lack of dynamic elements in primary exports, based to a large extent on the negative experiences of primary exporting countries during the Depression of the 1930s and on the shortage of industrial imports during World War II, made many developing countries launch import-substituting strategies for industrialisation. By the 1960s, these policies which had tended to dominate the picture, had not, as is well known, yielded particularly successful results.[37]

Ronald Findlay takes a different attitude. His paper shows that primary exports may be quite compatible with industrialisation without import substitution and that in the long run primary exporting countries may well become industrial exporters instead.

Findlay deals with three inter-related issues. The first part of his essay is dedicated to the Ricardo-inspired model constructed by Bent Hansen of economic development with unlimited supplies of land.[38] In the second section, this model is turned into a Ricardian model of primary exports and manufacturing. The last section analyses resource-based industrialisation in an open economy.

The Hansen model depicts a colonial economy where plantations monopolise high-quality land and where peasants have a choice between working on these plantations and settling on 'unlimited' land of marginal quality. Findlay examines the results of population growth, increases in the supply of superior land and technological progress in the plantation sector as well as the impacts of price changes and points out that plantation agriculture in this setting is an 'enclave' in the economy in the sense that a rise in the price of plantation crops does not change the real incomes of the native population. Moreover, the interests of planters and natives are opposed to each other. Thereafter, manufacturing is introduced and Findlay demonstrates that if both the return to capital and product prices are given, the real wage that manufacturing can afford to pay is also given. If this wage is above what the peasants can earn on marginal lands, peasant agriculture will be wiped out, and plantation wages will rise.

With given real wages in the plantation sector, the phenomenon known as 'Dutch disease' can be introduced. When the peasant sector has been wiped out and plantations and manufacturing compete for labour, an expansion of the latter sector, will drive up the wage rate and force capital to leave the country and thus lead to deindustrialisation.

In the second section of this paper, Findlay uses the Hansen model as a point of departure and shows how an economy which starts as an exporter of primary products becomes a producer of manufactures which it may eventually even export. In the Hansen model production was instantaneous. Findlay now assumes that it takes time. In this way capital enters the model. Agricultural workers receive their wages (food = circulating capital) at the beginning of the period and the output appears at the end. Since the workers in the plantation and manufacturing sectors earn less than their marginal product, due to the existence of an unlimited supply of marginal lands profits arise in these two sectors. Findlay demonstrates that if capital is competitively allocated, the size of the plantation sector becomes determined.

Going one step further, allowing for savings and capital accumulation out of profits, Findlay subsequently shows that, after the initial expansion of the plantation sector, when the rate of profit has been driven down in this sector as a result of diminishing returns to land, all further expansion will take place in the manufacturing sector at a constant profit rate (due to a given price of manufactures in combination with a given wage rate and constant returns to scale). This expansion may even result in the export of manufactures, provided that capital accumulation is sufficiently rapid in relation to population growth, while food production on marginal lands will shrink.

The final section points specifically to the role of raw materials in international trade in a model with one raw material, requiring 'land' and labour for its production and one final good using the raw material and labour. Here, Findlay first determines the optimum allocation of resources in the closed economy and the properties of this optimum before he goes on to demonstrate what the country's equilibrium will look like if the two goods can be traded for each other internationally at given prices and the country exports its raw materials.

Michael Roemer deals with the opposite side of the primary exports problem. A boom in primary exports may be a 'curse in disguise'. During the 1970s a number of developing countries had such booms. However, far from all of these countries saw any overall growth in the economy. One reason for this was the 'Dutch disease', experienced where a boom in primary exports may have negative repercussions on the rest of the economy that stifle growth.

The impact of Dutch disease has been analysed in a three-sector model by Max Corden and Peter Neary,[39] and Roemer also makes use of this model. In addition to the expanding sector, there is a 'lagging' sector of other traded goods as well as a non-tradeables sector (services, transports etc.). In the short run, only labour is mobile between these sectors. First, there is the spending effect: the price of non-tradeables increases and this in turn leads to an appreciation of the domestic currency in real terms. At the same time, labour moves from the lagging to the non-tradeables sector. There is, however, also a 'resource movement' effect. The export boom pulls labour away from both the lagging and the non-tradeables sector into the expanding one. Thus, the net effect is that the output of the lagging sector will fall, whereas, as far as non-tradeables are concerned, the two effects counteract each other.

In the long run, all factors are mobile, and then the results are no longer as clearcut. It is uncertain which of the sectors will suffer contraction. Roemer stresses this point, since most analyses have concentrated on the short run. Economic development, however, is by definition a *long-run* phenomenon and this must be kept in mind when the effects of a primary export boom are analysed. However, it cannot be denied that a number of less developed countries have suffered from Dutch disease. Roemer examines the validity of Dutch disease models for that type of economy, as well as some alternatives to the Corden-Neary model and some empirical data on Dutch disease in developing countries.

He subsequently poses the question of whether Dutch disease is really a disease at all, i.e. whether it needs to be 'treated'. After all, the core of the disease lies in the shift of relative commodity prices in favour of the booming sector, and shifts in relative commodity prices by their very nature must favour certain sectors over others. Hence they could be regarded as a recurrent feature of economic life. Nevertheless, Roemer argues that we *are* dealing with a disease. If a boom is expected to be short-lived, there is a need to protect the rest of the economy from the price signals emanating from it and even in the case of more long-run trends, the government does not necessarily want the economy to progress along the path which results from primary export-led growth, especially not if the boom is based on an exhaustible resource like petroleum. A more diversified development pattern may be desirable.

The most obvious treatment of Dutch disease is sterilisation of the revenues of the expanding sector by the government, by accumulation of foreign reserves and by limits on expenditure. Such a policy may, however, be politically difficult to carry out, since in less developed economies there is always, for various reasons, heavy pressure on the government to spend and it is unlikely that governments are able to resist such pressure. There are, however, other remedies. A dual exchange rate which pays an appreciated rate to the booming sector and a devalued one to all other tradeables could be used, but this would presumably only create incentives to circumvent the dual system in various ways. Taxing the expanding sector and subsidising all other tradeables would have the same effects, but in the typical political environment in less developed countries, the result could easily be that sectors dominated by political favourites would end up with the fatter share of the subsidies. Finally, there is tariff protection, where especially in the case of a lagging manufacturing sector, the primary export boom leads to deindustrialisation. However, as is well documented in the development literature, this has a number of drawbacks. Thus Roemer concludes that there are well-known remedies for Dutch disease, but that from the political point of view those that are economically to be preferred have a bitter taste. Hence the persistence of Dutch disease in many developing economies.

Frank Kirwan's paper points to some second- and third-round consequences of a boom in primary products: migration from non-expanding less developed economies into expanding ones and the effects that this migration has had for the economy from whence the migrants come. The case dealt with is the OPEC-triggered rise in oil prices in the 1970s and its impact on labour-exporting states in the Middle East, particularly Jordan.

When the price of oil rose in the 1970s, the demand for labour grew in the oil-exporting Arab states. Much of this demand was met by migration from such non-oil-exporting countries as Egypt, Jordan and the two Yemens. These migration waves reached such proportions as to create a labour scarcity in some of the source countries, which in turn led to a replacement wave from such countries as Bangladesh, Korea, Pakistan and China. Since most of this migration within the Arab world is not of a permanent character, it has given rise to a flow of remittances back to the source countries where, due to lack of supply elasticity, balance of payments problems and an upward pressure on the price level have arisen. Furthermore, given the relatively undeveloped state of the capital markets, many of these funds has been channelled into land acquisition and residential construction instead of into productive capital formation.

Kirwan chooses the case of Jordan to illustrate how these mechanisms work. Perhaps as much as one-third of the Jordanian labour force is employed in the neighbouring oil-producing states while Jordan itself imports Egyptian and other labour to fill the gap created by these departures. These migrants remit part of their earnings back to Jordan to the effect that substantial sums are entering the country each year.

Kirwan employs a two-by-two model with one non-traded good to analyse the possible impact of remittances on the source country. If no remittances at all take place, and everybody in the source country, including the emigrants, has the same homothetic tastes, the welfare of those remaining behind falls.[40] As Kirwan shows, if remittances are introduced that are sufficiently large to maintain the nominal income of the source country at its pre-migration level, the welfare of the source country will still be lower than if no migration had taken place, assuming that the emigrants consume in their home country. On the other hand, should remittances be even larger, the impact on welfare may be either positive or negative.

In the concrete case of Jordan, the combined effect of emigration and remittances was probably positive, since during the first part of the seventies there was unemployment and hence very little output ought to have been lost when migration began, while the gap left by the migrants was filled by foreign workers. Thus, according to Kirwan, the effect of remittances alone ought to have been by far the most important one.

Finally, Kirwan examines several macroeconomic consequences of emigration from Jordan. Due to emigration, unemployment fell drastically from 1970 to 1975 — from 14 per cent to 2 per cent — at the same time as GDP rose. A large part of the remittances from the emigrants ended up being invested in real estate which created a boom in the construction sector. Over the same period, agriculture contracted, but Kirwan does not find any evidence which indicates that this fact was a consequence of emigration.

Generating Change

Many of the articles in the first three sections of the present volume demonstrate different ways in which the development of the primary sector in Third World economies is blocked, and how a lagging primary sector may constitute a brake on the overall dynamism of these economies. The last two sections, in turn, deal with the generation of change in the primary sector to break this impasse.

It is not difficult to point to areas where change is needed, particularly in agriculture. As we have seen in the foregoing, the land ownership and land tenure systems in many countries tend to foster inefficiency, underemployment and skewed distributions of income. Land reforms are needed to correct this, but also to ensure a redistribution of political power away from the feudal or semi-feudal hierarchies that still characterise many rural areas, in favour of more broadly defined, economically less powerful, groups.[41] Land reforms cannot, however, do the trick alone, but must be complemented by other reform measures as well. Without provision of such services as credits, irrigation, seeds, fertiliser, marketing, education etc., the probability that land reforms will become 'negative' events is high as the historical experience eloquently demonstrates.[42]

Rural credit markets are often hopelessly imperfect. This is not necessarily the result of monopolistic power, as described above, but frequently information problems fragment these markets in such a manner as to make for a systematic misallocation of funds, away from high-yielding investments towards unproductive ones instead.[43] In both these instances, credit reforms are needed to make investment in agriculture possible. The lack of credit also bears directly on the lack of modern inputs in agriculture. Such innovations as the Green Revolution have a bias towards increased use of material inputs like fertiliser, irrigation and sometimes also towards mechanisation. If such needs cannot be met, the innovations may turn out to be inferior from the point of view of the individual farmer, who consequently will not adopt them but continue with a technology that is low-yielding.[44]

It is, however, not only direct provision of inputs that is needed. For agriculture to become dynamic, a number of overhead facilities are also needed. When landless workers take over the land, following a reform, they will be facing a number of problems that are new to them. They need education and extension services which enable them, for example, to understand technological change and to make economic calculations. Even though sometimes the argument is heard that farmers in developing countries do not need any formal education to become efficient producers, as Theodore Schultz has pointed out, it is virtually impossible to find any instances where educated farmers who continue to farm are coupled with a stagnant agricultural sector.[45]

Similarly, farmers need marketing outlets. Land reforms often face problems during the first years after the reforms have been undertaken in that the institutional structures that existed before the reform, for example with respect to collection and transport of agricultural produce, break down or go out of existence when the reforms are undertaken. New systems will then have to be devised rapidly, if the marketed surplus which the non-agricultural sectors of the economy need is not to fall drastically.

Technological change represents another big headache for the individual farmer. Naturally, such change can be introduced spontaneously, but often it tends to be very uneconomical for the individual to search for suitable new techniques without assistance. Since agricultural technology to a large extent has the character of a public good whose returns cannot so easily be appropriated by the innovating individual, research will have to be undertaken by other entities and extension services have to be organised to ensure the spread of technological change.

Other reform and support problems are common to agriculture and mining. These include, for example, income stabilisation schemes when supply or demand fluctuates in such a fashion as to make producer incomes fluctuate as well. Some type of stabilisation scheme may therefore be called for to smooth out these fluctuations over time in order to ensure, for example, that output of export produce does not fall drastically, giving rise to a reduction in the foreign exchange revenues needed to import investment goods.[46]

Related to this is the problem of creating adequate incentives to producers. In the foregoing, we have seen examples of how government pricing and other incentive policies have militated against the primary sector. There is frequently a strong need to correct different types of biases that have been introduced without due reflection on the possible effects on primary production.[47]

Finally, the integration of the primary sector with the rest of the economy must not be forgotten. It is a commonplace in much of the development literature that enclave mining and plantation sectors do not have any *patent* effects on the rest of the economy or that subsistence agriculture shows up in input-output tables with coefficients that are either zero or very close to zero. Thus, the linkage problem looms large. How can backward and forward linkages, as well as consumption and fiscal ones, to use the more ambitious approach, be created in order to involve the primary sector in a central role?

Ian Simpson examines the record of government intervention in agricultural development, in particular with respect to farm income stability and flexibility in the economic organisation of production.

The scope of government intervention has widened considerably after World War II. Prices are set by political decisions. Research programs are sponsored. Farmers receive subsidised credits and farm inputs. Institutions to control production have sprung up. Land reforms have been carried out in a number of countries. The results of these interventions, argues Simpson, have been generally unsatisfactory. The goals of income stability and flexibility in organisation have not been reached. Frequently, the necessary knowledge has been lacking. Intervention has not been based on facts. Inordinate delays in government decision-making has increased rather than reduced the uncertainty with which farmers have had to cope while institutions have been set up which, when no longer needed, have not been scrapped but turned into counter-productive, bureaucratic organisations instead.

Simpson stresses that specific forms of intervention have their limitations. If governments are to manipulate prices, reliable esti-mates, e.g. of supply elasticities, are needed, but in spite of a prolific use of regression analysis and programming models, much remains to be achieved. Nor does price intervention as a rule take into account the effects that such intervention has on land values.

Agricultural research programmes often build on estimates of rates of return which Simpson feels are biased upwards, due, for example, to comparative inefficiencies in research establishments. There is also the question of public versus private involvement. Agrobureaucracies often have a tendency to take over tasks which would have been more efficiently performed if left to private initia-tive. Governments also undertake to invest directly in agricultural infrastructure, such as in irrigation and transport facilities, but often both the identification and timing of such projects are faulty. Land reforms as well suffer from bad preparation and lack of infor-mation or failure to use the available information correctly.

Simpson compares the interventionist role of government with the regulatory role. The latter policy is more modest in its scope and interferes less with the way the agricultural economy works. This policy aims instead at providing positive incentives which make sta-bility and flexibility possible. Simpson identifies three important areas for regulation. Firstly, agricultural land markets have to be controlled to prevent land concentration and subsequent social unrest, while at the same time ensuring that land resources match capital and labour. The second area is stabilisation of agricultural prices which is felt to be necessary when farmers are averse to risk. Finally, the government should step in and ensure that the agricul-tural resource base is conserved. As is well known, erosion is severely threatening the ecosystems in many developing countries.

Tom Alberts provides a concrete illustration of the problems con-nected with ill-conceived land reforms. He analyses the effects of the 1969 Peruvian redistribution of land, undertaken by the military government.

The background to the Peruvian land reform is found in the ten-dency for agricultural production to stagnate. While in the 1950s agricultural output *per capita* grew by almost 2 per cent per annum, in the following decade, the growth rate fell to a mere 0.4 per cent. This stagnation had several causes. In the first place, arable land had become increasingly scarce. Secondly, during the period under consideration, the Peruvian government resorted to a policy of import substitution in the manufacturing sector behind tariff walls which penalised agricultural production via an overvalued exchange rate. In addition, food prices were deliberately kept low. The overall result was that the internal terms-of-trade turned against agriculture.

The change in relative prices in combination with mounting expectations of a land reform during the era of the Alliance for Progress in the 1960s apparently led to a fall in private investments in agriculture to a very low level during the decade preceding the 1969 reform. The latter, in turn, had two objectives. One was to increase the rate of growth in agriculture while the other was to create a more egalitarian distribution of incomes.

The land reform was comprehensive. Over a period of ten years, some 10 million hectares were expropriated and redistributed to some 400,000 rural families. Unfortunately, however, this redistribution was not followed up with a complementary input package. It would appear that the rate of investment was low and the volume of credits furnished by the Agricultural Development Bank was cut in half. Besides, the policy of favouring the urban food consumers at the expense of the rural producers continued until the late 1970s. The land reform affected almost 50 per cent of the agricultural population. These people received land against a quite modest payment to the former landowners, based on the declarations of asset values that the latter had made during the years preceding the reform. Furthermore, payment took place in bonds not adjusted for inflation.

When the land reform began, the Peruvian distribution of income was very skewed. Rural incomes were low on average with the result that a steady stream of people left the countryside to go to towns. However, the reform mainly involved the permanent workers on the large estates and benefited the upper 20 per cent of the rural population, whereas the poorest, i.e. mainly the landless, were left outside. Thus, it is highly uncertain whether the distribution target of the reform was ever reached. Nor does the reform seem to have been very successful in terms of the growth objective. During the 1970s, agricultural production *per capita* became negative. Peruvian agriculture today appears to be as stagnant as it was twenty years ago.

Steven Englander's paper goes into the details of another of Simpson's themes: the importance of agricultural research and training in connection with the transfer of agricultural technology. The bulk of the evidence available on research and transfer of technology in agriculture seems to indicate that these two activities are complementary in relation to each other and not substitutes.[48] Using this finding as a background, Englander sets out to examine how domestic agricultural research capacity is acquired in developing countries.

He begins by constructing a model of agricultural research and technology transfer, to answer the question of whether a research system in a particular developing country should adapt a foreign technology to suit its needs or develop a purely local one. The analysis is conducted with the aid of expected research possibility frontiers:tradeoff curves between two desired characteristics of the cereal (wheat) which describe the combinations of expected best improvements of these two characteristics from a given research programme.

Englander introduces two regions in his analysis, containing different relative valuations for the two characteristics. It is assumed that neither of the two regions prefers the variety which is the goal of the other. Furthermore, it is postulated that neither region can produce a variety which from the standpoint of the other region is better than what that region can itself accomplish. However, research is not a deterministic process but a highly probabilistic one. Consequently the result may be a product which has markedly different characteristics from those desired by the researchers. Hence the possibility remains that a region involuntarily ends up with a product that corresponds well with the requirements of the other region.

If this is the case, how does the other region respond? Will it or will it not attempt to exploit the research results? Obviously, this will depend to a large extent on *how close* the characteristics of the new variety are to those preferred by the region. If the new variety is superior to the existing ones in terms of both demand characteristics, the choice is easy. The product will be adopted. On the other hand, a product that is a great deal better in terms of one of the characteristics but below the standards set in terms of the second, will present problems.

One possibility is that, via domestic research, the new variety may be adapted to the requirements of the second region. However, it has often been the case in practice that complementary changes occur in factor endowments that enable new varieties that were originally unsuitable to become adapted to the requirements of the second region.

Englander subsequently turns to a discussion of some empirical findings. He presents data which indicate that local wheat varieties compete favourably with those developed elsewhere. A comparison of Green Revolution varieties of wheat developed in Mexico with locally developed varieties from 21 countries indicates that on average the latter had an advantage of 425 kilos per hectare. Moreover, it is clear that foreign technologies may have characteristics that outweigh domestic advantages, since in the majority of the cases investigated, the Mexican improved varieties turned out to have higher yields than *traditional* domestic seeds. Finally, domestic adaptations of varieties developed in Mexico outperformed both traditional seeds and Mexican-developed ones.

The last question which Englander raises is why domestic research capacity is often too low. The reasons given are that domestic researchers are frequently inadequately trained and that researchers do not remain with their research organisations. Drawing on a two-period model where a research system can choose between doing research now and training people for future research, Englander points out that a rapid turnover of personnel in this system lowers research output both today and in the future. This, in turn, puts a squeeze on the training capacity of the country and may easily lead to overinvestment in training. When a research system is unable to hold on to its researchers a long-run shift in the focus of the system, towards low-productive research, may occur, since the underlying scientific base becomes eroded and the system starts to focus on minor variations instead of on major breakthroughs.

The Socialist Experience

Attempts to introduce change in the primary sector may lead to far-reaching effects. Thus, land reforms, while generally attempting to change a pre-reform system based on private ownership, may have very different outcomes, depending above all on the ideological outlook of those undertaking the reform. Private ownership of land may be replaced by either cooperative, collective or state farming.[49] By the same token, attempts to raise productivity in mining and to integrate a foreign mining enclave with the remainder of the economy, maximising the spread effects or linkages from the mining sector, can be carried out in different ways, ranging from simple taxation, via joint ventures, to a complete takeover of owner-ship by private or public domestic interests with or without compen-sation to the former owners.

Keith Griffin has identified three different styles of policy-making in developing countries all of which bear on the question of change.[50] The technocratic style is geared towards increasing output and relies heavily on technological improvements, free market forces and private ownership, while it pays little attention to ques-tions of income distribution. A 'reformist' strategy is more inclined to redistribute incomes, at least to some sectors, while it places a lower weight on the output objective. Finally, the 'radical' solution is heavily concentrated on achieving social change and redistribution of political power, and as a corollary of this primary goal, a redistribution of incomes in favour of the poor. The growth objective, insofar as it conflicts with that of equality, may have to be played down.

The last section of the present book deals with the experience of the 'radical' type of change. *Stefan Hedlund's* article centres on the socialisation of labour in attempts at rural cooperation, i.e. the sharing of rewards from labour operations that are performed jointly. Cooperatives can be formed both for ideological and for material reasons. The latter aims, for example, at realising economies of scale to obtain higher incomes for the members of the cooperatives. Hedlund's thesis is twofold. Firstly, in order for socialisation to be successful, an ideological motivation must be present. However, it is unlikely that such a motivation will exist when large-scale cooperatives are established. Secondly, as the size of the cooperatives increases, other complications arise that make success difficult to achieve.

Hedlund uses three examples to illustrate his thesis: Israel, the Soviet Union and Tanzania. In all three cases, three different modes of cooperation have been attempted: communes — with complete socialisation and equal distribution; collectives — with partial socialisation, permitting private plots and different kinds of remu-neration systems; and association — without socialisation but realising the economies of scale inherent in marketing, purchasing etc.

The evidence from communes indicates that these depend very heavily on the recruitment of members with similar, and strong, ideological outlooks. In that case material incentives are not needed, but solidarity motives are sufficient for this mode of production to be feasible. When the communes are part of an official policy, on the other hand, and a large-scale cooperative scheme is attempted, problems begin to show up. Ideology can no longer be trusted to work. Material incentives are needed. However, without compulsion there will not be any pressure to work and the free rider problem will be difficult to solve.

In his discussion of the second mode — collectives — Hedlund takes issue with some abstract economic models, which, by abstracting from some of the core elements of collective production — the intensity of work — have reached the conclusion that work incentives should be stronger in collectives than in the other two modes. Instead, Hedlund argues, there are strong incentives for shirking in the collective system, due on the one hand to the existence of the free rider problem when working on collective lands and on the other hand to the existence of private plots which compete with the collective.

In the final mode — association, as exemplified by the Soviet *zveno* system — the problems of collective production tend to disappear. Units are small and allow for peer group control. A link is established between efforts and rewards which minimises shirking. Thus, this system retains some of the advantages of private production, but it also realises external economies of scale in marketing and purchasing activities.

Hedlund concludes that collectivisation provides a doubtful basis for rural development. In order to be effective it must be comprehensive, but then shirking problems immediately present themselves. It is not easy to devise viable incentives for peasants to join collectives on a voluntary basis if at the same time the principle of socialisation of labour is to be maintained. It would appear that the less ambitious forms of cooperation — those which most closely resemble private agriculture — have turned out to be the most successful ones.

The paper by *Benno Ndulu* and *Lucian Msambichaka* provides a good illustration of the problems of devising suitable incentives under a socialist mode of production. Ndulu and Msambichaka analyse the development of Tanzanian agriculture from the beginning of the 1960s to the present.

The first issue which is raised is the evolution of agricultural policy. Before the Arusha Declaration in 1967 there was no major difference between colonial and post-colonial agriculture in

Tanzania. The Arusha Declaration began a different policy. A 'frontal' approach was adopted to obtain self-sufficiency in food production, increased cash crop production that could serve as a basis for industrialisation, and the development of a socialist mode of production and living. Agriculture was thereby given a central role in the overall development process, one which continues to form the basis of subsequent policy documents.

Ndulu and Msambichaka subsequently examine the actual contribution of agriculture. The new policy has not been a success. The share of agriculture in GDP fell from about 60 per cent at the beginning of the 1960s to 36 per cent twenty years later. This was hardly due to the dynamism of other sectors. The food self-sufficiency target has not been reached. However, as the population outgrows food production resort has been made to food imports. Finally the production of export crops has been very mixed, with negative trends for some of the most important crops.

The agricultural sector continues to provide most of the employment in the country (some 80 per cent) largely due to the failure of the non-agricultural sectors to develop sufficiently rapidly. Within the sector, the share of wage employment has declined from 50 per cent in 1961 to 23 per cent in 1981. The sector is also the largest earner of foreign exchange and has increased its share from 70 per cent prior to 1976 to 80 per cent at the beginning of the 1980s. However, once again, this is due to the failure of other sectors to contribute. The capacity of agriculture to pay for imports has been cut in half during the past decade.

There are several factors behind this gloomy picture. Investment in the sector has been inadequate. The peasants have not been able to save much themselves, and the government has starved the sector of investment funds, at least in relation to its significance in the national economy. Hence, simple production techniques, dominated by the hoe, continue to prevail, while modern inputs such as fertiliser, improved seeds and chemicals, are either not available or not delivered in time.

A second explanation is that of price factors. The output of export crops has declined due largely to the failure to adjust the Tanzanian exchange rate to take account of falling international prices. Moreover, since 1975 food crops have become relatively more attractive to produce. However, in real terms, the price of both types of crops has decreased. Food crops also present a special availability problem in that a parallel, unofficial market coexists with the official market and the price in the parallel market has been consistently higher. Also, producers have tended to shift out of crops that have to be marketed via official channels towards for example horticultural crops which are sold exclusively via the unofficial marketing system.

On top of these difficulties, the agricultural sector suffers from a number of organisation problems due to public policy: in the distribution of input subsidies, in the setting of production targets, in marketing and planning etc., which together tend to establish insufficient incentives for production and delivery and make expectations regarding the future unstable.

The last paper in the book, by *Melanie Beresford*, deals with a problem that is similar to that treated by Ndulu and Msambichaka: the role of agriculture in the transition to a socialist mode of production in South Vietnam, after the end of the Vietnam war in 1975.

When the Vietnam war ended, the southern part of the country presented a highly distorted picture, with no less than 30 per cent of the labour force being unemployed (55 per cent in urban areas), severe war damage which meant that exports could cover only 2–4 per cent of current imports and a concomitant heavy dependence on outside funding. The availability of funds was cut off as the United States withdrew from the scene. At the same time, Soviet and Chinese aid to the north was no longer forthcoming in as large a quantity and on as generous terms as during the war. Vietnam had to find a development strategy that was based on domestic resources. This new strategy focused on agriculture as a means for building an industrial base, and not on the traditional socialist priority given to heavy industry.

One of the key areas in this strategy was the Mekong delta: the largest producer and exporter of rice. Beresford examines the evolution of a structure in this area which relied heavily on a capitalist mode of production. During the French period, land had been concentrated in a few hands and a system where tenants were exploited by landowners had developed. The First Indochina War and the gradual takeover first by the Viet Minh and later by the NLF had produced a series of land reforms and some redistributive measures were undertaken by the Thieu government as well. In the Mekong delta, this resulted in the establishment of a fairly egalitarian structure of land tenure by 1975 with the majority of the peasants being placed in the 'middle-sized' category. Here, shortage of labour, due to the war, American modernisation efforts and the increased scope for capital accumulation when land rents had decreased had led to the emergence of dynamic, modernised and partly mechanised agriculture which showed very little interest in collectivisation.

This created a problem for the Vietnamese government. In 1975 the collectivisation drive began. The principle was that collectivisation was to be voluntary, and that the incentives to join should come from the economic superiority of the collectives. The Mekong peasants were, however, not eager to join. In central Vietnam, where both land and capital were scarce and where collectivisation, according to Beresford, permitted a better utilisation of these factors, the campaign had been successful, whereas these incentives were largely absent in the south.

In the late 1970s, an agricultural production crisis developed. This was the signal for an intensification of collectivisation and the breakdown of some of the capitalistic structures in the Mekong delta in order to appropriate a larger surplus from the peasants and increase agricultural production. However, the short-term results fell short of what had been expected, and within a year, official criticism of the campaign suggested that it may have been counterproductive.

The failure of agriculture to expand jeopardised the overall development strategy. Hence, in 1979 a new strategy was adopted where direct contracts were signed between the government and individual producers and where increasing resort was made to the market mechanism. State procurement prices were also brought closer to the prices prevailing in the free market and price differences between the north and the south were reduced.

The short-run result of the change in agricultural policy has been an increase in output and procurements that can be used for developing other sectors. Self-sufficiency in food production has been achieved in 1983, for the first time since World War II. Thus, the use of markets and of individual incentives may be expected to continue in the future.

However, Beresford concludes that this does not necessarily mean that the transformation of production has been abandoned by the policy makers. The socialisation of production does not preclude the use of markets and the influence of the state has after all increased, rather than decreased under the new policy. It would appear that the official policy now is that industrialisation will have to come before the consolidation of cooperative production in agriculture, and not vice versa.

To conclude, the vast majority of development strategies have placed a strong emphasis on industrialisation. However, even when an industrialisation strategy is pursued, the role of the primary sector must not be forgotten. As Arthur Lewis expresses it, 'the various sectors in the economy must grow in the right relationship to each other, or they cannot grow at all'.[51] Today, the primary sector constitutes the backbone of the economies of the Third World and it will presumably continue to do so for quite some time to come. Economic development is a long-term process. Hence, the problems dealt with in the present volume will continue to be of interest for many years. Primary sectors will continue to stagnate. Trade in primary products will continue to be fraught with problems. The need for change will continue to be great, and more or less radical reforms recipes will continue to be tried.

Notes

1. Fisher (1939), p. 26
2. Ibid., p 28.
3. Ibid., p. 25.
4. Ibid., p. 24.
5. Fisher (1933); (1935: 1); (1935: 2); (1939).
6. Clark (1940); (1957).
7. Clark (1957), p. 492.
8. Ibid., p. 492.
9. Ibid., pp. 496-7.
10. Kuznets (1957).
11. Hartwell (1973), pp. 368, 394.
12. Lipton (1977).
13. Cf. the papers by Ahmad, Lundahl and Alberts in the present volume.
14. Cf. the ideas presented by Johnson (1964).
15. See e.g. Johnston & Mellor (1961) and Ghatak & Ingersent (1984), Ch. 3.
16. Cf. e.g. Livingstone (1968).
17. For an introduction to the debate, see Meier (1964), pp. 250-66.
18. Cf. Mamalakis (1965), Ch. 4, where the role of Chilean mining as a quasi capital goods sector is discussed.
19. For a discussion of the symptoms of overpopulation, see Grigg (1976), (1980), (1982).
20. For the completely opposite view, see Simon (1981).
21. Grigg (1976) gives a good summary of such changes. The theme is more fully developed in Grigg (1980).
22. Boserup (1965). The theme is followed up in Boserup (1981).
23. Cf. the works by Griffin (1969), (1974), (1976). Stavenhagen (1970) and Feder (1971) give an excellent introduction to the Latin American situation.
24. See Lipton (1977), for an analysis of a number of policies that discriminate against agriculture. For a vehement criticism of Lipton, see Byres (1979). Corbridge (1982) provides criticism of both Lipton and Byres.
25. Cf. the discussion below of trade problems.

26. In this context, mention must be made of Johnson's (1967) eloquent plea for decreased protection in developed countries.
27. For an overview of dependency theory, see Blomström & Hettne (1984).
28. Myint (1958). See also Findlay (1970), Ch. 4, for an excellent exposition and critique.
29. Adams & Behrman (1982), pp. 3–6; Gillis et al. (1983), pp. 410–12.
30. Nurkse (1961).
31. For the staple theory see e.g. Baldwin (1956), (1963); Caves (1965), (1971); Watkins (1963); and Roemer (1970).
32. See the classic works of Singer (1950) and Prebifch (1950).Cf. also the article by Bhagwati (1958) on 'immiserising growth'. The empirical picture is investigated in Bairoch (1975), Ch. 6, and Spraos (1980), who show that no secular tendencies in either direction appear to exist.
33. The argument appears to be false, however. See e.g. MacBean (1966); Knudsen & Parnes (1975); and Adams & Behrman (1982).
34. Hirschman (1958).
35. Hirschman (1977).
36. Mamalakis (1978).
37. See Little, Scitovsky & Scott (1970); Bhagwati (1978); Krueger (1978), (1982), (1983), (1984). For a survey of trade, growth and development in economic models, see Findlay (1984). Roemer (1979) surveys the possibility of resource-based industrialisation in developing countries.
38. Hansen (1979).
39. See e.g. Corden & Neary (1982).
40. Cf. Rivera-Batiz (1982).
41. Cf. Dorner (1972), Chs. 1 and 3.
42. Cf. e.g. the material presented in Raup (1967).
43. See McKinnon (1973), for a discussion of this.
44. Cf. Griffin (1974), Ch. 3.
45. Schultz (1964), p. 181.
46. Commodity price stabilisation is discussed e.g. in Newbery & Stiglitz (1981).
47. These problems are dealt with e.g. in Schultz (1978) and Tolley, Thomas & Wong (1982).
48. An overview of the research and technology problem in agricultural development is given in Pinstrup-Andersen (1982).
49. Cf. Dorner (1972), Ch. 2.
50. Griffin (1973).
51. Lewis (1955), p. 276.

Bibliography

Adams, F. Gerard and Behrman, Jere R. *Commodity Exports and Economic Development. The Commodity Problem and Policy in Developing Countries.* (Lexington, Mass., 1982).

Bairoch, Paul, *The Economic Development of the Third World since 1900.* (London, 1975).

Baldwin, Robert E. 'Patterns of Development in Newly Settled Regions', *Manchester School of Economic and Social Studies*, vol. 24 (1956).

Baldwin, Robert E. 'Export Technology and Development from a Subsistence Level', *Economic Journal*, vol. 73 (1963).

Bhagwati, Jagdish N. 'Immiserizing Growth: A Geometrical Note', *Review of*

Economic Studies, vol. 25 (1958).

_____ *Foreign Trade Regimes and Economic Development: Anatomy and Consequences of Exchange Control Regimes*. (New York, 1978).

Blomström, Magnus and Hettne, Björn, *Development Theory in Transition: Third World Respondences to Dependency*. (London, 1984).

Boserup, Ester, *The Conditions of Agricultural Growth. The Economics of Agrarian Change under Population Pressure*. (London, 1965).

_____ *Population and Technology*. (Oxford, 1981).

Byres, Terry J. 'Of Neo-Populist Pipe-Dreams: Daedalus in the Third World and the Myth of Urban Bias', *Journal of Peasant Studies*, vol. 6 (1979).

Caves, Richard E. ' "Vent for Surplus" Models of Trade and Growth', in: Robert E. Baldwin *et al. Trade, Growth, and the Balance of Payments, Essays in Honor of Gottfried Haberler*. (Chicago, 1965).

_____ 'Export-led Growth and the New Economic History', in Jagdish N. Bhagwati, Ronald W. Jones, Robert A. Mundell and Jaroslav Vanek (eds.) *Trade, Balance of Payments and Growth, Papers in International Economics in Honor of Charles P. Kindleberger*. (Amsterdam, 1971).

Clark, Colin, *The Conditions of Economic Progress*. (London, 1940).

_____ *The Conditions of Economic Progress*. Third edition. Largely rewritten. (London, 1957).

Corbridge, Stuart, 'Urban Bias, Rural Bias, and Industrialization: An Appraisal of the Work of Michael Lipton and Terry Byres', in: John Harriss (ed.) *Rural Development, Theories of Peasant Economy and Agrarian Change*. (London, 1982).

Corden, W. Max and Neary, J. Peter, 'Booming Sector and De-industrialization in a Small Open Economy', *Economic Journal*, vol. 92 (1982).

Dorner, Peter, *Land Reform and Economic Development*. (Harmondsworth, 1972).

Feder, Ernest, *The Rape of the Peasantry, Latin America's Landholding System*. (Garden City, 1971).

Findlay, Ronald, *Trade and Specialization*. (Harmondsworth, 1970).

Findlay, Ronald, 'Growth and Development in Trade Models', in: Ronald W. Jones and Peter B. Kenen (eds.) *Handbook of International Economics*, vol. 1. (Amsterdam, 1984).

Fisher, Allan G.B. 'Capital and the Growth of Knowledge', *Economic Journal*, vol. 43 (1933).

_____ *The Clash of Progress and Security*. (London, 1935: 1).

_____ 'Economic Implications of Material Progress', *International Labour Review*, vol. 70 (1935: 2).

_____ 'Production, Primary, Secondary and Tertiary', *Economic Record*, vol. 15 (1939).

Ghatak, Subrata and Ingersent, Ken, *Agriculture and Economic Development*. (Brighton, 1984).

Gillis, Malcolm, Perkins, Dwight H., Roemer, Michael and Snodgrass, Donald R. *Economics of Development*. (New York and London, 1983).

Griffin, Keith, *Underdevelopment in Spanish America. An Interpretation*. (London, 1969).

_____ 'Policy Options for Rural Development', *Oxford Bulletin of Economics and Statistics*, vol. 35 (1973).

_____ *The Political Economy of Agrarian Change. An Essay on the Green Revolution*. (Cambridge, Mass., 1974).

_____ *Land Concentration and Rural Poverty*. (London and Basingstoke, 1976).

Grigg, David B. 'Population Pressure and Agricultural Change', in: *Progress in Geography*, vol. 8, (1976).

_____ *Population Growth and Agrarian Change: An Historical Perspective*. (Cambridge, 1980).

_____ *The Dynamics of Agricultural Change. The Historical Experience*. (London, 1982).

Hansen, Bent, 'Colonial Economic Development with Unlimited Supply of Land: A Ricardian Case', *Economic Development and Cultural Change*, vol. 27 (1979).

Hartwell, R.M. 'The Service Revolution: The Growth of Services in Modern Economy 1700–1914', in: Carlo M. Cipolla (ed.) *The Fontana Economic History of Europe. Vol. 3, The Industrial Revolution*. (Glasgow, 1973).

Hirschman, Albert O. *The Strategy of Economic Development*. (New Haven and London, 1958).

____ 'A Generalized Linkage Approach to Economic Development, with Special Reference to Staples', in: Manning Nash (ed.) *Essays on Economic Development and Cultural Change in Honor of Bert F. Hoselitz, Economic Development and Cultural Change*. Supplement, vol. 25 (1977).

Johnson, Harry G. 'Towards a General Capital Accumulation Approach to Economic Development', in: OECD Study Group in the Economics of Education, *The Residual Factor and Economic Growth*. (Paris, 1964).

____ *Economic Policies towards Less Developed Countries*. (New York, 1967).

Johnston, Bruce F. and Mellor, John W. 'The Role of Agriculture in Economic Development', *American Economic Review*, vol. 51 (1961).

Knudsen Odin and Parnes, Andrew, *Trade Instability and Economic Development*. (Lexington, Mass., 1975).

Krueger, Anne O. *Foreign Trade Regimes and Economic Development: Liberalisation Attempts and Consequences*. (New York, 1978).

____ *Comparative Advantage and Development Policy Twenty Years Later*, Working Paper No. 65, The Industrial Institute for Economic and Social Research (Stockholm, 1982).

____ *Trade and Employment in Developing Countries. 3. Synthesis and Conclusions*. (Chicago and London, 1983).

____ 'Trade Policies in Developing Countries', in: Ronald W. Jones and Peter B. Kenen (eds.) *Handbook of International Economics*, vol. 1 (Amsterdam, 1984).

Kuznets, Simon, 'Quantitative Aspects of the Economic Growth of Nations. II. Industrial Distribution of National Product and Labor Force', *Economic Development and Cultural Change*, Supplement to vol. 5 (1957).

Lewis, W. Arthur, *The Theory of Economic Growth*. (London, 1955).

Lipton, Michael, *Why Poor People Stay Poor, Urban Bias in World Development*. (London, 1977).

Little, Ian, Scitovsky, Tibor and Scott, Maurice, *Industry and Trade in Some Developing Countries. A Comparative Study*. (London, 1970).

Livingstone, Ian, 'Agriculture versus Industry in Economic Development', *Journal of Modern African Studies*, vol. 6 (1968).

MacBean, Alasdair I. *Export Instability and Economic Development*. (London, 1966).

McKinnon, Ronald I. *Money and Capital in Economic Development*. (Washington, D.C., 1973).

Mamalakis, Markos J. 'Public Policy and Sectoral Development. A Case Study of Chile 1940–58', in: Markos Mamalakis and Clark Winton Reynolds, *Essays on the Chilean Economy*. (Homewood, 1965).

Mamalakis, Markos J. *The Minerals Theory of Growth. The Latin American Evidence*. Diskussionsbeiträge No. 18, Ibero-Amerika Institut für Wirtschaftsforschung (Göttingen, 1978).

Meier, Gerald M. (ed.) *Leading Issues in Development Economics*. (New York, 1964).

Myint, Hla, 'The "Classical Theory" of International Trade and the Underdeveloped Countries', *Economic Journal*, vol. 68 (1958).

Newbery, David G. and Stiglitz, Joseph E. *The Theory of Commodity Price Stabilisation. A Study in the Economics of Risk*. (Oxford, 1981).

Nurkse, Ragnar, *Patterns of Trade and Development*. (Oxford, 1961).

Pinstrup-Andersen, Per, *Agricultural Research and Technology in Economic Development*. (London and New York, 1982).

Prebifch, Raul (United Nations), *The Economic Development of Latin America and Its Principal Problems*. (Lake Success, 1950).

Raup, Philip M. 'Land Reform and Agricultural Development', in: Herman M. Southworth and Bruce F. Johnston (eds.) *Agricultural Development and Economic Growth*. (Ithaca and London, 1967).

Rivera-Batiz, Francisco L. 'International Migration, Non-traded Goods and Economic Welfare in the Source Country', *Journal of Development Economics*, vol. 11 (1982).

Roemer, Michael, *Fishing for Growth, Export-led Development in Peru, 1950–1967*. (Cambridge, Mass., 1970).

_____ 'Resource-based Industrialization in the Developing Countries: A Survey', *Journal of Development Economics*, vol. 6 (1979).

Schultz, Theodore W. *Transforming Traditional Agriculture*. (New Haven and London, 1964).

Schultz, Theodore W. (ed.) *Distortions of Agricultural Incentives*. (Bloomington and London, 1978).

Simon, Julian L. *The Ultimate Resource*. (Oxford, 1981).

Singer, Hans W. 'The Distribution of Gains between Investing and Borrowing Countries', *American Economic Review*, vol. 40 (1950).

Spraos, John, 'The Statistical Debate on the Net Barter Terms of Trade between Primary Commodities and Manufactures', *Economic Journal*, vol. 90 (1980).

Stavenhagen, Rodolfo (ed.) *Agrarian Problems and Peasant Movements in Latin America*. (Garden City, 1970).

Tolley, George S., Thomas, Vinod and Wong, Chung Ming, *Agricultural Price Policies and the Developing Countries*. (Baltimore and London, 1982).

Watkins, Melville H. 'A Staple Theory of Economic Growth', *Canadian Journal of Economics and Political Science*, vol. 29 (1963).

PART ONE
THE ROLE OF THE PRIMARY SECTOR

1 THE PRIMARY SECTOR: COMPOSITION AND FUNCTIONS*

Markos J. Mamalakis

If the rod be bent too much one way, says the proverb, in order to make it straight you must bend it as much the other.
Adam Smith, *The Wealth of Nations*, p. 628.

Introduction

This paper hopes to restore, through the analysis of all components of the primary sector, a long lost balance in development economics and correct an analytical incompleteness which has existed ever since Adam Smith, David Ricardo and John Stuart Mill. The incomplete developmental framework and analytical thinking to which I refer is the dualistic agriculture–industry model. The missing part is that of 'services'. This model, which even today pervades the literature even though it ignores services, is based on two pillars. The first is the partially valid 'industrialisation mystique' which glorifies the catalytic role of manufacturing in opening and paving the path to self-sustained growth. The second has its roots in the physiocratic tenet and emphasis on the 'produit net' of agriculture as the sole source of income and wealth. The modern neophysiocratic 'agricultural economics approach' which suggests transforming neglected 'traditional' agriculture[1] is also partial and incomplete because it perceives the 'primary sector' problem as a mono-sectoral, agricultural one, when in reality it is a multisectoral regional one.

The analytical misconceptions of the agriculture–industry model that are embedded in the classical school have been reinforced by modern Nobel-prize-winning development economists such as Theodore Schultz (emphasising agriculture) and W. Arthur Lewis (emphasising industry) and development of elaborate but incomplete

* I am indebted to Andreas Savvides and two outside reviewers for comments on an earlier draft of this essay.

models such as those of Ranis and Fei[2] and Dale Jorgenson.[3] The more recent popular rural–urban model of Harris and Todaro,[4] a reaction to the incomplete agriculture–industry framework, also fails to treat explicitly either rural or urban services.

A basic theme of the present paper is that the primary sector consists as much of agricultural, forestry and fishing activities as it does of services (Colin Clark's tertiary) and industrial (secondary) ones.[5] Economic development, therefore, never was a process of transition from agriculture to industry and then to services. It has always been a process of transition from embryonic primary activities (rural agricultural, service and industrial ones) to advanced, modern and highly productive primary (rural) and post-primary (urban service and industrial) ones. During this process industrial and service activities have generally increased in relative importance as compared to agriculture.

Lack of, or only implicit, treatment of services by the classical school and modern development specialists has led to flawed analyses and diagnoses of the poverty and underdevelopment problem and fundamentally defective remedial strategies.

The paper is divided into three parts. The first examines the relationship between production of goods and services and the primary sector. Presented in it are four concepts of the primary sector and of labour surplus. Part 2 discusses some major dimensions of the relationship between the primary sector and income distribution. Part 3 deals with selected aspects of capital formation as they relate to the primary sector.

1. The Primary Sector and Production

The Four Concepts of the Primary Sector

What the primary sector is, what its functions and composition are, is far from clear. There can be at least four concepts or definitions of the primary sector. According to the first, 'narrow' definition, primary is synonymous with agriculture. The function of the primary sector is to produce agricultural consumer goods. In terms of the second 'intermediate' definition, the primary sector includes all activities needed to produce and deliver agricultural goods to the final consumer. The primary sector consists both of goods and services production. Storage, transportation, trade and even those personal services transforming the quantity, time and location dimension of agricultural goods[6] are an integral part of it. The second is basically the definition used by Colin Clark.[7]

The third notion of the 'extended primary sector' includes all rural activities producing agricultural, service and industrial consumer goods needed for the survival of a family. The function of the extended primary sector is to produce all consumer goods needed by rural households. As long as they are consumer-oriented and rural, all agricultural, service and industrial activities are part of it.

And then there is the fourth and 'broadest' notion which includes within the primary sector all consumer and capital goods produced by and needed for the survival of rural families. Primary now is synonymous with rural. The primary is a multifunctional, multi-activity, multi-product and multi-service sector.

The Four Types of Primary Sector Labour Surplus

This fourfold classification of the primary sector is the first step in the process of decomposing its structure, identifying its idiosyncratic features and developing novel development strategies. The usefulness of this classification can be seen by examining the four 'labour surplus' concepts that correspond to the four aforementioned notions of the primary sector. There exists, first, the well-known and celebrated notion of the 'agricultural labour surplus'.[8] Surplus agricultural labour (narrow primary-sector labour surplus) is that part of the rural labour force that *cannot* find productive employment in agriculture. Estimates exist suggesting that as much as 80 per cent of the rural population in developing countries cannot find, under prevailing production conditions, full employment within rural agriculture. By focusing on this 'narrow (agricultural) labour surplus' concept, development economists (Ranis and Fei, W. Arthur Lewis) using the dualistic agriculture–industry framework have perceived of industrialisation as the only path to prosperity. The industrialisation plus stagnation pattern of many developing countries has created, however, the need for better analysis and development strategies.

In the second concept, the 'intermediate primary sector labour surplus' is defined as that segment of the rural labour force that cannot be employed productively either in agricultural production or in the ancillary services that augment the value of agricultural products as they move towards final consumption. It can be estimated conservatively that as much as 30 per cent of the rural labour force is, or can be, employed productively in the service segment of the intermediate primary sector. Labour employed in services complementary to agricultural production and consumption[9] is neither free nor idle nor surplus. Furthermore, development cannot be achieved unless the quality and quantity of these complementary primary sector services are greatly strengthened. Economic development is characterised as much by a transition from non-existent or low quality to ample and high quality complementary to agriculture primary sector services as it is characterised by a transfer to labour from low productivity agricultural to high productivity agricultural and industrial jobs.

According to the third concept, which corresponds to the extended primary sector, labour surplus is defined as that segment of the rural labour force that cannot be employed productively in any type of agricultural, service and industrial rural consumer goods production. As much as 80 per cent of the rural labour force is, or can be, employed in the 'extended primary sector'. Of this 80 per cent, 20 per cent would be employed in agriculture (narrow primary sector), 30 per cent in complementary-to-agriculture services (the second component of the intermediate primary sector) and another 30 per cent in autonomous services, such as health, education and administration[10] and industrial consumer goods production (the third segment of the extended primary sector). Economic development involves as much an employment transition from low to high productivity rural non-agricultural consumer goods production as it involves a transition from low productivity non-agricultural rural to high productivity urban consumer goods production.

Labour surplus of the 'broadest primary sector' (all rural activities), which is the fourth concept, is defined as that segment of the rural labour force that cannot find productive employment in any rural consumer and capital goods production. As much as 90 per cent of the rural labour force may be employed in the broadest primary sector, with 10 per cent engaged in the production of such capital goods as roads, dwellings, fences, irrigation works, bridges, storage places and so forth. If the above 'estimates' are accepted as reasonable, a vast difference between the labour surplus of the 'narrow' and 'broadest' primary sector does emerge. While the 'narrow primary sector labour surplus' can be as high as 80 per cent of the rural labour force, the labour surplus of the 'broadest primary sector' (the rural labour surplus) may be only, or even less than, 10 per cent of the rural labour force. The implications in the formulation of strategies cannot be ignored.

Agricultural, Service, Primary and Rural Revolutions

A goal and consequence of economic development is the rise in the productivity of labour in all segments of the broadest primary sector, that is in agriculture, complementary to agriculture services, other rural consumer goods production and rural capital goods production. The hypothesis advanced here is that rural services, complementary and autonomous, provide the magic link between an *agricultural revolution*, which generates the food surpluses needed for growth, and a *rural revolution*, which makes rural life as, or even more, attractive than that in urban areas.

There exists the need of transforming the location, quantity and time dimension of agricultural products through trade, transport and financial services revolutions. There exists also the need of transforming the quantity and quality of all rural agricultural and non-agricultural inputs and outputs through revolutions in quality maintaining and improving health, educational, social security and governmental services.

A *primary sector revolution* will have materialised if and when the underlying agricultural, medical, transport, governmental, trade, financial and educational transformations have taken place. In order for all these changes to be carried out it will be necessary (a) to find a means of employing previously unutilised or underutilised labour; (b) to reduce the size of unilateral resource flows from primary-rural to urban regions; (c) to establish free terms of trade between agriculture, services and industry, whether these are urban or rural; and (d) to restore a balance between rural and urban services by reducing the concentration of services in cities.

Many of the aforementioned changes are likely to occur simultaneously. However, I believe, there is one change that must come first. That is *decentralisation* of governmental services and political power. Such a decentralisation is needed to enable the primary sector to utilise its own resources for its own and the general social benefit. Such a decentralisation would also enable the primary sector to devise and implement the fiscal (increased local authority to tax and spend local government revenues), educational (locally provide primary, secondary and vocational education), legal (establish and promote locally needed executive, legislative and judiciary branches and services of government) health (provide and operate rural clinics and related medical services), labour (training, insurance and protection), financial (create and expand rural financial markets and services) and overall investment (especially overhead) policies that would mobilise all its human and natural resources and lead to an income-raising labour scarcity. This governmental decentralisation would be the first step in expanding the *Lebensraum* of primary sector inhabitants through employment- and income-generating opportunities in rural services and industry.

This political administrative change is, however, as Matos Mar and Mejía[11] and others have demonstrated for Peru, as difficult to materialise in socialist, as it is in social market or mixed developing countries with centralised bureaucracies. Governmental bureaucracies throughout most Latin American, African and Asian countries are capital-city-based and capital-city-oriented. One of their *de facto* functions is to use the resource surpluses they extract from the rural primary sector to enrich the semiprivileged and privileged urban households. The actors may change but the underlying primary sector discrimination seems to be embedded in granite. Clashes between private urban industry and private latifundio agriculture are superseded by clashes between private and state-owned industry and reformed agriculture. In turn, these are succeeded by clashes between state-owned industry and collective agriculture (Peru, Chile under Allende, Cuba). Only a *rural service revolution* would be able to remove these sectoral and regional clashes and eliminate the labour market pluralism that pervades the primary and post-primary sectors.

The primary sector has another angle which it is important to mention at this point. 'Primary' implies association with an internal, autochthonous developmental initiative. It is generally accepted that in England, Germany, the United States and Japan, the industrial revolution was intimately linked to agricultural and rural revolutions. In addition, however, these success cases are characterised by development of their primary, rural agro-service structures through internal rather than external initiative.

In many respects, the primary sector is the birthplace of the legislative, executive and judiciary legal system that determines the success of the long term development process. It is too difficult to draw any hard conclusions on this matter at this point. It is possible to speculate however, that, if a primary nation is to develop, its 'agro-service' base must give rise to services that reflect and cater to the needs of all people, classes, regions and sectors. These services may ultimately determine whether the 'agro-rural' surplus is released in a manner that stimulates or stifles primary sector and aggregate growth.

Both the agriculture–industry and rural–urban dualistic models are defective in that they ignore the indisputable presence of multiple service activities in rural areas. Their incomplete two-sector or two-region approach is responsible for their failure to recognise the existence and implications of land, labour and capital market pluralism within and outside the primary sector. Ignorance and omission of the role and presence of services within the primary sector, within rural areas and in the process of economic development is one of the legacies of classical economic thinking responsible for the failure of modern economics to eradicate world poverty.

2. The Primary Sector and Income Distribution

Many income distribution problems of less developed countries are linked to the diverse segments of the primary sector.[12] Thus, first, income and productivity in agriculture are low with much of the agricultural population of the primary sector belonging to the bottom 40 per cent that receives less than 18 per cent or 12 per cent of income. Second, there is the primary sector non-agricultural population engaged in services which, often, has an even lower *per capita* income than the agricultural one. Third, there is open, disguised, and seasonal unemployment and underemployment depressing the income levels. Fourth, much of the low income of primary sector labour and households can be explained by low levels of education and other capital endowments. It is worth noting that true, actual real income of the primary sector is likely to be underestimated because of inadequate measurement of the value of marketed or bartered non-agricultural activities within it.

The traditional approach of improving income distribution recommends generating agricultural labour scarcity by expanding aggregate labour demand through industrialisation. It recommends that labour be transferred from low productivity agricultural or rural to high productivity industrial (Lewis, Ranis and Fei) or urban (Harris and Todaro) jobs. This traditional approach has failed to a large extent as low productivity agro-service-rural labour has migrated to the cities becoming low productivity service labour.[13]

According to the new approach recommended here, if economic development and universal labour scarcity are to be achieved it will be necessary to upgrade transport, trade, government, health and educational services in both rural and urban settlements. The primary sector needs to be developed by the people and for the people to the point where lack of adequate basic services satisfying the basic human needs of health, education, transport and trade are no longer a cause of rural–urban, inter-regional, inter-city and international migration.

Reform, Incentives and Distribution

Reform, as it affects the income share of, and the distribution of income within, the primary sector, needs to be multifaceted. Best known are the two extreme cases of agricultural reform, namely total freedom of prices for its products (which frequently raises the agricultural income share) on the one hand, and a comprehensive, sometimes confiscatory, land reform (raising the income share of agricultural labour at the expense of the old landowning class) on the other hand. As shown elsewhere[14] the price reform is as partial as the land tenure reform in that each tackles only one aspect of the multifaceted primary sector and rural poverty problem. Higher relative agricultural prices generate the incentives for higher agricultural production. And land redistribution to small-scale private landlords (state ownership of land generally destroys incentives unless greatly modified) also increases the incentives for maximising agricultural output. Both may be needed simultaneously but are not sufficient to achieve a primary sector revolution. What is needed is an expansion of the primary sector production frontier through a generalised modernisation of all primary services (education, government, storage, trade and so forth) that raises the capacity to produce and respond to incentives. Such a modernisation should encompass all human capital, physical capital and financial capital endowments that are required for increased primary rural production.

Market incentives must be offered to agricultural, service, industrial and mineral rural-primary production. Incentives must be created for the accumulation of all capital forms that are scarce in the primary sector and rural areas. Furthermore, incentives must be the same for all activities whether they are rural or urban and for all capital forms, whether they are in the primary or post-primary sectors. This requires a government consumption reform, whereby government services are offered in all regions and to all sectors. It also requires a government investment policy reform, that is, a reduction or elimination of the regional, sectoral and class concentration of public capital and the services generated by it.

What is needed is an integrated reform where price, tax, government expenditure and all other benefits-incentives offered are the same for rural and urban areas and for the primary and post-primary sectors. Price and land tenure reforms must be accompanied by a rural services reform where rural services needed by the inhabitants are offered at an opportunity (labour) cost that reflects and corresponds to the lower labour costs of the rural areas using locally unemployed or idle labour, rather than the high wages of the capital city or the advanced industrial-service nations. The primary sector should avoid bringing in high cost service workers from the cities.

The growth of non-agricultural services and industrial activities in the rural-primary economic complex is an appropriate means of generating the labour demand that breaks down the monopsony power of landlords. Land reform and price increases may not increase, by themselves, the non-agricultural rural labour demand to the point where it would create universal labour scarcity, technological progress and increased productivity.

The Catalytic Role of Services

A major function of the S-sector is to break down the cleavages that separate the haves from the have-nots; to provide the poor with the capacity to produce and participate in output increments; to act as a bulldozer (the 'Bulldozer Theory'?) that opens up a path in the jungle of poverty so that the poor can move out and into new activities, regions and sectors. Services and service activities are the path from rural agricultural to rural non-agricultural activities, from low income to high income rural employment and from low income rural to high income urban employment. Services link and pave the path from agriculture to industry. Thus, the transition from poverty to prosperity is a transition from a primary, embryonic, predominantly rural agriculture–service–industry society to a post-primary advanced agriculture–service–industry society.

Within the process of income distribution, services break down the monopoly or oligopoly of education that leads to and reinforces distributional and skill pluralism. And they curtail landlord monopsony power by stimulating the growth of human, physical, technological and financial capital forms which increase output capacity while requiring minimum quantities of land. Thus, a *service revolution* is characterised by, coincides with and generates the transition from land-applied and agriculture-supported service activities of the primary sector to labour-applied and service- and industry-related and supported service activities of the post-primary economy.

3. The Primary Sector and Capital Accumulation

Capital formation can be defined narrowly in the classical and national accounting sense as capital goods production, or it can be defined broadly as any act or measure that can lead to an increased future output of goods and services by raising the stocks of physical, human, technological and financial capital. The second concept is so widely used in economic development and is so relevant to the treatment of the primary sector that an explicit analysis of it is needed. Furthermore, there is no need to be bound to concepts or frameworks which are incomplete and can hinder our efforts to eradicate this modern pest of repulsive poverty.

Developing nations possess different combinations of natural (land and mineral), human (quantity and quality), financial and physical (machinery and equipment and housing) capital. Within each nation, the primary sector possesses also different *per capita* endowments of these capital forms. A major development goal is to stimulate and achieve the growth of those scarce capital endowments that will permit maximum growth of agricultural output, maximum growth of rural, autonomous, agriculture- and industry-related services, and the maximum growth of rural industrial output.

There can be no economic development without the establishment and operation of a physical capital-goods-producing sector, a human capital-producing sector (health, education and social security services), a financial capital-producing sector (financial services), a political capital-producing sector (education, administrative services) and a social capital-producing sector (education). All these capital-producing sectors exist in an embryonic or advanced form within the primary sector of each country. They need to be increased and modernised within and beyond the primary sector.

A final comment on the issue of saving. Saving can arise from a variety of actions and under a variety of economic circumstances. First, saving means *not consuming*, that is producing capital rather than consumer goods. This concept of saving presupposes full labour and production capacity utilisation. It emphasises the *ex ante* action of releasing inputs from consumer to capital goods production. This *ex ante* saving is a classical notion. Unless you reduce consumption you cannot increase investment.

Second, however, saving means using inputs to produce capital goods. Saving here is an *ex post* concept and arises whether investment goods are produced by utilising idle (underemployed or unemployed) resources or previously fully employed resources released from consumer goods production. If maximum consumer goods production has been attained within the primary sector and there is still idle labour available, capital goods production can be augmented and saving will arise by using idle labour. If there is seasonally, cyclically, secularly or disguisedly unemployed-idle labour, investment and saving can be increased by using it. Under these circumstances what is reduced is labour idleness and unwanted leisure rather than consumption in the sense of consumer goods production. This then becomes a dominant developmental (capital formation, production and income distribution) issue in the primary sector: how to use low productivity, partially or totally idle labour to expand production of non-agricultural consumer (services and industrial) and capital goods. Ragnar Nurkse[15] pioneered this idea. Its implementation, however, has met with limited success because suggested strategies have ignored the critical role of services.

Conclusions

The issues raised by the analysis of the primary sector are highly complicated. There may indeed exist an advantage in totally abandoning the term 'primary' and using instead more specific descriptions for each of its component activities as these were explained in Part 1.

By using four different, increasingly inclusive notions of the primary sector in the present essay, it was demonstrated that the 'primary' sector poverty problem of the third world is more than an agricultural one and that it has numerous production, income distribution and capital formation related aspects.

The main idea that has evolved from the analysis of the primary sector is that we need in economic development an explicit treatment of the role of services within the primary sector, within rural and urban areas and in terms of their impact on production, income distribution and capital formation. In addition, it has been argued that agricultural, whether price or land tenure, and industrial revolutions cannot generate economic development or even occur without parallel service revolutions. Rural reform and modernisation of the primary sector require combined agricultural, service and industrial revolutions.

Notes

1. Schultz (1964).
2. Ranis & Fei (1961); Fei & Ranis (1964).
3. Jorgenson (1961).
4. Harris & Todaro (1970).
5. Clark (1940).
6. Mamalakis (1976), pp. 174–81.
7. Clark (1940), pp. 337–73.
8. Lewis (1954); Ranis & Fei (1961); Fei & Ranis (1964).
9. Mamalakis (1976), pp. 174–210.
10. Ibid., pp. 191–204.
11. Matos Mar & Mejía (1980).
12. Ahluwalia (1974),
13. Mamalakis (1976), pp. 176–210.
14. Mamalakis (1981).
15. Nurkse (1957).

Bibliography

Ahluwalia, M.S. 'Income Inequality: Some Dimensions of the Problem', *Finance and Development* (September), pp. 3–7 (1974) Reproduced in G.M. Meier, *Leading Issues in Economic Development* (Oxford University Press, New York, 1976).

Clark, Colin, *The Conditions of Economic Progress*, 1st ed. (Macmillan, London, 1940).

Fei, J.C.H. and Ranis, G. *Development of the Labour Surplus Economy: Theory and Policy*. Irwin, Homewood, Illinois, 1964.

Harris, John S. and Todaro, Michael P. 'Migration, Unemployment and Development: A Two-Sector Analysis', *American Economic Review*, vol. 60 (1970).

Jorgenson, Dale, 'The Development of a Dual Economy', *Economic Journal*, vol. 71 (1961).

Lewis, W. Arthur, 'Economic Development with Unlimited Supplies of Labour', *The Manchester School*, vol. 22 (1954).

Mamalakis, Markos J. *The Growth and Structure of the Chilean Economy: From Independence to Allende* (Yale University Press, New Haven and London, 1976).

_____, 'Estrategias generales de empleo e ingreso,' *El Trimestre Económico*, vol. 48 (1981).

Matos Mar, José and Mejía, José Manuel, 'Reforma agraria y cooperativismo rural en el Perú, 1968–78', *Estudios del Tercer Mundo*, vol. 3 (1980).

Nurkse, Ragnar, *Problems of Capital Formation in Underdeveloped Countries* (Basil Blackwell, Oxford, 1957).

Ranis, G. and Fei, J.C.H. 'A Theory of Economic Development', *American Economic Review*, vol. 51 (1961).

Schultz, Theodore W. *Transforming Traditional Agriculture* (Yale University Press, New Haven and London, 1964).

2   THE PRIMARY SECTOR IN AFRICAN DEVELOPMENT

Ester Boserup

In subsistence economies individual families consume within the family all that they have produced. A primary sector emerges when a large number of families begin to sell food or other commodities, which they have produced. Such products may either be exported for use by consumers or industries in other countries, or the development of a primary sector may be simultaneous with the development of a secondary sector to process the materials and food sold by the primary sector.

In large parts of Africa south of the Sahara[1] nearly all of the production of the primary sector is exported, because secondary sector development remains far behind that of the rest of the world. No less than 37 out of 40 African countries derived less than 15 per cent of their domestic product from manufacturing in 1970; worldwide, three-fifths of all countries with such low degrees of industrialisation were African countries.[2] Moreover, Africa is behind not only in development of the secondary sector, but also in primary sector development. In many African countries, the rate of urbanisation is low, and nearly all food consumed in rural areas is produced for subsistence only. In African countries with some urbanisation there is also little commercial food production, so that a large share of the food produced in urban areas is imported from other countries, usually from countries in other continents. Thus, primary production of non-food crops, forest products and minerals are of crucial importance for the African economies. These exports are virtually the only source of foreign exchange; further, in many African countries, taxation of these primary exports supplies the bulk of government revenue.

Africa is not the only part of the world that developed primary production for exports before the development of a secondary sector. Exchange between producers or gatherers of primary products and producers of secondary products has taken place during several millenia, not only through trade within the same village or country, but also by long distance trade. Often densely populated, urbanised areas ran short of building materials, certain types of food, metals and other materials and acquired them by long-distance trading, by plunder, or both.[3] Some peoples specialised in long-distance transport and trade, and many urbanised societies extended their military domination in order to protect trading routes and sources of supply. Thus, over time, a development took place with primary sectors producing a surplus for trade appearing in regions of previous subsistence production. Sometimes the primary producers were independent producers selling to foreign merchants; in other cases the primary producing areas became colonies of foreign powers which acquired the products by trade or as tribute.

The ancient societies in Mediterranean Europe got supplies of materials and food both from other shores of the Mediterranean and the Black Sea and from Western and Central Europe. Later when the latter areas became urbanised societies, they got supplies of raw materials and food from the less developed areas in North and East Europe, causing the emergence of large primary sectors in these areas. With improvement of transport technology before and after the Industrial Revolution, areas in other continents also developed primary sectors to supply Europe with raw materials, food and tropical products. Further, the primary producing regions in North and East Europe developed secondary sectors and became importers of overseas raw materials.

It is implied in what is said above that nearly all European countries were exporters of food and other primary products before they developed their own secondary sectors. This is true even of England, which relied on exports of wool and cereals to Continental Europe before becoming an exporter of manufactures and an importer of food. Also the non-European countries which are industrialised or semi-industrialised today began as exporters of primary products, before they developed industrialised sectors. But there was an important difference between the primary exporters in Europe and those in most overseas countries. The primary sector in European countries belonged wholly or mainly to indigenous producers, and the profits earned by export production financed the development of secondary and tertiary sectors in these countries. By contrast, in many overseas countries, a large part of the primary sector was foreign owned, and part of its profits was transferred to the homelands of the foreign owners and so did not finance investments in development of secondary and tertiary sectors in the overseas countries and colonies.

Both in most European colonies and in overseas countries which had remained independent, small indigenous family enterprises or settlers gathered, or produced, primary products and sold them to foreign or indigenous merchants in competition with large scale companies running mines or plantations. Some of the large companies were integrated enterprises, which not only produced primary products, but also processed them, either on the spot or in Europe, and transported and traded them. Competition between multinational companies, operating in several countries and colonies, and small indigenous primary producers is by no means a recent feature.

It is interesting to note that for many mining products the primary sector has nearly disappeared on a world scale, because large national and international companies handle not only the extraction of one or more minerals and ores, but also the secondary activities (processing) and the tertiary activities (transport, trading and research) related to these products. A similar development can be observed for some types of food, especially horticultural products. For these products the primary sector seems to be gradually disappearing; if such development spreads to more and more products, it is conceivable, although it seems improbable, that we may end up with vertically integrated economies without an independent primary sector.

Obstacles to Development in Africa

In the 19th century, when non-European areas developed into important exporters of primary products to the industrialising regions, many parts of Africa developed large primary sectors producing for exports. However, both in the 19th and in this century, the development of secondary sectors proceeded much more slowly in Africa than elsewhere. Several features characteristic of Africa contributed to make development of secondary sectors particularly difficult. Overall population density was low, population widely scattered, and infrastructure was extremely poor.

The colonial powers built a few railway lines, linking rich mineral deposits to export harbours, or strategic lines, but except for the Union of South Africa, no African country has more than 6 metres of railway line per square kilometre, and many have no railways. European countries have 75 to 100 metres per square kilometre.[4]

Most African railway lines run through sparsely populated or empty areas. They have little traffic, so little that it is uneconomic to build feeder roads serving the lines. Road density in Africa is also extremely low. While Western European countries have more than thousand metres of road per square kilometre, mostly hard surface roads, only a few African countries have as much as a hundred metres and some have less than ten, nearly all of much poorer quality than European roads.[5] Building of good roads in sparsely populated areas is uneconomic; therefore transport becomes prohibitively expensive for most types of products.

In an area with the overall population density of Africa there will live 100,000 persons in a circular area with a radius of 60 kilometres but in the same area with the overall density of European there will live one to two million people. In a densely populated area with reasonably good transport facilities the home market may be sufficiently large for the establishment of local industries, even when the majority of the population are poor and have a low *per capita* purchasing power for industrial goods. This helps to explain how manufacturing industries could be installed in densely populated areas of Asia in spite of colonial resistance to industrialisation and how, after independence, industrialisation has been more rapid in Asia than in Africa.

Overall population density in Latin America is not much different from that of Africa, but because Latin America was populated to a large extent by immigration, most of the population lives in coastal areas with high population densities and much better infrastructure than that of African countries. It is mainly these coastal areas and the densely populated plateau of Mexico that are becoming rapidly industrialised. In Africa, some mining towns grew up in the colonial period, but because they were located in sparsely populated areas they did not, as usually happened elsewhere, attract other industries. They remained small enclaves of extracting and crude-processing industry in a largely unindustrialised continent which failed to develop secondary sectors in spite of its rich, unutilised resources of land, minerals, and water for hydropower.

The low population density, the scattered population, and the poor infrastructure in Africa were serious obstacles not only to the development of manufacturing industries, but also to the development of a commercial food producing sector. As is usual in areas of low population density, the predominant African subsistence systems are forest fallow, bush fallow, and pastoralism.[6] In a region where forest and bush fallow systems are used, the land is cultivated for a few years, usually with hand tools, and left in fallow for many years. Adult men and young boys fell the trees and bushes when land is retaken into cultivation after several years, but most or all of the other field operations are done by women and children with very primitive tools or without any tools.[7] Only in small parts of Africa with relatively high population densities has this system of subsistence food production become supplemented or replaced by development of a primary sector of commercial food production.

Several factors have combined to produce this result. One is the lack of rural infrastructure, which makes long distance transport uneconomic, if not impossible, except for high value and durable crops. Another factor that causes delay in development of commercial food production is the organisation of work, and especially the sex distribution of work, in traditional African agriculture. The large increase of rural population in recent decades and expansion of the areas under export crops have forced the women, who produce food crops for family consumption, to cultivate poorer land with shorter fallow periods, or to cultivate land far from the villages. Thus women have had to put more time into food production and transport of crops from the fields. Since African women must combine food production with domestic work, gathering fuel and fetching water, and must often help the men with the production, transport and processing of cash crops, they are of course unable to produce any significant surpluses of food above the quantities needed to feed their own families. So even the small minority of African villages which are linked to urban areas with good transport facilities have little to sell.[8]

In regions where efforts were made to modernise and expand agricultural production, both male farmers and male government officials focused on the export crops for which the men are responsible, while the women's food crops were neglected. Women received no information about improved agricultural methods and if they had, they lacked both time and money to change and expand their production of food. Add to this the fact that African food production is exposed to severe competition from imports of subsidised food from the industrialised countries. Owing to heavy income and/or price support to farmers in industrialised countries, their exportable surpluses of many agricultural products have been rapidly increasing, resulting in the need to get rid of this surplus. This availability of surpluses has kept food prices low in the world market, and costs of sea transport from the industrialised countries to Africa are also quite low. Further, imported food has also benefited from overvalued exchange rates and from direct government subsidies to keep food prices low in the towns.[9] Because rural infrastructure in Africa is so poor, producers in rural areas generally obtain only a small fraction of the prices paid in urban areas. As a result, prices in most of Africa at the village level are too low to encourage commercial food production. Food continues to be subsistence production with traditional methods and low productivity, and food imports are growing rapidly. Moreover, the subsidised food exports from the industrialised countries prevent African countries with good natural conditions for commercial food exports from engaging in export production of food.[10]

Under these circumstances, producers can usually earn more by producing traditional non-food export crops than by producing food crops in spite of the high taxes, which are levied on many export crops.[11] Moreover, some large government projects, designed to establish commercial food production, had to close down or be kept alive with heavy subsidies because they could not compete with imports. Examples are projects for sugar and rice production linked to large scale irrigation projects.[12] In spite of the mounting imports and shortages of foreign exchange, government policies in most countries continue to encourage food imports. The politically powerful, urban, middle class, including civil servants and military personnel, benefit from low prices for the type of food which they prefer to consume. Moreover, by importing food, the towns can obtain sufficient supplies without the government having to use part of the revenue to finance rural infrastructure investment and other expenses which would have been necessary if the country were to remain self-sufficient in food in spite of the rapid increase of urban populations.

The surplus production of food in the industrialised countries has not only depressed world market prices, it has also induced the industrialised countries to grant large amounts of these surpluses as food aid in order to prevent an even greater pressure on world market prices. When African governments received food imports as food aid, not only did they save foreign exchange, they could also sell the food supplies and use the counterpart funds from these sales as budget aid. Except for countries which have large mineral exports which can be taxed, African government budgets are fed mainly by taxes on export crops and from counterpart funds related to food aid. In both cases African agriculture bears the burden.

Although some governments are becoming worried about the increasing dependence on foreign supplies of basic foodstuffs, there is little sign of a radical change of government policy. Food imports into Africa continue to increase by leaps and bounds, while African food production stagnates. In a number of countries, food production is declining due to competition from imports.

There were small food imports into Africa already in the colonial period, because the European and Asian populations in African towns imported and consumed non-African types of food. But for the rural population and most Africans in the towns, the basic foods were sorghum, millet, yams or bananas. Because imports are multiplying and the prices of imported food are favourable, more and more African families add foreign types of food, like wheat, rice, maize, sugar, and dairy products, to their diet, often abandoning the use of traditional foods. The foreign types of food have become so popular that change in taste is a frequently used argument against suggestions to promote the production of African types of food. However, the experience both in Africa and elsewhere is that food habits adapt to changes in relative prices of various foodstuffs. Therefore, it seems likely that import duties on imported food would be an effective means to encourage African food production and reduce imports especially if simultaneous efforts were made to reduce costs of internal transport and to improve methods of food production.

Perspectives for Development of the Primary Sector

Except for wheat, the types of food imported into Africa can be grown in most of the continent. Moreover, growing sufficient food for the rapidly increasing African population need not reduce the rate of growth of production of export crops. More food can be grown around the existing villages by changing the traditional system of bush fallow into a more intensive system of permanent land use with much more use of fertiliser and other inputs. Moreover, nearly all African countries have unused or underutilised cultivable land, which can be taken into use either for food production, or for export crops, or both. What is needed is making this land accessible by means of investment in transport networks and other infrastructure, and sometimes by radical changes in the traditional use of forests and pastures.[13]

A considerable share of the African rural population lives so far away from centres of export production or towns, that it is uneconomic for them to produce either food or other crops for sale. They produce most of what they need themselves and earn money income by labour migration. This migration may be either seasonal migration to mines, plantations, towns, or farms in other regions, or it may be more permanent migration by the head of the household or one or more adult children who transfer part of their earnings to the family members who have remained in the home village.

Labour migration from peripheral areas to regions of primary production for exports had already become large in the colonial period, and it has continued to be of major importance. But emigration of a substantial share of the able-bodied, adult population makes development of a peripheral area by infrastructure investment less urgent and even less economic than it would have been without emigration. Both public and private investments tend to be attracted to the areas of immigration of labour, and so bypass those of labour emigration. Thus, the contrast between areas overcrowded by immigrants and other empty or nearly empty areas becomes more and more pronounced. The low population density, which makes transport and other infrastructure uneconomic, is the main cause of these labour exports. Therefore, the continued rapid natural population growth in the labour exporting areas is a potential advantage. With a larger local population establishment of commercial production and improvement of infrastructure might become feasible in many such regions, assuming that the emigration could be contained. It would require considerable investment in long distance transport, local transport and other infrastructure, but it would increase primary production and raise employment also in construction, food processing industries and services. By such a policy of rural development, increasing congestion in the traditional centres of immigration, especially the metropolitan areas, could be avoided.

The rapid increase of population in Africa, which will continue far into the next century,[14] will also improve the possibilities for industrialisation. Many more parts in Africa will have a sufficiently large and dense population for economic operation of homemarket industries, as well as industrial processing of food and minerals for exports and domestic use. But to finance this industrialisation African countries must still, during a long period, rely mainly on income from exports of primary products, crops as well as minerals and forest products, to more industrialised countries in other continents.

It has been suggested that Africa should avoid depleting its mineral resources for the benefit of industries in other parts of the world and preserve them for use in future African industries. Delay of exploitation has also been recommended in the hope that increasing scarcity of raw materials will result in a more favourable development of export prices. However, in our world of rapid advancement of science and technology, it is more than likely that threatened scarcities of a particular raw material will be averted by technological improvements and new substitutes. Appearance of new substitutes and other technological changes may also reduce the future value of some natural resources.

In any case, African countries have little choice. Today, the secondary sector in African countries is too small to make any significant contribution to exports from the continent. Only gradually, as this sector expands, can the primary sector become less predominant as supplier of foreign exchange for many decades, but this is not necessarily a serious handicap. It must be taken into account, when evaluating the future prospects for Africa, that Latin America, Asia and the Arab world are industrialising rapidly. These areas have not only much lower wage costs than the highly industrialised countries, they also possess recently established industries in many branches, while many industrial enterprises in the older industrialised countries are of earlier date. For these reasons, the highly industrialised countries restrict the access to their home markets for imports of manufactures from developing countries, but they have no means to avoid competition in their export markets in the developing world from low cost producers in these areas.

It is likely, therefore, that export markets for most industrial manufactures will become so competitive that the old industrialised countries cannot continue to adapt their export prices to increasing wage costs in their own countries, without losing market share. Thus, there is some reason to believe that exports of manufactures will become less attractive than they were when the old industrialised countries had a near monopoly on this type of exports. If for that reason, the price gap between manufacture prices and prices of raw materials becomes reduced in the future, countries which like the African ones rely mainly on raw material exports will gain, and they may be able to finance their industrialisation by means of the foreign exchange earned by primary exports. But this requires that they do not use their foreign exchange earnings on imports of food, which could better be supplied by African agriculture.

Notes

1. All references to Africa in this paper are to Africa south of the Sahara.
2. Boserup (1981), p. 155.
3. Boserup (1981).
4. International Railway Statistics.
5. UNIDO (1974), World Road Statistics.
6. Boserup (1981); Boserup (1965).
7. Boserup (1970), pp. 16–23.
8. Presvelou and Spijkers-Zwart (1980); Lewis (1981).
9. World Bank (1982).
10. International Food Policy Research Institute (1981).
11. World Bank (1981).
12. Dumont and Mottin (1983).
13. Boserup (1965).
14. Tabah (1982).

Bibliography

Boserup, Ester, *The Conditions of Agricultural Growth*. (London and Chicago, 1965).
____ *Woman's Role in Economic Development*. (London and New York, 1970).
____ *Population and Technology*. (Oxford and Chicago, 1981).
Dumont, R. & Mottin, M.F. *Le défi sénégalis* (Dakar, 1983).
International Food Policy Research Institute, *Agricultural Protection in OECD Countries*. (Washington, 1980).
International Road Federation, *World Road Statistics*. (Geneva and Washington, annually).
International Union of Railways, *International Railway Statistics*. (Paris, annually).
Lewis, Barbara C. *Invisible Farmers: Women and the Crisis in Agriculture*. (Washington, 1981).
Presvelou, Clio and Spijkers-Zwart, Saskia, *The Household, Women and Agricultural Development*. (Wageningen, 1980).
Tabah, Leon, 'Population Growth', in Just Faaland, (ed.) *Population and the World Economy in the 21st Century*. (Oxford, 1982).
UNIDO, *Industrial Development Survey*. (Vienna, 1974).
World Bank, *Accelerated Development in Sub-Saharan Africa*. (Washington, 1981).
____ *World Development Report 1982*. (Washington, 1982).

3 WHAT DO SMALLHOLDERS DO FOR A LIVING?
SOME EVIDENCE FROM KENYA

Arne Bigsten

Introduction

Many analyses of the process of development in the dual economy tradition have made a distinction between a rural–agricultural and an urban–industrial sector, and focused on the shift of labour from the former to the latter through a process of rural–urban migration.[1] The point which I want to make in this paper is that if one analyses the Kenyan rural economy in these simple terms one misses essential aspects of the process of change in rural Kenya. Typically, there is a whole spectrum of economic activities in the rural areas, and a typical smallholder family has a multiplicity of income sources. Model-builders and policy-makers should be aware of the fact that the smallholder families do not live by income from their farm alone, but that their level of income also depends a great deal on the availability of complementary sources of income.

There is a piecemeal, gradual transformation of the smallholder agricultural sector in Kenya today. The importance of subsistence agriculture relative to production for the market is declining, and at the same time the smallholders earn substantial non-farm incomes. The relative importance of subsistence production is thus declining in the Kenyan economy, but this change has not primarily been brought about by a shift of labour from the smallholding areas to the urban areas, but rather through an increased monetisation and diversification of the rural economy. Moreover, for most migrants rural–urban migration is still of a temporary nature. Most employees in the urban areas intend to return to the rural areas after a shorter or longer spell of work.

The purpose of this paper is to analyse the composition and change of the income pattern of smallholder families in Kenya, and to discuss the implications on policy and model building of an explicit recognition of the diversity of the rural economy. The development of the Kenyan smallholder sector will be illustrated by means of data from central Kenya, since roughly comparable smallholder data are available for 1963/4 and 1974/5. These make it possible to illustrate the trend over time.

The central part of Kenya is mostly fertile, and this is reflected in the high population density of the area. It is the best developed smallholder agricultural area in Kenya, where, by 1963, a great deal of agricultural modernisation had already taken place. One should therefore be somewhat cautious about generalising about all of Kenya from the observations from this area, but the trends observed there seem to be similar to those of other parts of the country. IRS1-data show that the income pattern in Central Province is not that different from those in other provinces.[2] The share of farm operating surplus in household income is 50 per cent in Central Province compared to the national average of 57 per cent. The share ranges from 25 per cent in the Coast Province to 71 per cent in Nyanza Province. The degree of diversification may thus differ between regions, but the basic pattern is similar.

The outline of the paper is as follows: First, a brief description of the development of Kenyan agriculture is given. Then the income structures of central Kenya smallholders in 1963/4 and 1974/5 are calculated and compared, and the reasons behind the changes are tentatively discussed. The implications on model building of the explicit recognition of the complexity of the smallholder economy is then discussed. Finally, the main points are summarised and the policy implications of the diversity of smallholder incomes are discussed.

Some Facts About Kenyan Agriculture

Since the colonial days an agricultural smallholder sector and a large-scale sector coexist in Kenya. In the colonial period up to the 1950s a number of restrictions impeded the development of smallholder agriculture. In the 50s however, there was a change in policy along the lines outlined in the Swynnerton plan,[3] which implied a reorganisation of the land-holding system to private ownership of land. It also meant that smallholders now were allowed to grow high-value cash-crops, and accompanying services were beginning to be provided for the African smallholders. The policy which was initiated then has, by and large, been pursued also after Independence. The share of smallholder production in marketed agricultural output has gradually increased from 41 per cent in 1964 to 56 per cent in 1975. Thus, even today, large-scale agriculture is not only important in terms of production, but is also an important employer in the formal wage market.

The focus of interest here will be the period 1963/4 to 1974/5, i.e. roughly the first decade of independence (since these years are the only ones for which we have comparable data). To put the analysis in perspective some further information on the pattern of structural change in Kenya in this period will be given. The change in the sectoral composition of output is shown in Table 3.1.

Table 3.1:   Sectoral Shares in GDP (current prices)

	1964	1975
Primary sector	44.2	36.8
Secondary sector	12.5	16.7
Tertiary sector	43.3	46.5

Source: Statistical Abstract, annual

The primary sector in Kenya is practically equivalent to agriculture, and we can see that its relative share in output declined from 44 to 37 per cent. In terms of employment, however, it is vastly more important, although it is very difficult to give reliable figures on employment changes in agriculture. It may, however, be assumed that, over the whole period, more than 80 per cent of the labour force were to some extend dependent on agriculture. Unfortunately, there are reliable data only on those employed in the modern sector of the economy. Employment in this sector grew at the same rate as the labour force. Its share in total employment did not therefore increase. Depending on assumptions chosen, the share can be estimated to constitute 14–17 per cent of the labour force.[4] Those formally employed were distributed among sectors as shown in Table 3.2.

Table 3.2:   Modern Sector Employment by Sector (per cent)

	1964	1975
Primary sector	35.5	29.8
Secondary sector	10.1	17.2
Tertiary sector	54.4	53.0

Source: Employment and Earnings, annual

We see that the share of agriculture in modern sector employment declines slightly, while the share of industry goes up. However, this table disregards both those self-employed and those working as casual labour in the smallholder sector. It is to the smallholder households we now turn. In what follows, we shall consider the smallholder households as the unit of observation, not the small-holdings. It is thus the incomes of these families, whatever the source, which will be discussed here.

A Comparison of Smallholder Incomes in Central Kenya 1963/4 and 1974/5

The data which will be used to analyse the structural change in rural Kenya are derived from two smallholder surveys, namely the *Economic Survey of Central Province — 1963/4* and the *Integrated Rural Survey 1974/5*. The former covered the Central province according to the old (pre-1963) boundaries, while the latter covered all the major smallholder areas of the country. The comparisons between the two surveys will be confined to those districts included in the first survey, i.e. roughly what is now the districts of Kiambu, Muranga, Nyeri, Kirinyaga, Embu and Meru. The borders differ somewhat between the two surveys, but this should not introduce too much of a bias (see the note to Table 3.3). Kirinyaga and Embu were treated as one district in the first survey; the data for Kirinyaga and Embu are therefore aggregated for the later year.

Since the IRS was a national survey, it had smaller sample sizes in the districts included than the first survey — 384 as compared to 900 households. This means that one should not read too much into individual district figures for 1974/5 but mainly look at the pattern.

What we will do here is to calculate the structure of the income of smallholder families in central Kenya in 1963/4 and 1974/5 and to compare the two sets of observations. It is always difficult to compare sets of data which have been collected in different surveys the definitions and concepts of which are not necessarily the same. These data are, nevertheless, the best we have for Kenya for the purpose at hand.

Our first problem is with the concept of the household or the family, and there are some important differences between the two surveys here. In the first survey the household was defined as 'a group of persons generally of the same family, normally living together, sharing meals and operating a common cash account'.[5] In IRS1 the household was defined as 'a person or group of persons living together under one roof or several roofs within the same compound or homestead area and sharing a community of life by their dependence on a common holding as a source of income and food, which usually but not necessarily involves them in eating from a common pot'.[6]

The second definition is broader than the first, since in the 1963/4 survey it was possible that only part of a big polygamous family was included. If we compare the average household sizes for the two sets of data, we also find that while it was 5.5 in 1963/4 it was 7.2 in 1974/5 for the same region. Since it is unlikely that the average household size did increase to such a degree, this means that two types of biases are introduced. First, we tend to exaggerate the growth in smallholder households' real income over the period, if the total household incomes are to be compared. Second, since in the first case parts of the polygamous households were excluded and these were wives and their children, the proportion of production coming from agriculture in the first period may have been under-estimated. This is due to the fact that those excluded probably got most of their income from agriculture, while, normally, the man of the household is more involved in extraneous activities. This implies that the growth of agricultural output may be overestimated.

There are also some problems with the comparability of the income concepts used. These are mainly due to the fact that the IRS1 took into account valuation changes that were disregarded in the 1963/4 survey. Since there were considerable changes in, for example, livestock during the latter period due to the drought, many farmers got a negative farm operating surplus due to the fact that a number of the livestock died. It is, of course, theoretically correct to consider this to be a negative income, but the comparability of the two surveys would have been better if 1974/5 had been a more 'normal' year in agriculture. However, it has been possible to divide the income into four categories with roughly similar contents. They are farm income (that is operating surplus on the *shamba* including subsistence production), wage incomes, transfers, and non-agricultural operating surplus. These taken together give household income. The percentage breakdown of income and the level of household income in the districts included are shown in Table 3.3.

Table 3.3: Percentage Distribution of Income of Smallholder
Households in Kenya 1963/4 and 1974/5 (Current
prices)·

1963/4	Kiambu	Muranga	Nyeri	Embu and Kirinyaga	Meru	Total
Farm income	27	46	62	63	70	51
Wage income	60	30	17	20	18	32
Transfers	8	10	14	7	7	9
Non-agric. op. surpl.	6	14	7	10	5	8
Household income (shs)	1964	1187	2022	1002	1098	1417
Sample size	205	167	110	138	280	900

1974/5	Kiambu	Muranga	Nyeri	Embu and Kirinyaga	Meru	Total
Farm income	33	57	52	72	67	58
Wage income	30	44	28	12	17	28
Transfers	9	17	10	10	6	11
Non-agric. op. surpl.	28	-19	10	6	10	3
Household income (shs)	5421	4394	3349	4742	4151	4353
Sample size						384

The Meru district was the same in the two surveys. Nyeri has been expanded
somewhat between the two surveys. Kiambu and Muranga of today incorporate part of the old Thika district which was excluded in the old survey.
Embu of the first survey has been split into Embu and Kirinyaga since then,
but these two districts are aggregated in the analysis. Enterprise expenditures other than wages for 1963/4 had to be allocated pro rata with wages
between agriculture and non-agriculture, since no breakdown was
presented in the report.
Sources: Kenya, 1968, pp. 33–4 and IRS1, own computations.

If we take into account that the price level was 75 per cent higher in
1975 than in 1963, we find that real household income increased by
76 per cent, or about 5 per cent per year. The increase in real income
from agriculture was 101 per cent, from wages 52 per cent, from
transfers 112 per cent and from non-agriculture – 33 per cent. There
is reason to believe that this estimate of total income growth is an
overestimate, since the household was defined differently in the two
surveys. If we assume that the household size was the same in 1963/4
and in 1974/5, the aggregate increase is reduced from 76 per cent to
35 per cent. This reduction is probably too drastic, since the sections
of the households which were left out in 1963/4 certainly produced
less per head than those included. The extent to which the production of this group was covered by the survey is also unclear. We may
tentatively consider that real income per family increased by 2.5–5
per cent per year between 1963/4 to 1974/5 in central Kenya, and

this is certainly an impressive rate of increase.

It is not possible to check these figures against regional accounts for this period, but an estimate for the period 1967 to 1975 shows that production in agriculture in Central province increased by 41 per cent in real terms during the period 1967/75.[7] When account is taken of the population increase the *per capita* increase becomes about one per cent per year. Total regional production over the same period increased by about 5.9 per cent per year, or 2.5 per cent per year in *per capita* terms. It is thus clear that there was an increase in aggregate production in Central province in this period, although the growth particularly in agriculture seems to have been less than that which our previous estimates suggest. This discrepancy may be explained in several ways: First, our original estimate of 5 per cent is probably an overestimate; second, as was pointed out earlier, there was a shift of agricultural production from large-scale farms to smallholders, so it is likely that smallholders did better than the aggregate agricultural figures suggest; third, either the family size may have increased, which then would explain part of the increase, or there may be a bias due to differences in coverage between our original estimates. All things considered, we may assume that the household income increase probably was in the lower part of our range of 2.5 to 5 per cent per year. Now, let us look at the different income sources one by one.

One may be confident that smallholders in central Kenya experienced a substantial increase in their farm income during the period studied, and it also seems likely that its share in income did increase. Since this is the most successful period for smallholder agriculture in Kenya, and since central Kenya is the part of the country where it was best developed, this unexpected result is not inconceivable. However, since the early 70s agriculture in Kenya has faced difficulties and growth has slowed down. A decline in the share of agriculture since 1974/5 is therefore possible, even if the coffee boom gave it a temporary boost.

Wage incomes, which in part of course come from agriculture, also increased substantially in real terms, even if their share in total household income decreased. There was some expansion of wage employment in central Kenya during the period, but on the whole it only kept pace with the population increase. In Central province the share of the labour force in modern sector wage employment amounted to 13.2 per cent in 1963, 14.2 per cent in 1964, 15.9 per cent in 1974 and 14.3 per cent in 1975. Thus, there was hardly any increase in the proportion of the labour force in wage employment. If the figure for farm income is adjusted downwards, it seems possible that incomes from wages grew at about the same rate as total income. Income from wage employment during the period thus, at best, retained its share in total household income. This share might have increased since 1974/5, but the wage labour market has also grown slowly during the late 1970s and early 1980s.

We note that transfer incomes increased more rapidly than wage incomes, which indicates that employment of relatives outside the area increased in importance relative to employment within the area. Employment in other areas, primarily Nairobi, thus had a substantial impact on the incomes of smallholders as well, particularly in central Kenya.

Finally, incomes from various other activities, such as manufacturing and business are difficult to measure properly, but there was a very significant increase in Kiambu. There may also have been increases in Nyeri and Meru, but this is difficult to verify due to the small sample sizes. The large negative income for Muranga in 1974/5 is difficult to explain.

From these comparisons one may conclude that there was a considerable diversity of income sources throughout the period, and that the income structure showed considerable stability. The smallholder in central Kenya had already by 1963/4 been extensively integrated into the monetary economy. One may note, however, that even if the relative importance of *shamba* production increases somewhat, the importance of production for subsistence in agricultural output declined (see Table 3.4). If we disregard the cases with a negative operating surplus in agriculture, which probably are nontypical for the 1970s generally, we find a much more substantial decline in the subsistence share. The 'subsistence' element in smallholder incomes is thus diminishing. Even if subsistence production probably remains at approximately the present level in absolute terms, its relative importance will dwindle as production for the market expands.

Various studies of Kenya have given the impression that there is a very rapid rate of urbanisation. This is not quite true. The national rate of population growth during the 60s and 70s was around 3.4 per cent per year. If we look at Central province alone we find that it grew by 3.4 per cent annually between 1962 and 1979, thus at exactly the same rate as the country as a whole. The major urban agglomeration, Nairobi, grew by 5.8 per cent annually between 1962 and

1969 and by 5.0 per cent between 1969 and 1979. Kiambu and Muranga, the districts closest to Nairobi, grew faster than the national average, i.e. by 3.7–3.8 per cent annually. Thus, the population in the rural areas we study is increasing at a very rapid rate. In spite of this we observe a considerable increase in *per capita* incomes during the period we study. Changes are occurring within the rural areas to accommodate the increasing population.

Table 3.4: Percentage Share of Subsistence Production in Gross Agricultural Production in Kenya 1963/64 and 1974/75

	1963/64	1974/75	
		All Cases	All cases with a positive farm op. surplus
Kiambu	62	68	42
Muranga	72	48	45
Embu and Kirinyaga	59	40	39
Nyeri	60	46	45
Meru	58	66	59
Total	62	59	47

Sources: Kenya, 1968, pp. 33–4; IRS1, own computations

Radical changes had been brought about in the smallholder sector by the Emergency and the implementation of the Swynnerton plan. Both of these pushed the smallholders into the cash economy. In his study of Embu, Moris for example notes that 'the extreme hardship of the Emergency period forced the people to live by their wits',[8] in other words, they had to rely on the cash economy to a much greater extent than earlier. Also the land adjudication and land registration initiated in the 1950s meant a drastic change for the farmers. Moris points out that

the transition to a 'closed' economy where agrarian resources are sharply limited has been particularly painful because the indigenous economic system has been organised to exploit an 'open' economy where cattle and women were in short supply but land was not. In a situation where farming was risky and land abundant, the traditional way for a farmer to increase his productivity was to expand his acreages and to diversify his enterprises. This solution was highly successful as long as population was rising (and so maintaining the market) and there was fresh land to cultivate.[9]

However, when this was no longer the case, the household had little choice but to enter the cash economy to be able to pay taxes and even to buy food. It should therefore be noted that a drive towards diversity rather than specialisation had existed for quite some time because of the inherent riskiness of farming. Already in the 1960s it was found that among the men in Embu, 'farmers who pursue farming as a single, specialised occupation are in the minority'.[10] Only a small minority of farmers were full-time farmers in the western sense.

Thus, the diversification of income sources has been going on for a long time and it is difficult to say how soon it reached the degree of diversity which we observe in the 1960s and the 1970s. It is not certain that the diversity increased during the 1950s with the expansion of smallholder agriculture, since this may instead have initiated the weak trend we find in our material towards increased reliance on agriculture. Before that time it was difficult for smallholders to grow the lucrative cash crops.

To throw further light on the income pattern we will do some further disaggregations, even if we then, of course, really run into the problem of small cell sizes. The only comparison we can make between the two surveys is by income classes. The data from the 1963/4 survey was broken down in seven income classes, but for the 1974/5 survey we only split the data into four classes because of the smaller sample sizes. The results are presented in Table 3.5, and the income class limits are given in the note to that table.

Although we must be careful about drawing conclusions from this limited sample, certain general tendencies in the material should be noted. Looking at the share of farm incomes it is not easy to observe any distinct pattern in either period. Maybe one can note an inverted U-pattern. In the national data for 1974/5, however, the farm income share increases with income (see Table 3.6). It seems also that poor families with little land have to rely on other sources of income. Thus, their farm income share tends to be small. On the other hand a family that can earn good wage incomes will by definition be in the high income brackets, and should have a small farm income share. However, since it is common practice in rural areas to buy land or invest wage incomes in agriculture, families with high wage incomes will also tend to get high agricultural incomes. There are thus two counteracting tendencies, and it is therefore conceivable that the share of farm income even increases with income.

Table 3.5: Percentage Distribution of Income of Smallholder
Households in Kiambu, Muranga, Nyeri and Meru,
1963/4 and 1974/5

	Income classes*							
1963/4	I	II	III	IV	V	VI	VII	Total
Farm income	65	64	70	62	62	57	35	54
Wage income	24	22	20	29	26	33	46	34
Transfers	11	11	7	4	5	5	4	7
Non-agric. op. surpl.	1	3	3	5	6	5	16	6
Size of household	4.0	6.0	7.1	8.4	8.7	8.9	9.6	5.6
Size of holding (acres)	3.4	5.3	6.3	8.4	9.6	10.2	15.2	
1974/5	I	II	III	IV				Total
Farm income	*	55	59	54				49
Wage income	*	22	25	30				27
Transfers	*	17	8	6				14
Non-agric. op. surpl.	*	7	7	10				9
Size of household	5.5	7.0	7.2	9.3				7.2
Size of holding (acres)	5.7	4.4	4.7	10.4				2.5
Sample size	101	86	47	90				324

*   The income classes in the

1963/4 survey are	*1974/5 survey* (in current prices) are
I = less than 1000 shs	I = less than 2000 shs
II = 1001–1500	II = 2001–4000
III = 1501–2000	III = 4001–6000
IV = 2001–2500	IV = 6001 +
V = 2501–3500	
VI = 3501–5000	
VII = 5001 +	

The income concept used in the 1963/4 survey in the tables disaggregated by
income classes differs slightly from the one used in Table 3.3. This means that
transfers and, to a small extent, also non-farm operating surplus is underestimated in this table.

No estimates for Embu/Kirinyaga are reported for the 1963/4 survey, so these
districts are excluded throughout.

Our table for 1963/4 is aggregated from district tables; since the number of
observations in each income class is not given the same districts weights have
to be applied to all income classes. For 1974/5 the number of observations by
income class by district is used for the aggregation.

Sources: Kenya 1968, pp. 40–3; IRS1 – own computations

The share of wages tends to increase with incomes. This pattern
existed both in 1963/4 and 1974/5. Of course, quite a few of the
smallholders working for wages were still engaged in agriculture. In
1963/4 half of the men and three-quarters of the women working for
wages were engaged in agriculture.[11] In terms of income, however,

Table 3.6: Percentage Distribution of Household Income by Source of Income and Household Income Group, 1974/5

	Less than 0.K.Shs	0–999 K.Shs	1,000–1,999 K.Shs	2,000–2,999 K.Shs	3,000–3,999 K.Shs	4,000–5,999 K.Shs	6,000–7,999 K.Shs	8,000 K.Shs and over	Total
Farm operating surpl.	*	23	44	53	56	61	61	64	57
Wages	*	29	24	19	20	15	25	21	22
Transfers	*	31	21	18	13	12	8	4	10
Non-farm operating Surpl.	*	16	11	10	12	12	6	11	10
Total value of household Inc. K.Shs	−2,840	551	1,485	2,505	3,456	4,815	6,953	12,217	3,652

Source: Kenya, 1977, p. 56

the share of agricultural wage incomes will be substantially lower, since agricultural work is a poorly paid occupation. There is no similar industrial classification in IRS1, but the Labour Force Survey of 1977/8 shows that about one-third of rural employees work in agriculture.[12] Some of these, however, may not be engaged in farming, and therefore the proportion of smallholders working for wages in agriculture should be higher. Still most of the income smallholders derive from wage employment should originate outside agriculture.

The share of remittances shows the reverse pattern in both periods. It is of great importance to those with smaller incomes. It thus seems as if outmigration is more extensive in the poorer groups or at least their remittances are of greater importance to their families.

When it comes to non-agricultural operating surplus the material indicates that it increased by level of income in both periods.

Looking at the share of subsistence production in agricultural output (Table 3.7) we note a falling tendency as household income increases. This is clear, at least, if we only consider the cases with a positive operating surplus in agriculture in 1974/5. The falling share is, of course, a reflection of the fact that a household, normally, will provide for family consumption before it diverges into cash crop production.

Table 3.7: Percentage Share of Subsistence Consumption in Agricultural Output 1963/4 and 1974/5

	1963/4	1974/5	
		All cases	All cases with a posi-tive operating surplus
Kiambu	60	68	42
Muranga	68	48	45
Nyeri	58	40	39
Meru	57	66	59

Source: Kenya, 1968; IRS1, own computations.

Of the total number working in agriculture in 1977/8, 16 per cent gave both work on holding and agricultural work off holding as their two occupations, while 15 per cent gave agricultural work off holding as their only occupation.[13] The latter figure might possibly be taken to indicate that 15 per cent of the agricultural work force are landless, while the former may indicate the proportion which is short of land. The use of hired labour is widespread among Kenyan smallholders. During the long rainy season in 1980 two-thirds of smallholders in Embu used some hired labour, although most spent fairly small sums on this.[14] Farm size and farm income was clearly correlated during the first period. There is a less clear pattern during the latter period,[15] which may indicate that agricultural incomes have become less dependent on farm size and now, to a greater extent, are determined by factors like investment in cash crops.

Family size has a great effect on family income during both periods. If incomes are adjusted for family size, the differences are reduced substantially. It is particularly the households with the lowest incomes that are small, with *per capita* incomes that are higher than inter-family comparisons suggest. However, above a certain level of family incomes, the reduction of the differences is very small, if we adjust for differences in family size. These differences must then be explained by other factors.

Differences in land ownership obviously matter, but education is also a powerful influence on the level and structure of smallholder incomes. Analysis of IRS1 data shows that families with heads with no education derive most of their income from farming, while this share decreases with the educational level.[16] Instead, the importance of wage incomes increases with education. Trade and handicraft is of importance to all categories, but in particular to those with primary education. The pattern thus can be said to be one where farming is the major income for farm households with little education. When the educational status is improved they start to diversify into various non-farm income-generating activities, and when they get access to secondary education wage employment becomes the dominating income source. The degree of diversification is thus highly correlated with education.

This section has shown that a complex economy with a multitude of income sources is the basis for the existence of smallholder households in Kenya. The multitude of income sources requires a high degree of flexibility and mobility, and in many cases the farm income is not even the main income. It may even be difficult to determine which is the main source.

On the Modelling of Smallholder Households

Many people are under the delusion that urban economies are complex, while rural economies are simple. In Africa, this is definitely not the case. In this paper I have tried to show that the African smallholder family has a wide range of income sources. Thus, the smallholder is faced with a multitude of difficult economic choices. These concern not only the allocation of resources in agricultural production but also the allocation between agriculture and a range of other pursuits.

The modern theory of the farm household[17] explicitly recognises the possibilities of hiring-in and hiring-out of labour. It is normally assumed that the labour of the smallholder households may elect to work either on the farm, or in the external wage labour market. There is a marginal trade-off between incomes from farm production and wage labour. These models have thus started to take rural diversity into account, even if much of the diversity described above is difficult to capture. To complicate matters even more, it is also debatable whether the smallholder family can be treated as an integrated economic unit. Obviously, all resources are not under the control of the head of the household. Some decisions are normally made by the man, while others are made by his wife or wives. Maybe the standard pattern of Kenyan smallholder agriculture can be described as follows. The man allocates a parcel of land to each of his wives for cultivation. Each wife uses the proceeds from her land to feed herself, her children and (partly) her husband. The husband retains some land for cash crop cultivation (or for livestock), but women and children have to contribute labour also to these crops. This is thus an arrangement with sub-autonomous units which to some extent compete with each other for resources.

The question is how the system of incentives should be modelled. There is a measure of conflict between man and wife, and it is difficult to decide exactly how to define it. Should the decision process be treated as a game between man and wife, or should the man be considered to be the dominating decision maker, who not only allocates land to different uses, but also the labour of all working household members? This issue, has not as yet been adequately dealt with in the modelling of smallholder agriculture.

Concluding Remarks

I have tried to show that the rural economy is highly complex, and that smallholder families depend on a whole range of economic activities. The process of monetisation and diversification is ongoing in all parts of Kenya, but mostly *within* the rural areas and *within* the rural households. Rural–urban migration is still very much of a temporary nature, and remittances from the urban areas form an essential part of the income of smallholder families.

Our attempt to measure the change in the structure of smallholder incomes suggests that the degree of diversity remained fairly stable between 1963/4 and 1974/5. The share of farm incomes may even have increased somewhat. During this period the importance of transfers increased somewhat in relation to wage incomes, while non-agricultural pursuits seemed to flourish mainly in Kiambu. The relative importance of our four categories did not change much. However, within agriculture the share of subsistence production did decline. In the aggregate the rural households of central Kenya did see considerable economic progress during the period. Net migration from the area was very limited. The changes that occurred within the rural areas made is possible for the rural smallholders to increase the average income of a rapidly increasing rural population.

The pattern of income, of course, varies between different categories of smallholders. There was some evidence for 1974/5 that the poorest households had to rely more on the external sources, but the income pattern did not vary much by this factor. We also noted that remittances are relatively most important to the poorest households.

Our comparison also suggests that farm size was a better predictor of income in 1963/4 than in 1974/5. Other factors may now be assumed to be more important. Investment in cash crops in a case in point. Family size affects family incomes, but beyond a certain household income level the households seem to be of similar size. This factor does not therefore explain much of the income variation, particularly not towards the upper end of the income spectrum.

Our analysis suggests that the view of structural change implied by the dual economy model misses important aspects of the process. The Kenyan experience suggests that over a long period of time, there is an extensive economic diversification within the smallholder households. This, internal, diversification may be at least as important as the rural–urban migration in the process of economic transformation. The Kenyan economic structure is being transformed, but this process does not imply that large masses of people permanently leave smallholdings and subsistence agriculture for secondary and tertiary sectors in the urban areas. What is happening is that smallholder agriculture is becoming increasingly commercialised at the same time as the smallholders are becoming extensively — but partially — involved in other sectors of the economy. In this transition stage smallholder family incomes are therefore only in part dependent on what is happening in agriculture. Thus, the welfare of smallholders is also very much dependent on the scope for other economic activities in the rural areas and, to some extent, on the employment possibilities in urban areas. A development policy aimed at improving the incomes of smallholders should therefore not be confined to agriculture alone. Particular efforts should be made to create alternative, rural employments or market opportunities.

Thus, smallholders can gain from economic opportunities both in rural and urban areas, but it is obvious that they stand a better chance, if the opportunities are created in the rural areas or in nearby towns. A regional policy aimed at equalisation of economic opportunities should therefore play a part in a development strategy aimed at improving smallholder incomes.[18] The agricultural and non-agricultural activities in a region are obviously interdependent. The expansion of non-agriculture thus may mean an increase in both non-agricultural and agricultural incomes of smallholders. The ambition of policy makers should therefore be to, generally, increase the level of economic activity in rural areas and to improve communications between rural and urban areas which would make it easier for smallholders to gain from urban growth. It is not by accident that the smallholder areas which have the strongest links with the urban economy also have done best in agriculture. During the transition stage at which Kenya will be for the foreseeable future, policy makers should therefore strive for improved economic integration, which makes it possible for smallholding families to have a diversity of income sources.

Notes

* Thanks for comments are due to Per Lundborg. Financial support from the Swedish Agency for Research Cooperation with Developing Countries (SAREC) and J.H. Palmes fund is gratefully acknowledged.

1. Harris and Todaro (1970), and many others.
2. Kenya (1977), p. 56.
3. Kenya (1955).
4. See Bigsten (1980).
5. Kenya (1968), p. 3.
6. Kenya (1977), p. 20.
7. Bigsten (1980), Ch. 11.
8. Moris (1971), p. 17.
9. Ibid., pp. 356-7.
10. Ibid., p. 13.
11. Kenya (1968), p. 13.
12. Bigsten (1984).
13. Labour Force Survey 1977/8, own computations.
14. Haugerud (1981), p. 19.
15. See Kenya (1977), p. 57.
16. IRS1-data, own computations. Supporting evidence is found in Paterson (1980) pp. 5-6 and Haugerud (1981).
17. Barnum and Squire (1979).
18. Bigsten (1980).

Bibliography

Barnum, H.N. and Squire, L. 'An Econometric Application of the Theory of the Farm Household', *Journal of Development Economics*, vol. 6 (1979).

Bigsten, A. *Regional Inequality and Development. A Case Study of Kenya* (Farnborough, 1980).

_____ *Education and Income Determination in Kenya* (Aldershot, 1984).

Harris, J.R. and Todaro, M.P. 'Migration, Unemployment and Development: A Two-Sector Analysis', *American Economic Review*, vol. 60 (1970).

Haugerud, A. *Development and Household Economy in Two Eco-Zones of Embu District*, Working Paper no. 382, IDS, Nairobi (1981).

Kenya, *Economic Survey* (Nairobi, annual).

_____ *Employment and Earnings* (Nairobi, annual).

_____ *Statistical Abstract* (Nairobi, annual).

_____ *A Plan to Intensify the Development of African Agriculture in Kenya* (Nairobi, 1955).

_____ *Economic Survey of Central Province — 1963/4* (Statistics division, MEPO, Nairobi, 1968).

_____ *Integrated Rural Survey 1974-5. Basic Report* (CBS, Nairobi 1977).

Moris, J.R. *The Agrarian Revolution in Central Kenya: A Study of Farm Innovation in Embu District*, PhD dissertation, Northwestern University (1971).

Paterson, D.B. *Education, Employment and Income. Incipient Economic Stratification in Land-Scarce Bunyore*, Working Paper no. 371, IDS Nairobi (1980).

PART TWO
PROBLEMS OF STAGNATION AND INCOME
DISTRIBUTION

4 THE EFFECT OF POPULATION GROWTH ON A PEASANT ECONOMY: THE CASE OF BANGLADESH *

Alia Ahmad

The main purpose of this paper is to analyse the process of stagnation under heavy population pressure in the peasant economy of Bangladesh. The relationship between population growth and economic development is a controversial topic in economics, and in spite of the existence of a vast literature the issue has remained somewhat unresolved. A brief review of the literature on economic development and population growth before the main discussion is deemed necessary in order to formulate the main hypothesis underlying the present study. The first part of this paper will, therefore, be devoted to a discussion on the main lines of thought in this area. The second part will consider the case of the Bangladesh peasant economy.

Theories of Population Growth and Economic Development

The Malthusian Theory

According to the Malthusian theory of population, population has a tendency to grow at a higher rate than output, and in the race between output and population growth, a peasant economy may eventually reach the 'subsistence equilibrium level'. This equilibrium is maintained only at a subsistence level, the reason being that an increase in output above the subsistence level leads to population growth which brings *per capita* income back to the subsistence level again. On the other hand, population cannot grow once the subsistence level is reached. If *per capita* income falls below the subsistence level, the mortality rate will increase so that equilibrium at the subsistence level is maintained.[1] Population in the Malthusian

* The author gratefully acknowledges the financial support provided by the Swedish Agency for Research Co-operation with Developing Countries for carrying out this study. She would also like to thank Dr Inga Persson-Tanimura for her helpful comments.

model is a function of the deviation of the actual *per capita* output from the subsistence level.

Nearly 200 hundred years ago, Malthus could not anticipate that technological changes would raise output at a rate surpassing the rate of population growth, so that equilibrium at a higher level of income was, in fact, conceivable. Malthus' only solution to human misery was thus deliberate prevention of birth.

Malthus has been accused of overlooking not only the possibility of technical change but also the fact that under certain circumstances, population can grow in spite of a decline in *per capita* output.[2] The latter phenomenon can be observed in many Third World countries. Moreover, Malthus' solution of deliberate birth control appears to be rather ineffective in controlling population growth in many countries.

The Theory of Ester Boserup

The inapplicability of Malthus' theory of population in the case of less developed countries facing high rates of population growth has given rise to a search for new explanations for the rate of population growth and for the growth of output in a peasant economy. The most commendable work in this line has been done by Ester Boserup who takes a completely different stand from that of Malthus.[3]

In Malthus' model we find population growth as a dependent variable which changes in response to changes in the condition of food supply. Boserup, on the other hand, regards population growth as an independent variable which induces the growth of output in a peasant economy. The mechanism through which equilibrium is maintained is different in these models. In Malthus' model, any fortuitous change in technology which leads to the growth of output encourages population to grow, and consequently, *per capita* income has a tendency to get stuck at a low level.

In Boserup's model, on the other hand, an increase in population takes place autonomously. Population growth exerts pressure on the subsistence level of income (which may be culturally determined). This eventually leads to the search for improved and increasingly labour-intensive techniques of food production. The increase in output through increased application of labour helps to counteract the fall in *per capita* income. According to Boserup, peasants try to increase output from a given supply of land to meet a greater demand for food as a result of population growth. The need to use existing land more intensively leads to a reduction of the fallow period and also to the application of greater labour inputs.

Population growth, by increasing the supply of labour, helps to make greater intensification possible.

The hypothesis that population growth induces technical change rather than vice versa fits well with the experience of many peasant economies. It may be observed that total food production in many developing countries has a tendency to grow in response to population growth, even though in many cases the former falls short of the latter.[4]

Boserup's main hypothesis relates to the development over centuries during which slow and steady growth of population led to gradual changes in agricultural techniques and the agrarian structure in the pre-industrial societies. But today, developing countries are faced with the problem of bringing about changes within decades, and most of them are experiencing a rapid growth of population. Boserup clearly distinguishes between the possibility of agricultural change under slow versus rapid population growth. In the case of the latter, peasants find it much more difficult to respond positively to population growth.[5]

A steady growth of population exerts pressure on *per capita* output (given the technology), and induces peasants to change agricultural technology to counteract the fall in output. The ability to counteract population pressure by changing the technology is greater in a community where the man/land ratio is not excessively high.[6] However, even in cases where the intensification of agricultural practices is achieved relatively easily, it is doubtful that population growth can result in a substantial growth of output.

The adjustment between population and output as envisaged by Boserup is a slow process through which peasants try to restore *per capita* income.[7] The endogenous changes which take place in response to population growth are usually not very productive. Moreover, peasant economies may differ with respect to knowledge of new techniques or the ability to utilise the existing knowledge effectively.[8] Hence, it cannot be expected that a higher level of investment and, consequently, a higher *per capita* income can be maintained. This is in line with Boserup's idea of growth. According to her,

This process, however, can hardly be described as economic growth in the generally accepted sense of the term, since the proximate effect upon output per man-hour is to lower it. But sustained growth of total production and of total output in a given territory has secondary effects which at least in some cases can set off a genuine process of economic growth, with rising output per man-hour, first in non-agricultural activities and later in agriculture.[9]

Boserup also emphasises the need for agricultural investment, flexibility of the land tenure system and appropriate agricultural taxation and price policies so that peasants are able to intensify agricultural practices in response to population growth.[10] It appears that often the growth of the agricultural sector depends crucially on the stimulus from the non-rural sector.[11] The possibility of over-population and stagnation of income is thus not ruled out. Grigg's coherent analysis of agricultural changes in response to population growth in pre-industrial societies confirms the fact that peasants try to introduce various changes in agricultural practices in search of a new optimum when population grows autonomously.[12] But in this process, a point eventually comes when the peasant community exhausts its knowledge of new techniques, and faces over-population with all its attendant evils. According to Grigg, it is through indus-trialisation that a peasant economy can be transformed into a commercial one, and it is hard to find a direct relationship between population growth and the rate and pattern of industrialisation conducive to agricultural development.[13]

Once the density of population becomes high it is increasingly difficult for peasants to raise output through their own effort. In her later book, Boserup emphasises that the greater the density of popu-lation the greater is the need for public support to agricultural devel-opment.[14] But population growth itself may also be a hindrance to the growth of output. In a land-scarce country with a slow rate of growth of industries and high concentration of land, factor markets do not operate efficiently, and resources, especially land, are not used optimally. The high rate of growth in such cases may cause additional problems for intensive use of land in spite of the fact that it exerts downward pressure on the existing level of living. We shall see later that population growth influences the agrarian structure in a negative way and hampers further intensification of agricultural practices.[15]

The difficulty of raising output in response to population pressure through the *peasants' own effort* seems to be even more pronounced in some wet rice agricultures that have several unique features. Wet rice agriculture is highly labour intensive, and the adoption of this system has been encouraged by population growth. Most of the wet rice regions were occupied by migrant people from the drier regions.[16] At the outset, people started cultivating the deltaic soils annually and left the high lands which were later occupied as a result of the increase in population. Annual cultivation was possible due to the fact that deltaic soils regained their fertility from annual floods and did not require the fallow period of rest.

As population continued to grow, the need for further intensification of agricultural practices arose. Peasants in many rice growing areas thus tended to adopt double or multiple cropping with varying degrees of success. But it appears that once the stage of annual cropping is reached, peasants find it increasingly difficult to raise output in response to population growth, because successful multiple cropping which can counteract the problem of over-population involves modern labour-intensive technologies which not only need labour inputs but also various off-farm inputs such as quick-maturing varieties of seeds, artificial irrigation and drainage, chemical fertilisers and pesticides. The supply of these inputs and the appropriate institutional structure depend essentially on the economic policies which can induce and shape the development of the non-rural sector in a manner which is conducive to agricultural growth. The problems of over-population in many wet rice regions confirm that appropriate economic policies do not necessarily take place in response to population growth.

We consider it important to distinguish between those agricultural changes which occur in response to population growth without any stimulus from the non-rural sector, and those changes which can only materialise when the government takes the initiative in agricultural development. Such a distinction helps to direct our attention to the importance of conscious economic policies at a stage when population growth fails to stimulate growth in a peasant economy.

The discussion so far points towards the conclusion that when a population which is already large grows steadily at a high rate, a peasant economy cannot counteract the state of over-population and stagnation of income for very long through endogenous technical changes which take place in response to population growth. We shall see later in this paper that stagnation of income under steady increase of population is an inevitability where the non-rural sector fails to stimulate the peasant sector. This is more true in a wet rice agriculture where annual cropping is already practised.

The Case of Bangladesh

The validity of the above conclusion may be tested through the study of the peasant economy of Bangladesh which has been experiencing steady increases in population for several decades. Bangladesh has been selected for several reasons. First of all, Bangladesh agriculture is characterised by wet rice cultivation which presents special problems of intensification along labour intensive lines. Secondly, Bangladesh has been experiencing rapid growth of population since the beginning of this century. The trends of growth of output and population indicate that total agricultural production has increased with the increase in population although *per capita* output has a tendency to stagnate. It appears that population has been growing in spite of a decline in *per capita* output. It can also be assumed that the peasants have probably resorted to certain measures to deal with population pressure. The study of Bangladesh agriculture thus allows the test of both Malthus' and Boserup's hypotheses regarding population growth and output.

The stagnation of rural income in Bangladesh under steady growth of population may be attributed to two main factors. First, the demographic responses to population pressure and falling incomes are weak even when sufficient time lags are allowed. Secondly, the peasants are constrained to raise output through improved labour intensive techniques.

Demographic responses

Bangladesh has been experiencing high rates of population growth since the beginning of this century. This high rate of growth (about 3 per cent on average) has been mainly due to a decline in the mortality rate (from 45 per thousand in 1911 to 19 in 1965) which has not been matched by a corresponding decline in the fertility or massive emigration. The high fertility rate (total fertility being 6 per woman) among rural women even under conditions of extreme poverty, and in spite of the availability of various contraceptive methods, appears as a challenge to Malthus' theory of population. Population in Bangladesh has been growing in spite of the worsening condition of food supply, and Malthus' solution of deliberate birth control also remains ineffective. Fertility behaviour among rural households is found to be a result of a complex interaction of socio-economic, cultural and institutional forces rather than a direct response of individuals to the condition of food supply.[17]

Changes in Agricultural Practices

The question is how far peasants have been able to maintain *per capita* income in response to population growth which they accept as a datum. According to Boserup, the main response of peasants to population growth constitutes intensive use of land through frequent cropping, i.e. by reducing the fallow period which also involves application of more labour input. Following Boserup's arguments, Grigg has identified the agricultural changes which took place in pre-industrial peasant economies of Europe.[18] These changes were:

1. Bringing less fertile lands (which were under long fallow) into cultivation.
2. The intensive use of existing arable land through (a) increased intensity of cropping; (b) application of more labour input per hectare of land per crop season; and (c) changes in the crop-mix and crop rotations.

The growth of output in response to population growth is also supposed to occur from non-monetised investment such as the use of surplus family labour for capital formation.[19]

1. *Changes on the Extensive Margin.* The process of extension of the cultivated area in Bangladesh has been influenced by the interaction of natural and demographic factors. Historical evidence roughly indicates that the agricultural changes which took place on the extensive margin in response to population growth did not follow the sequence of forest fallow to bush fallow and annual cropping. Wet rice agriculture in Bengal was, no doubt, induced by population growth. But the deltaic regions were first occupied by people who migrated from the drier regions of India. An important point to observe here is that people who settled here resorted to the annual cultivation of the deltaic soils while leaving the high lands which were later brought under cultivation as population increased further.[20] The colonisation of newly formed alluvial lands in the active delta and the reclamation of forest and uncultivable land continued throughout the 19th and the early part of this century due to population growth, the components of which were both immigration and natural growth.

By 1950 more than 80 per cent of the cultivable area in Bangladesh was already under cultivation, i.e. cropped at least once. The lands which could be cultivated with simple tools and investment of labour had been exploited by the peasants. The possibility of reclamation of less accessible lands through peasants' efforts thus became extremely limited, even though population did exert pressure on the rural community.

2. *Changes on the Intensive Margin.* As most of the lands in Bangladesh have been placed under annual cropping long ago, it will be interesting to observe how further intensification along labour intensive lines has been possible with the increase in population. Empirical studies of the sources of growth of agricultural output in Bangladesh indicate that total output has increased due to increased intensity of cropping, greater application of labour input per crop season and changes in the crop-mix and rotations.[21]

The intensity of cropping has increased, on average, from 130 per cent in 1950 to 153 per cent in 1978/9.[22] There are, however, regional variations ranging from more than 200 per cent in some areas to just 100 per cent in others. The degree of intensity of cropping has largely been determined by natural factors. The availability of water remains the most important constraint to frequent cropping as the temperature in Bangladesh allows farming throughout the year. In order to meet their growing food needs, the peasants try to grow two or three crops in a year on the same land with the help of indigenous irrigation methods. But these are highly labour intensive, low productive and dependent on the availability of surface water near the field. The insignificant contribution of indigenous irrigation methods to the growth of output confirms that population growth serves as an insufficient stimulus. The lack of public support for the development of infrastructural facilities and the underdeveloped industrial sector have crippled the ability of the peasant sector in Bangladesh to respond effectively to the needs of the growing population.

Peasants have also failed to raise output substantially through proper fertilisation and improved cultivation practices. There is a lack of knowledge of improved techniques of production and also of a market which can supply modern farm inputs.[23]

The scope for increasing output through changes in the crop-mix is limited in a wet rice agriculture. In the main agricultural season when cultivation is based on the arrival of monsoon and flood, no crop other than wet paddy can be cultivated. The only possibility to increase agricultural production is to introduce quick-maturing, high-yield varieties of rice which may be suitable to agronomic conditions in different regions. Such changes can be carried out through publicly or otherwise supported adaptive research and continuous trial and error on the farm. The substitution of high-yield varieties for local varieties of crops in Bangladesh has not taken place on a large scale due to the inadequate support given to the agricultural sector. The cultivation of a variety of food crops during the winter season, and the cultivation of labour intensive cash crops have also been adversely affected by inappropriate economic policies. We shall see in a later section that economic policies remain the most important determinant of agricultural change while population growth may have acted as a necessary condition.

Peasants in Bangladesh have also been unable to raise output through increased capital accumulation, because capital formation requires financial capital to go with the surplus family labour. Population growth, by reducing the rate of rural savings has, in fact, deterred capital formation in the peasant sector of Bangladesh.[24]

The high man/land ratio in rural Bangladesh where each worker has less than one acre of land to work with (if one divides the cultivated area by the number of agricultural workers) and the extremely low average level of income, less than $100 *per capita* per annum, indicate that the peasant economy has failed to act either on the demographic or on the production front. The peasants have tried to introduce a few changes in response to steady increase of population. These changes have helped to counteract a precipitant fall in *per capita* output. However, the economy has reached a stage where endogenous techniques of greater intensification are exhausted, and population has now little opportunity to stimulate growth. The problem of increasing agricultural production in Bangladesh is not solely confined to a lack of appropriate techniques. We shall see in the following section that at a high density of population, further growth of population creates deleterious effects on the agrarian economy and its ability to utilise resources and available technology optimally.

Negative Effects of Population Growth

The peasant economy of Bangladesh is not a collection of homogeneous farm units each striving for the same degree of intensification in response to population growth. The difference in the degree of intensification among farms of different sizes and tenurial arrangements is reflected in the pattern of allocation of labour, the most important input in traditional agriculture. The amount of labour input per unit of land determines the productivity of land. Empirical studies of Bangladesh agriculture indicate that large farmers and tenant farmers make less intensive use of land (low labour input).[25] This is reflected in their productivity level which is lower than that obtained by small owner farmers. The main reasons behind such inefficiency at a sectoral level are the inefficient agrarian structure and the imperfect factor markets. The point which should be stressed here is that while, on the one hand, population growth induces peasants to intensify agricultural practices, on the other hand, it creates constraints to the growth of output.

Laws with respect to the ownership of land in Bangladesh leave sufficient room for unequal distribution of land. The ceiling on land ownership was fixed in 1950 at 33 acres per family or 3.3 acres per person whichever is larger. The ceiling was too high for the peasant economy where, on average, the cultivated area per family would be 2 acres. The farm structure had the tendency to become more unequal under conditions of high ceiling on land ownership, and low agricultural taxation. Our discussion of the land market will show that, given these exogenous factors, population increase and slow growth of the non-rural sector have contributed to further concentration of land in the rural areas. The increasing concentration of land has given rise to a discrepancy in the land/labour ratio across farms. The discrepancy in the land/worker ratio is the main cause of inefficiency in the traditional agriculture of Bangladesh. We shall now observe that rural factor markets in Bangladesh do not operate efficiently to remove this discrepancy.

1. *The Land Market.* The demand for agricultural land in Bangladesh is extremely high due to the high rate of population growth and the lack of job opportunities and avenues for investment outside the farm. The price of land is, therefore, so high that small farmers who have excess labour in relation to land cannot hope to buy land in order to complement their surplus labour. On the contrary, most small farms are forced to sell their land out of economic hardship.

Small farms have a greater tendency to become uneconomic than the larger farms due to the sub-division of holdings under the steady increase of population. Uneconomic farms are eventually bought by large farmers. Land transactions in Bangladesh thus involve the transfer of land from small farmers to large farmers.[26] Under the steady increase of population, the land market operates in such a way as to accentuate the discrepancy in the land/worker ratio.

2. *The Labour Market.* The labour market is influenced by the land market, and it operates along dualistic lines. Large farmers depend mostly on hired labour and small farmers on family labour, and the costs of hired and family labour differ a great deal. As small farmers cannot take up employment any time they like due to uncertainty and seasonality involved in traditional monsoon agriculture, their decision to allocate family labour to their own farms is not affected by the prevailing wage rate. In other words, the wage rate does not reflect the opportunity cost of family labour on small farms. Large farmers, on the other hand, are guided by the wage rate in allocating labour inputs on their farms.

In the regions where the supply of labour mainly comes from small farmers, and the number of landless agricultural labourers is relatively small, large farmers face a labour shortage during the peak seasons, because small farmers cannot leave their farms even though the wage rate may be high. The labour shortage is also aggravated by the uncertainty of rainfall and poor transport communication which hinder the movement of labour from the labour surplus areas. Thus, large farmers have to offer a high wage rate during the peak seasons.

During the slack seasons, the wage rate does not go below the minimum subsistence level as some of the labourers are completely landless and do not have any other source of income. It is the custom in the society to pay at least the minimum subsistence wage. The demand for labour at this wage is usually low and small farmers face difficulty in getting regular jobs. The valuation of family labour by small farmers is not influenced by the prevailing wage rate. Small farmers thus supply labour as long as it adds to total output, whereas large farmers apply labour up to the point where the marginal productivity of labour is equal to the prevailing wage rate. Empirical studies of Bangladesh agriculture show that while all farmers have resorted to greater intensification along labour intensive lines, the gap between large and small farmers with respect to the application of labour input remains the same.[27] The high cost of labour borne by large farmers because they use hired labour instead of family labour, is partly affected by cultural factors, which forbid women to work in the fields and also discourage men from performing manual work.

The important point is that the dualistic tendencies in the labour market are becoming intensified under the steady increase of population as the latter accentuates the discrepancy in the land/worker ratio.

3. *The Credit Market.*[28]   The rural credit market in Bangladesh is segmented and localised. The market is divided into two broad segments — the formal and the informal. The former consists of different lending institutions, and caters mainly to the needs of large farmers. Small farmers and tenants depend on the informal market where private individuals operate. The price of capital faced by small and large farmers differs a great deal because the rates of interest in the formal market are much lower than the ones prevailing in the informal market.

The formal market is not guided by market forces. The rates of interest are exogenously determined, and they bear little relation to the risk premium, administrative costs and the returns from alternative uses. The informal market, on the other hand, is more influenced by market forces but it cannot be called a perfect one either. The high rates of interest are mainly due to the high rates of time preference on the part of both borrowers and lenders, the high premium on risks and administrative costs. The market, however, operates imperfectly due to the monopoly position of some lenders, the extra-economic relations which exist between borrowers and lenders, and the interlinkage among land, labour and credit markets. The market becomes localised and fragmented because of the interdependence of factor markets, and the lack of information and general insecurity under extreme poverty in the economy.

Our main concern here will be to see how population growth is connected with the imperfect credit market in Bangladesh, and how the imperfect credit market influences the degree of agricultural intensification at a sectoral level.

The effects of population growth on the process of land concentration and greater impoverishment of small farmers have already been mentioned. These, in turn, have far-reaching consequences on the credit market because land concentration in fewer hands implies that a small group of farmers is able to procure special privileges from the government such as access to cheap institutional credit. The impoverished condition of the majority of farmers, on the other hand, adversely affects their creditworthiness, and leads to a high demand for short-term consumption loans. The interest rate for such loans is usually very high because of the limited supply in relation to the high demand.

As mentioned earlier, the scope for substitution of capital for labour is limited in Bangladesh traditional agriculture. Thus the relative price of capital in relation to labour faced by large farmers has not resulted in the adoption of less labour intensive cultivation practices. However, the low price of capital has helped the purchase of land by large farmers, and thereby intensified the discrepancy in the land/worker ratio and dualistic tendencies in the labour market.

The imperfect credit market is one of the important contributory factors towards the emergence of share tenancy in Bangladesh agriculture. Given the land and labour markets, both large and small farmers find it convenient to enter into a tenancy contract on a share-cropping basis. Under this arrangement, large farmers can procure labour at a lower price whereas small farmers obtain a secure way of using family labour and a stable income. The extension of credit along with the conferment of the right to cultivate to small farmers, is one efficient instrument at the disposal of large farmers to make productive use of their land. However, share-cropping which emerges largely as a result of imperfection in the factor markets and unequal agrarian structure, is an inefficient arrangement compared to owner farming with family labour. Empirical studies indicate that share-cropped lands are less intensively cultivated than owner-cultivated lands.[29]

Our discussion of the agrarian structure and the factor markets in Bangladesh indicates that population growth, by exacerbating the concentration of land, the dualistic tendencies in the labour market and the imperfections in the credit market, has adversely affected the degree of intensification along labour intensive lines in Bangladesh agriculture. The peasant sector cannot even attain the level of production which is feasible under the existing technology.

The Role of the Non-rural Sector

The pattern of adjustment between population and agricultural production in Bangladesh confirms our hypothesis that population growth is not a sufficient condition to stimulate growth in a peasant economy. The stagnation of income in Bangladesh is an inevitable consequence in view of the fact that population growth has had no impact on the most important determinant of agricultural development, i.e. the growth of the non-rural sector. Although the non-rural sector consists of both public and private sectors, for several reasons the former plays a relatively more important role in Bangladesh. First of all, in a land-scarce country where biochemical research assumes more importance than mechanical research, public support is essential for indigenous basic and applied research, since private enterprise does not usually venture into such areas. Public support is also needed in the development of infrastructure and in carrying out institutional changes, areas where the private sector can contribute little. Lastly, the development of the private sector itself is influenced by the economic policies of the government.

The peasant sector of Bangladesh has never received adequate public support for technological advancement. Since the time of independence from British rule, economic policies have been biased against the agricultural sector. This sector thus received only a small proportion of total public expenditures, and indigenous research on crop-breeding, the development of irrigation technology, and the building of infrastructure and necessary institutional change suffered due to lack of funds.[30]

Private incentives to farmers and to the small industrial sector have also been adversely affected as economic policies with respect to taxes, subsidies, foreign exchange and credit were designed to favour the large industrial sector. During the Pakistan period, a substantial amount of agricultural surplus was transferred from the rural to the urban sector.[31] The growth of large industries did not, however, make a favourable impact on the peasant sector of Bangladesh. The large industries which used capital intensive techniques could not absorb rural labour, nor could they supply cheap farm inputs and utilise farm products as raw materials.[32]

The flow of resources from the peasant sector to the urban sector seems to have decreased in recent years, simply because of the shrinkage of agricultural surplus as population has increased. The bias of economic policies against the peasant sector still persists, as is evidenced by the low proportion of public expenditure devoted to agriculture and the reluctance of the government to introduce necessary institutional changes.[33] It is also alleged that the policy of maintaining the food ration system through food imports rather than through domestic procurement of food grains has kept food prices low, and often creates disincentives to large farmers who produce for the market.

It is a fact that the government finds it easier to solve the food supply problem through food aid rather than by intensifying the effort to increase domestic production as the latter involves radical changes in the socio-economic structure. However, over the last two decades, there have been some attempts by the government to push the new seed-fertiliser–water technology in order to attain food self-sufficiency. But the pressure of population in the rural community has become so acute and poverty so widespread that most of the peasants do not have the ability to bear the costs of the new technology such as investment in farm inputs. The private sector supplying modern inputs could not develop because of the lack of purchasing power of the peasants.

The government has been trying to supply subsidised inputs with the help of the bureaucracy. But the results have not been satisfactory due to the inegalitarian farm structure, the limited supply of modern inputs such as fertilisers, improved seeds, irrigation equipment, and poor infrastructure. Today, less than 20 per cent of the cultivated area is devoted to modern high-yielding rice. As a consequence, food production has persistently been falling short of the demand of the rising population. The peasant economy is, in fact, facing retrogression rather than stagnation.

Main Conclusions

1. Population growth appears as an independent factor in a peasant economy and it induces the peasants to adopt labour-intensive cultivation practices. This supports Boserup's theory regarding the positive effects of population growth on agricultural technology, and refutes the Malthusian theory which views population growth as a dependent factor of food supply.

2. However, population growth *by itself* is a weak stimulus to agricultural change.

The range of endogenous techniques of greater intensification may eventually become exhausted in any peasant economy experiencing a steady growth of population. At a high density of population, further population growth often creates a negative influence on the agrarian structure and rural factor markets. This can also offset the positive effects of population growth on agricultural output.

3. When the man/land ratio is high, a peasant economy under steady population growth can counteract stagnation if the non-rural sector that consists of both the public and the private sectors, helps to introduce modern technology.

4. The study of the Bangladesh peasant economy indicates that the scope for introducing changes in response to population growth through peasants' own efforts is limited in wet rice agriculture, because multiple-cropping, which is the most labour-intensive practice, involves modern technology and can be successfully introduced only with the help of the non-rural sector. In the absence of appropriate economic policies, steady population growth over a long period of time has thus failed to generate a significant growth of output, and recent experience shows that population growth is contributing towards the stagnation of output by intensifying the distortions in the factor markets and the agrarian structure.

5. The case of Bangladesh shows that there is a greater need for public support for agricultural development in wet rice agriculture with a high density of population than in sparsely populated areas where population growth can still have positive effects on output through the reduction of the fallow period. It also confirms that the stagnation of income under a continuous growth of population is not an unexpected outcome because population growth does not necessarily stimulate the private industrial sector nor help to elicit government support to agricultural development.

Notes

1. Harvey Leibenstein has further developed this concept. A graphical exposition of 'subsistence equilibrium' can be found in Leibenstein (1957).
2. It may be *per capita* domestic production of basic foods, or even *per capita* consumption of basic foods among certain income groups. It should be noted here that supporters of Malthus tend to think that the subsistence level at which positive checks start operating has not yet been reached. Besides, there are countervailing factors like the control of epidemics through inoculation and cheap antibiotics, and the supply of foods from food-surplus countries, which Malthus probably did not foresee.
3. Boserup (1965).
4. This is what Malthus had predicted. But, contrary to Boserup, Malthus did not consider that population growth induced the growth of output through technical change.
5. Boserup (1965) pp. 63–4.
6. Ibid.
7. According to Boserup, peasants have to work harder to maintain the subsistence level, as there is a tendency to declining output per man-hour. Ibid, Ch. 4
8. Boserup has also considered these possibilities.
9. Boserup (1965) p. 118.
10. Ibid. Ch. 12.
11. Grigg (1976) and Robinson and Schutjer (1984).
12. Ibid.

13. According to Robinson and Schutjer (1984), p. 363, 'the model currently used (Boserup's) does not, however, make explicit the interaction between population-related technical change and continued agricultural development . . . the key to this issue is the agricultural surplus and its relationship to population growth and the rise of the urban industrial sector.'

14. Boserup (1981) p. 171.

15. According to Boserup, unless exogenous factors like colonial rule come into play, the land tenure system goes through changes in response to population growth so that greater intensification becomes possible. But in today's developing countries, the agrarian structure tends to become more inefficient due to both exogenous and endogenous factors causing distortions in the peasant economy.

16. Grigg (1974).

17. Ahmad (1984).

18. Grigg (1980).

19. Simon (1977).

20. Ganguli (1938).

21. Hossain (1980).

22. The Yearbook of Agricultural Statistics, 1979/80.

23. Ahmad (1984).

24. Ibid.

25. Master Survey of Agriculture in Bangladesh, 1967/8 (1972); Hossain (1977) and Jabbar (1977).

26. Alamgir (1978).

27. Hossain (1977).

28. The reader is referred to Ahmad, (1984) for a detailed discussion.

29. Hossain (1977) and Jabbar (1977).

30. Ahmad (1984).

31. Lewis (1970).

32. Ahmad (1984).

33. Ibid.

Bibliography

Ahmad, Alia, *Agricultural Stagnation under Population Pressure—the Case of Bangladesh* (New Delhi, 1984).

Alamgir, Mohiuddin, *Bangladesh: A Case of Below Poverty Level Equilibrium Trap* (Dhaka, 1978).

Bangladesh Bureau of Statistics, *Master Survey of Agriculture in Bangladesh, Seventh Round, Second Phase, 1967* (Dhaka, 1972).

____ *The Yearbook of Agricultural Statistics, 1979/80* (Dhaka, 1980).

Boserup, Ester, *The Conditions of Agricultural Growth* (London, 1965).

____ *Population and Technology* (Oxford, 1981).

Ganguli, Birendranath, *Trends of Agricultural and Population in the Ganges Valley* (London, 1938).

Grigg, David B. 'Population Pressure and Agricultural Changes', in *Progress in Geography* vol. 8 (London, 1976).

____ *The Agricultural Systems of the World: An Evolutionary Approach* (Cambridge, 1974).

____ *Population Growth and Agricultural Change* (Cambridge, 1980).

Hossain, Mahabub, *Agrarian Structure and Land Productivity: An Analysis of Farm Level Data*, Unpublished Ph.D. Dissertation, Cambridge, 1977.

____ 'Foodgrain Production in Bangladesh: Performance, Potential and Constraints', in *Bangladesh Development Studies*, Vol. 8, Nos. 1 & 2, 1980, pp. 39-70.

Jabbar, Mohammed A., *Farm Structure and Resource Productivity in Selected Areas of Bangladesh* (Dhaka, 1977).

Leibenstein, Harvey, *Economic Backwardness and Economic Growth* (New York, 1957).

Lewis, Stephen, R. *Industrialisation and Trade Policies — Pakistan* (London, 1970).

Malthus, Thomas R. *An Essay on the Principles of Population* (London, 1798).

Robinson, Warren and Schutjer, Wayne, 'Agricultural Development and Demographic Change: A Generalisation of the Boserup Model', in *Economic Development and Cultural Change*, Vol. 32, No. 1 (1984).

Simon, Julian L. *The Economics of Population Growth* (New Jersey, 1977).

5 AGRICULTURAL STAGNATION IN CHILE, 1930-55: A RESULT OF FACTOR MARKET IMPERFECTIONS?*

Mats Lundahl

From 1930 to 1955, Chilean agriculture presents a picture of stagnation in the sense that the growth of output had difficulties in keeping pace with the growth of population. Two different types of explanations have been advanced for this stagnation. The first one stresses the role of economic policies. In an endeavour to further industrialisation, the agricultural sector was neglected and even discriminated against. In various ways, allocation policies tended to favour industry over agriculture with the result that the latter sector stagnated.[1] The second explanation points to imperfections in rural factor markets as the prime cause of stagnation. To a varying extent, land, labour and credit markets in rural Chile were characterised by monopolistic and monopsonistic elements which in turn acted as a brake on agricultural development.[2]

This chapter will be concerned with an investigation of the second of these explanations. We will start by sketching the situation in Chilean agriculture at the end of the 1920s and demonstrate that the available evidence indicates that agricultural output stagnated on a *per capita* basis from 1930 to 1955. Thereafter data regarding the development of imperfections in each one of the three major factor markets during the same period will be scrutinised. In the final section these threads will be pulled together and it will be shown that, if anything, the evidence would appear to indicate that the degree of factor market imperfection remained constant or decreased rather than increased over the period under consideration. Consequently, the explanation of agricultural stagnation which runs in terms of factor market imperfections does not appear to be a particularly convincing argument.

* The research was financed by the Swedish Council for Research in the Humanities and Social Sciences and SAREC. This support is gratefully acknowledged. Thanks are due to Markos Mamalakis for constructive criticism.

105

Output and Productivity in Chilean Agriculture, 1930–55

During the 1910–30 period, the rate of growth of agricultural output in Chile had been approximately 3 per cent per annum, or 1.5 per cent on a *per capita* basis.[3] The export-oriented growth process which the country had undergone during the latter half of the nineteenth and the first three decades of the twentieth century had in different ways created strong growth impulses in agriculture.[4]

The end of the 1920s represented the end of a growth epoch. Over the next two and a half decades stagnation prevailed. To see this clearly, let us examine some of the available statistics.

Table 5.1 contains six different estimates of agricultural production *per capita* from the early 1930s to the mid-1950s. During this period the Chilean population grew by less than 1.5 per cent per annum before 1940 and by 1.9 per cent between 1940 and 1955. As the table shows, agricultural output had problems keeping up with the growth of population. The Ballesteros estimate, which covers some 80 per cent of the total value of agricultural production, as it was composed during the first half of the 1950s,[5] points not only towards stagnation but even retrogression. The second estimate, produced by ECLA, likewise shows that agricultural production *per capita* fell by some 20 per cent from the beginning of the 1930s to the mid-1950s. The third estimate, derived by the *Dirección de Estadísticas y Censos* (DEC), paints an even gloomier picture, according to which *per capita* output fell from a peak index value of 118 in 1934 to one of 77 in 1955. The remaining three series cover a shorter period, from around 1940, but provide similar data, both in agriculture proper and in livestock production. Given the inherent uncertainty regarding the magnitude of errors in the estimates,[6] individual figures in Table 5.1 are not particularly significant, but the trends consistently indicate stagnation from the beginning of the 1930s to the mid-1950s.

The overall result of the failure of agricultural output to expand *pari passu* with the population is shown in Table 5.2. During the 1930–55 period, Chilean economic development policy concentrated strongly on the promotion of domestic industrial production at the expense of imports, with the result that the traditional export branches were neglected.[7] One of the consequences of this policy was that foreign exchange became scarce which in turn led to increased difficulties in importing foodstuffs in sufficient quantities to compensate for the inadequate performance of domestic agriculture. At least from the early 1940s, and presumably during the 1930s

Table 5.1: Indices of Agricultural Production *Per Capita*, 1929–55 (1940 = 100)

	Ballesteros	ECLA	DEC	ODEPLAN Agriculture proper	Animal prod.	Ministry of Agriculture
1929	110.0	108.4	—	—	—	—
1930	115.0	111.1	—	—	—	—
1931	88.1	90.4	—	—	—	—
1932	83.8	91.4	93.2	—	—	—
1933	111.5	108.9	108.9	—	—	—
1934	124.7	114.9	117.5	—	—	—
1935	100.2	101.4	100.1	—	—	—
1936	96.0	103.3	101.7	—	—	—
1937	100.1	102.4	103.0	—	—	—
1938	104.1	97.9	102.4	—	—	—
1939	110.3	106.2	107.0	108.0	98.0	—
1940	100.0	100.0	100.0	100.0	100.0	100.0
1941	90.5	96.3	97.2	95.6	101.1	97.2
1942	92.0	94.8	92.1	101.1	99.3	98.9
1943	96.8	96.9	91.4	104.9	101.9	104.1
1944	103.9	103.2	99.9	109.4	105.0	112.8
1945	98.6	97.1	92.0	100.1	103.3	102.8
1946	97.2	96.1	90.9	98.6	110.0	100.5
1947	94.0	92.8	84.0	96.0	103.4	98.1
1948	100.1	96.5	87.4	99.2	102.5	107.3
1949	92.7	103.2	85.7	97.5	103.7	100.4
1950	84.2	90.9	86.3	92.9	102.4	96.9
1951	84.2	88.6	77.4	91.1	104.0	96.3
1952	84.5	87.8	77.5	88.3	99.9	92.9
1953	90.7	92.5	83.7	96.3	98.9	101.6
1954	90.1	90.1	82.2	97.4	102.7	103.8
1955	95.0	—	77.1	102.7	99.0	108.6

Sources: Output: Ballesteros: Ballesteros (1965), p. 29;
ECLA: Ballesteros & Davis (1963), pp. 170–1;
DEC: Mamalakis (1967), p. A-217;
ODEPLAN: Ibid., pp. A-210–A-217;
Ministry of Agriculture: Ibid., p. A-234.
Population: Mamalakis (1980), p. 4.

as well, the net result was that the *per capita* availability of basic foodstuffs *decreased*.

Table 5.2: *Per Capita* Availability of Basic Foodstuffs 1940/4–1950/4 (kilos per inhabitants)*

	Average 1940–4	Average 1950–4
Wheat	169	168
Barley	11	8
Beans	9	6
Corn	14	11
Potatoes	87	77
Meat	28.7	24.6
Mutton	7.6	4.9
Pork	4.5	4.2
Goat	0.4	0.3

* Presumably, the population figures employed to calculate the figures for meat mutton, pork and goat differ from those employed for the rest of the table.
Sources: Wheat, barley, beans, corn and potatoes computed from output figures in Instituto de Economía (1956), p. 115 and population figures in Mamalakis (1980), p. 4. Rest of table: Instituto de Economía (1956), pp. 118–20.

The Role of Market Imperfections

The argument which states that imperfections in the factor markets were an important cause of agricultural stagnation in Chile between 1930 and 1955 rests heavily on the system of land tenure:

It is widely held that the land tenure system in Chile has resulted in a generally inefficient use of land, water, labour, and capital and has retarded the rate of adoption of new, more productive inputs. This is a theme that runs through most of the discussions of Chilean agriculture that have appeared over the last few decades, and it has provided the motivation and the argument for the various land reform measures adopted in this period.[8]

In an extensive study of the land tenure system in Chile and its impact on the socio-economic development of the agricultural sector undertaken by the Inter-American Committee for Agricultural Development (ICAD, or CIDA — the Spanish abbreviation) between 1962 and 1965, it was concluded that

Almost nowhere is full advantage being taken of land and water resources. This is especially notable on large farms. In addition there is considerable underemployment of labour, especially among those families which depend on the operation of sub-family-size holdings. However, underemployment is also evident on the large farms. The amount of capital invested is relatively low and much of it is inefficiently used. Both case studies and data for the country as a whole indicate that this failure to take full advantage of available economic resources is correlated with the traditional system of latifundio-minifundio.[9]

The underutilisation of productive resources in agriculture is intimately connected with the latifundio-minifundio system, both directly — via the land market, and indirectly — via the influences of the land market on the labour and credit markets. Imperfections in these factor markets lead to static inefficiency in production, and if the degree of imperfection increases over time, agricultural production *per capita* may also stagnate or even fall. In more extreme cases, an absolute decline may even occur.

Towards the end of the chapter, the influence of factor market imperfections on production will be taken up again in greater detail. However, before entering that discussion we will take a look at each one of the three major factor markets to find out whether the degree of imperfection in each one of them increased or decreased from around 1930 to the mid-1950s.

The Development of Land Concentration

The ownership structure of Chilean agriculture in the mid-1950s did not differ much from that of the mid-1920s. In 1924, the *Dirección General de Estadística* reported a distribution of agricultural property, shown in Table 5.3, which indicated that over 60 per cent of all agricultural land was held in lots exceeding 5,000 hectares, and that almost 90 per cent belonged to farm units exceeding 1,000 hectares. This corresponds to 0.7 and 2.7 per cent of all farm *units* respectively.[10]

Table 5.3:   The Distribution of Agricultural Land, 1924

Size in Hectares	Number of Properties	As Percent of Total Properties	Area in Hectares	As Percent of Total Area
<5	46,136	42.5	73,069	0.28
5–20	27,475	23.3	292,411	1.10
21–50	13,853	12.7	470,414	1.80
51–200	12,503	11.5	1,288,048	5.02
201–1000	7,236	7.3	3,242,582	12.80
1001–5000	2,080	2.0	4,245,124	16.70
5001–	570	0.7	15,813,796	62.30
Total	109,853	100.0	25,425,444	100.00

Source: Loveman (1973), p. 95.

This distribution should be compared to the one given by CIDA for the year 1955. The CIDA study makes a distinction between four different types of landholdings:

1. sub-family holdings: required less than two man-years of labour,
2. family holdings: required two to four man-years of labour,
3. medium multi-family holdings: required four to twelve man-years of labour and
4. large multi-family holdings: required more than twelve man-years of labour.

Most of the agricultural land was concentrated in the hands of a minority of owners of large multi-family holdings. Thus, as shown in Table 5.4, while these holdings only represented 7 per cent of all farm units, they controlled 79 per cent of all agricultural land,[11] 65 per cent of all arable land,[12] and 78 per cent of all the irrigated land in the country. The most typical units on the other hand, the family farms, which accounted for 40 per cent of all farms, controlled only 8 per cent of the agricultural land, 12 per cent of the cultivable land and 7 per cent of the irrigated area. The sub-family holdings which in terms of numbers were almost as important as the family farms (37 per cent) accounted for a mere 0.3, 0.1 and 2.1 per cent, respectively.

The concentration of land in the hands of a minority[13] created a monopoly in the land market or rather, a series of local monopolies. The main manifestation of these monopolies was the difficulty encountered by small farmers in buying small parcels of land. Thus, Oscar Domínguez in a study of four communities in the Aconcagua

Table 5.4: Number and Size Distribution of Landholdings, 1955

	Number of units	Area (hectares)			Average cultivable per unit	Average irrigated per unit
		Agricultural	Cultivable	Irrigated		
Sub-family	55,761	67,400	57,500	23,400	1 ha	0.4 ha
%	37.0	0.3	1.0	2.1	—	—
Family	60,388	1,762,800	642,600	80,000	11 ha	1.4 ha
%	40.0	8.1	12.0	7.3	—	—
Medium multi-family	24,427	2,823,400	1,220,400	138,300	50 ha	5.7 ha
%	16.0	13.0	22.0	12.6	—	—
Large multi-family	10,383	16,983,900	3,623,000	856,200	349 ha	82 ha
%	7.0	78.6	65.0	78.0	—	—
Total	150,959	21,637,100	5,543,500	1,097,900	—	—
%	100.0	100.0	100.0	100.0	—	—

Source: CIDA (1966), p. 168.

valley in the late 1950s reported that 55 per cent of all the farmers could not buy any land from the *fundos* in the neighbourhood.[14] As a rule the large landowners only sold land in order to meet immediate economic necessities. In these cases, the sales were made either against prompt cash payment or against payment in the immediate future. An idea of the importance of these imperfections in the land market may be gained from the fact that an agricultural worker who saved some 20 per cent of his yearly income in order to buy and pay cash for a lot of 10 hectares of irrigated land in the Central Valley or 30 hectares in the Valdivia zone in the Lagos region, would have to wait for some 40–55 years before he could realise the transaction. His landlord, on the other hand, could buy four to seven lots of this type per year by saving 20 per cent of *his* income.[15] Thus, in most instances the lack of a supply of *small* parcels effectively precluded landless workers and small farmers from access to agricultural land. Only large farmers and some, but not all, owners of family farms could afford to buy and pay cash for parcels of the size that were put on the market.

The data in Table 5.3 and 5.4 are not strictly comparable, since in the former case the definition is made in terms of area whereas the 1955 figures are based on the employment capacity of a given farm. Nevertheless, both sets of figures provide a strong indication that land tenure was concentrated in a few hands. It seems, however — taking the figures at face value — that a slight decrease took place in the degree of concentration. The 1924 figures indicate that 79 per cent of the land was held by at most 3 per cent of all rural farm units, while in 1955, the latter figure had increased to 7 per cent.[16] In Figure 5.1, the information of Tables 5.3 and 5.4 has been translated into Lorenz curves. We find that the one for 1955 lies inside the one for 1924, indicating a lower degree of concentration, the Gini coefficients being 0.91 (1955) and 0.93 (1924).

The 1924 figures are presumably fairly unreliable. However, regional data indicated that the direction of change from 1924 to 1955 indeed appears to be the correct one and in addition that, if anything, Figure 5.1 *under*estimates the real magnitude of the change. Thus, Gene Martin Ellis, in a study of the Santiago province, found that the share of agricultural land held in properties of over 250 hectares fell from 79 to 41 per cent of the total between 1928 and 1954.[17] Thus, to conclude, it appears as if the degree of land concentration decreased somewhat in Chile from the early 1930s to the mid-1950s.

Figure 5.1:   Distribution of Land in Chile, 1924 and 1955

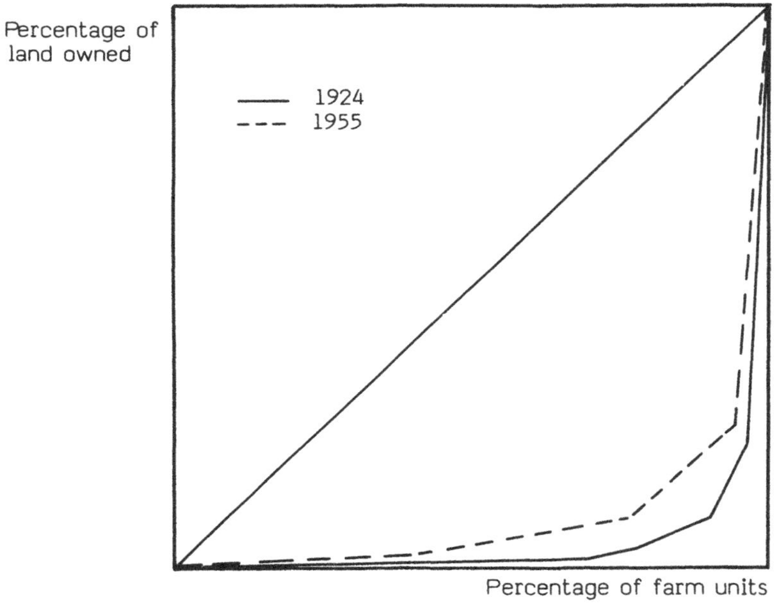

Percentage of
land owned

——— 1924
– – – 1955

Percentage of farm units

The Rural Labour Market

A common feature of the rural factor markets of most Latin American economies is that the high degree of monopoly prevailing in the land market creates monopsony power, i.e. a series of local monopsonies or oligopsonies in the labour market. This, in turn creates a problem for the worker when he enters into an agreement with a landlord as to the conditions of employment. In the general case, the worker is illiterate, unorganised, and competes with large numbers of workers who are in exactly the same position. The landowner, on the other hand, can count on a good education and backing by a landowner association which both reinforces his monopsony position and which provides legal expertise if needed. In addition, he either handles the enforcement of law and order in the countryside himself, by employing a private police force, or otherwise has recourse to the official police who provide him with the necessary support. Finally, the workers may be tied to him by virtue of debts incurred previous years and cannot leave without the settlement of these debts.[18] In short, all the advantages are with the landowners, but the factor of greatest importance is their control over the access to land via purchases or renting. These uneven power relations in turn allow the landowner to contract labour by means of individual bargaining with each worker at wage rates which are generally much lower than would be forthcoming in a market characterised not only by competition among workers but among landowners as well, i.e. a market where land ownership is more widely distributed. The landlords are able to hire workers either by setting a single wage rate which lies below the marginal cost of hiring labour, or by discriminating as perfectly as possible between the workers.[19]

Up to the mid-1920s, the authority of the landed oligarchy had been virtually unchallenged in the Chilean countryside. The hacienda and fundo labour system rested mainly on *inquilinaje* where resident labourers provided work for a determined number of days in exchange for the right to use a small plot, pasture rights, housing and food rations. This labour was supplemented during periods of peak activity with temporary farm hands. The rural labour contract was basically 'free' in the sense that no legal prohibitions existed regarding its contents. 'This meant the landowner could require whatever the market could bear, short of slavery, as a condition of employment and residence within the hacienda,' concludes Brian Loveman in his well-researched study on politics and the rural land and labour markets from 1919 to 1972.[20] There were no legal possibilities of forming any labour unions, and all extra-legal efforts to this end were met with fierce resistance from the hacendados. Before 1931, the rural labour movement in Chile was unable to register anything but the most ephemeral gains.

Alternative employment was hard to find. Temporary workers could of course move from one hacienda to another, but paid a high price for this freedom in that they had to forego whatever minimal security that permanent residence on an hacienda could offer.[21] The inquilinos, on the other hand, were scarcely in a much better position since they were not allowed to work outside the estate where they were living.[22]

Outside the agricultural sector, employment opportunities were not abundant. During the 1920s, nitrate mining displayed heavy fluctuations in labour demand from year to year which periodically brought back waves of unemployed to rural districts.[23] To some extent, workers transferred into the large-scale copper sector which was taking shape in the 1920s, but in 1930 the Braden company which accounted for approximately one-half of total sales in that sector employed a mere 8,250 workers.[24]

After 1920, migration from rural districts in central Chile was no longer directed towards the north but towards urban areas instead.[25] The manufacturing sector, however, was unable to absorb a substantial number of the growing surplus of hands. If we use the figures of Ballesteros and Davis, we find that total employment in manufacturing and construction increased by only 48,000 people from 1907 to 1930. (During the same period, the total labour force grew by some 215,000.)[26]

From 1931 to the mid-1950s, the rural labour market in Chile underwent certain changes. In 1931, a Labour Code was promulgated. According to this code, share-crop contracts had to specify the obligations of the contracting parties. Written contracts were made compulsory in the case of inquilinaje. An explicit prohibition was issued against contractual requirements that resident labour sell their produce to their employers, and hacendados were compelled to pay the current market price in such transactions. A factor of even greater importance was that general provisions regarding mandatory collective bargaining and unionisation were made applicable to agriculture. Strikes, labour petitions, unionisation etc. could no longer be opposed on legal grounds. The 1931 Labour Code was later supplemented with provisions regarding family allowances (1947), minimum wages (1953), a fixed minimum percentage of the agricultural minimum wage in cash (1953) and a housing code (1954). All these laws increased the obligations of the landlords toward their workers and somewhat limited their authority.

Other steps were, however, taken in the opposite direction. In 1933, rural union rights were suspended by an administrative decree from the Department of Labour after hacendado pressure. From that date, no new rural labour unions could be legally registered until 1937, when the 1933 decree had more or less fallen into oblivion. Rural unions were again formed, and again, the landowners moved to stop unionisation. A 1939 decree again suspended rural unionisation — this time until 1946.[27] In 1947, a special law stipulated that in order to constitute a rural labour union, a minimum of twenty workers was required. These workers had to be more than 18 years old, had to have been on the farm for more than a full year, and had to represent 40 per cent of all the workers on the farm. Ten of them had to be literate.

These were strict requirements. All the landowners had to do was to keep a maximum of 19 permanent workers on the hacienda or to convert inquilinos to sharecroppers, since the latter did not count as 'workers'. In addition, no outside labour organisers were allowed to help in the formation of the union, and union leaders were not made immune to dismissal. Finally, all rural unions which had been formed prior to the 1947 law had to be dissolved.

In 1948 the Communist Party was outlawed and its cadres were excluded from taking any part in labour organisation. This was a severe blow to the union movement, since the Communists had been one of the most active organising groups in the countryside.

The legal problems facing the rural union movement did not crush it but made unionisation difficult in practice. The landowners could count on the support of the government throughout the period and it was mainly when presidential elections were due that unionisation was allowed. The various groups that attempted to organise the rural labourers were thus forced to work underground for long periods of time. This was true especially of the Communist Party which had become active in rural unionisation at the end of the 1930s. Here, not only the negative attitude towards unionisation, but in addition the general suppression of communism, made activities difficult. Other groups had problems as well. A Trotskyite organisation — the *Liga Nacional de Defensa de Campesinos Pobres* — met with a certain success but this group did not survive the thirties. The Christian left — what was finally to become the Christian Democratic Party — did not become active in rural affairs until the early 1950s.

The landowners, on the other hand, were extremely active throughout the period. A recurrent pattern was established where severe repression followed whatever short-run gains the workers managed to make. The landowners persistently, and in most cases successfully, opposed all attempts — legal and others — to strengthen the bargaining position of the rural workers. Loveman concludes that from 1931 to 1964 'only slight improvement occurred in the enforcement of most labor laws in the country-side'.[28] The landowners also began a policy of shifting away from inquilinaje, which was covered by labour legislation, towards sharecropping which was not, since a sharecropper was not considered a 'labourer'. The landowners also increased their employment of temporary wage labour in order to escape the social security payments which applied to resident labour.

The availability of outside employment did not improve much between 1930 and 1940. It is even possible that the share of agriculture in total employment *rose* between these two dates,[29] but this may also be a statistical misrepresentation of the true development, due to an underestimate of agricultural employment in 1930.[30] At any rate, the available statistics do not allow for any distinct trend in the share of agriculture until after 1940. That year, 37 per cent of the active population were employed in agriculture (654,600) while fifteen years later the share had fallen to 30 per cent (694,100).[31] Employment in mining increased slightly from 1930 to 1940, by about 2,600 people per year.[32] Thereafter, however, it stagnated. The 1955 figure was only 8,600 people higher than the one for 1940,[33] due to layoff of blue-collar workers in large-scale mining.[34]

The industrial sector failed to provide much relief. Industrial employment appears to have fallen by 13,000 people between 1920 and 1940, to rise over the next fifteen years by 134,000.[35] During the latter period, the total labour force increased by 546,000 people. Hence, industry absorbed one-quarter of the growth of the labour force. Most of the new employment offered instead came from the service and commerce sectors. During the 1930s these sectors absorbed more than 100,000 people. Subsequently, in the period up to 1955, they accounted for almost 45 per cent of the increase in the labour force.[36] It would appear that most of the employment in the sector came from service and commerce excluding transport, storage and communications.[37] Trade especially was a category which contained the most diverse undertakings. Presumably, 'the smaller number of farmers' markets dealing in food and second-hand or low-price products'[38] absorbed most of those who would otherwise have been in agriculture.[39] From the point of view of the rural population, the employment situation does not appear to have been very much better in 1955 than immediately before the Depression.

Were the Chilean rural labourers in a better or worse bargaining position *vis-à-vis* the landowners in 1955 than in 1931? As we have seen, virtually every advance by the labour movement was followed by stern repression from the landowners, and the laws which aimed at improving the position of labour were revoked or suspended time after time. Still, it seems as if the amount of hacendado control over the rural labour market was no greater in 1955 than twenty-five years earlier.

In the first place, as we saw in the section on land tenure, the concentration of landownership was reduced from the early 1930s to the mid 1950s, i.e. the degree of monopoly exercised in the land market was probably slightly reduced during this period.

Secondly, before 1931 *no* kind of rural labour movement was conceivable. However, during the 1931–55 period a labour movement was established in the countryside in spite of all the difficulties arising from the combined action of landowners and governments. This labour movement did its utmost to change the terms of the labour contracts, and it does not seem possible to contend that these changes were *negative*. With or without the support of the legislators, the landowners provided a strong, sometimes too powerful, resistance, but they hardly managed to set the clock back.

The third factor which allows us to draw the conclusion that the power of the landowners over the workers was somewhat reduced between 1931 to 1955 is one which we have so far not touched upon: the rise of a bureaucracy dealing with rural affairs that basically acted according to rules that had not been determined by hacendado interests but had instead become an autonomous force without any direct relationship with either landowners or workers: in agencies dealing directly with labour questions, health services, schools, post and telegraph offices, civil registers, etc. These groups contributed to breaking down the relative isolation of rural areas from urban centres. In addition, road communications improved considerably over the period, allowing for improved two-way communication between city and countryside.

By and large the bureaucracy managed to distance themselves from landowner interests. Even though the latter placed very severe obstacles in the way of the actions of the bureaucracy, they were never successful in neutralising its influence altogether. These bureaucrats were in the main recruited politically. All governments from 1938 to 1958 contained Socialist or Communist participants as well as people from the *Partido Radical*, which was ideologically very heterogeneous but which certainly allowed for people with leftist outlooks. Consequently, as the number of people with populist or Marxist political ideologies increased in the bureaucracy, the likelihood that worker complaints would receive a favourable treatment in government agencies also increased.

To sum up our argument: The monopsony hold over the rural labour market exercised by the hacendados appears to have loosened somewhat from 1931 to 1955. The concentration of land in the hands of a minority decreased. The first rural labour unions were formed and immediately began attacking landlord prerogatives, with or without help from the law. Finally, the relative isolation of the countryside was broken. Communication with urban districts led to the penetration of new ideas in the countryside, often communicated by a bureaucracy among whom radical ideas were slowly absorbed. However, the *extent* of change in power positions was very limited. The landowners managed to resist most attempts to break their power and only yielded marginally to worker pressure. Nevertheless, it does not seem possible to contend that worker power was *less* in 1955 than in 1931.

The Rural Credit Market

To complete our picture of the rural factor markets, we must also examine the distribution of credit between different types of farmers. It would appear that the terms for access to credit differed very markedly between large and small farmers. Moreover this situation did not change between the early 1930s and the mid-1950s.

The extension of credit to the agricultural sector via the banking system began in Chile during the 1850s. Mortgage laws made rural property an excellent security for loans.[40] In the *Caja de Crédito Hipotecario*, property worth at least 2,000 pesos could be mortgaged. The long-term loans from the Caja were available only to the larger landowners. Arnold Bauer remarks that 'a list of Caja loan recipients in 1880 would be barely indistinguishable from a list of members of the Club de la Unión, the Club Hípico, or Congress',[41] and Jean Borde and Mario Góngora in their study of the development of rural property in the Puangue valley, close to Santiago, term the Caja 'a docile instrument in the hands of the landowners'.[42] This was the case at least up to 1930.[43] In addition to this source, the landowners also had access to the commercial banks which readily lent their services to the hacendados,[44] albeit mainly in the form of short-term loans.[45]

Small farmers, on the other hand, did not generally have any recourse to organised credit. In order to obtain a loan of 1,000 pesos during the latter half of the nineteenth century, property worth at least 2,000 pesos had to be presented as a mortgage. However, a property of that size was much larger than a single family farm.[46] This situation continued up to the Depression. Owners of sub-family and family farms in the main had to be content with whatever loans they could receive in the informal credit markets.

Moving from around 1930 to 1955, not very much seems to have changed in the formal credit market. Among private banks, regular, conservative banking principles were adhered to in the screening of applicants for agricultural loans. The asset position of the borrower was the single most important criterion.[47] The Banking Department of the *Banco del Estado* followed exactly the same principles, clearly favouring large farmers with substantial assets over small ones of low creditworthiness.[48] Together, private banks and the Banking Department accounted for more than 50 per cent of all organised lending to agriculture between 1951 and 1955.[49]

These loans were, however, available only for short periods — hardly ever for more than a single year.[50] The only agency providing longer-term credits was the Agricultural Department of the Banco del Estado which gave loans of up to 3 years for 'development' purposes. This institution was supposed to employ criteria other than strictly commercial ones in its judgement of proposals from small farmers, sharecroppers, and tenants, but in practice the bank showed 'little evidence of carrying out this professed policy'.[51] Ernest Feder, in a scrutiny of the lending activities of the Agricultural Department in 1959 concluded from a random sample of 163 loan applications by 137 applicants that, 'considering the small size and randomness of the sample, it is remarkable that part of the list of the Bank customers should read like a social register'.[52] 82 per cent of the farmers in this sample held farms exceeding 100 hectares, and 69 per cent owned a net capital exceeding 25,000 1958 escudos.[53] Feder also found that the value of the landholdings in general was grossly understated in the applications, and concluded that 'many, if not the majority of the potential recipients of loans from the Bank are the "upper crust" of Chilean families',[54] and that as much as one-third of the total value of Bank loans to agriculture went to one or two per cent of all farms in the country.[55]

It was mentioned above when describing the credit opportunities available for smallholders etc. at the beginning of the 1930s that this category of borrowers was normally confined to the informal credit markets. The same was true in 1955. Before 1959, no important formal credit sources were available to the low-income sectors of the Chilean economy.[56] Unfortunately, no analysis of the informal credit markets is available before the mid-1960s. However, there is no reason to believe that any significant changes took place between

1930, 1955 and the former date. Consequently we will proceed to give an account of the situation in 1964–5.[57]

In 1964–5 Charles Nisbet undertook a field study of 200 farm operators ('owners, sharecroppers, administrators, commoners, and renters'),[58] in ten of the most typically agricultural provinces in Chile. On the basis of this sample he estimated that some 70 per cent of the rural population did not have any opportunity to borrow in the formal credit market. 74 per cent of the sample owned a maximum of 5.1 hectares, if they had any land at all. More than 80 per cent had had less than six years at school. These borrowers dealt with two different groups of lenders — commercial and non-commercial. The latter consisted of friends, neighbours, relatives and *patrones*,[59] while the former were mainly village stores and moneylenders (and to a minor extent itinerant traders). Generally, the size of the loans was small — 78 per cent less than US$200 and 97 per cent less than US$1,000. (These figures should be compared to the average size of loans to farmers in the largest commercial bank: US$10,000 in 1965–6.) The loans obtained were very short-term (the most common term being 'until the harvest'). In only a single case (out of 104) did the term extend beyond a single year.

The informal credit markets of rural Chile in the mid-1960s were characterised by limited competition among the lenders. Since the non-commercial sources were not able to satisfy more than part of the demand for credit among the borrowers, the commercial sources played an important role, accounting for more than 50 per cent of all loans in the sample. On average these sources charged over 83 per cent per year (against a mean of 18 per cent in the formal credit market). The rate of interest consists of four different components: the opportunity cost, transaction costs, risk premia and monopoly rents. Nisbet did not investigate the first three components other than indirectly, but found that the lenders had an intimate knowledge of the borrowers and that no financial securities entered the picture in two-thirds of the cases. From this we may conclude that neither transaction costs nor risk premia played any important role. The opportunity cost can in turn be measured by the rate of return on other risk-free investments like government bonds, which yielded much less than 18 per cent. Thus, the overwhelming part of the average interest rate, 82 per cent, must by definition be considered as a monopoly profit.

Several factors accounted for the existence of local monopolies or collusive duopolies or oligopolies. In the first place, only a limited number of commercial credit sources were found in each *comuna* (township), and in all the cases examined both moneylenders and village stores limited their radius of action to the immediate neighbourhood. Moneylenders seldom worked beyond one or two miles from their point of location (less than the entire comuna) and the village store owners did not go into neighbouring villages in their operations. The number of moneylenders in each 'rural credit market area' ranged from zero to three and the number of village stores engaged in moneylending varied from two to five. The mean numbers were one and three, respectively.

The reason for limiting the scope of activities to the immediate neighbourhood is to be sought in the difficulties of gathering information about people who were not known locally or from previous business transactions. Thus, the local monopoly positions held by commercial lenders were to a great extent a result of the lack of information regarding the creditworthiness of borrowers from 'outside'. The borrowers, in turn, were in a yet worse position when it came to information regarding the sources available to them. As a rule, they did not know of the existence of commercial informal lenders outside the local credit market area, let alone what such sources would be likely to charge on different types of loans. Especially in the case of moneylenders knowledge was lacking — very much due to the fact that moneylending activities were illegal. (Only ten per cent of the people interviewed in the sample could identify other than the local moneylenders.)

The commercial lenders did not compete with each other. No borrower had switched from one moneylender to another who offered a lower rate of interest. Market shares among the moneylenders appeared to be virtually stationary. No lender dared to go outside his customary territory and into nearby areas where he lacked the necessary local knoweldge. Moneylending activities were illegal and were hence most easily kept under cover if the volume of operations was limited. Finally, most of the moneylenders were farmers, who could at best put 50 per cent of their annual gross income into moneylending. The market share of each village store also appeared to be stationary.[60] The borrowers were tied to the stores through old, overdue debts or through current commitments. At times the collusion between village stores went to the point where different stores financed each other's lending activities over the agricultural year. The terms offered a particular borrower were approximately the same regardless of whether he went to a store or to a moneylender.

Thus, to conclude: large and small farmers had access to credit on very different terms both in the early 1930s and around 1955. The former could as a rule borrow in commercial banks or government credit agencies at the prevailing market rate of interest which was frequently negative in real terms due to a high rate of inflation — simply because they could offer land as collateral. The latter, on the other hand, were virtually cut off from access to organised credit and had instead to rely on the informal rural credit markets where interest rates were perhaps four times as high, mainly because in the latter markets borrowers were facing collusive oligopolists, duopolists or even pure monopolists. Strictly speaking, available data for the informal markets do not allow us to find out whether monopoly tendencies were stronger or weaker around 1930 than in 1955. However, in the section on the rural labour market we mentioned that from the early 1930s to the mid-1950s much of the relative isolation of the countryside was broken. Contacts increased between town and country.[61] It would be strange if this improvement did not have at least some corroding influence on local monopolies, although the magnitude of the impact was presumably marginal. As we have seen, Nisbet's field study which was undertaken in 1964-5, indicated that the amount of competition in the formal market at that time appeared to be limited.

Factor Market Imperfections and Agricultural Production

The analysis above has provided us with some insights as to the nature of the imperfections prevailing in the rural land, labour, and capital markets and their development during the 1930–55 period. Armed with this knowledge, we are now in a position to try to answer the question posed at the outset, namely whether changes in the agricultural factor markets increased the inefficiency of resource use in agriculture from 1930 to 1955.

We may then draw on the analytical framework suggested by Keith Griffin in *Underdevelopment in Spanish America*.[62] Denoting rent (the return to land) by r, wages by w, and interest (the return to capital) by i and letting subscripts l and m stand for latifundio and minifundio, respectively, we find that the following relative factor prices prevailed in the agricultural sector from 1930 to 1955:

$$r_m > r > r_l, \qquad (1)$$

$$w_l = w_m < w, \qquad (2)$$

and

$$i_m > i > i_l. \qquad (3)$$

Factor prices without subscripts denote the prices that would have been established, had the factor markets in question been competitive.

Thus, it is evident that in the land market, small farmers (including inquilinos, other tenants, and landless workers) had to pay a price which lay above the competitive level. Actually, in many instances, as we found, the price must be considered infinite, since land was sold only in large blocks and small farmers would not be able to bid for these at all but only for small parcels which seldom were put on the market. The monopolist hacendados on the other hand could get land at an imputed price below the competitive level, given by a point on the marginal revenue product of land in latifundio production which must lie below the total demand (latifundio plus small farmers) curve.[63]

In the labour market, monopsonistic conditions, derived mainly from the monopolisation of land, prevailed. Thus, the hacendados paid a wage rate which lay below the competitive one — a wage which was equal to what the workers would have received if they had remained on their own land (an imputed figure) or worked for other smallholders.

In the capital market, finally, we found that the hacendados had access to credits at the going bank rate of interest — one which in practice was often negative. Since the large majority of the farmers were excluded from the formal credit market, the interest rates that prevailed there were below their competitive level. The small peasants had to rely on the informal rural credit markets, where due to the monopolistic and semi-monopolistic conditions prevailing, the going rates of interest as a rule were well above the competitive rate.

The fact that small and large farmers faced two different sets of relative land-labour and capital-labour prices ought to have made production on larger farms more intensive in the use of both land and capital per man-hour. Table 5.5 shows that this was true for 1955 at least as far as the land–man ratio is concerned. In all the agricultural zones for which data were available this ratio increased according to the size of the farm units. (Unfortunately, no comparable data are available regarding the use of capital inputs per person employed. However, with the tremendous differences in access to credit for large and small farmers, it should go without saying that the use of capital inputs was higher on latifundios than on smaller farms. Where does a farmer find an investment that gives an 82 per cent yield — the average found by Nisbet?)[64]

Table 5.5: Land–Man Ratios and Farm Size, 1955 (hectares per person active in agriculture)

Zone*		Sub-family	Family	Multi-family		Total
				Medium	Large	
I	Norte Grande & Norte Chico	0.5	1.9	3.8	10.3	4.5
II	Central Chile	0.7	2.4	5.0	9.4	6.4
III		0.9	4.1	8.4	14.7	8.8
IV	La Frontera	0.7	4.6	9.0	17.3	10.6
V	Los Lagos & Chiloé	0.7	2.7	10.8	20.7	8.4
Chile		0.7	3.5	8.6	14.2	8.3

* Zone VI (Los Canales) is included only in the national total.
Source: CIDA (1966), p. 162.

Other observations also lend support to the argument that resources were inefficiently allocated in agriculture in the mid 1950s. One such observation is that the land worked by small farmers, inquilinos, and other tenants was often subject to severe erosion.[65] The CIDA report quotes a 1950 study by the *Departamento de Conservación de Recursos Agrícolas y Forestales*[66] which pointed out that the small size of the plots worked by these categories was conducive to an excessively intensive use of the land and that tenant farmers and sharecroppers faced with the fear of eviction attempted to obtain as much as possible out of a given plot as quickly as possible without paying any attention to the detrimental effects that this had on soil fertility. A comparison between efficient resource allocation under competitive conditions and a situation characterised by monopoly in the land market and monopsony in the labour market, shows that the large estates tended to employ too much land (and capital) per unit of labour while the smaller farms over-utilised the available land.

So far, we have seen that resources were inefficiently used in Chilean agriculture in the mid-1950s. This raises the related question, indicated at the beginning of the paper, namely, whether or not the efficiency of the resource allocation at this time represented an improvement in comparison with the early 1930s.

Our analysis of the rural factor markets led to the following three tentative conclusions:

1. The degree of monopoly in the land market appears to have declined from 1930 to 1955, but only marginally.
2. The bargaining position of the workers *vis-à-vis* the land-owners had possibly improved slightly, or at worst, remained constant.
3. The degree of imperfection in the capital market shows no signs of having changed from 1930 to 1955.

This knowledge, in turn, allows us to advance the hypothesis that resources were slightly more efficiently used in 1955 than in 1930. Returning to the relative factor prices facing large and small farmers we should have that *ceteris paribus*:[67]

$$r_m^{1930} > r_m^{1955} > r > r_l^{1955} > r_l^{1930} \tag{4}$$

$$w_l^{1930} = w_m^{1930} \leqslant w_l^{1955} = w_m^{1955} < w \tag{5}$$

$$i_m^{1955} = i_m^{1930} > i > i_l^{1955} = i_l^{1930} \tag{6}$$

The degree of imperfection was somewhat lower in the land market, slightly lower or unchanged in the labour market and unchanged in the capital market. This, in turn means that in 1955 less land and capital were used per unit of labour on large farms than in 1930 whereas small farmers at least used more land per unit of labour (and possibly more capital as well). The fact that factor prices were as close to competitive equilibrium values in 1955 as in 1930, or even closer, suggests that the degree of inefficiency in resource use ought to have fallen, although presumably only slightly. It seems that the difference between the marginal productivity of large and small farms did not change in the case of capital but was reduced some-what for land, while the (implicit or explicit) wage rates moved closer to the value of the marginal product of labour.

There was a slight improvement in resource allocation within the agricultural sector between 1930 and 1955; the land tenure system served to constrain agricultural production mainly in a *static* sense — production would have been higher at any given point in time if competitive conditions had prevailed instead of the monopoly-monopsony relationships which characterised the land, labour and credit markets. In the *comparative static* perspective, the economic policy pursued by Chilean governments would appear to have been the villain of the piece.[68] As a result of the reduction in the degree of imperfection prevailing in agricultural factor markets, a slight tendency towards increased output arose. However this tendency was counteracted and swamped by the negative influences emanating from the discriminatory policies pursued by respective governments. The positive changes in the factor markets were far too small to have had any noticeable impact on the framework of discrimination.

Notes

1. See e.g. Mamalakis (1965), Ch. 3; Crosson (1970).
2. See e.g. CIDA (1966).
3. Mamalakis (1976), p. 122 indicates that agricultural production grew by 2.8 per cent per annum 1910/12–1918/22 and by 3.1 per cent 1918/22–1928/32. Over this period, the population was growing at an annual rate of 1.5 per cent (Mamalakis (1980), p. 4).
4. These are discussed in Lundahl (forthcoming).
5. Ballesteros (1965), p. 9.
6. For a discussion of the methods used, see Ballesteros (1965); Mamalakis (1967).
7. See Mamalakis (1965); Reynolds (1965).
8. Crosson (1970), p. 34.
9. CIDA (1966), p. 205.
10. The table underestimates the real concentration of landed property. It was not uncommon for a single owner to have more than one estate.
11. Agricultural land was defined as land which can be used for cultivation, for grazing or for forestry.
12. Cultivable land includes actually cultivated land, artificial (cultivated) pastoral land and fallow land and natural grazing land provided that these had been cultivated during the last ten years before the 1955 census.
13. It is probable that Table 5.4 underestimates the real degree of concentration in the same manner as Table 5.3, since a single owner could also have owned more than one unit in 1955.
14. Quoted by CIDA (1966), note, p. 66.
15. CIDA (1966), pp. 172–3.
16. Note, that the definition of agricultural land probably differs between the two estimates.
17. Quoted by Loveman (1973), p. 125.
18. See e.g. Feder (1971), Part II, for details.
19. Cf. Robinson (1969), Chs. 18 and 26.
20. Loveman (1973), p. 60. Except where otherwise indicated, the data presented in this section are drawn from that study.
21. Ibid., pp. 72–3.
22. McBride (1936), p. 156.
23. Johnson (1978), p. 363; Loveman (1973), pp. 440–2.
24. Reynolds (1965), p. 391.

25. Johnson (1978), p. 366.
26. Mamalakis (1967), p. A-436 a.
27. Loveman (1973), p. 241.
28. Ibid., p. 138.
29. Cf. Mamalakis (1976), pp. 11, 134.
30. Ibid., p. 11.
31. Mamalakis (1980), pp. 198–201.
32. Using the Ballesteros and Davis participation rates and share of mining in the total (Ballesteros and Davis (1963), p. 176) and the 1930 census population figure (Mamalakis (1980), p. 5), mining employment in 1930 was 74,600 people.
33. Mamalakis (1980), p. 200.
34. Herrick (1965), p. 48.
35. Mamalakis (1976), p. 165; (1980), p. 198.
36. Computed from figures in Ballesteros and Davis (1963), p. 176; Mamalakis (1980), pp. 5, 201.
37. Cf. Mamalakis (1976), p. 177.
38. Ibid., p. 186.
39. Mamalakis notes that 'while export orientation and dependence were linked and associated with high productivity services, industrialisation and urbanisation have been associated with declining or low-productivity service sectors'. (Ibid., p. 208.)
40. Bauer (1975), p. 89.
41. Ibid., p. 91.
42. Borde and Góngora (1956), p. 126.
43. Bauer (1975), p. 91.
44. Ibid., pp. 91–2.
45. Ibid., p. 95.
46. Ibid., pp. 93–4.
47. Crosson (1970), p. 13.
48. Ibid., pp. 13–14; CIDA (1966), p. 175.
49. Crosson (1970), p. 13.
50. Ibid.
51. Ibid., pp. 13–14.
52. Feder (1959), p. 48.
53. CIDA (1966), p. 176.
54. Feder (1959), p. 48.
55. Crosson (1979), p. 16.
56. Nisbet (1967), p. 85.
57. The following is an account of the most important findings of Nisbet (1967).
58. Ibid., p. 86.
59. 'The *patron* has been traditionally the hereditary owner of a farm property, but currently he is any immediate supervisor of farm labor on whom farm laborers are economically dependent.' (Ibid.)
60. Most of the village store credit was handled by large stores carrying a full line of consumption goods, hardware items and combustibles, while the smaller stores that only carried a few consumption items did not account for more than a minor share.
61. Cf. also Hurtado (1966), pp. 108–9.
62. Griffin (1969), pp. 79–80.
63. The situation is one of price discrimination. Each latifundista is in principle a local monopolist faced with allowing small farmers to have land at a monopolistic price and using the land himself, i.e. obtaining the marginal revenue product of land in latifundio production. It is then easily demonstrated that small farmers pay more and latifundistas less than the competitive price.

64. Cf. Also CIDA (1966), p. 161. Inquilinos and other tenants usually had very few tools and implements at their disposal.
65. Ibid., pp. 160–1.
66. Ministerio de Agricultura (1958).
67. This condition is important. The inequalities (4)–(6) do not, for example, imply that rural wages were necessarily higher in 1955 than in 1930.
68. This is analysed in Mamalakis (1965). Cf., however, the caveats in Swift (1971), Ch. 2.

Bibliography

Ballesteros, Marto, 'Desarrollo agrícola chileno, 1910–55'. *Cuadernos de Economía*, vol. 2 (1965).

Ballesteros, Marto & Davis, Tom E. 'The Growth of Output and Employment in Basic Sectors of the Chilean Economy, 1908–57', *Economic Development and Cultural Change* vol. 11 (1963).

Bauer, Arnold J. *Chilean Rural Society from the Spanish Conquest to 1930* (Cambridge, 1975).

Borde, Jean and Góngora, Mario, *Evolución de la propiedad rural en el Valle del Puangue. Tomo I. Texto.* (Santiago de Chile, 1956).

CIDA, *Chile. Tenencia de tierra y desarrollo socio-económico del sector agrícola.* (Santiago de Chile, 1966).

Crosson, Pierre R. *Agricultural Development and Productivity. Lessons from the Chilean Experience* (Baltimore and London, 1970).

Feder, Ernest, 'Controlled Credit and Agricultural Development in Chile' (Mimeo, University of Nebraska, 1959).

____ *The Rape of the Peasantry. Latin America's Land-holding System* (Garden City, 1971).

Griffin, Keith, *Underdevelopment in Spanish America. An Interpretation* (London, 1969).

Herrick, Bruce H. *Urban Migration and Economic Development in Chile* (Cambridge, Mass. and London, 1965).

Hurtado Ruíz-Tagle, Carlos, *Concentratión de población y desarrollo económico — El caso chileno* (Santiago de Chile, 1966).

Instituto de Economía de la Universidad de Chile, *Desarrollo económico de Chile, 1940–56* (Santiago de Chile, 1956).

Johnson, Ann Louise Hagerman, 'Internal Migration in Chile to 1920: Its Relationship to the Labor Market, Agricultural Growth, and Urbanisation' PhD thesis, University of California, Davis, 1978.

Loveman, Brian E. 'Property, Politics and Rural Labor: Agrarian Reform in Chile, 1919–72'. PhD thesis, Indiana University, 1973.

Lundahl, Mats, *Foreign Trade and Economic Development in Chile* (Forthcoming).

McBride, George McCutchen, *Chile: Land and Society* (New York, 1936).

Mamalakis, Markos J. 'Public Policy and Sectoral Development. A Case Study of Chile 1940–58' in Markos Mamalakis & Clark Winton Reynolds. *Essays on the Chilean Economy* (Homewood, 1965).

____ (Compiled by). *Historical Statistics of Chile. Vol. 3.* (Mimeo,-1967).

____ *The Growth and Structure of the Chilean Economy: From Independence to Allende* (New Haven and London, 1980).

____ (Compiled by). *Historical Statistics of Chile. Demography and Labor Force. Volume 2.* (Westport and London, 1980).

Ministerio de Agricultura, Dirección General de Producción Agraria y Pesquera.

La sobrevivencia de Chile (Santiago de Chile, 1958).

Nisbet, Charles, 'Interest Rates and Imperfect Competition in the Informal Credit Market of Rural Chile', *Economic Development and Cultural Change* vol. 16 (1967).

Reynolds, Clark Winton, 'Development Problems of an Export Economy: The Case of Chile and Copper', in Markos Mamalakis & Clark Winton Reynolds. *Essays on the Chilean Economy* (Homewood, 1965).

Robinson, Joan, *The Economics of Imperfect Competition.* Second edition (London, 1969).

Swift, Jeannine, *Agrarian Reform in Chile. An Economic Study* (Lexington, Mass., 1971).

6 THE DISTRIBUTION OF INCOME IN BRAZIL AND ITS DEPENDENCE ON INTERNATIONAL AND DOMESTIC AGRICULTURAL POLICIES*

Per Lundborg

1. Introduction

Brazil has been one of the countries in the focus of the debate on income distribution in less-developed countries. There are several reasons for this. First, the Brazilian economy has been characterised by extremely high growth rates for several decades, and the question of income distribution is of a special interest during times of high economic growth. The high growth rate of Brazil has even been questioned with reference to an alleged worsening of the distribution of income during the period. Second, the economic policy of Brazil has been shifted during the last 20 years from being import-substitution oriented to being more outward looking and such policy shifts naturally stimulate the interest of researchers.

In this chapter we shall analyse the distribution of incomes with the distribution between the agricultural and the non-agricultural populations as a point of departure. This distribution of income will be dealt with in a model that emphasises the integration of the Brazilian economy in world trade. The model is of the general equilibrium type and treats global agricultural and non-agricultural production in a dynamic setting. Brazil is one of seven regions separated in the implementation of the model. We shall compare the effects on the income distribution of domestic policies to the effects of the policies that occur on international markets. For this purpose we have simulated the effects of:

1. lowered grain protectionism in the European Economic Community (EEC),
2. coordinated grain policies in the US and the EEC,

* This study has been financially supported by Jan Wallanders stiftelse för samhällsvetenskaplig forskning. I am indebted to Arne Bigsten and Charles Stuart for valuable comments.

3. changed wheat policies in Brazil and
4. alternative policies for coffee in Brazil.

These four simulations are compared to themselves and to a basic solution.

The study has the following structure. Section 2 reviews the existing literature on the distribution of income in Brazil and then explains in more detail the focus on agricultural policies. Section 3 gives some background information on the agricultural sector. The model is presented in Appendix 1 but commented on in section 4. Section 5 presents the simulations, and section 6 gives the conclusion.

2. Survey of the Literature

Most studies on the distribution of income in Brazil have arrived at, or are based on, the conclusion that the distribution became more unequal during the growth process of the 1960s and the 1970s.[1] The explanations of the increased inequality are of both a microeconomic and macroeconomic character. Langoni, in a much cited study,[2] stresses the educational changes that took place during the growth period from 1960 to 1970. According to this study, the educational expansion led to a marked increase in the number of university and secondary graduates compared to primary school graduates. Since income is more unequally distributed among the well educated, this expansion led to increased inequality.[3]

Langoni's results led to a number of other studies that examined the labour market more deeply. Morley and Williamson[4] utilised a dynamic input–output model to reproduce the historical output of each sector. Employment was then determined by its relation to output. The main conclusion drawn was that labour demand favoured the most highly skilled groups. The annual growth rate for 1960 to 1970 in labour demand for the most highly skilled was 4.8 per cent whereas it was only 3.2 per cent for the least-skilled group. Fishlow[5] raises the question how biased labour demand must have been in order to be consistent with the actual payments to each group. His conclusion from a partial equilibrium approach is that supply and demand alone cannot explain the differential earnings.

Cardoso[6] concludes that a large part of the income distribution shift toward the rich can be explained by shifts in the functional distribution of income. These results are consistent with conclusions drawn by Taylor *et al.*[7] whose model also predicts an increasing profit share in Brazil between 1960 and 1970. Their simulations also indicate decreasing wage differences during the period. The most important conclusion they draw is that skill differentials cannot be considered an acceptable explanation of the distributional change. Taylor *et al.* instead put forward the wage squeeze of the 1964 stabilisation programme as a more important explanation. This squeeze reduced the real income growth for the middle deciles and caused increased inequality. The effects of the wage policy were also examined in a study by Macedo.[8]

A feature of the Brazilian manufacturing sector is the existence of minimum wages, and an important question is to what extent this fact should be reflected in the modelling work. There are, however, several reasons to believe that a minimum-wage policy is so inefficient that the existence of minimum wages can be neglected and that a minimum wage does not constitute an income floor. Macedo[9] points out that the minimum wages are often evaded in the formal sector and do not apply at all in the informal sector. This means that urban and rural workers without regular jobs, the poor self-employed, domestic servants, and other people in the lower deciles of the size distribution are not affected. Macedo refers to studies showing that, in 1972, more than half of the income recipients earned less than the minimum wage.[10]

The studies are, in general, not focused on the agricultural sector. This is remarkable for several reasons. The first is that, in poor countries such as Brazil, the poorer segments of the population by necessity must include a large proportion of rural families. Table 6.1 shows the extent of poverty for the rural and urban populations in 1974/5. As can be seen from Table 6.1, 61 per cent of the poor resided in rural areas in 1974/5. Furthermore, Fishlow and Meesok[11] have claimed that, in 1960, 60 per cent of the poorest 40 per cent were agricultural families and, in 1974/5, 66 per cent were rural. From this point of view, it seems as if the agricultural sector could play a crucial role in explaining the development of the distribution of income in Brazil.

Another reason to concentrate on the agricultural sector is that other studies, notably those of Adelman and Robinson[12], de Melo[13] and Lundborg[14] point out the crucial role that the agricultural terms of trade play in the distributional process. The Adelman and Robinson study is of particular importance as it deals with the Korean

Table 6.1: Extent of Poverty in Urban and Rural Areas —
Families Under Two Minimum Wages, 1974–5

Area	Total Number of Families, 000	Number of Poor Families, 000	Poor Families as a Percentage of Total Families
Urban	12,239	2,157	17
Rural	8,061	3,409	42
Total	20,300	5,566	27

Source: Pfefferman and Webb (1979).

economy which has experienced growth rates comparable to those of the Brazilian.

Some authors, such as Bergsman[15], Leff[16], von Doellinger et al.[17], Veiga[18] and Baer[19], recognise a discrimination against agriculture in the postwar period without, however, making much reference to income distribution. There is one obvious reason for this discrimination: the overvalued exchange rate which inhibited production of the agricultural export crops. In 1960, for instance 63 per cent of the total exports originated in the agricultural sector and, in such a situation, an overvalued exchange rate would discriminate against agriculture. At the same time, a program for support of the wheat sector was implemented in the beginning of the 1960s.

Another aspect which could have discriminated against agriculture is the change in the agricultural terms of trade on the world market. The quite successful reductions in tariffs that the world has experienced during the last 20 to 25 years have been concentrated on trade in manufactured goods. For agricultural products, the tendency has been toward increased protection, particularly in developed western European countries. These facts have led to lower agricultural terms of trade than otherwise would have been the case. It could, therefore, be possible that the international policies discriminated, in particular, against the Brazilian agriculture sector. To illustrate this point, Table 6.2 shows the Brazilian and other South American agricultural trade in 1960. In Brazil, wheat dominated on the import side, and exports were dominated by coffee. It should be remembered that wheat policies in the Common Market and in many other developed countries were very protectionistic which led to lower wheat prices on the world market than otherwise would have occurred. Such policies would affect the agricultural terms of trade in Brazil and counteract the domestic measures that were taken to support the wheat sector. The main purpose of the present study is to test to what extent the international trade policies for agricultural commodities have affected the Brazilian economy and, in particular, the distribution of incomes. The effects, if any, will then be compared to those of domestic policies.

Table 6.2: Exports Minus Imports, Selected Agricultural Commodities, 1960

Crop	Brazil US$Million	Other South American Countries
Wheat	-143	68
Other cereals	- 3	176
Meat	14	166
Fruit and vegetables	12	103
Sugar	58	99
Coffee, tea cocoa, spices	818	377
Feedstuff	12	82

Source: Computed from FAO Trade Yearbook. Annual.

With this background, it is necessary to approach the problem of the distribution of income in Brazil by means of a model that describes in some detail not only the Brazilian economy but also the world economy and emphasises the world integration of the Brazilian economy. What we shall do is to use a global model of agricultural trade as earlier described in a study by Lundborg,[20] though with some important modifications. By means of this model we simulate the consequences on the distribution of incomes, migration, etc., of different policies for the agricultural sector for the period 1960-8. This restricted time period has been chosen as the most interesting since the development of the agricultural terms of trade then were unfavourable to agriculture.

3. The Agricultural-Non-agricultural Distribution and the Performance of Agriculture

Compared to other Latin American countries, the Brazilian agricultural sector grew at impressive rates during the 1960s and the 1970s.

The annual average growth rate of 4.6 per cent for the period 1960 to 1977 was close to double that of other Latin American countries. The average annual growth rate for crop agriculture during the period 1959 to 1977 was 3.9 per cent and for animal agriculture 4.7 per cent. Still, compared to Brazilian manufacturing industries, agriculture did not perform as well: manufacture experienced a growth rate of 6.37 per cent for the same period. A salient feature of the economy during these years is, furthermore, the very strong rural–urban migration that took place. This indicates an unbalanced sectorial growth and implies disparities in income increases between the agricultural and non-agricultural population.

Table 6.3 shows the changes in non-agricultural and agricultural populations from 1960 to 1970 in Brazil and other South American countries. If we assume that the relative indigenous growth rates of the agricultural and non-agricultural populations are approximately the same in the two regions, then the figures imply a higher relative labour outflow from agriculture in Brazil than from agriculture in other South American countries.

Table 6.3: Changes in Non-agricultural and Agricultural Populations. Brazil and Other South American Countries, 1960–70

| Country | Population, millions | |
	Non-agricultural	Agricultural
Brazil		
1960	34	36
1970	52	41
% change	+ 56	+ 12
Other South American countries		
1960	47	29
1970	64	33
% change	+ 36	+ 14

Source: Computed from FAO Production Yearbook. Annual.

A crucial variable for relative sectorial incomes is the agricultural (or internal) terms of trade, i.e., the price relationships between agriculture and non-agricultural commodities. The time series in Table 6.4 show a measure of the agricultural terms of trade. In general, the terms of trade deteriorated during the 1960s. The fall of the internal terms of trade is consistent with the increased rural–urban migration during the period.

Table 6.4:   Internal Terms of Trade (1960 = 100): Farm Product Wholesale Prices/Industrial Product Wholesale Prices

Year		Year	
1960	100	1969	86
1961	93	1970	94
1962	101	1971	100
1963	93	1972	100
1964	101	1973	106
1965	89	1974	110
1966	95	1975	110
1967	95	1976	106
1968	85		

Source: Computed from ECLA Statistical Yearbook for Latin America. Annual.

4. The Global CGE-model

The global dynamic computable general equilibrium (CGE) model[21] is characterised by endogenously determined world market prices and sectorial and regional factor prices. All of these prices are determined so as to equalise supply and demand. The model is highly non-linear and allows for substitution among factors of production and among commodities. Each commodity is treated as homogeneous irrespective of origin of production. The model consists of two parts: the first is a set of equations that makes up a static model; the second consists of a set of equations that, when added to the first part, makes the model dynamic. The second part we refer to as dynamic linkages. We first go through the static model (part one). Country and time indexes have been deleted. The equation system is represented in Appendix 1.

Equations (1) and (2) describe the price system. The governments in each region may let domestic producers' and buyers' prices deviate from world market prices by the introduction of *ad valorem* tariffs and subsidies.

Production technology is described by means of Cobb-Douglas production functions — equations (3) and (4) — for labour and capital and fixed input–output coefficients for intermediate goods — equation.(5). Equation (3) is for agriculture and equation (4) for non-agriculture. Within each time period, the factors may not move from agriculture to non-agriculture (nor the other way). (However, a migration function, introduced later, is included to determine the flow of labour from agriculture to non-agriculture between the time periods.)

From the farm household theory, we have derived equations (6) and (7). Equation (6) determines the labour supply of those farmers or farm workers to which this theory applies (specified in the section below). Equation (7) determines (also for specific agricultural groups) the demand for the non-marketed quantities. The supply of labour from other groups is assumed to be given as in equations (12) and (13). The supply of capital is exogenous as in (14) and (15).

From the production functions, we derive factor demand functions reproduced in their general forms in equations (8) to (11). All factors are assumed to be fully employed as in equations (16) and (17).

On the demand side, we first determine expenditures for food and non-food items by means of the linear expenditure system (equation 18).[22] This equation is used for each income group, ℓ. To determine the demand for the individual agricultural products, we use a log-linear demand function as in equation (19),[23] with total expenditures on food and buyers' prices as arguments. This function is not used for the individual income groups (no index ℓ), however.[24]

Equation (20) determines the total income. Tariff revenues appear explicitly in this function.

We allow for foreign ownership of the means of production. The international distribution of profits and capital yields is represented by equations (21) and (22) — the former for regions being net owners of foreign capital and the latter for regions not controlling the total capital stock used domestically. The distribution of income between the domestic income groups is determined in the section below. Each world region is given an accounting relationship (equation (23)) constituting balance conditions and from which we may determine foreign trade. Equation (24) specifies the current account which is affected by the international flows of income between the regions.

The model includes exogenous trade with the centrally planned economies, and equation (25) shows that for each commodity the sum of endogenous and exogenous imports should equal the sum of endogenous and exogenous exports. To obtain balanced trade for the centrally planned economies, trade in the non-agricultural commodity is determined by means of equation (26). This completes the description of part one of the model.

Part two of the model describes how the supply of factors changes from one time period to another. This part includes labour growth rates, migration, savings, and investments as central concepts. The notion of dualism has been leading in determining the intertemporal allocation of labour. Migration is assumed to be a function of relative urban–rural *per capita* income and of the relative sizes of the agricultural and non-agricultural populations. The function is of the log-linear type as expressed in equation (27). According to equations (28) and (29), the supply of agricultural and non-agricultural labour is assumed to grow by exogenous rates and to be affected by migration.

Savings is determined by means of income group–specific savings ratios, and total investment is assumed to adjust to total savings. Since we allow for foreign ownership of the capital stock, the restriction that total savings equal total investment is a global restriction and is not imposed upon each region. This is represented by equation (30).

Total investment will be used to increase agricultural and non-agricultural capital as in equations (31) and (32) in which allowance for depreciation has been made. A coefficient, σ_A, determines the share of agriculture; σ_{NA} ($= 1 - \sigma_A$) determines the share of non-agriculture. By means of a logistic function, we determine a coefficient, $\hat{\sigma}_A$ ($0 < \hat{\sigma}_A < 1$) as in equation (33). To arrive at σ, we also take the relative factor stocks into consideration as is done in equation (34). The value of σ_A is, however, restricted by $\sigma_A^{min} \leq \sigma_A \leq \sigma_A^{max}$ to guarantee positive investments in agriculture and non-agriculture.[25] This completes part two of the model.

The algorithm used to solve the model is straightforward, and the price changes are determined as functions of excess demands.[26]

Regions, Sectors, and Income Groups

The model has been simulated for six endogenous regions; and one region, consisting of the centrally planned economies, is treated as being exogenous. The six endogenous regions are: the United States, the European Economic Community, other developed market economies, Asia and Africa, Brazil, and other Latin American countries. To keep the presentation simple, we report only the results for Brazil.

The agricultural sectors included in the simulations are: wheat, rice, other cereals, coffee, other cash crops, animal foods, and non-caloric agricultural commodities. The rest of the economy is treated in one sector called non-agriculture. Important intermediate deliveries occur from other cereals and wheat to animal foods.

We specify the farm income groups as landless rural workers, small farmers, the rural rich, and the urban population. Landless rural workers only obtain incomes from work. The supply of labour of this group is determined by means of the farm household theory. Small farmers obtain incomes from work on the farm and capital. The supply of labour is fixed. The quantities that are not marketed are retained by this group.

The rural rich include large owner-operators and landowners. For this group, incomes from land and capital dominate to such an extent that incomes from work are neglected.

The urban population obtains all returns from factors in the non-agricultural sector, less the shares of capital yield that accrue to foreign owners.

The Data

There are two basic sources for the data used in this study. For the global model, we rely on the data in the Lundborg study.[27] For Brazilian data, we rely, to a certain extent, on the study by Taylor *et al.*[28]

5. The Simulations

In addition to a basic solution to describe the actual development, we perform two simulations for international policies and two for Brazilian policies. The international simulations concern policies for grain in the United States and in the EEC. For Brazil, we do one simulation for wheat, which dominates agricultural imports, and one for coffee, which dominates exports. Lundborg has examined the sensitivity of the model.[29]

We have chosen the period from 1960 to 1968 with three-year averages (three time periods). We first give formal descriptions of the basic and policy runs.

BASRUN.——This run is the basic solution to which the four policy experiments will be compared. BASRUN is meant to be a description of actual world developments.

EECWH.——In this simulation we assume increasing imports of wheat for the Common Market instead of the increasing protectionism that characterises the basic solution. In BASRUN, the European Economic Community shifts from being an importer in the first time period to being an exporter. In EECWH imports increase by 10 per cent each period following the initial one.

EECUSGR.——Here, we assume a coordinated policy in the United States and in the European Economic Community for all grains. The policies are very restrictive for wheat, rice, and other cereals: the United States doubles the taxes or cuts subsidies by 50 per cent per time period. The EEC pursues the same policy as in EECWH for wheat and doubles the imports of other cereals and rice per period.

BRAWH.——In BASRUN, the Brazilian wheat sector obtained substantial support. In BRAWH we have increased these support measures — tariffs and subsidies — even further: both measures are doubled as compared to BASRUN.

BRACO.——This is the second simulation of domestic Brazilian policies for the agricultural sector. The policy is one of increasing subsidies to the coffee sector: The subsidies are double those of BASRUN. During a large part of the time period that we analyse, coffee trade was regulated by the first International Coffee Agreement (ICA), which was negotiated in 1962 and terminated in 1968. No attempts have been made here to determine whether the simulated coffee policy is consistent with the agreement.

In Table 6.5, we have summarised the effects of the policy measures on the distribution of incomes. We provide three different measures of the distribution: the variance of the log of incomes, the coefficient of variation, and the Gini-coefficient. These calculations have been carried out under the assumption of no within-group income differences. Table 6.6 shows the effects of the policies on rural–urban migration. In both tables, we express the effects by means of index values that compare each run to the basic run, BASRUN, for each time period, respectively.

It should be stated first that increased incomes in the agricultural sector as compared to non-agriculture do not necessarily improve the distribution of incomes. This is so since not all agricultural income groups are poorer than the non-agricultural group; 'the rural rich' are, *per capita*, considerably better off. So, whether increased incomes in agriculture improve the distribution or not depends on the distribution within the agricultural sector. The international policies, as represented by EECWH and EECUSGR, do not seem to affect the distribution very much. The variance of the log of incomes shows, though, an increase in the first time period for EECUSGR. In the third time period, however, this measure indicates a distribution which is very close to the one in BASRUN. The Gini-coefficient also indicates a slightly more unequal distribution for this time period. The coefficient of variation appears very insensitive and does not change, as compared to BASRUN, for any of the three time periods.

Table 6.5: Measures of Income Distribution: Index Values as Compared to BASRUN for Each Time Period

Time period	EECWH	The variance of the logs of income EECUSGR	BRAWH	BRACO
1	100	108	105	103
2	100	98	88	95
3	100	101	99	94
		The coefficient of variation		
1	100	100	100	100
2	100	100	100	100
3	100	100	99	100
		The Gini-coefficient		
1	100	101	101	100
2	100	100	101	99
3	100	101	104	98

Table 6.6: The Effects on Migration of the Different Policies Index Values as Compared to BASRUN for Each Time Period

Time period	EECWH	EECUSGR	BRAWH	BRACO
1	100	99	98	99
2	100	99	91	99
3	100	99	91	97

The basic reason for the appearance of shifts in the distribution from one time period to another is the counteracting effects that migration has on the distribution. An income redistribution affects migration so that the relative labour supplies in the agricultural and non-agricultural sectors change for the subsequent time period. The coordinated policy of EECUSGR leads to a general increase in agri-cultural prices which increases agricultural incomes. (This mitigates migration which falls by a little more than half a per cent.) Even though the urban population on average is richer than the two poorest agricultural income groups, landless rural workers, and small farmers, the increased agricultural incomes have not improved the distribution of incomes. The rural rich have increased their incomes more than the two poorer agricultural income groups. Hence, the positive income redistribution which arises out of improved agricultural terms of trade, is counteracted by a negative redistribution within the agricultural sector.

To the extent that rural–urban migration as such is considered to be a problem, more restrictive policies (that tend to increase the world's agricultural terms of trade) would be favourable to the Brazilian economy. It should be pointed out, however, that the effects on migration even after rather drastic policy changes in the United States and the EEC are small. The changes in the Gini-coefficient and the coefficient of variation indicate also that the effects on the distribution of income are small. Considering that the distribution of the third period of EECUSGR is very close to the one in BASRUN, this conclusion can also be said to be supported by the variance of the log of incomes. The policy run EECWH has had hardly any noticeable effects either on migration or on income distribution.

The first of the two domestic policy runs, BRAWH, implies increased support to the wheat sector in Brazil as compared to BASRUN. The effects on world prices of wheat are negligible. The policy, however, implies increased agricultural incomes which slows down rural–urban migration quite considerably. Migration in the last period, for instance, is 91 per cent of the BASRUN migration. The distribution of incomes is affected positively according to the variance of the log of incomes (except for the initial time period) and according to the coefficient of variation for the last period. The Gini-coefficient, however, increases as compared to the basic run. Note also that, according to the variance of the log of incomes, the distribution in the third time period is much closer to the base run distribution than is the case in the second period.

It is difficult to evaluate the distributional effects of this policy since our measures do not yield clear-cut results. The fact that our measures yield different results not only quantitatively but also qualitatively can be explained by the different properties of the measures.[30] The log-variance measure and, to a certain extent, the Gini-coefficient measure, have the property of decreasing more if a poor person is given an increase than if the same sum is subtracted from a rich person. Thus, a greater weight is given to lower income earners. The coefficient of variation, on the other hand, is equally sensitive to transfers at all income levels. The Gini-coefficient has the property of being insensitive to changes near the centre of the distribution.

Due to the Brazilian dominance on coffee production, the last policy simulation, BRACO, in which the subsidies are double those of the basic run, lowers the world market price for coffee. In the first time period, for instance, the price of coffee in this run is 2.87 per cent lower than in the basic solution. The prices for the producers, which include the subsidies are, however, higher in this simulation than in BASRUN which indicates that the Metzler paradox is not present. This policy simulation yields stronger effects on rural-urban migration than do the international policies. They are, however, not as strong as the effects in the policy run on wheat policy; in the last period, it is 97 per cent of migration in the basic solution compared to 90 per cent in BRAWH.

Our measures of income distribution now yield more clear-cut results. The variance of the log of incomes and the Gini-coefficient both show that this policy yields a more equal distribution of incomes compared to BASRUN even though the former indicates an initial increase. The coefficient of variation is not affected (at the level shown).

6. Overall Conclusions

This paper set out, among other things, to test whether the international trade policies to any considerable extent affect the distribution of incomes in Brazil. The simulation EECUSGR, which implies a substantial reorientation of the policies for grain in the EEC and the United States, indicates that this is not the case. The domestic conditions in terms of distribution and migration also seem insensitive to international policies concerning wheat despite the fact that this is the dominating agricultural import commodity.

The domestic policies seem to be more important. Except for the coefficient of variation, the distributional measures indicate that the trade policy for agricultural commodities has a substantial impact on the distribution of incomes. Our simulations, however, give no indication as to whether this policy is more important than the educational policy as explored by Langoni or Fishow *et al.* or the wage policy as examined by Taylor *et al.*

Appendix I: The Model

System of Notation

The notations in the following list will be used. Time subscripts and country index have been dropped.

A_i	=	Constant of the production function, Sector i.
a_1, a_2	=	Constants for determining the distribution of investments.
BP_i	=	Buyers' price, Commodity i.
C_i^ℓ	=	Consumption quantity, Commodity i, Socio-economic group ℓ.
D	=	Factor for the fulfilment of the budget constraint.
d_A	=	Rate of depreciation of agricultural capital.
d_{NA}	=	Rate of depreciation of non-agricultural capital.
E_i	=	Income elasticity of demand, Commodity i.
Exp^ℓ	=	Expenditures, group ℓ.
e_{ij}	=	Price elasticity of demand for Commodity j with respect to the price of Commodity i.
g_A	=	Growth rate of agricultural labour.
g_{NA}	=	Growth rate of non-agricultural labour.
g_{LM}	=	Annual rate of labour inflow in non-agriculture.
h_1, h_2, h_3	=	Constants of the migration function.
i_{ji}	=	Total input of Commodity j in the production of Commodity i.
INV	=	Investments.
$K_{i, A}$	=	Agricultural capital used in Sector i.
$K_{m, NA}$	=	Non-agricultural capital used in Sector m.
$L_{i, A}$	=	Agricultural labour used in Sector i.
$L_{m, NA}$	=	Non-agricultural labour used in Sector m.
M_i	=	Imported quantity of Commodity i.
$\overline{M}_i$	=	Imports from the exogenous region, Commodity i.
$(MPS)^\ell$	=	Marginal propensity to save, Socio-economic group ℓ.
N_A	=	Agricultural population.
N_{NA}	=	Non-agricultural population.
O_i	=	Gross output, excluding non-marketed quantities. The marketed surplus. Commodity i.

PP_i	=	Producers' price, Commodity i.
$\hat{PP}_i$	=	'Net price' expressed in producers' price, Commodity i.
Q_i^ℓ	=	Constant of the demand function, Commodity i. Socio-economic group ℓ.
r_A	=	Capital yield per unit of agricultural capital.
r_{NA}	=	Capital yield per unit of non-agricultural capital.
$\bar{r}$	=	The average of agricultural and non-agricultural capital yields.
s_i	=	Subsidy rate, Commodity i, Policy variable.
(SAV)	=	Savings ratio.
t_i	=	Tariff rate, Commodity i, Policy variable.
t	=	Time period.
TC_i	=	Rate of technical change, Commodity i.
w_A	=	Unit wage in agriculture.
w_{NA}	=	Unit wage in non-agriculture.
WP_i	=	World market price, Commodity i.
X_i	=	Exported Quantity of Commodity i.
$\overline{X}_i$	=	Exports to the exogenous region, Commodity i.
Y	=	Total Incomes.
Y^ℓ	=	Incomes of Socio-economic group ℓ.
$\tilde{Y}$	=	Incomes corrected for foreign ownership of the means of production.
$(YPC)^\ell$	=	Per capita incomes, Socioeconomic group ℓ.
$\widehat{(YPC)}$	=	Ratio of non-agricultural to agricultural *per capita* incomes.
Z_m	=	Traded quantity from the rest of the world, Commodity i.

Greek Letters

α_{ji}	=	Input–output coefficients.
β_i^L	=	The elasticity of O_i with respect to inputs of agricultural labour.
β_i^K	=	The elasticity of O_i with respect to inputs of agricultural capital.
β_m^L	=	The elasticity of O_m with respect to inputs to non-agricultural labour.

β_m^K = The elasticity of O_m with respect to inputs of non-agricultural capital.

θ_i^ℓ = Marginal propensity to spend, Commodity i, Socio-economic group ℓ.

π_i = Net profits in Sector i.

μ^{ji} = Constants.

σ_A = Factor denoting the proportion of investments used to increase agricultural capital.

σ_{NA} = Factor denoting the proportion of investments used to increase non-agricultural capital.

$\hat{\sigma}$ = Auxiliary variable.

Indexes

m = Number of Sectors and the index number of the non-agricultural sector.

n = Number of Countries.

r = Number of Socio-economic groups.

Model Description

Part I

1. $BP_i = \begin{cases} (1 + t_i)\, WP_i \text{ for } M_i > 0 \\ WP_i \text{ for } X_i > 0 \end{cases} \quad i = 1 \ldots m$

2. $PP_i = \begin{cases} (1 + s_i + t_i)\, WP_i \text{ for } M_i > 0 \\ (1 + s_i)\, WP_i \text{ for } X_i > 0 \end{cases} \quad i = 1 \ldots m$

3. $O_i = A_i e^{TC_i \cdot t}\, L_{i,A}^{\beta_i^{L'}}\, K_{i,A}^{\beta_i^K} \qquad \beta_i^L + \beta_i^K < 1$
   $$i = 1, \ldots, (m-1)$$

4. $O_m = A_m e^{TC_m \cdot t} \cdot L_{m,NA}^{\beta_m^L} \cdot K_{m,NA}^{\beta_m^K} \qquad \beta_m^L + \beta_m^K = 1$

5. $i_{ji} = \alpha_{ji}\, O_i \qquad\qquad j, i = 1, \ldots, m$

6. $-_WA L_r^s = -_WA Q_{LS} + \beta_L^\ell\, [\, Exp^\ell -_WA Q_F^\ell - BP_1 Q_1^I$
   $$\qquad\qquad - BP_m Q_m^\ell - \sum_{i=2}^{m-1} BP_i C_{NM_i}^\ell\,]$$

7. $BP_j C_{NM_j}^\ell = Q_j^\ell BP_j + \beta_j^\ell\, [Exp^\ell -_WA Q_F^\ell - BP_1 Q_1^I$
   $$\qquad\qquad - BP_m Q_m^\ell - \sum_{i=2}^{m-1} BP_i C_{NM_i}^\ell\,]$$

8. $L_{i,A}^d = L_{i,A}^d\, (\hat{PP}_i, w_A, r_A)$

9. $K_{i,A}^d = K_{i,A}^d (\hat{PP}_i, w_A, r_A)$

10. $L_{m,NA}^d = L_{m,NA}^d (\hat{PP}_m, r_{NA}, w_{NA})$

11. $K_{m,NA}^d = K_{m,NA}^d (\hat{PP}_m, r_{NA}, w_{NA})$

12. $L_A^s = \bar{L}_A^s$

13. $L_{NA}^s = \bar{L}_{NA}^s$

14. $K_A^s = \bar{K}_A^s$

15. $K_{NA}^s = \bar{K}_{NA}^s$

16. $\sum_i L_{i,A}^d = L_A^s - L_r^s \qquad L_{m,NA}^d = L_{NA}^s$

17. $\sum_i K_{i,A}^d = K_A^s \qquad K_{m,NA}^d = K_{NA}^s$

18. $Exp_i^\ell = BP_i Q_i^\ell + (1 - MPS^\ell) \theta_i^\ell [Y^\ell - \sum_{j=1}^{m} BP_j Q_j^\ell]$

19. $C_i = D Y_i (Exp)^{E_i} . \prod_{j=2}^{n} BP_j^{e_{ij}} \qquad i = 2, \ldots, n$

20. $Y = \sum_{i=1}^{m} WP_i O_i - \sum_{i=1}^{m} \sum_{j=1}^{m} WP_j i_{ji} + \sum_{i=1}^{m} t_i WP_i O_i - \sum_{i=1}^{m} \sum_{j=1}^{m} t_i WP_i i_{ji} + \sum_{i=1}^{m} t_i WP_i M_i$

21. $\tilde{Y}^k = Y^k + \sum_k (\frac{K_j^k}{K_j}) . (r_A^j K_A^j + r_{NA}^j K_{NA}^j + \sum_{i=2}^{m-1} \pi_i^j)$

22. $\tilde{Y}^j = Y^j - \sum_k (\frac{K_j^k}{K_j}) (r_A^j K_A^j + r_{NA}^j K_{NA}^j + \sum_{i=2}^{m-1} \pi_i^j)$

23. $O_i + M_i = C_i + \sum_{j=1}^{m} i_{ij} + X_i \qquad i = 1, \ldots, m$

24. $\sum_i WP_i M_i - \sum_i WP_i X_i + (Y - \tilde{Y}) = 0$

25. $\sum_k M_i^k + \bar{M}_i = \sum_k X_i^k + \bar{X}_i \qquad i = 1, \ldots, (m-1)$
$\qquad\qquad\qquad\qquad\qquad\qquad\qquad i = $ agricultural commodity

26. $Z_m = \dfrac{\sum\limits_{i=2}^{m-1} WP_i (\bar{M}_i - \bar{X}_i)}{WP_m}$

where $Z_m = \begin{cases} X_m \text{ for } Z_m > 0 \\ -M_m \text{ for } Z_m < 0 \end{cases}$

Part II.

27. $g_{LM} = h_1 \cdot (\widehat{YPC})^{h_2} \cdot \left(\dfrac{N_A}{N_{NA}} \right)^{h_3}$

28. $L_{t,A}^s = L_{t-1,A}^s (1 + g_A) - g_{LM} \cdot L_{t-1,A}$

29. $L_{t,NA}^s = L_{t-1,NA}^s (1 + g_{NA}) + g_{LM} \cdot L_{t-1,A}$

30. $\sum\limits_j BP_m^j \cdot (INV)^j = \sum\limits_k \sum\limits_\ell (SAV)^{k\ell} Y^{k\ell}$

31. $K_{t,A}^s = K_{t-1,A}^s + \sigma_A \cdot INV_{t-1} - d_A \cdot K_{t-1,A}^s$

$\quad = (1 - d_A) K_{t-1,A}^s + \sigma_A \cdot INV_{t-1}$

32. $K_{t,NA}^s = K_{t-1,NA}^s + \sigma_{NA} \cdot INV_{t-1} - d_{NA} \cdot K_{t-1,NA}^s$

$\quad = (1 - d_{NA}^s) K_{t-1,NA} + \sigma_{NA} INV_{t-1}$ where $\sigma_{NA} = 1 - \sigma_A$

33. $\hat{\sigma}_A = \dfrac{e^{(\hat{r}-a_1) a_2}}{e^{(\hat{r}-a_1) a_2} + e^{-(\hat{r}-a_1) a_2}}$

where $\hat{r} = \dfrac{r_A - \bar{r}}{\bar{r}}$

$\bar{r}$ = Average capital yield, defined as

$\dfrac{k_A}{k_A + k_{NA}} \cdot r_A + \dfrac{k_{NA}}{k_A + k_{NA}} \cdot r_{NA}$

34. $\sigma_A = \hat{\sigma}_A + (1 + \hat{\sigma}_A) \dfrac{\dfrac{K_A}{K_A + K_{NA}} - 0.5}{0.5}$

where $\sigma_A^{min} \leq \sigma_A \leq \sigma_A^{max}$

Notes

1. See for instance, Langoni (1973); Taylor *et al.* (1981); Hoffman and Duarte (1972); Hoffman (1973); Tavares (1969); Bacha (1976); Wells (1974); and Fishlow (1972). Fishlow's claim that the Gini-coefficient increased from 0.59 in 1960 to 0.63 in 1970 is consistent with the increase reported by Langoni for the same period, namely, from 0.49 to 0.56. The difference between the two may be explained by Langoni's exclusion of zero-income people. Other studies, such as Fields (1977) arrived at the conclusion that the Brazilian poorest improved their situation more during the 1960s than did the non-poor. Specifically, Fields found that the poor increased their real income by 60 per cent during the 1960s while the real income of the non-poor increased by only 25 per cent. Fields (1977), is however criticised in, for instance, Taylor *et al.* (1980). A third group of studies, e.g., Morley and Williamson (1975) claims that the debate is pointless because the data and methods are inadequate.

2. Langoni (1973).
3. This is not to deny the positive impacts of the educational expansion in the form of, for example, a considerable decline in illiteracy rates.
4. Morley and Williamson (1975).
5. Fishlow (1973).
6. Cardoso (1978).
7. Taylor *et al.* (1980).
8. Macedo (1977).
9. Ibid.
10. See also Drobny and Wells (1983).
11. Fishlow and Meesok (1972).
12. Adelman and Robinson (1978).
13. de Melo (1978).
14. Lundborg (1982).
15. Bergsman (1970).
16. Leff (1967).
17. von Doellinger (1974).
18. Veiga (1974).
19. Baer (1965).
20. Lundborg (1982).
21. The model presented here is an extension of a model exhaustively presented in Lundborg (1982). A major difference is that in the present paper the modelling of the farm household is strongly influenced by the so called farm household theory.
22. Note the inclusion of a savings ratio.
23. The log-linear function has been adjusted to correct for the fact that the budget constraint is not fulfilled. See Lundborg (1982); Adelman and Robinson (1978).
24. The primary rationale for using both demand functions is data limitations; the parameters of the log-linear function cannot be obtained easily for each individual income group, but the parameters of the Linear Expenditure System can be determined easily. (See an extensive discussion in Lundborg (1982)).
25. For a more detailed account of the properties of these functions, see Lundborg (1982).
26. For details, see Lundborg (1982).
27. Lundborg (1982).
28. Taylor *et al.* (1980).
29. See Lundborg (1982).
30. See, for instance, Szal and Robinson (1977); Champernowne (1974).

Bibliography

Adelman, Irma, and Robinson, Sherman, *Income Distribution Policy in Developing Countries: A Case Study of Korea* (Oxford University Press, The World Bank 1978).
Bacha, Edmar L. *Os mitos de uma década: Ensaios da economia Brasiliera.* (Paz e Terra, Rio de Janeiro, 1976).
Baer, Werner, *Industrialisation and Economic Development in Brazil.* (R.D. Irwin, Inc., Homewood, Illinois, 1965).
Bergsman, Joel, *Brazil: Industrialization and Trade Policies* (Oxford, 1970).
Cardoso, Eliana A. *Growth and Real Wages: Modelling the Brazilian Economic Miracle* (M.I.T., Department of Economics, Cambridge, Mass., 1978).
Champernowne, D.G. A Comparison of Measures of Inequality of Income

Distribution, *Economic Journal*, December 1974.

de Melo, Martha H. 'A General Equilibrium Investigation of Agricultural Policies and Development Strategies: A Case Study of Sri Lanka', unpublished PhD dissertation, University of Maryland, 1978.

Drobny, Andres, and Wells, John, 'Wages, Minimum Wages, and Income Distribution in Brazil', *Journal of Development Economics*, vol. 13 (1983).

ECLA, Statistical Yearbook for Latin America. United Nations. 1976-9.

FAO Production Yearbook, vol. 16-35. 1963-83.

FAO Trade Yearbook, vol. 16-35. 1963-83.

Fields, Gary S. 'Who Benefits from Economic Development? A Reexamination of Brazilian Growth in the 1960s', *American Economic Review*, vol. 67, no. 4 (1977) pp. 570-82.

Fishlow, Albert, 'Brazilian Size Distribution of Incomes', *American Economic Review*, vol. 62 no. 2 (1972) pp. 391-402.

_____, *Brazilian Income Size Distribution: Another Look* (University of California, Department of Economics, Berkeley, 1973).

Fishlow, Albert, and Meesok, Astra, *Technical Appendix: Brazilian Size Distribution of Incomes, 1960* (University of California, Department of Economics, Berkeley, 1972).

Hoffman, Rudolfo, 'Consideracões sobre a evolucão recendente da distribução da renda no Brazil', *Revista de administração de empresas*, vol. 13, no. 4 (1973) pp. 7-17.

Hoffman, Rudolfo, and Duarte, J.C. 'A Distribuição da Renda no Brazil,' *Revista de administração de empresas*, vol. 12, no. 2 (1972) pp. 46-66.

Langoni, Carlos G. *Distribuição da renda e desenvolvimento economico do Brazil*. (Editora Expressão e Cultura, Rio de Janairo, 1973).

Leff, Nathaniel H. 'Export Stagnation and Autarkic Development in Brazil. 1947-62', *Quarterly Journal of Economics*, vol. 81, no. 2 (1967) pp. 286-01.

Lundborg, Per A.H. 'Trade Policy and Development: Income Distributional Effects in the Less Developed Countries of the U.S. and EEC Policies for Agricultural Commodities', *Ekonomiska Studier Utgivna av Nationalekonomiska institutionen vid Göteborgs Universitet*, PhD dissertation no. 9, 1982.

Macedo, Roberto B.M. 'A Critical Review of the Relation Between Post-1964 Wage Policy and the Worsening of Brazil's Size Income Distribution in the 1960s', *Explorations in Economic Research*, vol. 4, no. 1 (1977) pp. 117-40.

Morley, Samuel A., and Williamson, Jeffrey G. *Growth Wage Policy and Inequality: Brazil in the 1960s*. Social Systems Research Institute Workshop Series No. 7519 (University of Wisconsin, Madison, Wisconsin, 1975).

Pfefferman, Guy P., and Webb, Richard, 'The Distribution of Income in Brazil', *World Bank Staff Working Paper* no. 356 (1979).

Szal, Richard, and Robinson, Sherman, 'Measuring Income Inequality,' in Frank and Webb (eds.) *Income Distribution and Growth in the Less Developed Countries* (The Brookings Institution, Washington DC, 1977).

Tavares, Maria C. *Caracteristicas da distribuição da renda no Brasil* (Escritorio CEPAL/JLPES, Rio de Janeiro, 1969).

Taylor, Lance *et al.*, *'Models of Growth and Distribution for Brazil'* (A World Bank Research Publication, Oxford University Press, 1980).

Veiga, A. 'The Impact of Trade Policy on Brazilian Agriculture: 1947-67', unpublished PhD dissertation, Purdue University, 1974.

von Doellinger, Carlos *et al.*, 'A Politica Brasileira de Comercio Exterior e Seus Efeitos: 1967-73', *Relatorio de Pesquisa*, No. 22, Rio de Janeiro, JPEA/JNPES 1974.

Wells, John, 'Distribution of Earnings, Growth and the Structure of Demand in Brazil during the 1960s', *World Development*, vol. 2, no. 1 (1974).

7 GROWTH AND STAGNATION IN THE MALAYSIAN RUBBER SMALLHOLDER INDUSTRY

Christer Gunnarsson

Introduction

For long, the rubber industry served as a fairly secure source of income for Malaysian small-scale farmers. This appears no longer to be the case for the 'real' smallholders, i.e. holders of small plots of land, although production is growing for the smallholder sector as a whole.[1] In this essay an attempt will be made to determine the mechanisms of growth in the early expansion of the smallholder sector and to evaluate the potentialities for future growth within the sector following the same patterns of growth. By tracing the factors which rendered expansion of rubber production possible among smallholders during the initial decades of this century the limits to growth after the Second World War may be determined. Thus, a study of the introduction of rubber among smallholders is not only a matter concerning Malaysian economic history but also of great significance for present allocation issues.

The analysis is concerned with two different periods, the period of expansion before 'the Great Depression' and the period of recovery and renewed expansion after independence in 1957. During both periods the smallholder sector has statistically proved more dynamic and expansive than the estate sector in spite of a fast growth of output in the latter sector. It will be argued, however, that the expansion of the smallholder industry has followed entirely. different patterns of growth in the two periods. Whereas in the early period production expansion rested upon the advantages contained in the existence of a complementarity between subsistence and commercial agriculture on very small units of production, the growth of the post-1957 period is more a reflection of structural changes and reallocation of resources, the consequence being a great differentiation of production, organisation and income within the smallholder sector. Today, the expansive and fairly prosperous part of the smallholder industry is the part in which the production units are large enough to benefit from the technological advantages of the 'Green Revolution' and in which economies of scale have been introduced. Simultaneously, poverty is increasing among petty farmers with only a few acres of land and with only limited access to new technology.[2]

An attempt to analyse the initial dynamics of the smallholder economy will be made by applying three conflicting theoretical explanations: the dependency theory, the comparative cost theory and the vent for surplus approach. We shall argue that the vent for surplus theory (with certain modifications) is the theory that most accurately helps to reveal the forces behind the early expansion. For the post-war period the vent for surplus theory is inapplicable and a specialisation approach more valid.

The Statistical Picture

Empirical studies of the Malaysian rubber smallholder industry are not easily performed. Until recently it has been nearly impossible to obtain reliable information about the number of farmers, size of farms, yields, etc for the smallholder industry. In fact, even today the facts about the unhealthy smallholder industry are to some extent concealed by official statistical figures, according to which the rate of growth is higher for the smallholder industry than for the plantations. However, this is only a statistical fiction. The Malaysian rubber industry has always been classified into two sectors, estates and smallholdings. The estate sector includes all production units of a size larger than 100 acres and, consequently, all units smaller than 100 acres have been classified as smallholdings.[3]

As a result of this method of classification, the official statistical figures are highly misleading. According to these figures the output of the smallholder sector has been growing faster than that of the estate sector since the early 1960s. Thus, the smallholder sector appears to be prosperous whereas the estate sector gives the impression of being a highly unhealthy industry. In fact nothing could be more wrong. The declining estate output is basically a sign of diversification. Output per acre on estates has never been higher than today and the gap in productivity between estates and smallholdings is constantly widening. These productivity gains in rubber production have made possible a diversification into other products, such as palm oil and cocoa.[4]

However, the rather approximate definition of smallholdings is an even more serious problem. By classifying all units of production of a size below 100 acres as smallholdings no account is taken of the various forms of organisation of production within the sector. There is no denying that, on the average, output and productivity are growing fast also on holdings smaller than 100 acres. However, there are no reasons to believe that the growth is evenly distributed between holdings of different sizes. Considering that the majority of the smallholders are petty farmers with only a few acres of land, and the evidence of increasing poverty, there is little reason to assume that a significant proportion of the growth of output is accounted for by the 'real' smallholders, the petty producers. On the contrary, there is reason to believe that the medium size or large holdings account for the bulk of the growth of smallholder output.

The Early Expansion of Smallholder Rubber

Although the expansion of rubber production had been initiated by European capital it was soon to be followed by a remarkable growth of production on non-European holdings. Around 1907, Asian smallholders had begun planting rubber trees and by the end of the First World War the first results of these efforts had reached the market.[5]

By 1920 the smallholder sector had developed to an extent that it was beginning to become noticed by contemporary commentators and (not least) competitors. In fact, the rate of growth was so remarkable that it was regarded as a threat to the future prosperity of the plantation sector. In 1921, it was estimated that more than one million acres had been planted by non-Europeans, primarily on smaller plots of land.[6] Of these planted acres at least 400,000 must have reached maturity by 1921. By 1939, almost 40 per cent of the acreage planted to rubber in Malaya fell under the category of small-holdings. Of a total acreage of 3,300,000, about 1,300,000 had been planted by smallholders. Although this was an area of considerable size, the ratio of smallholdings to estates had actually been higher in 1921. The decline was mainly due to restriction policies practised by the colonial government. Thus, the rapid growth of planting on small holdings was primarily a phenomenon of the 1910s, whereas the 1920s and, in particular, the 1930s meant a relative and, eventually, absolute decline of the importance of the smallholder sector.

To explain this early expansion of the smallholder sector three different theories will be tested in the following sections.

The Dependency Approach

Until recently the neo-marxist version of the theory of imperialism, the so-called development of underdevelopment analysis or the dependency approach has been in the focus of Third World studies.[7] According to the theory, underdevelopment is a direct effect of the expansion of the capitalist system into non-capitalist areas of the world. Not only were the colonies deprived of their economic surplus and, thereby, their means of sustained economic growth, they were also integrated into the system of international trade by means of force.

According to the dependency approach, cash crop production was introduced into the colonies on European initiative and by means of coercion. The argument is that subsistence farmers were obliged to abandon their status as self-sufficient peasants and produce for the distant European markets. Forced production and various methods of taxation were used to persuade smallholding peasants of Africa and Asia to become export crop producers. Presumably, the smallholders had little interest in engaging in export oriented enterprises, since their needs of subsistence were satisfied in the traditional society. The result of the European penetration of the subsistence economies was a breaking-up of the traditional mode of production and a total reallocation of productive resources towards cash crop production, i.e. a creation of monocultural economies.

It can easily be shown that the dependency approach is a misjudgement of the mechanisms of growth in the colonial smallholder economics. Admittedly, compulsory methods were occasionally employed to create export oriented farmers out of subsistence peasants. The French in West Africa and the Dutch in the East Indies used various means of coercion to achieve such goals. However, in a majority of cases, the introduction of cash crops in the colonies occurred without coercion and was a perfectly voluntary act on the part of the producers. In taking up production of cash crops they merely responded positively to the stimulus created by the widening of the market created by the colonial system. The Malaysian case is remarkably illuminating. Rubber production on smallholdings owned by Asians was surely not encouraged by colonial interests, and thus coercive methods were naturally out of the question. In fact, the Europeans had little interest in having Asians as competitors. The plantation owners would rather have seen that the indigenous smallholders had remained subsistence farmers isolated from the market economy.[8]

Still, it has been argued that the Malayan peasants were forced to switch from subsistence to cash crop production in order to obtain cash to pay taxes imposed by the colonial government.[9] This is hardly a plausible argument. Firstly, in the early years, land rents were generally kept low to encourage settlers to open up more land. However, for non-Europeans the new land was not intended for commercial purposes. The government thought it best to encourage the traditional types of agriculture. Thus, the commercial activities of smallholders would not obstruct the progress of plantation agriculture. Secondly, before the establishment of British rule, there hardly existed a substantial landowning peasantry on which taxation on a large scale could be imposed.[10]

The dependency approach fails to recognise the dynamic elements of the peasant economy. In fact the approach has a striking resemblance to Chayanov's theory of 'peasant mode of production'.[11] The peasant economy is regarded as a static, self-sufficient mode of production where the farmers are not profit maximisers and behave irrationally from the point of view of the market economy. Therefore, the peasants can only become involved in the market economy by means of some kind of external force imposed on the economy. Climatic changes, population growth and changes in the institutional setting are factors that might disrupt the state of equilibrium in the peasant economy. In the peasant mode of production the producer is unlikely to react to positive stimuli created by the market. Force is then required to make the farmers switch from subsistence to commercial agriculture.

Since colonialism was introduced by force upon the countries of Asia and Africa it has been assumed that practically all types of enterprise undertaken during the colonial era were forced upon the indigenous peoples. Colonialism was just another external threat to the equilibrium (sometimes called the ecological balance) of the peasant economy. Such views are far from being realistic. In fact, in the case of the Malayan rubber smallholders, coercion would have been necessary to *prohibit* the peasants from becoming involved in cash crop production. That the introduction of the market economy was a result of colonialism is an obvious and trivial fact, and as such it is not very interesting. The important thing is to find the mechanisms which enabled the peasants to respond to the stimuli created by the market. Obviously, factors prevailed in the agrarian economy which made export crop production a feasible and promising enterprise also amongst smallholders. The interesting thing is to trace these mechanisms. The dependency theory offers little help in this respect.

Specialisation or Vent for Surplus

The dependency theory cannot be used as an explanation to the opening up of the Malayan subsistence economy to cash crop production. In this section it will be argued that the vent for surplus theory offers a more plausible explanation than the conventional comparative cost approach. On the other hand, for the present situation the reverse seems to be the case.

The vent for surplus theory of trade is one of the more forgotten aspects of classical economic thinking. Although the principle was originally suggested by Adam Smith, and named by J.S. Mill, it was totally overshadowed by the comparative cost theory until restored and adapted to Third World conditions by Hla Myint.[12] The original formulation of the theory can be traced to a few passages in the *Wealth of Nations*. Smith regarded trade as a dynamic factor of economic growth and argued that 'by means of it the narrowness of the home-market does not hinder the division of labour in any particular branch of art or manufacture from being carried to the highest perfection'. Furthermore, he stated that '(by) opening a more extensive market for whatever part of the produce of (their) labour may exceed the home consumption it encourages them to improve its productive powers and to augment its annual produce to the utmost and thereby to increase the real revenue and wealth of society'.[13]

As Myint has pointed out these statements reflect two different lines of thought. Firstly, trade may contribute to an increased division of labour and thereby lead to a rise in productivity. Secondly, by opening up a country for foreign trade the narrowness of the home market is overcome and markets are created for utilisation of a surplus for which there is no outlet on the home market. The first aspect, i.e. the role of trade as instrumental in raising productivity should of course be separated from the comparative cost approach. The principle of comparative costs is based on the assumption of a given set of resources and given technique and postulates that static gains can be obtained by reallocating available resources without technological changes. For Smith, trade was a dynamic factor altering the division of labour and accelerating the introduction of technological innovations. Still, the theories are similar in assuming specialisation and rising productivity to be the factors behind the growth of output.

In the Malayan case there is little evidence of a specialisation in the early phase of rubber production. The smallholders seldom became specialised rubber producers. There is no evidence of a decline in the production of food crops together with the growth of rubber output or an increase in productivity. Thus, it seems as if the peasants took up rubber as a commercial crop as an addition to the production of food crops. At least this was true for the majority of the petty producers, the Malay peasantry. For the Chinese small-holders the situation may have been somewhat different.

So far we have questioned both that commercial rubber production was imposed on the peasants by means of coercion and that a reallocation of productive resources and commercial specialisation were necessary conditions for the expansion of production on small-holdings. In order to understand how the smallholder economy of early 20th century Malaya could become market oriented without a reallocation of resources or without coercion we must turn to the second aspect of the Smithian principle, the vent for surplus aspect. The core of the theory postulates that an economy may be in posses-sion of a dormant capacity to produce a surplus, but that this capacity could only be realised by an extension of the market, preferably by external trade.

The vent for surplus aspect differs from the comparative cost theory by not assuming full utilisation of resources. According to the comparative cost principle the relative costs will function as instruments of allocation, directing resources to sectors with lower costs and higher productivity. Thus, export production could only occur after the reallocation of resources away from home market oriented or subsistence activities. Apparently this was not the case in Malaya.

In contrast, the vent for surplus theory does not assume full employment or full utilisation of resources.[14] The function of trade is to create an effective demand for a potential surplus capacity in the economy. Export production may therefore prove feasible without resources having to be moved from one sector of the economy or from one activity to another so as to raise productivity. A crucial difference between the two theories is that the comparative cost theory assumes complete factor mobility between different sectors of the economy. This presupposes the operation of a smoothly functioning price mechanism, which is completely unrealistic as an assumption for early 20th century Malaya. The vent for surplus theory needs no such assumption. Trade expansion did not involve an allocation problem, the basic necessary precondition being that in export oriented production there did not exist obstacles to a realisation of the potential surplus.

Generally, neoclassical theory does not accept the idea that there could exist a vent for surplus production in any economy. In the Heckscher–Ohlin version of the comparative cost theory an economy could never produce at a point inside the production possibility curve. Although there may, for instance, exist unoccupied land, there is never, at the point of equilibrium, a productive surplus capacity available, since the relatively scarce resource, labour, will be fully employed. In other words, the fact that land is lying idle is due to the fact that labour is fully employed and, thereby, idle land resources contain no surplus capacity.

Still, history gives many examples of how agrarian economies on subsistence level have been integrated into the international system of trade without improvements in productivity or reductions in other types of industrial productivity. Examples could be found not only in the colonial areas but perhaps in European history as well.[15] Neoclassical theory cannot give any reasonable explanation of this phenomenon, unless it assumes an introduction of external factors of change. If new resources are brought from outside the economy, the state of equilibrium may be disrupted. However, the point is that this was seldom the case in smallholder economies and certainly not in Malaya.

Whatever the merits of equilibrium theory, it has little relevance for historical analyses of the opening up of subsistence economies to external trade. In non-monetised, sparsely populated agrarian societies on subsistence level the mechanisms of change were entirely different from those suggested by the comparative cost approach. There existed underemployed resources owing to the limited size of the market. This is neither a restoration of the myth of 'the lazy farmer' nor an idealisation of 'the happy savage'. It does not imply that subsistence economies were affluent societies or that full utilisation of resources was unnecessary in an absolute sense. On the contrary, the isolated subsistence economy was, if not primitive, certainly characterised by a lopsided production structure. The supply of necessities may have been limited although there need not have been a shortage of basic food supplies in which the economy was self-sufficient. Local and regional trade had little impact on either the pattern of consumption or resource allocation. The farmers had few opportunities of exchanging their produce for manufactured products. As a consequence, in the isolated economy, relative prices had little impact on the allocation of resources. Thus, it seems quite plausible to assume that subsistence farmers could be in possession of a dormant surplus capacity without being idle or having all their needs saturated. However, it is important to note that the surplus capacity consists of *both land and labour resources*.[16] If only one factor is said to be abundant the neoclassical criticisms are correct and the theory fails to explain the mechanisms of growth in the smallholder economy. In considering four possible cases of relationship between utilisation of land and labour we shall find the vent for surplus aspect to be valid in one case only, and that is the case which could be applied to the Malayan example.

In the first case (A) both land and labour are fully employed. This has little validity for Malaya. Although there were examples of

Figure 7.1:   Different Combinations of Land and Labour Utilisation

Land / Labour	fully utilised	abundant
fully employed	A	B
under-employed	C	D

producers switching from other crops to rubber especially on the plantations it should be emphasised that Malaya was a land surplus economy. The real expansion of cultivated acreage came with the introduction of rubber. However, land could not be the only surplus resource (as in case B), although the experience of plantation rubber seems to indicate that. Obviously the plantations suffered from a shortage of labour since they were forced to import large quantities of labour from India to develop the vast land resources. For the subsistence economy, however, the situation was quite different. Large resources of land could be developed without imports of labour. Thus it seems as if labour was underemployed as well. This has nothing to do with the case of disguised unemployment (in case C).[17] Disguised unemployment may exist in an economy where the marginal productivity of labour is low as a consequence of a population pressure on the land resources. An extension of the market is not likely to lead to a realisation of a surplus. In fact, the mechanisms would work completely in reverse. Where the marginal productivity of labour in subsistence agriculture is low and land is the scarce resource, labour supplies will be abundant. If that had been the case for the traditional Malay peasant community it would have been a perfect source of labour supply for the plantations. We know that the reality was different. The Malay subsistence economy was a meagre source of labour supply. Of course it could be argued that a supply of labour from the subsistence economy was hindered by non-economic obstacles in the traditional economy or by 'non-rational' preferences amongst the rural population. Still, the fact remains that the farmers not only stayed on their land, they also opened up new land for the purpose of producing rubber. Furthermore there is no evidence of a substantial decline in the acreage under paddy or in the production of rice.

Thus we may conclude that in the subsistence economy of Malaya both land and labour must have been abundant (case D). If there is no reallocation of resources and consequently little specialisation on cash crops, new resources must have been employed. If these new resources were not brought from outside the subsistence economy they must have been dormant within the subsistence economy and set free with the opening up of new market opportunities. For the Malayan case this explanation seems plausible, i.e. that subsistence farmers sacrificed leisure time to develop idle land resources.

The Mechanisms of Growth

Output of plantation rubber grew extremely fast during the two decades following the turn of the century. In spite of this the output originating from indigenous smallholders increased even faster, in fact it grew at a rate only exceptionally experienced in tropical agriculture.[18] The growth of plantation rubber rested upon a utilisation of the land surplus and on imports of labour from India. A third crucial factor was the large amounts of capital supplied from the capital markets of Europe. The development of the smallholder sector, on the other hand, involved practically no capital imports from Europe. This raises the question of capital formation in the process of economic growth. It might appear surprising that indigenous smallholders could have accumulated capital from domestic sources of a magnitude equal to that of the European estates.[19] However, this would be a misunderstanding of the important aspect that the progress of the smallholder industry rested primarily on the foundation that larger capital supplies were unnecessary. What were then the mechanisms of growth? Using the vent for surplus theory the following pattern of growth can be established.

The incentive to engage in foreign trade was provided by the growing demand for rubber and the means were provided by the establishment of British rule, improvements of transport facilities and credit institutions. Furthermore, the Europeans introduced the new crop, they brought the technology and established contacts with distant markets. They also imported the goods which gave subsistence farmers the incentive to adopt a new pattern of demand. The European-owned estate sector was important in its role as a leading sector. However, this does not imply that the presence of an estate sector was a necessary condition for the expansion of smallholder production.

In fact, a similar development occurred in West Africa, where European ownership was totally absent. The important European connection was created by merchant firms who brought the produce to the market and provided credits to middlemen and producers.

If the presence of European capital as a necessary condition for the development of the smallholder industry might be questioned, it can certainly be argued that it was not a sufficient condition. The crucial factor was that rubber production could be easily adapted to traditional agriculture. Whereas plantations required large supplies of hired labour the smallholders found their productive basis in the family unit and hired labour was used only exceptionally. Although the rubber tree had been imported into Southeast Asia from South America it fitted well into the ecological setting of the Malay kampung. It could be interplanted with food crops and once a tree had been planted it needed little nursing and could be abandoned for six to eight years until it reached maturity. Especially in hilly terrain, the areas planted with dry paddy there was a complementarity between existing agricultural practices and rubber planting.

Another important factor was the simple technology of rubber production. After 1910 seeds were freely available and any grower could gather them. Tapping knives were easily available, and collection and processing of the latex could be done with very simple equipment: cigarette and kerosene tins and hand mangles. Thus, there was no apparent technological dualism between production on holdings of different size.[20]

In other words, the success of the Malayan rubber smallholder industry during the first decades of this century can be attributed to the relative ease with which the cash crop was taken up as a complementary commodity. According to McHale the rubber trees 'did not represent tied-up capital, involved no long term labour or managerial commitments and merely required limited and easily learned skills to be transformed into actual productive assets'.[21] The primitive methods of cultivation have also been stressed by Bauer as the prime factors behind the expansion. 'So easy is rubber cultivation on Asian smallholdings that the smallholders often simply add rubber to the cultivation of food crops.'[22]

Sir Arthur Lewis has remarked that simple techniques of cultivation were a common feature of practically all development of cash crop production in the tropics in the late 19th and early 20th century.[23] There were no technological reasons why production should take place on estates rather than on smallholdings. Provided there were no institutional obstacles all economies with abundance of both land and labour could have engaged in export crop production. In Malaya there were no technological obstacles to the production of rubber on smallholdings. Rubber produced on estates generally was of higher quality but, on the other hand, yields per acre were higher on smallholdings due to closer planting.

Finally, costs of labour and administration worked against the estates. It seems that economies of scale were largely absent in the early years of rubber production in Malaya. As long as the vent for surplus could be utilised the smallholder sector proved, in fact, more expansive than production on large estates. Whereas the large estates required control of ground conditions, a network of roads and drains and functioned by means of a staff of European supervisors and Indian labourers, the smallholders could manage with little capital. Drabble puts it in the following way:

> The Malay smallholder initially cleared and planted the land, and once the trees were established did little until they reached maturity. Tapping was then done by the family or labourers engaged on a sharecropping arrangement. The general practice among the Asian producers was to do minimal weeding and to process the rubber with the simplest of equipment. Limited capital resources therefore were not an obstacle to entry into the industry especially where other means of livelihood provided subsistence until the trees matured or where loans were raised from private moneylenders.[24]

The Chinese Settler — Peasant or Specialised Agriculturalist?

Although much empirical research remains to be done it could be claimed that the vent for surplus theory is a reasonable explanation for the adaptation of rubber as a commercial crop by the Malayan peasantry. The majority of the peasants were Malay subsistence famers. However, there is also the question of the Chinese immigrant settlers. Should the Chinese be described as subsistence farmers and could the vent for surplus theory explain their switch to rubber production? Most Chinese immigrants did not come to Malaya to settle as subsistence farmers but as commercially oriented entrepreneurs, in many cases with an open intention to make money. To a large extent these settlers were responsible for the introduction of rubber in the Malayan smallholder economy. It might even be argued that the Chinese penetration of the rural community was more important than the European influence for introducing 'the spirit of enterprise' among the rural smallholders.

The Chinese migrated into the 'hinterland' and settled on unoccupied land. Planting was generally undertaken on a small-scale basis, but the Chinese settlers were hardly peasants in the traditional sense. They were generally well acquainted with the market economy and had established contact with Chinese dealers and creditors. As Fryer and Jackson put it: 'Chinese smallholders form part of an integrated local economy with regular and numerous contacts with the mainstream of national economic life. In no sense they can be classed as rural peasants.'[25] A study by Drabble confirms the differences between Chinese and Malay small-holders.[26] Drabble found that from the very beginning the Chinese were engaged in activities other than rubber production, in tin mining, a contracting business or trading, and that capital was provided from such sources. The Malays on the other hand lacked such sources. Cultivation of rice was their only alternative.

The Chinese holdings were generally larger than the Malay holdings, 8–10 acres as compared to 3–5 acres. Furthermore, the Chinese marketed a higher proportion of the output in processed form as smoked sheet. Still, Drabble argues that there is no reason to differentiate the two groups of smallholders. 'Technological constraints such as the yielding power of the trees, extensive reliance on family labour and marketing through a chain of middlemen were common to both groups.'[27]

This, however, rather points to the apparent similarities in production and organisation and says little of the mechanisms of growth in the early period. That the Chinese were not part of a 'truly peasant economy' could be claimed without much doubt. A more interesting question, however, is whether the switch to rubber production could be characterised as a vent for surplus mechanism. This is a very difficult question and before answering in detail much more empirical research should be done. We should need to know to what extent resources were being transferred to rubber production from other activities and if labour resources were being underemployed. At the present state of research the question must be left unanswered, but obviously the applicability of the vent for surplus theory is less apparent than in the case of the Malay subsistence farmers.[28]

The Limits to Growth

Availability of abundant land resources and underemployed labour were the necessary static preconditions for a growth of rubber production in the Malayan smallholder economy. The production structure established in the early years has, in fact, remained unchanged until today for a large section of the smallholder economy. During a considerable period of time production could continue to increase. As long as surplus resources could be utilised, production increased in spite of the absence of structural changes. However, when one of the resources becomes relatively scarce, a reallocation of productive resources is needed to increase output. Unless there is a structural shift, population pressure will lower the marginal productivity of labour and lead to underemployment of labour which is impossible to utilise in the agrarian economy. At this point a specialisation approach is required to explain both expansion and stagnation.

With a growing population, the pressure on the land resources increases. Land resources become less available and the price of land is raised. Thus the farmer has no means of increasing his productive acreage and the marginal productivity of labour decreases. The scarcity of land leads either to an increased proportion of food crops and a declining production of cash crops or to out-migration of labour to other sectors of the economy. Thus the economy either moves towards a specialisation on cash crops or slides back into the subsistence economy.

In the following sections an attempt will be made to show that during the decades after independence the development of the Malaysian smallholder industry has been entirely different from that in the early years of expansion. It will be argued that for the medium size or larger holdings a substantial growth has been possible due to structural changes. The smaller holdings, on the other hand, have remained largely unchanged. The absence of such structural changes is the main cause of stagnation of production and the increase in poverty. Thus, whereas in the early years, expansion was possible without structural changes, present growth of output is dependent on structural changes. Consequently, the vent for surplus theory has no validity for the present situation. It can neither explain the growth of production nor the absence of structural changes.

Expansion and Growth of Poverty

Still, from 1957 onwards the Malaysian rubber industry has experienced a period of considerable expansion. Production increased from a low level of 626,000 tonnes in 1956 to over 1,500,000 tonnes in the early 1980s. The growth rate was fairly stable during the period, but the years between 1963 and 1969 were the most expansive with an annual average growth of 9.3 per cent as compared to 2.2 per cent between 1956 and 1962 and 3.4 per cent in the 1970s.[29]

In addition, the 1960s was a period of recovery for the smallholder sector in terms of output. The gap between it and the estate sector was rapidly closed. By 1969 it had almost reached parity with the estates and in 1973 output from smallholdings was for the first time in history recorded as larger than that of the estates. To understand the shifts between the two sectors it is necessary to analyse the characteristics of the new rubber policy introduced in the 1950s and to study the impact on both estates and smallholders.

Generally, the most severe problem facing the newly independent countries of South and Southeast Asia in the 1950s was the rapidly growing populations and the stagnation of agriculture. Therefore, many governments undertook to solve the problem of rural poverty through various types of reform policies. To an increasing extent it was also becoming apparent that the stagnation of agriculture could not possibly be resolved unless the discrimination against smallholdings *vis-à-vis* plantations was reconsidered. In Malaysia population pressure was not considered to be a problem as severe as in many other countries. The inequality between the sectors was an effect of administrative discrimination regarding alienation of land for rubber planting purposes and restrictions on new planting. Thus, there was no immediate shortage of land and a policy of land redistribution was considered unnecessary. There existed large areas of uncultivated land suitable for rubber exploitation.

In the mid 1950s it was thought that an increasing utilisation of unoccupied land could be a way of countering rural stagnation. As a consequence, the restrictions on alienation were removed and new planting was no longer discouraged although replanting of cultivated land may have been preferred.[30]

In Malaysia, however, the picture was complicated by the unequal ethnical distribution of ownership in the rubber industry. Whereas most plantations were controlled by Europeans or Chinese and only exceptionally by Malays, the smallholder sector involved both Malays and Chinese. In 1952, 47 per cent of all smallholdings were owned by Malays and 41 per cent by Chinese. The holdings were, however, not equally distributed in terms of size. The smaller holdings, below 25 acres, which constituted the majority, were 55 per cent owned by Malays, whereas on holdings of a size ranging from 25 to 100 acres only 5 per cent of the owners were Malays as compared to 66 per cent Chinese.[31] This of course points to the inadequacy of the term smallholding mentioned above. Those planters who had suffered most from the previous restrictions were the petty producers, the majority of whom were Malays. The ethnical problem was further emphasised by the fact that the political leadership within the ruling Alliance Party lay in the hands of Malays and naturally the government felt obliged to remedy the consequences of the discriminatory colonial policy. The two major government institutions of control over the rubber industry were the *Rubber Industry Smallholders' Development Authority* (RISDA) and the *Federal Land Development Authority* (FLDA and later FELDA).

The post-independence rubber policy has taken the following forms:

— replanting and technical assistance
— land settlement and new planting
— central marketing
— intensified research.

Two aspects are particularly important for our purposes; replanting and new planting. Replanting schemes were undertaken under the auspices of the forerunners of the RISDA. One of these was the *Rubber Industry Replanting Board* founded in 1953 and another was the *Smallholders' Advisory Service* of the Rubber Research Institute.

The Replanting Board aimed at restoring productivity of existing rubber land on both estates and smallholdings. From a specific fund financed by export taxes the government gave financial support to planters willing to replant their holdings. This policy was markedly different from the policy practised by the colonial administration. Before 1953 practically all replanting took place on estates. Not more than 20,000 acres had been replanted on smallholdings as compared to 500,000 acres on estates between 1937 and 1952. The existence of the replanting fund enabled many smallholders to undertake replanting, by 1957 at a rate equal to that of the estates. By 1973 a total of 1,261,000 acres was recorded as having been replanted under the scheme. A smaller part, some 100,000 acres of the acreage classified as replanted may in reality have been new planting, but this does not alter the impression that smallholders were also involved in and affected by the replanting schemes. In fact in 1973 almost 50 per cent of the total planted rubber acreage on smallholdings consisted of replanted land under RISDA schemes.[32]

Land settlement and new planting was the main task of the *Federal Land Development Authority*, FELDA, founded in 1956. Its function was to initiate and finance cultivation and settlement on new, previously unoccupied land by landless rural settlers. From 1960 FELDA was given direct managing responsibility for all settlement projects undertaken in the various states of Malaysia. The FELDA schemes certainly contributed to the increase in planting from 1959 onwards, on the average some 35 per cent of the new planting between 1959 and 1972. Between 1955 and 1973 a total of more than 1,700,000 acres of smallholder land were replanted or newly developed under RISDA or FELDA schemes. This means that in 1973 some 60 per cent of the total acreage of 1,700,000 under rubber on smallholdings had been developed under these schemes, and that high yielding varieties had been introduced on these holdings.[33]

The Effects on the Smallholdings

The increasing replanting and new planting activity after 1953 has undoubtedly had a great impact on the smallholder sector as a whole. The increase in planted acreage was a direct response to the loosening of the restrictions and the stimulus created by the Replanting Fund in 1953. During the 1950s planted acreage increased steadily, the growth averaging 20,000 acres per annum.[34]

By 1959/60 the growth of planted acreage was further accelerated and in 1972 acreage under rubber on smallholdings was twice the pre-war level. In 1959 smallholder acreage for the first time in history had grown larger than acreage of the estates and by 1973 the smallholder sector was almost double the size of the estate sector in terms of acreage.

However, figures for mature acreage were quite different. Between 1947 and 1965 the acreage under mature rubber decreased considerably. This means that in spite of the increase in planted acreage, the rate of new planting had not been fast enough to eliminate the effects of acreage going out of production. This was a consequence of the rubber policy of the early 1950s when replanting was encouraged, whereas new planting was maintained on a low level. The increase in mature acreage from 1966 onwards can then be attributed to the increase in new planting — partly under FELDA schemes — after 1959. A relative stagnation of mature acreage between 1971 and 1975 also corresponds well with a decrease in new planting around 1965.

From 1963 onwards output from the smallholder sector has grown rapidly. The previous stagnation is hardly surprising considering the loss of mature acreage. By 1973–5 productivity per mature acre had almost doubled as compared to productivity in 1955. The large increase in smallholder output can, therefore, be attributed to the effects of replanting with high yielding material.

Thus the production growth of the smallholder sector after independence has not been caused by the mechanisms that formed the basis for the early expansion after the turn of the century. Whereas pre-war expansion rested upon occupation of easily available land resources and a reduction of leisure time and took the form of new planting, post-independence expansion has been a result of an administrative policy undertaken by the government. This means that a structural change has occurred and has raised productivity on larger holdings, including parts of the smallholder sector.

The remarkable expansion of smallholder output after 1963 cannot be attributed primarily to the increase in acreage under rubber. The introduction of high yielding varieties on smallholdings has played a dominant role in restoring the viability of the smallholder economy. The rubber policy of the independent Malaysian government aiming at a rural development based on smallholder expansion might, therefore, be looked upon as a partial success. Since a large proportion of smallholdings has been replanted, resulting in improved productivity per acre, it might even be accurate to talk of a 'Green Revolution' in the smallholder sector during the last 25 years. The question is, however, if the goals of the land development schemes, i.e. to ensure 'full employment and adequate returns for the farmer and his family', were achieved. Evidence seems to suggest that this has not been the case.

It is often argued that price fluctuations impose the most severe threat to the prosperity of primary commodity producers. In the case of Malaysia falling market prices for rubber might have counterbalanced the growth of smallholder output. A dramatic fall in prices meant that revenue from rubber production hardly improved at all between 1955 and 1968. However, from 1969 prices have improved, in particular after 1973, which might have improved the revenue of the smallholders. To some extent the increase in revenue has been followed by increasing cost of living but, nevertheless, on average, smallholder incomes seem to have stabilised somewhat during the last few years. This average is not a good account of the situation for the majority of the smallholders, but it would be misleading to emphasise price fluctuations as the sole factor behind falling returns to smallholders. Thus, other factors must be considered, such as the inherent structural weakness of the small-holder economy.

Population growth has not been halted. Although the rural per-centage of the total population actually decreased somewhat between 1957 and 1970 (from 73.5 to 71.2) the number of people increased from 4.7 million to 6.3 million in 1970. On average, the growth of rubber output has been faster than the growth of popula-tion but the pressure on the land resources has increased. Land is becoming less abundant and more expensive. In 1960 an over-whelming majority of the smallholdings were of a size below 10 acres. On the other hand, farms larger than 10 acres covered an area three times as large as the area of the smallholdings below 3 acres. Although the figures are from 1960 and may not be accurate in detail, there is no reason to believe that the pattern of today is significantly different, and the skewness less pronounced. On the contrary, an opposite assumption would be more realistic.[35]

These figures indicate that smallholders do not constitute a homogeneous group, and, consequently, the rubber policy may have affected smallholders unevenly. Considering the fact that by 1972 almost 1 million acres had neither been newly planted or replanted with high yielding varieties it is quite reasonable to assume that it was the smallest holdings that were not planted with high yielding material. Those who could afford the capital investments involved in replanting were of course the larger producers. The Replanting Fund assisted a large number of middle-sized or large holdings with the required capital but the costs remained too high for the small producers. The area of acres planted increased during the period but considering the population growth and the fact that one-third of the new planting took place on government sponsored settlements and involved 65,000 households it might be argued that the land settle-ment policy has even aggravated rural poverty.[36] It has created a small minority of prosperous peasants with incomes several times those of the smaller rubber producers. Settler farms are usually between 7 and 14 acres and planted entirely with high yielding varieties. An investigation from 1968 suggested that settlers' incomes were ten times the mean income of the poorest 20 per cent of the population. It has also been suggested that while incomes for the highest quintile of the population were growing between 1957 and 1970, household incomes were greatly worsened for the poorest quintile. An assumption that the poorest strata of the population are also the holders of small plots of land is hardly sensational.[37]

The question is whether the growing inequality between large producers or settlers and smaller producers has also been accompanied by an absolute pauperisation of the petty producers. The pressure on the land has not decreased and declining rubber prices inevitably leave the producers with falling incomes unless organisational changes are undertaken. The best method is of course to replant with more productive varieties, to introduce yield stimulants, herbicides and pesticides, and fertilisers and to improve exploitation and processing techniques.

Holders of small plots have had little opportunity to undertake replanting or benefit from technological improvements. The replanting fund has probably benefited the medium-sized or large sections of the smallholdings. As a consequence their output per acre has increased rapidly, whereas productivity for the smaller holdings has remained low or stagnant. Evidence shows that productivity on large high yielding farms may be as high as 0.5 tonne per acre which is well above the average for smallholdings and certainly much higher than productivity on small plots with low yielding varieties.[38]

Findings from a study of rubber smallholdings in South West Parak, a region dominated by older, small-size holdings, suggested that the volume of smallholder output declined by 6.6 per cent between 1968 and 1973, in spite of an increase in the size of the workforce by 8.8 per cent. This implies a decline in output per person by 3 per cent annually.[39]

An alternative method to increase production would be to extend the planted area. As we have seen the total area under smallholdings increased during the period. Between 1958 and 1972 smallholder acreage under rubber increased by a total of 783,000 acres, which is quite remarkable. However, this increase includes a subdivision of estate land to smallholdings amounting to some 257,000 acres. Furthermore, as we have seen, 188,000 acres were planted under Settlement Schemes. Consequently, only 338,000 acres represent a real extension of planted acreage. This shows that the expansion of the smallholder sector during the post-war period has not followed the same mechanisms as in the early expansion. Between 1910 and 1922 about 1 million acres were planted, i.e. *three times the acreage planted between 1959 and 1972.* Thus, area extension has not been a dominant feature of the post-war 'recovery' of Malaysian rubber smallholdings.[40]

What are the causes of the slow rate of new planting? Why has not the vent for surplus mechanism functioned? One reason could be the lack of market stimulus due to declining prices during the period. Of course falling prices have resulted in lower incomes for smaller farmers with little or no opportunities of technical reorganisation but they do not explain the absence of new planters entering the business. Prices in the 1910s and the 1920s were also declining, but because of low opportunity costs new smallholders could with little risk engage in rubber production. Consequently, decreasing prices cannot alone explain the slow rate of planting.

Another factor could be a shortage of land. However, there is no reason to believe that there is a land shortage in an *absolute* sense. The settlement schemes have shown that there exist large areas of available land suitable for rubber cultivation. The problem faced by smallholders is that the land, because of the population growth and the emergence of other crops such as palm oil, is too expensive even for smallholders using mainly family labour. Consequently, there is no vent for surplus available.

Thus, only those planters who have been accepted as beneficiaries on settlement land have actually benefited from the rubber policy after 1953. Furthermore those who could afford to replant could avoid a decline in income whereas those who could neither replant, extend the area of cultivation nor become accepted as settlers have suffered a sharp fall in income.

The following mechanism seems to be in operation. In the beginning of the century, when the rapid population growth had not begun, farmers were in a position to invest some of their leisure time in rubber planting. When population growth accelerated, family sizes were increased and the dependency ratio increased. Consequently, farmers were under pressure to use their labour resources on activities which gave quick returns, and less time was spent on rubber planting which is a long-term investment. Farmers simply cannot afford to abstain from an income which is needed for immediate consumption. Thus, the capital/labour ratio declines and eventually the rubber land has been either planted with other crops or has been taken back by the jungle.

The rubber policy of the independent government has been successful in the sense that output has been raised and a declining trend has been turned into an upward trend for the smallholder sector as a whole. On the other hand, the effects on the poorer strata of the smallholders are very dubious. The official support to individual smallholders on small plots of land seems to have been negligible, relatively seen. Although the government's policy cannot be regarded as being of a *laissez-faire* type since it has involved large institutional changes it has done little to solve the poverty problem for the smallholders created by the colonial policy of the 1920s, 1930s and 1940s. Instead, it has quite likely contributed to the strengthening of the group of rather wealthy medium-size or larger smallholders.

The Need for Structural Change

In contract to the early years the present expansion of production on Malaysian smallholdings is an effect of a reallocation of resources and a rise in productivity. Structural changes that were largely unnecessary for the early expansion have formed the basis for the present progress in the smallholder sector, whereas the contribution of the vent for surplus mechanism is insignificant.

On the other hand, a large proportion of smallholders have been unable to undertake replanting or benefit from other technological improvements, which has resulted in a stagnation of output. The reason for the slow rate of replanting on small holdings is easy to understand: the holdings are quite simply too small. Continuous replanting on plots of, say, 1 to 3 acres means a considerable loss of income over a long period of time, a loss many smallholders cannot afford. Since little unoccupied land is available for new planting (except to the beneficiaries of the government-sponsored schemes) the poor smallholders are stuck with small plots which are becoming less and less economic.

Why, then, has a majority of the holdings (especially those owned by Malays) remained small? There seems to be no tendency towards an overall aggregation of land into individual hands. At least this seems to be the fact in terms of holding sizes. Absentee ownership is common, which means that one owner could be in possession of several holdings, but the size of the holdings remains small, which is an obstacle to structural change. Thus, productivity remains low. In fact, evidence seems to confirm that a countervailing tendency is at work, a tendency towards fragmentation. Fragmentation is partly an effect of population pressure and partly of complicated rules of inheritance.

Multiple ownership of land is more frequent amongst Malays than for Chinese smallholders. Whereas Chinese smallholders tend to have an individualistic outlook and prefer properties of their own, the system of landownership amongst Malays is complicated by Malay customary and Islamic laws. According to the latter the properties of a deceased should be divided among all rightful heirs, 'God thus directs you as regards your children's inheritance: to the male a portion equal to that of two females'.[41] With a growing population the effect has been extreme land fragmentation and multiple ownership. Aggregation of holdings seems to be hindered by an unwillingness among heirs to part with their shares owing to the prestige, status and security of being a landowner.[42] In addition, however, insufficient accumulation could have contributed to the fragmentation. The returns from rubber production have generally been spent on consumption, but the cash received has seldom allowed for accumulation on a larger scale. Thus, smallholders have difficulties in acquiring enough capital to buy out relatives or to acquire land from other smallholders.

With population pressure, fragmentation and low returns smallholders cannot afford to replant their holdings, but have to concentrate their efforts on activities which yield quick returns. Thus, rubber land reverts to jungle-like conditions. One would imagine that abandoned rubber land could be regarded as free and open to acquisition, clearing and planting. In that case the vent for surplus mechanism would be functioning. However, counteracting tendencies are at work. The land is not free in a legal sense. If abandoned land is reopened and brought back into cultivation, the land could be claimed by the legal owner. In contrast to the years of early expansion there is little free land to be developed in a legal sense. On the contrary the system of land registration seems to protect the interests of absentee owners and prevent smallholders from opening up new land.[43]

The prospects for the poor rubber smallholders seem extremely gloomy. The need for structural change is urgent and it is difficult to foresee any future for the small-scale peasants unless such changes are achieved. The official rubber policy seems to have been successful in promoting structural change leading to improvements in productivity for larger and medium size holdings. On the other hand the policy has done little to improve the position of the poorest strata of smallholders. Land development programmes appear expensive and seem to benefit only small sections of smallholders, whereas the market forces work towards fragmentation, falling returns and increasing poverty. This process involves losses of socio-economic welfare of considerable magnitude. One might hope that people expelled from agriculture could find employment in the rapidly growing modern sector. However, although this might be the case of a certain extent, most people will be exchanging rural poverty for urban poverty.

Notes

1. Peacock (1979), p. 377.
2. In 1975, 59 per cent of the families who relied on rubber smallholdings for their income were living below the poverty line. It has been estimated that 4 acres of high yielding rubber is needed to raise a farmer above this line. Half of all rubber holdings are below this size. See ibid., p. 384.
3. See Figart (1925).
4. For a further discussion see Gunnarsson (1979), pp. 65 ff.
5. For a discussion on the introduction of rubber in Malaya, see Barlow (1979).
6. Figart (1925). See also Gunnarsson (1979), pp. 20-3.
7. See for instance the works of Baran (1957); Frank (1967); Amin (1975).
8. Knowles (1924), discusses discrimination against smallholders.
9. Lee (1973), p. 441.
10. Drabble (1979), p. 74.
11. Chayanov, (1966).
12. Myint (1958).
13. Ibid., p. 317 ff.
14. For a critical discussion on the vent for surplus theory see Findlay (1970), pp. 70-3.
15. Lundgren (1984) argues that the vent for surplus is relevant as an explanation of the integration of the forestry region of Northern Sweden into an internationally controlled system between 1870 and 1910.
16. Thus, the term 'land surplus economy' used by Helleiner is inappropriate. Helleiner (1966).
17. Lewis (1954).
18. The experience of cocoa in West Africa is, however, similar. For a discussion see Gunnarsson (1978).
19. Thoburn (1978).
20. Drabble (1979), p. 73.
21. Mc Hale (1965), p. 42.
22. Bauer (1953), p. 91.
23. Lewis (1970), p. 19.
24. Drabble (1972), pp. 247-61.
25. Fryer and Jackson (1966), p. 199.
26. Drabble (1973), pp. 70-1.
27. Drabble (1979), pp. 75-6.
28. There is an interesting debate regarding the relevance of the vent for surplus theory to the early expansion of cocoa in West Africa. For a review see Berry (1975), pp. 1-8.

29. Gunnarsson (1979), p. 52.
30. Barlow (1978).
31. The discussion following is basically derived from Gunnarsson (1979), pp. 52–85.
32. Ibid., p. 56.
33. Ibid., p. 57.
34. Ibid.
35. Census of Agriculture 1960, quoted in Gunnarsson (1979), p. 62.
36. Lee (1977).
37. Ibid., pp. 8–9.
38. Figures derived from Rubber Statistical Handbook 1975, quoted in Gunnarsson (1979), p. 74.
39. Crotty (1978), p. 231.
40. For further discussion, see Gunnarsson (1979), pp. 52–78. For a thorough discussion on rubber policy see Rudner (1970), (1979), (1981) and (1983).
41. Crotty (1978), p. 237.
42. Voon Phin Keong (1972), p. 73.
43. Crotty (1978), p. 73. See also Rudner (1981), who argues that the emerging strata of high-yielding producers use their political influence to secure policies that deny resources to the smallest and poorest producers, who if they would or could modernise would become low cost competitors.

Bibliography

Amin S. *Accumulation on a World Scale* (New York, 1975).
Baran, P. *The Political Economy of Growth* (New York, 1957).
Barlow, C. *The Natural Rubber Industry* (London, 1978).
Bauer, P.T. 'Malayan Rubber Policies', *Political Science Quarterly*, vol. 72, (1953).
____, *The Rubber Industry* (London, 1948).
Berry, S. *Cocoa, Custom and Socio-Economic Change in Rural Western Nigeria* (London, 1975).
Chayanov, A.V., in D. Thorner (ed.) *The Theory of Peasant Economy* (Homewood, 1966).
Crotty, R. 'Constraints on Smallholder Treecropping in Malaysia', *Internationales Asienforum*, vol. 9 (1978).
Drabble, J.H. 'Investment in the Rubber Industry in Malaya 1900–22', *Journal of Southeast Asian Studies* vol. 3 (1972).
____, *Rubber in Malaya 1876–1922, The Genesis of the Industry* (Kuala Lumpur, 1973).
____, 'Peasant Smallholders in the Malayan Economy: An Historical Study with Special Reference to the Rubber Industry,' in Jackson and Rubber (eds.) *Issues in Malaysian Development* (Singapore, 1979).
Figart, D.M. *The Plantation Rubber Industry in the Middle East* (U.S. Government Printing Office, Washington, 1925).
Findlay, R. *Trade and Specialization* (Harmondsworth, 1970).
Fisk, E.K. 'Productivity and Income from Rubber in an Established Malay Reservation', *Malayan Economic Review*, vol. 6 (1961).
Frank, A.G., *Capitalism and Underdevelopment in Latin America* (New York, 1967).
Fryer, D.W. and Jackson, J.C. 'Peasant Producers or Urban Planters? The Chinese Rubber Smallholders of Ulu Selangor', *Pacific Viewpoint*, vol. 7 (1966).
Gunnarsson, C. *The Gold Coast Cocoa Industry 1900–39* (Lund 1978).
____, *Malaysian Rubber Production, Patterns of Growth 1900–1975*, Meddelande

från Ekonomisk historiska institutionen, nr 6, Lund 1979.

Helleiner, G.K. 'Typology in Development Theory: The Land Surplus Economy', *Food Research Institute Studies*, vol. 6 (1966).

Knowles, L. *Economic Development of the Overseas Empire* (London, 1924).

Lee, E. *Rural Poverty in West Malaysia 1957 to 1970*, World Employment Programme Research, ILO, 1977.

Lee, G. 'Commodity Production and Reproduction amongst the Malay Peasantry', *Journal of Contemporary Asia*, vol. 3 (1973).

Lewis, W.A. 'Economic Development with Unlimited Supplies of Labour', *Manchester School*, vol. 22 (1954).

____ *Tropical Development 1880–1913* (London, 1970).

Lundgren, N.G., *Skog för export* (Timber for Export; Forest Work, Technology in the Lule Valley 1870–1970) (Umeå, 1984).

McHale, T. 'Rubber Smallholdings in Malaya', *Malayan Economic Review* vol. 10, (1965).

Myint, H. 'The Classical Theory of International Trade and the Underdeveloped Country', *Economic Journal*, vol. 68, (1958).

Peacock, F. 'The Failure of Rural Development in Peninsular Malaysia, in Jackson and Rudner', (eds.) *Issues in Malaysian Development* (Singapore, 1979).

Rudner, M. 'Rubber Strategy for Post-War Malaya 1945–1948', *Journal of Tropical Geography*, vol. 34 (1972).

____, 'The State and Peasant Innovation in Rural Development: The Case of Malayan Rubber', *Asian and African Studies*, vol. 6 (1970).

____, 'Development Policies and Patterns of Agrarian Dominance in the Malaysian Rubber Export Economy', *Modern Asian Studies*, vol. 15 (1981).

____, 'Changing Planning Perspectives on Agricultural Development in Malaysia', *Modern Asian Studies*, vol. 17 (1983).

Thoburn, J. *Primary Commodity Exports and Economic Development* (London, 1978).

Voon Phin Keong, 'Size Aspects of Rubber Smallholdings in West Malaysia: A Case Study of Bentong, Pahang', *Journal of Tropical Geography*, vol. 34 (1972).

PART THREE
TRADE IN PRIMARY PRODUCTS

8 THE IMPACT OF PRIMARY EXPORTS ON THE GHANAIAN ECONOMY: LINKAGES AND LEAKAGES FROM MINING AND COCOA 1956-69

Edward Horesh and Susan Joekes

1. Introduction

The value of international trade to development used to be assessed simply in terms of comparative advantage. In the last 25 years or so, assessment has shifted towards a less abstract consideration of the contribution of specific economic activities in fostering others within the domestic economy. 'Linkages' and 'leakages' are two of the ruling concepts in this type of evaluation. Linkages exist whenever an ongoing activity gives rise to economic pressures that lead to the taking up of a new activity. Leakages are the loss to the national economy of some of the income generated by an activity; they are one set of economic factors which hinder or prevent the development of linkages. In this paper we examine the economic effects of the two main exporting activities in Ghana in relation to these two concepts.

Neither term has a standard operational definition. The concept of linkage was related first to the production characteristics of particular activities. Baldwin[1] argued that what would now be called 'direct production linkages' — deriving from the input-output matrix[2] — stem from the characteristics of the production function which differ between industries. He cited mining as an example of a common type of activity from which few local linkages could be expected in a poor country. The economic activities linked to mining (refining and smelting of ores downstream, production of mining machinery and equipment as it were upstream) could be done at lower cost in the metropolitan countries because of economies of scale in each case. 'Indirect production linkages' occur when otherwise unrelated activities can benefit — through reduced production costs — from infrastructural and other services set up to service the first activity.

Hirschman's 'generalised linkage approach'[3] widened the definition of linkages in an attempt to formalise 'staple theory' and display

181

the set of conjunctures within an economy which would favour development. Two of his themes are relevant to this paper. First, Hirschman proposes that 'consumption linkages' arise as export revenues grow and retained incomes are spent on consumer goods. The possibilities for import substitution are obvious. He points to a less obvious *negative* linkage which might then follow. Local traditional industry might be undermined or destroyed as a result of the combined effect of the withdrawal of labour into import substituting industry and the competition from imports. Secondly, 'fiscal linkages' are realised through the ability of the State to tax staple exports and channel the proceeds into productive investment. He argues that these fiscal linkages are strongest in the case of 'enclave' activities which are characterised by the absence of other types of linkage. To the extent that such an industry (unlike a peasant industry) is controlled and owned by foreigners, it is easier to tax.

The 'leakage' concept has similarly become vague and multifarious. Weisskoff and Wolff for example count the export of raw materials as a leakage since it precludes the possibility of a forward linkage to processing.[4] Without quarrelling with this approach, the conventional accounting definition of income not retained locally but lost through remittances from labour incomes and profits is more attractive for practical purposes. Such outflows hinder the growth of consumption and investment by reducing disposable personal incomes and the local supply of investible funds. The 'leakage' concept is closely related to the 'development of underdevelopment' analysis which emphasises the negative effects of metropolitan investment on peripheral economies.

It is of course extremely difficult to quantify linkages and leakages according to almost all of these definitions for any economy. In the case of Ghana, however, there is enough data to analyse the more concrete and immediate effects stemming from the two main exporting activities. The purpose of this paper is accordingly to examine the linkages and leakages associated with mining and cocoa production in Ghana. Mining and cocoa are large industries whose production accounted for 4.5 per cent and 15 per cent of Ghana's GDP at factor cost respectively at the end of the 1960s and which at that time, with their output all exported in both cases, between them accounted for over three-quarters of Ghana's total exports. The limitations of published data mean that it is unfortunately only possible to present estimates for a short period, 1956–69; nevertheless, this period is of some special historical interest as it relates to the economic situation during the first fourteen years of Ghana's independence.

The main empirical base for this paper is data on industrial income in mining and cocoa. In the following sections we first derive the functional distributions of income in the two sectors between labour (local and foreign), the government and profits. It is well known that the mining industry employed a considerable number of highly paid European staff whose remittances could account for significant leakages. Less obvious is the fact that the cocoa industry employed a significant number of foreign low paid workers and the possibility of significant leakages from their incomes must be considered. In fact, these leakages were small, but in order to establish this, it is necessary to discuss in some detail the organisation of labour and, therefore, the distribution of income between nationals and foreigners in cocoa as well as in mining. We go on to consider the consumption and fiscal linkages and leakages of income associated with the two activities. We then briefly examine the production linkages promoted by the two industries since their inception at the end of the nineteenth century. In the concluding section we draw out the implications from the Ghanaian experience for the theorising which has been done in this area.

2. Mining

The establishment of mines and plantations in less developed countries seems historically to have been almost invariably done in 'enclaves' dependent on the introduction of foreign capital, management and technology. With respect to mining the literature normally stresses the heavy capital intensity and scale economies which necessitated foreign initiative. It is therefore well to remember Hopkins' contrary view that in a number of cases 'the prominence of expatriate companies could be more accurately explained in terms of the need to confer rights to encourage prospecting and the convenience of collecting royalties and taxes'.[5] Of the three main minerals exported from Ghana in the period 1956–69 only manganese, the least important, has always been wholly under non-African ownership. The mining of manganese began during the first World War. During the 1960s production fluctuated about a falling trend due to the exhaustion of the single mine in production. Export volume in 1969 was little more than half the 1956 amount.

Gold is more important to the Ghanaian economy. It had been mined long before the first concession was granted to Europeans in 1874. The Europeans used African knowledge to prospect efficiently; the destruction of the indigenous industry which followed and allowed gold mining to become a European expatriate enterprise by the 1890s was not the result of normal market competitive forces.[6] Thenceforth, gold was produced by a small number of foreign companies of varying size and productivity. By 1965, however, they had all — with the major exception of the single largest firm, Ashanti Goldfields, which produced about half of industrial output — been nationalised; Ashanti Goldfields was finally nationalised as well as in 1972.

The diamond sector is the most complex part of the mining industry in Ghana. Throughout the colonial period and beyond, a mixture of local and European capital was involved in what was a heavily dualistic industry. In the foreign, large mines sector the multinational Consolidated African Selection Trust (CAST) dominated four other very small mining companies; all used large-scale mechanised techniques. Alongside them, producing about as many diamonds again, worked a large number of 'diggers' who extracted diamonds by manual surface sieving. The diggers were individual licensees, who each contracted a small number of labourers to carry out the actual sieving on payment of a fee and with the obligation to sell all the diamonds back directly to the digger. Most of the diggers and their contracted labourers were foreign, from nearby African countries. This sort of small scale mining tends to be ignored by development theorists[7] even though it was clearly a major source of employment and foreign exchange, accounting for about two-thirds of employment and one half of output in diamond mining in 1960.[8]

Neither the colonial nor the independent government encouraged small scale diamond sieving, in spite of its high labour productivity. After 1965 licenses were no longer granted at all, contrary to expert advice.[9] The decision was made, curiously, when loss-making mines were being nationalised and kept in operation with the stated objective of maintaining employment. The diggers' licensing system was supposedly stopped to allow one of these companies, the State Diamond Mining Corporation, to expand (though a more direct response would have been to limit the issue of licenses to Ghanaian nationals). The State Corporation was so badly managed, however, that it not only failed to expand but in 1965 produced only one-quarter of the previous year's output. Various other reasons were given at the time to explain the government's move. It was alleged that sieving was technically inefficient (though experts held the contrary opinion), and that it was the only way to stop the drain on the foreign exchanges through smuggling. The latter point interestingly reflects Hopkins' suggestion that large-scale foreign operations give governments greater control over industrial activity. It has also been suggested more prosaically that the responsible minister was corruptedly encouraged to withdraw licences by appointees to the Board of the State Corporation.[10] Finally, it is not impossible that CAST also encouraged prejudice against the diggers, who competed for the same ores. After the suppression of licences CAST markedly increased its capital investment and was able subsequently to expand production and increase its share of the world market without any downward pressure on prices.

2.1 *Employment and Labour Income in Mining*

According to the *Census* there were in total 48,000 workers in the mining sector in 1960, of whom nearly 12,000 were in the small-scale diamond mining sector. The number fell drastically to 24,000 in 1969.

The total labour income series for this workforce is set out in Table 8.1. Labour income accounted for a variable but on average falling share of total mineral export earnings from 1956–69. The fall in the income share and in total employment is due to the elimination of the diggers. Table 8.2 shows that within the company sector labour's income share, though fluctuating from year to year, did not show any tendency to fall.

2.2 *Labour Incomes of Foreigners and their Remittances*

A large number of workers in mining were foreigners whether from other African countries or Europe. As well as many of the diamond diggers and their labourers, companies employed mostly migrant workers, a substantial minority of whom were foreign. A reasonable estimate of the number of foreigners in 1960, based on the *Census* for that year, is 20,600, i.e. 43 per cent of the total mining workforce.

There is no published information about remittances from mining. It is known that European expatriate savings' rates from basic salaries and benefits are usually high, so we have assumed that 50 per cent of skilled income (which is given separately in the company sector accounts) is remitted. As for foreign African workers, we take a much lower proportion (20 per cent). Seasonal migration by high saving 'target' workers has never been important in Ghanaian mining. The remittance series included in Table 8.1 is the sum of these two streams.

2.3 *Mining Companies Profits and Remittances and Total Leakage*

Total mining sector profits fell substantially during the period 1956–69. In the early years, all mining companies were foreign owned and all post-tax profits available for repatriation. In our estimates in Table 8.1 we assume a repatriation rate of 100 per cent.

After 1961 the government proceeded to nationalise the industry firm by firm and the position became more complicated. Information about the subsequent operations of the state owned enterprises is incomplete, though it seems that, like other public enterprises at the time, they operated at a loss.[11] Paradoxically, therefore, profit remittances were probably *greater* than total mining industry profits after the first nationalisations. For example, in 1964 and 1969 the net profits of *foreign* mining companies were 12 per cent and 11 per cent respectively compared to total industrial company profits of 5 per cent in 1964 and losses of 2 per cent in 1969.[12] Unfortunately data does not exist for all the relevant years, so it is impossible to calculate the share of profits in total income of foreign owned companies, and therefore to estimate exactly the level of profit remittances. The share of total company profits in income, 17 per cent over the whole period (Table 8.2), sets the floor; we can say that profit remittances were at least this high.

In 1949 an official but unpublished estimate gave the proportion of gross mining proceeds transferred abroad in profits and personal remittances by Europeans as approximately 50 per cent.[13] As this excluded transfers by African foreigners, it underestimated the *total* income leakage. The foreign company leakage was evidently less in the ensuing period. From 1956–60, when foreign company profits averaged 32 per cent of export proceeds and total personal remittances were just under 6 per cent the leakage was 38 per cent of company income. During the whole of the period 1956–69 the leakage was probably less than this. The average level of company profits (and to a lesser extent the level of profits eligible for repatriation) fell to 17 per cent; with personal remittances roughly constant at 6 per cent, this means that the total income leakage was something

Table 8.1: Exports, Labour Income and Income Shares in the Ghanaian Mining Industry 1956–69

	1956	1957	1958	1959	1960	1961	1962	1963	1964	1965	1966	1967	1968	1969
A. Exports (N¢ million)*														
Gold	15.0	19.6	21.2	22.4	22.2	21.5	22.5	22.6	20.6	18.8	17.5	23.3	28.1	28.9
Diamonds	19.1	18.0	16.0	17.4	16.3	15.0	12.4	8.7	12.1	13.0	13.1	20.4	9.4	12.3
Manganese	14.1	18.0	17.3	13.6	12.8	12.0	11.0	8.0	8.7	10.0	11.8	10.4	9.8	6.8
	46.2	55.6	54.5	53.4	51.3	48.5	45.9	39.3	41.4	41.8	42.4	54.1	47.3	48.0
B. Labour Income (N¢ million)														
Total labour income[a]	19.5	20.1	21.0	20.3	18.6	16.8	15.4	15.2	13.7	10.0	11.7	12.9	14.4	15.9
of which:														
Income to Ghanaians	7.0	7.2	7.6	7.6	7.1	6.7	6.5	6.5	5.9	4.6	5.4	6.5	7.5	8.7
Income to African foreigners[b]	9.6	9.9	10.2	9.7	8.4	7.3	5.9	5.7	4.5	3.1	3.8	3.6	4.1	4.7
Income to non-African foreigners	2.9	3.0	3.2	3.0	3.1	2.8	3.0	3.0	3.3	2.3	2.5	2.8	2.8	2.8
Remittances	3.4	3.5	3.6	2.4	3.3	2.9	2.7	2.6	2.5	1.8	2.1	2.1	2.2	2.0
C. Income shares (percentage)														
Labour income	42	36	39	38	36	35	34	39	33	24	28	24	24	33
Payments to government[c]	8	9	15	16	15	24	25	33	31	43	44	23	37	40
Company post-tax gross profits	30	35	22	21	24	13	14	–8	5	4	7	33	2	–2
Total remittances out of labour incomes and profits	38	41	29	26	31	19	20	–1	11	9	12	37	7	2

* Throughout these tables conversions are at the following rates: £G = N¢ 2, ¢ = N¢ 1.2

Notes: (a) Includes diggers' self-employed incomes.
(b) For calculation of African foreigners' income and remittances see Section 2.2.
(c) Data on payments to government and company profits presented in Table 8.2.

Sources: Ghana Central Bureau of Statistics, Ghana Chamber of Mines; Killick (1966) (for manganese).

Table 8.2:   Gross Earnings, Disbursements and Profits of Ghanaian Mining Companies 1956–69

	1956	1957	1958	1959	1960	1961	1962	1963	1964	1965	1966	1967	1968	1969
A. *By Value* (N¢ million)														
Gross Earnings:														
Exports by mining companies	37.0	45.9	44.6	43.9	44.2	42.7	42.7	36.5	40.3	41.5	42.1	54.0	47.2	48.0
Disbursements:														
Wages	10.1	10.4	11.1	10.7	11.4	11.1	12.2	12.4	12.6	9.9	11.4	12.7	14.3	15.8
Inputs (imported & locally purchased)	9.2	11.0	13.0	13.4	12.4	13.8	14.4	14.0	12.8	11.6	8.8	11.4	14.4	14.2
Payments to Government	3.6	5.2	8.4	8.5	7.9	11.7	11.7	13.1	13.0	18.1	18.7	12.2	17.5	19.3
Gross Profits post-tax:														
Earnings less Disbursements	14.1	19.3	12.1	11.3	12.5	6.1	6.4	-3.0	1.9	1.9	3.2	17.7	0.9	-1.2
B. *Income Shares* (Percentage)														
Labour income	27	21	25	24	26	26	29	34	31	24	27	24	30	33
Payments to Government	10	11	19	19	18	27	27	36	32	74	44	23	37	40
Post-tax gross profits	38	42	27	26	28	14	15	-8	5	5	8	33	2	-2
Total remittances out of factor in-comes[a]	38	41	29	26	31	19	20	-1	11	9	12	37	7	2

Note: (a) Remittances are underestimated from 1961 onwards. See Section 2.3.
Sources: As Table 8.1.

above 23 per cent — still of course a very sizeable proportion of export proceeds.

2.4 *Payments to Government*

The fall in net company profits in the latter part of the period 1956–69 was due not to the nationalisations of foreign companies but to the shift in the distribution of total mining income to the government in taxes. The mining companies were subject to two different corporate taxes. The first, Minerals Tax, was a tax specific to the industry, applied above a certain level of profitability. Although the rate of this tax did not change, increased profits among some companies led to higher tax payments in the latter half of the 1960s.[14] Secondly, companies had to pay standard corporation tax. Some increases in the rate raised the tax bill somewhat, but more importantly the Central Revenue Department tightened up its definition of 'assessable and chargeable' income.[15] No allowance has been made for nationalised companies losses (see Section 2.3 above).

2.5 *The Distribution of Mining Income*

The following features stand out from Tables 8.1.C and 8.2.B. First, over the period labour income fell, both absolutely and as a share of total mining income. The size of the labour force also fell, by 53 per cent. In money terms the average rate rose by 70 per cent — but prices doubled in the period,[16] so that despite the increases in labour productivity suggested by the data, real wages fell and with them the potential for consumption linkages.

Secondly, there was a complementary fall in the share of post-tax profits, from 36 per cent in 1956–8 to 12 per cent in 1967–9. It was only in the last year of the period, when companies were ordered to pay a retrospective excess profits tax, that they registered an actual loss.

Thirdly, the most striking feature is the steady increase of the state's share of total mining income reflecting the declining shares of labour and corporate income. Over the total period 62 per cent of gross operating profits were paid over in taxes. The tax changes described above allowed the state to increase its share of operating income in mining from 8 per cent of export proceeds in 1956 to 40 per cent in 1969. The precondition for realising fiscal linkages was therefore met on a considerable scale.

3. Cocoa

3.1 *Cocoa Farming — a Peasant Enclave?*

The Ghanaian cocoa industry only partially conforms to the conventional picture of a peasant export industry, with small family farms specialising in the production of a cash crop exported through the agency of middlemen or a marketing board. Although ownership of cocoa farms is exclusively local and farms are typically small, labour is by no means wholly 'family'. There is a complicated labour market with substantial migration, both seasonal and long term, and a large number of foreigners in the labour force. Undoubtedly, however, the role of the State Marketing Board with its monopoly on sales abroad has been important in the recent period, especially in relation to the distribution of cocoa income within Ghana.

The story of the introduction of cocoa and its rapid spread during the last decade of the nineteenth and first decade of the twentieth century in the face of the hostility of the colonial government is well known. Export crops were already being grown by a number of farmers; new cocoa farms were financed from the surpluses of rubber production. Hopkins has explained the absence of concessions to foreign plantations in terms of the political opportunism of local traders and the bourgeoisie who stood to gain from continued production in African hands.[17] Szereszewski's explanation of the growth in cocoa, based on a vent for surplus model,[18] has often been challenged, recently by Ingham who argues convincingly that the innovative cocoa farmers were activated by conventional entrepreneurial calculations.[19] This corroborates Hill's description of changes in land use as well as labour migration — a denial of the vent for surplus model which depends on new uses for idle land and labour.[20] Though the cocoa industry was established without European assistance, the expatriate buyers moved in early (around 1908) and soon the international trade was in their hands. It was quickly cartelised; by 1925, cocoa farmers were facing monopsonistic traders.[21] The leakage of cocoa income through the abnormal profits of the cartel was stemmed by the introduction of the Cocoa Marketing Board after the second World War whereby the surpluses could be appropriated by the State and retained locally.

3.2 *Labour Organisation in the Production of Cocoa*

There is a wide variation in cocoa farm size and type.[22] Large farms tend to be worked by hired and small farms by family labour.

Almost all farms have food crops interspersed with the cocoa trees and most labour is also engaged in off-farm activities. This continued lack of specialisation is mainly due to the highly seasonal pattern of demand for labour, which is concentrated at main harvest time between October and December. There is a second minor peak in July when weeding has to be done on both young and mature bearing trees.

There have been several field surveys and other investigations into cocoa employment patterns, where the situation is analysed in terms of types of employment contract.[23] A four-way classification of employment types is generally used:

1. FARMERS: the self employed owners of cocoa land who may hire in extra labour.

2. ABUSAMEN: who work unsupervised on bearing farms for which they are paid a share, most commonly one-third, of the crop they help to produce. They may themselves hire labour. The abusa system signifies a particular form of payment and the existence of an open-ended employment contract, not an autonomous 'managerial' position.

3. ANNUAL or SEASONAL LABOURERS: are employed mainly on new farms tending young trees before they come into bearing. They are provided with food, clothes and lodging by the farmer as well as cash wages. The contract may be for a year or only six months.

4. CASUAL or 'BY-DAY' LABOUR: is used widely in preparing new ground for cocoa and in work on mature bearing trees. According to the degree of supervision required there is either a short-term employment contract or supervised 'by-day' work. Wages are paid in cash and often food is provided as well.

This variety of contracts is well adapted to the particular processes in cocoa cultivation. The clearing and preparing of ground for planting is a one-off job for which by-day labour can be used; once seedlings are planted they require continuous care for which a supervised annual fixed payment contract is most suitable. The sharecropping abusamen have an interest in the successful completion of the harvest; the farmers spread the risk of crop shortfall by this arrangement and avoid the need for costly supervision.

3.3 *Estimating the Relative Size of Employment Categories*

No single estimate of the numbers, or even the proportions, of workers in each of these categories exists. The supposedly comprehensive 1960 *Census of Population* seriously underestimates the true numbers: the reference day was in March, a slack period, so that temporary full-time harvest-time (as well as all part-time) workers were excluded. Using other sources to correct the *Census* data[24], estimates of the relative labour contributions and income shares over a representative year are shown in Table 8.3.

Table 8.3: Estimated Labour Contribution, Income Share and Proportion of Foreigners by Category of Worker in the Ghanaian Cocoa Industry: Percentages

Category of Worker	Labour Contribution	Income Share	Number of Foreigners
Farmers	34	75	0
Abusamen	27	15	50
Annual and seasonal	24	4	45
By-day	15	6	33

The labour contribution estimate relates to the age structure of the tree stock, the distribution of tasks across labour categories and the production techniques current in the particular regions and dates at which the various source studies were carried out. There is not enough information about changes in any of these variables through time and place for it to be possible to suggest how the estimates should be modified to provide a more reliable picture to cover the whole period. The figures should be taken therefore only as a very partial attempt to indicate orders of magnitude.

3.4 *Shares of Personal Incomes by Employment Category*

The categorisation of labour contracts is based on specialisation of function rather than differentiation of skills. Most workers seem able to do each others' jobs, though farmers and abusamen tend to be more experienced. However, because of the partially segmented nature of the cocoa labour market earnings are not equalised by mobility of labour between categories. Annual labourers are explicitly bound to a single employer; the provision of lodging helps to enforce this. By-day labourers cannot take up other kinds of contract during the season. On the other hand, both abusamen and farmers can supplement their earnings by supplying extra casual labour at peak times. Rourke and Sakyi-Gyinae estimate that abusamen may increase their earnings by half as much again in this way.[25] Thus inter-category mobility within the season is practised by those who are primarily abusamen or farmers, but not by annual or by-day labourers.

There is some direct and indirect empirical evidence on cocoa workers' incomes. Combining this with the estimates of labour contributions presented in Table 8.3 gives the relative shares of personal incomes estimates set out in the second column of the table. Farmers earn by far the largest share (75 per cent of gross income) followed by abusamen with 15 per cent. Short and longer fixed term labourers each get less than 10 per cent of total income. Farmers' share of net income is reduced by the amount they have to spend on current and capital inputs, which seem to be very small although there are no quantitative estimates of average expenditure. It should also be noted that farmers' income is in one respect distinct from other personal incomes: it includes a part which represents a return on the capital invested in land and cocoa trees.

These estimates tally with information from two surveys of cocoa farm income carried out between 1956 and 1957 in the two large growing regions together producing about half the total cocoa crop in Ghana.[26] In one case the division of income between farmers and hired labour of all kinds was 77:23 and in the other 73:27. Our estimate falls between these two, which lends it plausibility. However, both these surveys and our estimates overestimate the share of income going to farmers. Only farms with mature bearing trees generate any current cocoa income; owners of entirely new cocoa farms without any mature trees are normally excluded from income surveys. Okali suggests that a large number of cocoa workers are employed on entirely new farms, wage payments to them often being financed by credit raised by the employer-farmer against expected future cocoa income.[27] In any case, it is clear that farmers' net cocoa income is reduced and the shares of annual and casual labour employed on young trees correspondingly increased. But it is impossible to quantify the adjustment.

Another factor to consider is the return attributable to the labour of cocoa workers' families, whose share cannot be assessed separately. Farmers, and probably to a lesser extent abusamen, have family labour to call on, but not other categories of cocoa workers. Therefore the true personal incomes of farmers and abusamen are lower than appears from our estimates, but again it is impossible to quantify the necessary adjustment.

3.5 The Distribution of Foreigners by Employment Category and their Income Share

There is general agreement that there are no foreigners among the cocoa farmers but a substantial number in each of the other three groups. That is to say, foreigners are concentrated in the lower paid categories and are therefore unlikely to earn the same proportion of total personal income as they contribute to total labour input. The proportion of foreigners among abusamen was 50 per cent according to the 1960 *Census* which is unreliable as a guide to the number of foreigners in other categories, because of the seasonality problem noted above. Our estimates suggest that the total contribution of foreigners to labour input was 29 per cent. But foreigners' share of total income is less — of the order of half this amount. (As noted above however, foreigners' incomes derived from the creation of new farms are not included.)

3.6 Remitted Income

Again there is no direct evidence of the propensity of foreign workers to save or remit cocoa earnings. However, among migrants in West Africa in general, both the proportion of workers who make remittances and the proportion of income they send tend to be high.[28] The large number of seasonal migrants who provide by-day and annual cocoa labour fit the stereotype of foreign target savers aiming to save the maximum possible out of their earnings and then go home quickly. On the other hand wage levels are low with little margin for saving. It therefore seems reasonable to take an intermediate fraction for their remittances (25 per cent) so that remittances would amount to only about 2½ per cent of total cocoa income.

3.7 The Cocoa Marketing Board (CMB) and the State

All cocoa in Ghana is statutorily purchased by the CMB, a parastatal agency, which then sells the crop on the world market. The CMB therefore receives as revenue the total realised export value of the cocoa crop. The CMB surplus is what remains after payments for purchases of cocoa at the official producer price have been made to the farmers, the cocoa export duty has been paid, the CMB has defrayed the cost of some of the production inputs supplied to the farmers at a subsidised rate (bags, spraying machines and insecticides), and has covered its own operating expenses. The surplus was originally intended as a means of maintaining reserves to stabilise the producer price and to finance improvements in the production of cocoa. But this purely sectoral role has long been superseded. The CMB surplus and reserves now represent an important source of extra finance for general public expenditure.

Cocoa duty constitutes by far the largest sole item in government revenues attributable to export earnings and it has often been the largest item in government revenues altogether, averaging 20 per cent of the total from 1956 to 1969. The way that cocoa duty is formulated however has made the state revenues from cocoa very unstable about this average (Table 8.4). Cocoa duty is a 'progressive' *ad valorem* tax, the rate varying directly with the volatile world price of cocoa. As a proportion of total government revenues cocoa duty fluctuated between 7 per cent in 1965 and 1966 and 30 per cent in 1969.[29]

Table 8.4 shows the distribution of export revenues from cocoa between the State and the farms.[30] Over the whole period cocoa duty and CMB operational costs and surpluses accounted for about one-third of export earnings, with the remaining two-thirds going to the farms. The pattern of distribution varied from year to year in accordance with the size of the crop and the world cocoa price, which were inversely related throughout this period.[31]

The period 1956–69 was marked by a series of very large harvests and low world prices in the first half of the 1960s, when cocoa duty payments were low and the distribution of cocoa income was greatly in favour of the farms. In the culminating 1964/5 season the farmers were paid more than the CMB received from export sales as the world price virtually collapsed below the cocoa producer price (low as it was) set at the beginning of the cocoa season. The distributional picture was soon reversed as the tonnage exported fell back and the world price doubled between 1965 and 1968. Even in 1964/5, despite the receipt of an unprecedentedly high share of export incomes, farmers' gross receipts were less than half the real value of five years before. The slight recovery in farmers' gross receipts in the last two years of the period was undermined by a rapid reduction in expenditure out of the CMB surplus on subsidised production inputs for farmers. The index of public expenditure on the cocoa sector fell from 100 in 1960/1 to 21 in 1968/9.[32]

Table 8.4: The Distribution of Cocoa Income

	1956/7	1957/8	1958/9	1959/60	1960/1	1961/2	1962/3	1963/4	1964/5	1965	1966	1967	1968	1969[a]
A. *By Value* (N¢ million)														
Export sales	101.4	125.7	141.9	139.8	143.3	138.1	138.2	153.8	51.4	(119.7)	127.0	156.4	217.2	245.4
Cocoa duty	23.9	53.8	51.1	38.8	31.0	25.6	26.9	33.9	9.9	(15.9)	21.6	40.4	84.9	119.7
Cost of purchases = farmers' gross receipts[b]	86.5	60.6	74.3	90.3	121.7	127.6	124.4	109.4	52.1	(112.1)	95.3	78.9	103.9	123.5
CMB costs	12.4	9.0	10.6	13.6	22.0	26.2	20.8	23.0	11.9	(12.9)	21.3	20.8	17.2	10.7
CMB current operating surplus[c]	−21.4	2.3	5.9	−2.9	−31.4	−41.3	−33.9	−12.5	−22.5	(−21.2)	−11.2	16.3	11.2	−8.5
B. *Income Shares*[d] (Percentage)														
Farmers' gross income	85	48	52	65	85	92	90	71	101	(94)	75	50	48	50
Income to the state														
Cocoa duty	24	43	36	20	22	18	19	22	19	(13)	17	26	54	49
Cocoa duty plus CMB surplus	2	45	40	30	0	−12	−6	14	−25	(−5)	−8	36	59	46

Notes:

(a) The data years are not consistently crop or calendar years, as the CMB changed the basis of its accounts from the former to the latter in 1965. 1965 data cannot be adequately compiled from either or both the 19th and 20th *Reports* and are reproduced in brackets to indicate the lack of comparability.

(b) Farmers' receipts refers to production rather than export of cocoa.

(c) CMB surplus is taken as a residual after cocoa duty, farmers' receipts and marketing costs are subtracted from export sales proceeds. The official published statement of CMB surplus includes changes in cocoa stocks and income from investments. See note 30.

(d) Farmers' gross income and income to the state as percentages of the value of export sales each year. In years when these two 'variables (plus CMB costs which do not enter into this calculation) summed to more than the value of export receipts the deficit was made up from accumulated CMB reserves.

Source: Ghana Cocoa Marketing Board

In broad outline therefore the functional distribution of income evolved similarly in cocoa as in mining. Personal labour incomes fell, while the share of the state rose dramatically in both absolute and relative terms. The government of the newly independent state showed itself vastly more effective than its colonial predecessor in capturing a portion of value added in both the main export sectors.

4. Linkages and Leakages in Mining and Cocoa

We have now to relate the data on mining and cocoa incomes to the various aspects of the concepts of linkages and leakages identified as crucial to the evaluation of the economic impact of an activity. We consider income-related linkages and leakages first, and then go on to production linkages.

4.1 *Consumption Linkages*

The early period of national independence in Ghana which is the subject of this paper was marked in both the main export industries by a sustained reduction in the share of personal labour incomes and a concomitant increase in the share of income going to the state in tax. An examination of the distribution of industrial incomes makes it clear that there may often be in practice a trade-off between consumption and fiscal linkages — an increase in one is likely to be at the expense of the other.

The potential for consumption linkages associated with both mining and cocoa was eroded during the years 1956–69 as real wages and total local disposable personal incomes fell. Such evidence as there is suggests that the consumption patterns were not in any case conducive to stimulating local activity. The income elasticity of demand for imports of consumer goods (mainly food and textiles) was high, and significantly higher in the rural than in the urban areas.[33] In many areas of the country, cocoa provided the main source of income to the rural population, so these effects can also be ascribed to expenditure out of cocoa earnings. Even personal savings (considerable for larger cocoa farmers) did not boost local production and accumulation: personal investment expenditure was mainly on import-intensive housing, imported vehicles and education for farmers' children.

4.2 Fiscal Linkages

The shift in the distribution of incomes away from personal incomes could therefore have had some justification in macro-economic terms. The potential for developing local productive activity might well have been greater out of public than private personal expenditure.

In both mining and cocoa the increase in the state's share of industrial income was very marked over the period studied. The most notable finding in relation to the literature on linkages is that Hirschman's proposition that the normally friendless foreign enclave is more likely than the peasant sector to have stronger fiscal linkages is not confirmed. Over the period 1956–69 payments to the state in cocoa duty totalled 28 per cent of total cocoa proceeds, compared to corporate tax payments from mining of 27 per cent. The relatively high figure in mining was only achieved through a steady and deliberate attempt on the part of the government to increase its share of mining income above the minimal level prevailing under the colonial administration. The previous history of the mining enclave was of virtual non-payment of any tax to the local government (either directly or indirectly: there were no inter-government developmental transfers):

> Until the 1930s income taxes were paid to the British and not to the Ghanaian Treasury, and in the 1940s and 1950s taxes paid to Ghana were from 10 to 15 per cent of output. Tariffs on fuel oil used by the mining sector have been kept low.[34]

It is a moot point whether occasional deficits of the Cocoa Marketing Board ought not also to be included in State income, bringing down its share of cocoa income from 28 per cent to 14 per cent from 1956 to 1969. In that case Hirschman's proposition would be valid for this particular period. The short period studied here, however, included an abnormally severe run of deficits by historical standards; even so it was largely financed out of accumulated reserves, testifying to the CMB's average surplus-generating performance over the long run. In the longer term, taking account of the greater accumulated marketing board surplus on the one hand and the low past tax payments out of mining on the other, it remains true that the local peasant sector was not a lesser contributor to the state revenues than the foreign owned enclave.

Hirschman also makes the point that fiscal linkage does not end with the gathering of taxes: it is strengthened by wise public spend-ing. Insofar as colonial governments tended not to spend and post-colonial governments tended to spend unwisely, the fiscal linkage was weakened. The parsimony of the former[35] and the recklessness of the latter[36] have been well documented. The failure of the inde-pendent government to invest effectively does not however alter the fact that the cocoa industry made a major contribution in *providing* investible resources to the public sector. The government could per-haps be charged with over-taxation of the cocoa industry insofar as low producer prices, the instrument of tax collection, were a cause of the chronic decline of cocoa production which has continued in Ghana to the present day. But the failure could be said to be one of investment rather than of taxation, that is that the resources returned by the state to the cocoa sector to expand and improve methods of production were insufficient. An appropriate level of investment might have been achieved as well out of public as private funds at the actual level of taxation.

4.3 *Leakages*

Income leakages are the direct consequence of foreign participation in an economic activity. It is a common charge against the 'enclave' that a high proportion of profit and managerial and other skilled expatriate income is leaked. In large scale mining in Ghana, it is estimated that from 1956 to 1969 with inputs imported, and profits and a portion of foreign workers' wages and salaries remitted abroad, only about half of gross export proceeds was retained in net foreign exchange earnings. The leakages out of export proceeds net of imported inputs was approximately 23 per cent in mining com-pared to only 3 per cent in cocoa, where the imported inputs were very small. Non-retained incomes in cocoa were almost all accounted for by leakage of foreign African workers' remittances.

The term 'enclave' does not fit the small scale diamond mining industry even though the diggers' activities seem to have been just as loosely articulated with the local economy as large-scale mining, the income leakage to have been comparable and the contribution to the State revenues probably even less. It is not just that diamond sieving is not visibly foreign: that its organisation and technology are closer to the peasant than the capitalist style. The crucial distinction between European and African enterprise lies in the consequences of repatriation of profits. European profit repatriation (unlike intra-African) contributes to the process of concentration of capital in the metropolis and thereby to the conditions ensuring the failure of capital accumulation in the periphery. This dual process was manifest in Ghana in the rapid suppression of indigenous gold mining in the nineteenth century alongside the establishment of foreign mines and the elimination of small-scale foreign-owned diamond mining and the expansion of the large-scale multinational industry in the 1960s.

4.4 *Direct Production Linkages*

The income and expenditure data examined for mining and cocoa does not illuminate the development or otherwise of production linkages. That is, it does not reveal to what extent the production backwards of inputs of intermediate and capital goods for mining and cocoa production or the further processing of minerals and cocoa was stimulated locally in Ghana.

The literature makes it clear that very little directly linked activity did spring up. Both cocoa and minerals continued to be exported almost entirely in their raw, unprocessed state. This was not merely the result of a weak local entrepreneurial response. The possibility of forward linkages in cocoa was curtailed by the oligopsonistic conditions of the cocoa market and the structure of import duties in the metropolitan countries which discriminated heavily in favour of the raw product. In mining, similar import duties were important together with the prevalence of foreign ownership. The local mines fitted into the vertically integrated and worldwide operations of multinational firms, which restricted their role to that of suppliers of raw materials.

As regards backward linkages all machinery and other capital equipment for mining was imported, accounting for more than 60 per cent of production costs.[37] While some stores were purchased locally, these were mainly traditional consumer goods and there was no upgrading of local products to meet what might have been a source of more sophisticated demand. Backward production linkages in the cocoa industry have been investigated by Gordon. The local production of jute bags was an important high-value added activity and a large vehicle repair and maintenance industry was established to service cocoa transport vehicles (the vehicles themselves were imported). On the other hand, there was a notable failure to develop local production of pesticide sprays and spraying machines.[38]

4.5 *Indirect Linkages: Mining, Cocoa and Economic Development*

There remains the indirect impact of the cocoa and mining industries on Ghanaian productive capacity to be investigated. Indirect linkages arise most obviously when infrastructural improvements made for the first activity stimulate new activities which can also make use of them or promote already existing ones whose efficiency is increased. The changes can be more or less far reaching. During the period 1891–1911 when the mining and cocoa industries were rapidly expanding dramatic changes in the structure of the Ghanaian economy did occur,[39] not all beneficial. The establishment of the gold industry induced infrastructural development such as the railway line from Kumasi terminating at Sekondi where harbour facilities were developed. But this choice of location was detrimental to cocoa producers whose principal growing areas lay far to the east. At first, the farmers themselves built roads and bridges to head-load their produce directly South to the coast. When the railroad was extended to link with the cocoa areas, it appeared as a negative linkage. Public road construction was limited to encourage profitability on the railway which farmers were forced to use, paying higher freight charges than the mining companies.[40]

Between the first decade of the century and Independence in 1957, the only further major infrastructural developments are those associated with Governor Guggisberg in the 1920s. Guggisberg's conception of linkages went thus:

For progress we must have Education. For Education of the right kind we must have bigger Revenue. To get bigger Revenue we must have bigger Trade, and to get bigger Trade, we must have more Agriculture and far better systems of Transportations than at present exist.[41]

Most of the Guggisberg expenditure accordingly went on transportation and some of it was probably helpful to the local farmers. Some of the new roads designed for the collection and marketing of cocoa may also have contributed to the commercialisation of food growing in remote areas.[42]

This beneficial effect of Guggisberg's expenditure for the cocoa industry seems likely to have been outweighed however by a more general negative factor. As has been shown, the structure of the cocoa industry is far removed from the textbook characterisation of a peasant export economy based on family farming. The labour force is drawn not only from local sources, but from far afield and abroad, contributing to a complex, flexible pattern of labour use in the countryside. The cocoa labour market provides a ready source of supplementary income for family members, landless labourers and others at harvest, and also a means of access to capital accumulation for individuals. On the other hand, the attraction to temporary migrants of work in the cocoa farms is to an extent due to the rural underdevelopment of their own regions. One of Ghana's main development problems has been the failure to expand food production. Although we cannot prove the point, it is possible that both mining and cocoa had a contributory effect in reinforcing the backwardness of the food growing regions in the north of Ghana by periodically drawing away an important portion of the labour force. Moreover, cocoa farmers were able to pay 'super-exploitative' low wages to workers who drew on their home regions for part of their subsistence, which gave little margin for the migrants for investment in their own agriculture.[43] Agricultural techniques, for example, have not changed for the past century in the northern regions. There was minimal public expenditure on agriculture to offset the dearth of investments by local people in the food growing regions.

This negative linkage effect of the primary export sector through the labour market is an example of the type of deleterious influence that Hirschman envisaged, though he did not explicitly mention food production in this connection. Nevertheless he is the only writer within this paradigm whose approach leaves a place for examining the impact of export industries on food supply. It is a major flaw of the 'linkages and leakages' approach that it neglects — mirroring (perhaps even influencing) the actions of many developing country governments — the fundamental importance of food production in the process of development.

4.6 Conclusions

On all counts the linkages associated with mining and cocoa have been weak or even negative, and the leakages from mining considerable, so that the developmental impact of both sectors has been feeble. Both industries were, however, a fruitful source of funds for the state, cocoa slightly more so than mining — the ranking of the two sectors not conforming to the expectations of Hirschman in this respect. The independent government was very effective in channelling resources from these two industries to the public sector. The full positive potential of the primary export industries on the Ghanaian economy depended on the subsequent policies of the government for its realisation. Had the state been as effective in investing as it was in collecting resources the developmental impact of mining and cocoa might have been more favourable.

Notes

1. Baldwin (1963).
2. Cf. Hirschman (1958) where this notion is developed.
3. Hirschman (1977).
4. Weisskoff and Wolff (1977).
5. Hopkins (1973).
6. Howard (1978).
7. Exceptions are Killick (1973) and Thoburn (1977).
8. Killick (1966).
9. Ghana (1971).
10. Ibid.
11. Killick (1978).
12. Ghana Chamber of Mines; Killick (1978).
13. Davidson (1973).
14. Ghana (1972).
15. Ibid.
16. International Monetary Fund.
17. Hopkins (1973); see also Howard (1978).
18. Szereszwski (1965); see also Myint (1974).
19. Ingham (1981).
20. Hill (1963), (1970).
21. Howard (1978).
22. Beckman (1976).
23. Hill (1963); Kotey, Okali and Rourke (1974); Robertson (1982).
24. Addo (1972); Okali (1974); Killick (1966); Rourke (1971).
25. Rourke and Sakyi-Gyinae (1971).
26. Ghana (1958), (1960a).
27. Okali (1974).
28. Miracle and Berry (1970); Amin (1974).
29. Manu (1974).
30. Beckman (1974 p. 278) publishes a similar calculation indicating that farmers receive a smaller share of cocoa income to the state. He includes income from investments derived from previous surpluses in the CMB's share. We believe this to be wrong and prefer to limit our calculation to the distribution of income directly derived from cocoa production. Moreover, Beckman's method is inconsistent, since he would need to include in farmers' incomes the return from their investments outside the cocoa sector financed by cocoa earnings.
31. Since 1969, Ghana has lost its portion as a dominant world producer of cocoa and this adverse relationship has weakened.
32. Manu (1974).
33. Gordon (1974).
34. Hymer (1972).
35. Kraus (1971).
36. Krassowski (1974).

37. Ghana Chamber of Mines.
38. Gordon (1974).
39. Szereszewski (1965).
40. Hymer (1972).
41. Gold Coast (1920/21).
42. Gordon (1974).
43. Cf Dos Santos (1970); Wallerstein (1976).

Bibliography

Addo, N.O. 'Employment and Labour Supply on Ghana's Cocoa Farms in the Pre-
    and Post-Aliens Compliance Era'. *Economic Bulletin of Ghana* Second Series
    vol. 2 (1972).
Amin, S. (ed.) *Modern Migrations in West Africa* (Oxford University Press, London,
    1974).
Baldwin, R.E. 'Export Technology and Development, from a Subsistence Level'
    Economic Journal vol. 73 (1963).
Baran, P. 'On the Political Economy of Backwardness' *Manchester School* reprinted
    in Agarwala and Singh, *The Economics of Underdevelopment*. (Oxford University
    Press, London, 1952).
Beckman, B. 'Government Policy and the Distribution of Cocoa Income in Ghana',
    in Kotey *et al.* (1974).
_____ *Organizing the Farmers: Cocoa Politics and National Development in Ghana*
    (Scandinavian Institute of African Studies, Uppsala, 1976).
Davidson, B. *Black Star: A View of the Life and Times of Kwame Nkrumah* (Allen
    Lane, London, 1973).
Dos Santos, T. 'The Structure of Dependence' *American Economic Review* vol. 60,
    Papers and Proceedings (1970).
Ghana, *Survey of Population and Budgets of Cocoa Producing Families in the Oda-
    Swedru—Asamakese Area*, 1955-6, Statistical and Economic Papers No. 6.
    (Office of the Government Statistician, Accra, 1958).
_____, *Census of Population* (Government Printer, Accra, 1960).
_____, *Survey of Cocoa Producing Families in Ashanti 1956-57* Statistical and Eco-
    nomic Papers No. 7. (Office of the Government Statistician, Accra, 1960).
_____, *Report of the Commission of Enquiry into the Affairs of the State Mining
    Corporation* (Government Printer, Accra, 1971).
_____, *Financial Statement* (1972).
_____, Central Bureau of Statistics *Economic Surveys* (Accra, various years).
_____, Chamber of Mines (GCM) *Annual Reports* (Accra, various years).
_____, Cocoa Marketing Board *Reports and Accounts* (Accra, various years).
Gold Coast, *Legislative Council Debates* (Government Printer, Accra, 1920–21).
Gordon, S. 'The Role of Cocoa in Ghananian Development' in Pearson S.R., and
    Cownie, J., (eds.) *Commodity Exports and African Economic Development*
    (Lexington Books, London, 1974).
Hill, P. *The Migrant Cocoa Farmers in Southern Ghana. A Study in Rural
    Capitalism*. (The University Press, Cambridge, 1963).
_____, *Studies in Rural Capitalism in West Africa*. (The University Press, Cambridge,
    1970).
Hirschman, A.O. *The Strategy of Economic Development* (Yale University Press,
    New Haven, 1958).
_____ 'A Generalised Linkage Approach to Development with Special Reference to
    Staples' *Economic Development and Cultural Change* vol. 2 (Supplement in
    honor of Bert Hoselitz, 1977).

Hopkins, A.G. *An Economic History of West Africa* (Longmans, London, 1973).
Howard, R. *Colonialism and Underdevelopment in Ghana* (Croom Helm, London, 1978).
Hymer, S. 'The Political Economy of the Gold Coast and Ghana' in Ranis, G., (ed.) *The Government and Economic Development* (Yale University Press, New Haven, 1972).
Ingham, B. *Tropical Exports and Economic Development* (Macmillan, London, 1981).
International Monetary Fund *Financial Statistics* (various years).
Killick, T. 'Mining' in Birmingham W, Neustadt I, and Omaboe E.N. (eds.) *A Study of Contemporary Ghana*, vol. 1. *The Economy of Ghana* (Allen and Unwin, London, 1966).
_____, 'The Benefits of Foreign Direct Investment and Its Alternatives: An Empirical Exploration' *Journal of Development Studies*, vol. 9 (1973).
_____, *Development Economics in Action. A Study of Economic Policies in Ghana* (Heinemann Educational Books, London, 1978).
Kotey, R.A., Okali, C and Rourke, B.E. (eds.) *The Economics of Cocoa Production and Marketing*. Proceedings of the Cocoa Economics Research Conference, Legon, ISSER (1974).
Krassowski, A. *Development and the Debt Trap. Economic Planning and External Borrowing in Ghana* (Croom Helm, London, 1974).
Kraus, J. 'Political Change, Conflict and Development in Ghana' in Foster and Zolberg *Ghana and the Ivory Coast: Perspectives in Modernisation* (University of Chicago Press, Chicago, 1971).
Manu, J.E.A. 'Cocoa in the Ghana Economy' in Kotey *et al.* (1974).
Miracle, M.P. and Berry, S.S. 'Migrant Labour and Economic Development' *Oxford Economic Papers*, vol. 22 (1970).
Myint, H. *The Economics of the Developing Countries* (Hutchinson, London, 1974).
Okali, C. 'Labour Inputs on Cocoa Farms' in Kotey *et al.* (1974).
Robertson, A.F. 'Abusa: The Structural History of an Economic Contract' *Journal of Development Studies*, vol. 18 (1982).
Rourke, B.E. *Wages and Incomes of Agricultural Workers in Ghana*, Legon ISSER Technical Publication Series no. 13 (1971).
Rourke, B.E. and Sakyi-Gyinae, S.K. 'Agricultural and Urban Wage Rates in Ghana' *Economic Bulletin of Ghana* Second Series vol. 2 (1971).
Szereszewski, R. *Structural Changes in the Economy of Ghana 1891-1911* (Weidenfeld and Nicholson, London, 1965).
Thoburn, J. 'Commodity Prices and Appropriate Technology. Some Lessons from Tin Mining'. *Journal of Development Studies*, vol. 17 (1977).
Wallerstein, I. 'The Three Stages of African Involvement in the World Economy' in Gutkind and Wallerstein (eds.) *The Political Economy of Contemporary Africa* (Sage Publications, London, 1976).
Weiskoff, R. and Wolff, E. 'Linkages and Leakages: Industrial Tracking in an Enclave Economy'. *Economic Development and Cultural Change*, vol. 25 (1977).

9 MINERAL-LED DEVELOPMENT: THE POLITICAL ECONOMY OF NAMIBIA

Bo Södersten

Namibia is a sparsely populated country in south-west Africa. It is today controlled by South Africa but will probably gain some kind of independence in the not too distant future. It has somewhere between 1 million and 1.25 million inhabitants and its gross domestic product amounted in the late 1970s to around $1,200 million; its *per capita* income was around $1,000.

Mamalakis has classified a country as a 'mineral' country according to whether 10 per cent or more of GDP was generated by the mineral sector.[1] According to this criterion, Namibia easily qualifies as a mineral nation since in the late 1970s almost 50 per cent of her GDP came from minerals; in fact it may be asked if Namibia does not top the list of the world's mineral nations according to this criterion. At the same time only around 17,500 persons were employed in the mining sector. Of these 3,500 were white, 1,000 coloured and 13,000 were blacks. It may be added that 37.5 per cent of government earnings came from the mineral sector and that it generated 70–80 per cent of Namibia's export earnings.[2,3] Hence less than 2 per cent of the population generated almost 50 per cent of the country's GDP. This creates quite a peculiar and special situation for a country.

The present chapter will start by sketching a theoretical framework applicable to the situation of a mineral country like Namibia along the lines of a 'minerals theory of growth'.[4] We will then continue with a discussion of some of the developing problems that confront a country with this specific endowment and point out some norms that may be applicable in the development process.

Capturing Mining Rents

Natural resources have played a great role in economic history. As economic development proceeded many observers believed that natural endowments would come to play a smaller role, and technology would become all-important. Many economists used to argue that man-made resources and synthetic materials would increasingly come to replace natural resources. This has not come about. On the contrary, natural resources and their pricing have in very definite ways influenced or determined recent world events. A case in point are the effects on the world economy of oil price increases during the 1970s.

In order to understand the role of natural resources in a country's economic development, one has to realise what are the characteristics of a natural resource such as a mineral or an oil deposit. In an ordinary industrial process, a good is produced with the help of raw material, labour and capital. When it comes to producing a natural resource like copper, diamonds or oil, labour and capital are indeed also needed. But the essential ingredient is the actual presence of the mineral or the oil itself. Much of economic analysis, especially neoclassical theory, has been geared to the study of renewable products. Such analysis is almost exclusively couched in terms of two-factor models in which labour and capital are the only two factors of production that appear to be of interest at the analytical level. This type of analysis is not suitable for a study of the economics of natural resources.

Minerals, oil and other natural riches are rarely found in readily usable form. Minerals come in various degrees of purity, and oil is often mixed with water and gas at various depths. There is always an extraction cost involved in producing a natural resource like copper or diamonds, and this cost will vary with the quality of the mine. Let us denote the richest existing diamond mine with D_3. We can then rank diamond deposits in the following order:

$$D_3 > D_2 > D_1 > D_0$$

where D_0 denotes the poorest or *marginal* deposits, and where D_3 denotes the richest deposit. The difference between D_0 and D_1 can be measured as the surplus per unit of volume (say per tonne or kilo) between the marginal deposit (D_0) which just covers its operating costs and the next more profitable deposit.

Historically speaking, a country may start to extract minerals which are easily located and where the price is just enough to cover the extraction costs. Here no scarcity or land rent may be present, but mining might still be worthwhile as long as it covers labour costs and gives a normal return to capital.

Let us then assume that the world develops and that overall

demand for minerals increases. This will lead to the mining of less easily exploited deposits at higher costs. The richer and more easily available deposits will start to earn what might be termed land rents.

Let us now take a static point of view and return to our earlier notations. Assume that there is equilibrium with all the aforementioned deposits in operation. The revenues from the poorest one, D_0, will just cover its costs and earn no surplus. All the other deposits will earn surpluses. The surplus earned by the third-best will be $D_1 - D_0$ and the surplus earned by the best will be $D_3 - D_0$. These surpluses have the character of pure land rents and will be called Ricardian rents.

The concept of Ricadian rents is important to understand since it forms the basis of the economics of natural resources. It seems that a country like Namibia is dominated by the existence of such rents. Naturally, due to lack of information, it is difficult to give any precise estimate of the magnitude of the land rent element in the Namibian economy. The following example may, however, be illustrative. The value added of the mining sector can be estimated to be around \$600 million.[5] Assume that the wage in this sector is five times the *per capita* income (\$5,000 per year) and that the return to capital equals the wage bill.

Hence the operating costs of the mining sector would be around \$200 million and the Ricardian rents in the Namibian mining sector could be estimated to amount to around \$400 million yearly! Although the example is rough and somewhat arbitrary, it still points to the fact that the rent element in the Namibian economy should be very important.

We might also distinguish another rent. As we all know, prices of minerals like copper and diamonds fluctuate widely. This gives rise to another type of rent which can be termed *short-period rent* or demand rent. This rent element may not always be positive. It can also be negative and cut into the Ricardian rent element. But why refer at all to a 'rent' in this context? Should not a profit above normal simply be referred to as 'surplus profit'? The reason why we prefer to speak about the short-period rent is that it has its rent element determined by the fact that when it comes to minerals, supply is inelastic; it may take five years or so to open a new mine. Recent history also shows that such short-period rents can be very important in connection with oil. If it were the case that perfect foresight existed, it could be argued that no such short-period rents could exist but that the price trend should be accurately forecast and all that would be left would be Ricardian rents plus normal profits. As perfect foresight does not exist, however, the concept of short-period rents should be acknowledged and realised as an important concept in connection with the economics of minerals.

Starting at time t, there is a 'normal' price P and given operating costs which then generate a 'normal' amount of Ricardian rent. Because of an increase in demand, the price of diamonds now increases. On top of the Ricardian rent a new short-period rent or demand rent is created. But the knife can cut both ways. From time t_1 onwards, the price of the mineral starts to decline. At time t_2 it begins to fall under the 'normal' price, and the short-period rent becomes negative and starts cutting into the Ricardian rent.

This reasoning is only meant to be a rough illustration of some of the essential aspects of the theory of minerals. The division between Ricardian rents and demand rents is somewhat arbitrary. Still, they do illustrate two essential points connected with the exploitation of natural riches like mines and oil-fields. We would normally expect a fairly stable surplus or Ricardian rent to exist. This rent can often be very large — and represent the bulk of the total revenue accruing from the natural resource in question. At the same time, total revenue will usually fluctuate and can be expected at times to show large and drastic fluctuations due to changes in demand and other factors. Both these phenomena have important implications for income distribution and development possibilities in countries where exhaustible resources form an important part of the country's endowments.

Furthermore it should be remembered that from a historical perspective, nothing lasts forever. Minerals will become depleted with time. New deposits may be found that wipe out the economic value of already existing ones. History has seen many examples of mining booms that have ended in ruin. Therefore it is all the more important to use the rents accruing from the minerals sector efficiently as long as they exist.

Rents, Income Distribution and Development

History shows that the struggle for the division of rents accruing in the primary sector has often been hard and sometimes violent. Today the mines in Namibia are controlled by South African interests. After independence it is natural to expect that they will be controlled by the state.

One important problem is how to divide the rents internally between the state and the capital and labour working in the mines. It is not self-evident how much should accrue to labour, how much to capital and how much to the state.

Capital might be the easiest factor to deal with, at least in principle. Here the Government should strive to get the mines run as efficiently as possible with a minimum input of capital, and try to minimise the total share going to capital.

When it comes to labour, things will be come trickier. Up until today, the black workers in the mines of Namibia have been very crudely exploited. After liberation they are certainly entitled to decent treatment, good working conditions and a fair share of the returns from the mines. Nevertheless it has to be remembered that the greater the share taken by the workers, the smaller will be the share available to the state. Once independence is established, we can expect the workers in the mines to form a class or group of elite workers. They should therefore also be asked to show a certain moderation in their wage demands, in the overall interest of Namibia.

History knows many examples where rents in the primary sector have been squandered. One case in point is that of guano in Peru which has been unusually well documented by Jonathan Levin in his classic study.[6] There a small minority of the population consisting of domestic entrepreneurs, soldiers, bureaucrats and insiders plus some foreign investors took the major part of the rents. The earnings coming from the exports of guano led only to 'a pattern of frustrated development . . . characterised by a stagnating domestic sector, few signs of general economic growth, and a level of effective general income that was pitifully low'.[7]

Something along these lines could naturally also happen in the Namibian case. A greater risk is, however, that the workers in the mines will appropriate an unduly large share of the rents and set themselves up as elite workers, building up enclaves around the mines, employing relatives and others in subordinate and service positions.

The development in Chile points in this direction. As a matter of fact, labour discipline may be better upheld by an authoritarian government than by a socialist one or one with more liberal leanings. Chile during the Unidad Popular government from 1970–73 is a case in point. Difficulties in maintaining copper production became pronounced; at the Chuquicamata mine 67 partial work stoppages are said to have taken place in 1972 alone.[8] An important incident which contributed to the downfall of the Allende government was the strike which took place at the El Teniente copper mine in May and June 1973.[9]

There is, actually, a certain risk involved in possessing a strong comparative advantage stemming from natural resources. It is all too easy to squander the rents that accrue from the mining sector. The government will therefore have to exert strong discipline when spending the rents. In several countries, rents have simply been used to inflate the government sector out of all proportion or spent on quite useless prestige projects. Reactionary regimes have also used them to set up a military class that has then been used to oppress the country's own people.

When it comes to getting a development process under way, the question of how governments spend the rents is therefore one of major importance.

Rents, Norms and Industrial Strategies

When Namibia reaches independence, large segments of the population will have high expectations of swift improvement. Political freedom and freedom from oppression can be achieved instantly. Economic development, on the other hand, will take longer. The demands on the resources available will also be great. Pressure on the government sector will be heavy. It will be costly to set up an effective administration. But it will also be tempting to let the government sector act as a creator of employment. The pressure to use the rents from the mining sector for government purposes will therefore be great.

In order to set aside specific resources for development purposes, it might be wise to create a specific development budget. Resources allocated to the development budget should not be used for any purpose other than development. Here, development of the industrial sector should be given a high priority. It might even be wise to allocate a certain share of the development budget specifically for development of the industrial sector.

As we have noticed, part of the rents accruing from the mining sector will have the character of short-term rents, which will fluctuate with time. This makes planning difficult. The government will have to take a cautious attitude to the spending of these rents, in order not to be left with the short end of the stick. From this point of view it could be wise to allocate only a share (and not a fixed sum) to the government sector itself. A *norm* could be devised and the rents coming from the mining sector shared between the current budget and the development budget in certain fixed proportions. If this is not done, it is easy to wind up in a situation where the allocations going to development purposes become simply a residual. If a norm is created, the development budget will always be guaranteed a certain share of the overall resources accruing to the government. One could even go so far as to make the allocation for development purposes a fixed sum, perhaps including an increasing trend. A certain stability in its development plans could thereby be created. At the same time, the government sector will have to show greater adaptability than would otherwise be needed. In the long run this might not be detrimental to the Namibian economy.

Development and Trade Policy

Aulakh and Asombang discuss the concept of balanced growth in their report for the United Nations Institute for Namibia entitled *Towards Economic Development Strategy Options for Independent Namibia.*[10] Balanced growth, as they rightly point out, can mean various things.

It is true that certain balances should always be kept in mind when trying to develop a country. One such balance is that between investment in physical assets and human capital. It is important to remember that the development of skills, health and training should go hand in hand with the development of material capital. We can thereby expect to broaden the base for development, and see to it that the absorptive capacity of the Namibian economy develops as much as possible, evenly and without bottlenecks. We should also remember that industry and agriculture ought to develop and grow hand in hand.

When referring to balanced growth, economists often think in terms of trade strategies, so that balanced growth is often seen as a form of import-substitution strategy, as opposed to some form of uneven development or export-push. Namibia, economically speaking, is quite a small country.

Namibia has a rather well-developed mining sector. It even seems to be the case that her industrial sector has a variety of small-scale industries that is not common in black Africa.[11] Still, it would hardly be advisable for Namibia to opt for a policy of import-substitution. The domestic market is simply too small. On the contrary, it would seem advantageous to opt for a policy of export-push, based on Namibia's rich mineral resources while at the same time keeping a certain independence in the production of basic goods for consumption, simple tools etc. based on the existence of small-scale domestic industry. Such a policy could also be combined with selective support to certain import-competing sectors of the economy.

Today, Namibia forms part of the South African customs union. This union was originally formed in 1910 with Botswana, Lesotho and Swaziland. After having come into the South African sphere of influence, Namibia also joined it.

The theory of customs unions is a fairly involved type of analysis. In its simplest version, it teaches us that a customs union will have two effects. On the one hand, it will lead to trade creation, i.e. trade between the members of the union will increase. On the other hand it will lead to trade diversion, i.e. trade with countries outside the union will be diverted, and imports from third countries will decrease.

Normally we would expect the exporters within the union (South Africa) to gain from trade creation, while the importers (Namibia, Swaziland, Botswana and Lesotho) would have their welfare lowered as they would have to pay more for their imports, which are being diverted from efficient low-cost producers to the less efficient customs union partner. This result can be modified, especially if the country's domestic trade is large compared to its foreign trade.[12] This is hardly the case for Namibia. Hence the implicit loss from membership of the customs union seems to outweigh the eventual gains.

Namibia should therefore try to leave the customs union with South Africa as quickly as possible after independence. The country already has a strong export base in her mineral endowments. Namibia is therefore in a strong position to start out, after independence, with a strong external balance. The country should use this advantage to import goods cheaply from the most competitive producers on the world market, at low or no tariffs. Such a policy should prove advantageous to both domestic consumers and producers. A policy of openness need not be applied indiscriminately. There will be sectors that — for a certain period of time — will require protection from competition. Here the argument for infant industry protection is applicable. Given the limited size of Namibia's domestic industry and domestic market, support to industry should be selective. From the standpoint of industrial expansion and general economic welfare, it therefore seems that trade policy should be based on the following three factors: first, the genuine comparative advantage of the mining sector should be used to provide export earnings; second, a policy of openness to cheap imports should be pursued; third, a policy of selected industry support ought to be given to help certain domestic factories develop and flourish.

Aspects of Industrial and Agricultural Promotion

When it comes to the promotion of more specific industries, I will be brief. It would be natural for Namibia to try to build its industries around its own natural resources. One such resource is obviously minerals, and it could be wise for the country to try to process and refine some of them. The construction of a copper refinery, and of plants using other domestic resources, such as lead, for producing batteries, cables and electric wires seem promising undertakings. Various larger-scale developments are also possible. Such mineral processing may involve fairly complicated undertakings and should be studied closely as to viability.

Another promising point of departure is to use fishing and agriculture as a base for an industrial promotion that can lead to the establishment of new export industries. When it comes to controlling fishing, some problems will undoubtedly arise. However an independent Namibia should declare a 200-mile fishing zone, and maintain control over catches. A stable resource base for the fishing industry could thereby be created. An effective canning industry could then be built up, which would lead to a broadening of the export base.

Agriculture provides a parallel case to fishing. The production of meat can be increased, and a canning industry developed. A tanning and leather goods industry can be built up and developed around the production of hides and skins, and karakul products. Vegetables and fruits can provide another base for domestic consumption, at the same time as they serve as input factors for an export canning industry. To help establish industries of this type, which will form part of a policy of export-push, the sort of low-tariff policy for which I have argued should prove effective. These industries will basically use domestic raw materials. At the same time they will need imported input-factors, such as machinery etc. in order to get started. A policy of low tariffs will permit the export industries to import such input factors at low cost. This will help these industries, and make them competitive.

A policy of low tariffs need not be applied indiscriminately. Namibia will also need to develop small-scale and medium-sized industries that are primarily geared toward the domestic market. Such industries could include textiles and the production of shoes, furniture, kitchen utensils and the like. Other industries of a similar nature could include mills, timber and wood processing industries, breweries, cigarette factories and construction works. In the case of such lines of production, tariffs, import quotas and other means of trade policy can be used to foster and protect domestic industries. Such protectionist measures should, however, be applied with caution and for specific purposes, in order to avoid creating unnecessary domestic monopoly rents and ineffective production units.

In general, industrial policy in Namibia should rely on working with *positive* means. These may include subsidies, which are usually more effective and direct, and also make it easier to determine the true costs for a certain type of production. The means for industrial subsidies should be made available from the surpluses generated in other sectors, primarily the mining sector. It is therefore of vital importance that the mining rents should be captured by the state, and used wisely for development purposes.

Another important factor is to try to provide a good general and vocational training for the workforce. After many years of neglect and destructive policies on the part of the South African racist regime, this is an area that needs attention and care. To upgrade the labour force and provide it with skills will be one of the most urgent tasks of industrial policy in independent Namibia.

Summary

Namibia is a country well endowed with natural riches, and with a strong comparative advantage in the mining sector. Today around half of its GDP is generated in the mining sector. Important surpluses or rents are created in this sector. One such type of rent is the Ricardian or pure land rent, while another type of rent can be characterised as a short-period or demand-influenced rent. Proceeds from the mining sector tend to fluctuate with business conditions. It is important that the state should be able to collect the largest share of these rents, and that an unduly large part should not go to foreign or particular domestic interests.

In order to foster development, a substantial part of the means collected in the form of rents should be spent for development purposes. In order to implement such a strategy, it might be useful for the government to adhere to certain norms, in order that development programmes will not be set aside or scrapped if economic gains from the primary sector should be lower than normal.

Today, Namibia's economy is intimately linked with that of South Africa. Namibia effectively forms part of the South Africa customs union. When independence is achieved, the country should sever these links and get out of the customs union.

Outside the union, Namibia will be able to form an independent trade policy and go for a development strategy of export-push, while at the same time taking advantage of cheap imports from the world market. A policy of industrial promotion can start by developing export industries based on the country's rich primary resources in mining, agriculture and fishing. Such a policy will also permit these industries to enjoy the privilege of access to cheaply imported machinery and other input factors. Other industries for the domestic market can be promoted and built up, if necessary with the help of subsidies and a cautious and selective application of certain protectionist measures. Care will also have to be taken in building up the necessary skills of the workforce that will form another important prerequisite for a policy of successful industrialisation in Namibia.

Notes

1. Mamalakis (1978).
2. Eriksen (1982).
3. Aulakh and Asombang (1982a).
4. Mamalakis (1978).
5. Aulakh and Asombang (1982a).
6. Levin (1960).
7. Ibid., p. 202.
8. De Vylder (1974), p. 137.
9. Södersten (1975).
10. Aulakh and Asombang (1982b).

11. German Development Institute (1978).
12. Södersten (1980).

Bibliography

Aulakh, H.S. & Asombang, W.W. *Mineral Development Strategy Options for Independent Namibia* (UNIN, Lusaka, Zambia, 1982).
_____, *Towards Economic Development Strategy Options of Independent Namibia* (UNIN, Lusaka, Zambia, 1982).
Eriksen, T.L. *Namibia* (Uppsala, 1978).
German Development Institute, *Multisectoral Study of Namibia* (Berlin, 1978).
Levin, J.V. *The Export Economies. Their Pattern of Development in Historical Perspective* (Harvard University Press, Cambridge, Mass., 1960).
Mamalakis, M. *The Minerals Theory of Growth. The Latin American Evidence* (Universität Göttingen, Göttingen, 1978).
Södersten, B. *Den svenska sköldpaddan* (Rabón and Sjögren, Stockholm, 1975).
_____, *International Economics* (Macmillan, London, 1980).
de Vylder, S. *Chile 1970–3: The Political Economy of the Rise and Fall of the Unidad Popular* (Unga filosofers förlag, Stockholm, 1974).

10 PRIMARY EXPORTS, MANUFACTURING AND DEVELOPMENT

Ronald Findlay

The theme of our conference is the role of the primary sector in economic development. One of the major aspects of that theme is the complex interdependence between the primary and manufacturing sectors in the development process, in which they compete with each other for the common pool of scarce inputs and also complement each other in a variety of ways. Much of this interdependence is mediated through the foreign trade sector and it is to this particular feature that the present paper is addressed.

The standard theories of international trade and comparative advantage generally do not lay any particular stress on the physical or technical characteristics of the commodities that are produced, consumed and traded. At the level of abstraction that usually prevails all that matters is that the goods require scarce inputs of some kind for their production and yield utility to someone in consumption. Thus the specific quality of output from the *primary* sector, that it requires inputs of scarce *natural* resources, is not of any particular importance. In the usual textbook and journal article statements of the Heckscher–Ohlin theory (though not in Heckscher and Ohlin themselves), for example, the 'factors' whose differing proportions govern the pattern of national comparative advantages are all assumed to be in fixed supply and are perfectly symmetric with respect to each other. In the Ricardian model of Chapter 7 of the *Principles*, involving the famous example of England and Portugal trading in cloth and wine, 'climate' is sometimes invoked as being responsible for the differences in relative labour productivities that determine the pattern of comparative costs but nothing of any consequence is made of this point.

In the general theory of value, distribution and growth, however, the name of Ricardo is almost synonymous with diminishing returns from the 'original and indestructible powers of the soil' and all the dire consequences of this for the rate of profit on capital. It is therefore surprising that only very recently have Ricardo's ideas on the operation of the Corn Laws, expressed in his *Essay on Profits*, been taken into account in a richer analysis of trade, growth and income distribution as expressed in works by Findlay[1] and Maneschi[2], the former drawing on Pasinetti[3] and the latter on Casarosa[4]. I shall adapt and develop some pertinent aspects of this analysis in the rest of this paper as it offers one of the few avenues open for even minimally rigorous theoretical work in this area. The famous 'staple' theory of H.A. Innis and other Canadian economic historians, the 'vent for surplus' theories of Myint[5] and Caves[6] and the related papers of Baldwin[7] are all suggestive and insightful but as yet loose and informal approaches, better suited as organising frameworks for historical case studies than for general equilibrium modelling.

The first section of this chapter will consider an interesting model of the primary sector in an underdeveloped economy put forward by Hansen[8]. The second section gives a dynamic Ricardian model of primary exports and the manufacturing sector. The third and final section is devoted to a simple diagrammatic model of resource-based industrialisation in an open economy.

1. The Hansen Model

Hansen's model is of a primary producing economy with a 'dualistic' structure. He envisages a limited quantity of specially fertile or productive land that is owned by a privileged group of colonial settlers (or their successors from a native elite), on which highly profitable plantation crops are grown, and an unlimited supply of 'marginal' land on which food crops are grown. The relative price of the plantation and food crops is given on world markets. The fixed population of native workers can either farm the marginal land as independent peasant producers, earning the average (equals marginal) product in that activity, or work as agricultural labourers on the plantations of the settlers for a wage in terms of food which competition will drive down to equality with the average product on marginal land that is a technically determined datum. The equality of the marginal product of labour on the plantations with this wage determines the division of the native labour force between peasant producers and total rent earned in plantations and the total output of food on the marginal lands.

The entire model is depicted in Figure 10.1. The horizontal axis measures the given supply of native workers, with employment on

Figure 10.1:   The Hansen Model

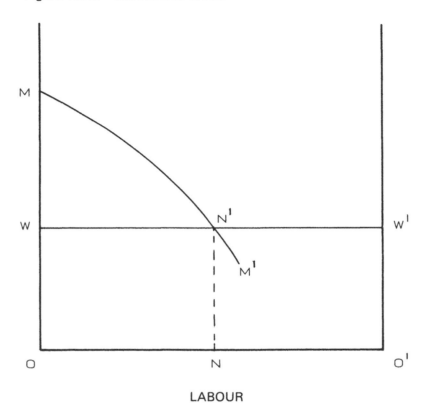

LABOUR

plantations measured from O and in food production on marginal
lands from O′. The distance O′W′ measures the fixed average (and
marginal) product of labour in food production and the equal distance OW the real wage in terms of food on the plantations. The
MM′ curve depicts the diminishing marginal productivity of labour
in plantation agriculture (since the appropriate land is fixed), evalu-
ated at the given world price of plantation products in terms of food.
The intersection of MM′ with WW′ at N′ determines employment on
plantations as ON, peasant producers as O′N, rent in plantations as
the triangular area MWN′, the plantation wage bill as OWN′N and
food output as O′W′N′N. Total plantation output is of course the
sum of rent and the wage-bill. Production, resource allocation and
income distribution are thus all completely determined. All income

earners can consume food, plantation products or imports of manufactures and other non-produced commodities at the fixed world prices.

It is now of course an elementary exercise to find the consequences of a change in any of the parameters. It is just a matter of reading it off from Figure 10.1. An increase in population increases OO', leaving MM' and WW' unchanged. It is thus entirely absorbed in additional food production at the extensive margin, leaving employment, output and rents unchanged in the plantation sector. An increase in the supply of scarce land, or neutral or labour-saving technical progress in plantation agriculture, shifts MM' to the right, increases rents and plantation employment and output and leaves the real income of peasants and workers unchanged. A rise in the relative price of plantation crops in terms of food, which Hansen takes as tantamount to an improvement in the terms of trade (though food need not necessarily be imported by the logic of his model), will have similar effects on plantation output, employment and rents. It will also leave real incomes of workers and peasants unchanged if the plantation products are not consumed by them, as seems likely. A rise in the relative price of food would have the opposite effects on the planters, while also leaving real incomes of cultivators and workers unchanged under the assumption that they do not consume plantation products.

Plantation agriculture thus has a typical 'enclave' property in Hansen's model since fluctuations in the world market do not essentially affect the living standards of the native population, though they do alter the distribution between cultivators and labourers. There is also a brutal opposition between the welfare of the natives and that of the planters. An increase in the efficiency of food production on the marginal lands raises the real wage OW on the plantations and hence reduces employment, output and rents, in that sector. Conversely, the infamous 'poll tax' on peasant cultivators reduces the real wage to plantation agriculture and hence stimulates employment, production and rents there.

We turn now to the introduction of a manufacturing sector into the model. Hansen first attempts to do this by postulating a constant returns to scale production function for industry, with 'capital' and labour as inputs and the return to capital also given from abroad, along with the relative prices of the goods. The given return to capital fixes the capital–labour ratio and hence the marginal product of labour and the real wage that industry can afford. If this is below the 'going' wage determined by peasant agriculture, industry cannot get started in the absence of protection. If it is above then peasant agriculture will eventually be wiped out, and the wage on plantations will rise to equal the industrial wage as determined by the international return to capital and the technology of manufacturing. All labour will be wage labour, either in plantations or factories, and food will presumably have to be provided solely by imports in exchange for exports of plantation products and manufactures. Note that the lower the international return on capital and the more efficient the industrial technology the higher will the real wage be in the economy and the lower therefore will be employment, output and rents in plantation agriculture, the sole surviving form of primary production in the economy. This result follows from the familiar negative slope of the 'factor price frontier', and the fact that greater efficiency is tantamount to shifting the entire frontier to the right, i.e. raising the real wage for any given return to capital.

With the real wage effectively determined by the 'unlimited supply of capital' from abroad, at the given rate of return, any expansion of agriculture, whether due to an increase in the supply of land, technical progress or rise in relative price will initially raise real wages and hence reduce the return to capital as the sectors compete for the given pool of labour. Capital will therefore leave the country until industrial employment is compatible with the rightward shift of MM' and the given wage. This phenomenon is precisely the so-called 'Dutch Disease' of de-industrialisation provoked by a primary sector boom. Corden[9] has provided a lucid survey, with extensive references. More on this topic later.

An alternative way to introduce industry is to give up the assumption that capital is perfectly mobile internationally at a fixed return, with the stock of capital endogenously determined, and instead take capital as fixed and let employment be determined by the point at which the marginal productivity of labour in industry is driven down to equality with the average product of labour in food on marginal lands. The work force is thus divided between *three* employments, peasant cultivation of food and employment (at the same terms as in food) in plantations and factories respectively. The food sector thus determines the real wage while the supplies of intramarginal land and capital determine employment in plantations and industry and hence rents and profits. What we have is essentially the so-called Viner–Ricardo or 'specific factors' model now very popular with trade theorists, with the wrinkle that there is a third activity, food production using labour alone, that independently ties down the real wage.

One quibble I have with Hansen's otherwise entirely admirable paper is his contrast of his own 'unlimited supply of land' model with the 'unlimited supply of labour' model of Arthur Lewis[10]. To my mind Hansen's food sector is simply a natural specification of the 'peasant hinterland' of Lewis, conditions in which determine the level of the real wage at which labour supply is perfectly elastic to the 'modern' or 'capitalist' sector, in which Lewis specifically includes mines and plantations. The difference between Hansen and Lewis is that the former stresses 'land' as the scarce input in the modern sector whereas Lewis stresses 'capital'. Both of them would presumably agree that both inputs are necessary for plantation agriculture, as I shall assume in the model to be presented in the next section.

The significance of thinking in terms of 'capital' rather than 'land' of course is that this paves the way for a dynamic model of accumulation and steady growth while the latter alone results in a static model such as Hansen's. What we shall see is that the inclusion of both scarce inputs can lead to a model in which there is expansion of the primary sector until it is eventually choked off by the diminishing returns on 'land', after which manufacturing becomes the leading sector of the economy in the absence of continuing land-augmenting technical progress in the primary sector.

My intention in pointing out the affinity of Hansen's model to that of Lewis and 'specific factors' models such as that of Jones[11] is in no way to belittle the originality and significance of his paper. What is common to all three authors is the Ricardian heritage of their ideas, Hansen and Jones stressing diminishing returns due to the fixity of the earth's natural resources and Lewis the possibility of accumulation out of profits by capitalist entrepreneurs.

2. The Ricardian Model

In this section we shall incorporate 'capital' into production in the primary sector and 'dynamise' the analysis in Ricardian fashion by linking capital accumulation to profits and income distribution. The objective is to construct the time path of a stylised economy that begins as a typical 'monocultural' primary exporter but then eventually moves into being a producer and perhaps even an exporter of manufactures.

The concept of capital that we shall use is of 'circulation' capital or 'advances to labour' in the physiocratic sense. I hesitate to use the term 'wage fund' since that conjures up the image of a heap of sacks of corn. In a 'small' open economy such as we shall be considering, with fixed foreign prices for all goods and, for simplicity, a fixed exchange rate as well, there is no reason not to think in common-sense everyday terms and consider capital as loans expressed in monetary terms but which are used by the workers to purchase consumer goods in whatever proportions desired. The Hicks composite commodity theorem can still allow us to think in terms of a single product 'corn' but this 'commodity' is of course a metaphorical one.

As in Hansen's model food cultivation on marginal lands requires no capital. It will be convenient to choose units such that one unit of labour produces one unit of food. Then the wage in plantations and factories will have to be the value of one unit of food, which will be denoted w.

The production function for plantation crops is

$$X_1 = f(L_1, T) \tag{1}$$

in which X_1 denotes output, L_1 the labour input and T the fixed quantity of intramarginal 'land'. The function is assumed to be linear homogeneous.

So far everything is identical to the Hansen model. We now assume, however, that production takes time and that wages have to be advanced to workers at the beginning of the agricultural production cycle while output only appears at the end. The rate of profit in plantation agriculture will therefore be

$$r_1 = \frac{p_1 (X_1 - \frac{\partial X_1}{\partial T}T) - wL_1 p_1}{wL_1} = \frac{\frac{\partial X_1}{\partial L_1} - w}{w} \tag{2}$$

in which p_1 denotes the price of plantation products and the second equality follows from Euler's Theorem. In other words plantations are enterprises in which a group of workers are hired at the going wage at the beginning of the season yielding output $p_1 X_1$ at the end, from which rent of $(\partial X_1/\partial T) T$ must be deducted in addition to the replacement of the 'advance of labour' of wL_1. The residual, divided by wL_1, gives the rate of profit earned over the season, which we shall take to be a year.

Manufacturing production is also assumed to use circulating capital only (though this assumption will be altered later without seriously affecting the results), and to have a uniform one-year lag between input and output as well. Letting x_2 denote output *per man* in manufacturing the rate of profit in that sector will be

$$r_2 = \frac{p_2 x_2 - w}{w}. \tag{3}$$

We shall now note a crucial property of the model. It is that r_1, the rate of profit in primary production, depends upon L_1 because of diminishing returns on 'land' and is hence an endogenous variable, while r_2 depends only on the parameters p_2, x_2 and w and hence is given once these are specified. Competitive allocation of capital is thus only compatible with $r_1 > r_2$ if the manufacturing sector does not operate at all. If manufacturing production occurs then the rate of profit in plantations must be equal to r_2. This immediately can be seen to place a limit on the size of the plantation sector in terms of employment, and hence output and rent as well. In other words

$$r_1 = r_2 \tag{4}$$

implies

$$\frac{\partial X_1}{\partial L_1} = \frac{p_2}{p_1} x_2. \tag{5}$$

Given T, we can define L_1^* as the unique value of L_1 that ensures equality of the marginal productivity of labour in plantations with the constant term on the right hand side, which is the relative price of plantation products and manufactures times the average (and marginal) productivity of labour in manufactures.

The stock of circulation capital in the economy is

$$w[L_1(t) + L_2(t)] = W(t) \tag{6}$$

in which the dependence of L_1, L_2 and W on time is indicated by the 't' in parentheses. Define

$$W^* \equiv wL_1^*. \tag{7}$$

From this it follows that if $W(t) < W^*$ then $L_1 < L_1^*$ and hence $r_1 >$ r_2, with the economy not producing any manufactures at all. If $W(t) > W^*$ then L_1^* workers will be employed on plantations and employment in manufacturing will be

$$L_2(t) = \frac{W(t) - W^*}{w}. \tag{8}$$

If we make the classical assumption that profits are the source of capital accumulation, and denote the capitalist propensity to save by s we would of course obtain what Joan Robinson called the 'Anglo-Italian' equation

$$g(t) = sr(t) \tag{9}$$

in which $g(t)$ indicates the growth rate of capital and hence of employment in manufacturing and commercial agriculture and r the ruling rate of profit in the economy. If $W(o) < W^*$ i.e. if the initial stock of capital were sufficiently small, the economy would special-ise completely in primary production and the initial growth rate would be $sr_1(o) > sr_2$. The expansion of employment of fixed 'land' would steadily drive down the rate of profit, and hence growth would decelerate, until $W(t^*) = W^*$. From that point t^* on the profit rate and growth rate would be steady at the value of r_2 specified by (3). Employment in plantations would remain constant at L_1^* from that point on, with all additional employment by capitalist entrepre-neurs being solely in manufacturing.

Some further properties of the model can now be briefly noted. First, the reader can check that the model is homogeneous of degree zero in p_1, p_2 and w i.e. changing all these prices in the same propor-tion leaves all real magnitudes unchanged. Raising p_1 alone will raise L_1^* by virtue of (5) and diminishing returns to labour in the produc-tion of X_1. It will *raise* the rate of profit if the economy is in the phase of complete specialisation on the primary sector. If manufac-tures are being produced, however, it is evident that r_2 will not be altered and hence the rate of profit in plantations must also remain unchanged. A rise in p_1 will provoke a switch in employment from manufacturing until the marginal productivity of labour in planta-tions declines in the same proportion. Raising p_2 alone will of course raise r_2 and hence the general rate of profit, with employment diverted from primary to manufacturing production. Raising x_2 will have a similar effect. An increase in T, the supply of 'land', will raise L_1^* in the same proportion. It will raise the marginal productivity of labour, and hence the rate of profit, if the economy is in the primary specialisation phase, but the profit rate will be unchanged if manufacturing production has already started. Increasing w, either because of a rise in the world price of food relative to other commodities or an increase in the physical productivity of peasants on marginal lands, will clearly reduce the rate of profit whether the economy is specialised or not. We see from (5), however, that it will not affect L_1^* and hence the entire contraction in employment, given the stock of circulating capital, will be in the manufacturing sector.

To sum up, what we have is a Ricardian model of a primary producing economy in which accumulation drives down the rate of profit because of diminishing returns on 'land'. Unlike Ricardo's original model however, the profit rate does not fall to zero. It is bounded above that by the rate of profit in manufacturing in which there is constant returns to scale. The production of plantation crops reaches a limit set by the alternative opportunities for capital and employment in manufactures.

The economy starts by exporting plantation crops and perhaps also food and depending exclusively on imports for its entire supply of manufactures. However, it eventually takes up manufacturing production, in at least some labour intensive lines. If the growth of capital is appreciably faster than that of the population food production will shrink relative to production of manufactures and the economy will export manufactures and import food. Plantation products will presumably always be exported since domestic demand for them is not likely to be sufficiently large to outstrip the supply.

A more 'realistic' postulate for the manufacturing sector is that production requires 'machines' rather than circulating capital. This does not alter the analysis in any essential respect. To see this, assume fixed coefficients and let x_2 be output per unit of labour as before and k the value (at world prices) of capital per unit of labour in this sector. Competitive equilibrium would then require

$$r_2 = \frac{p_2 x_2 - w}{k} \tag{10}$$

in which p_2, x_2, w and k are all parameters and so r_2 is determined independently by conditions in the manufacturing sector, just as before. The stock of 'capital' in the economy consists of two parts, 'advances to labour' in plantations and 'machines' in industry. Throughout our analysis we have assumed that the relative price of primary exports on world markets is fixed. Many LDCs however do have some monopoly power in primary exports such as coffee, tea, cocoa, rubber and so on. In this case the rate at which the world demand curve shifts to the right becomes an important consideration for the long run. In other words we have the prospect of diminishing returns in the *value* sense due to declining terms of trade if primary exports expand too fast rather than in the *physical* sense due to scarcity of 'land'. I have considered this problem in some detail elsewhere,[12] to which I would refer the interested reader. In the models presented there, manufacturing exports at fixed world prices appear as a possible escape route from the constraint of sluggish world demand for primary exports. There is considerable formal similarity with the 'supply-constrained' growth of the primary sector in the present analysis.

The relative price of primary products and manufactures is a key feature in what I have called 'North–South' models of trade and growth. I use the terminology to emphasise the contrast between the *asymmetric* interdependence of structurally dissimilar trading partners in such models with the rather bland 'Countries A and B' of the conventional literature, in which the partners are qualitatively identical, differing only in factor proportions or relative technical efficiency. The work of Prebisch, Singer and Emmanuel fits into this category. Again I cannot do justice to these views here and refer the reader to the relevant sections of my other works,[13] for detailed comments. In my own approach to the North–South problem,[14] the growth of the South is constrained in the long run by the growth of the North, with the terms of trade being the variable that brings the growth of the South into equality with that of the North. The analysis of that paper has been extended in various ways in as yet unpublished work by Andre Burgstaller, Miguel Kiguel, Neantro Saavedra-Rivano and Ian Wooton.

3. Resource-based Industrialisation

The output of the primary sector is frequently a raw material that is an input into the manufacturing sector. The division of the primary output between export and use as a raw material for domestic industry then becomes an important quesion. This and related matters are the subject of a growing literature on 'resource-based industrialisation', surveyed very thoroughly by Roemer[15]. Since the topic has been relatively neglected in the trade theory field it may be useful to lay out the essential resource allocation problems involved by means of a diagrammatic apparatus. We continue to deal with a two-sector economy but instead of two final goods we shall consider one raw material and one final good, both of which can be traded on world markets at a fixed relative price.

Production of the raw material requires 'land', which is in fixed supply and labour, the total supply of which is also given. Production of the final good requires the raw material and labour as inputs, with smooth substitution possible between them in the production of a given level of output. In Figure 10.2 the distance OO' measures the total labour available. With the fixed supply of 'land' diminishing returns to labour in the raw material sector result in a curve such as OR showing the level of raw material output corresponding to any level of labour input measured from O as the origin. A family of isoquants for the final output can be drawn in the diagram with O' as

Figure 10.2: Production of Final Goods from Raw Material

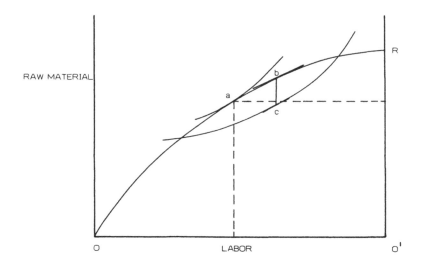

origin, labour input being measured horizontally and raw material input vertically. It is easy to see that in the absence of foreign trade possibilities the output of the final good will be maximised at point *a* in Figure 10.2, which is where an isoquant is tangential to OR. The slope of OR at *a* determines the marginal productivity of labour in the raw material sector and hence the real wage. The coordinates of point *a* also determine the allocation of the labour force between the two sectors and the raw material input into the manufacturing sector. Hence the marginal productivities of labour and raw material in manufacturing are also known. The ratio of these marginal productivities must be equal to the marginal productivity of labour in the raw material sector, by the tangency at *a*. Real wages and rent, both in terms of the raw material and the final good, are also determined by equality with the relevant marginal productivities. It is clear that the allocation determined by point *a* would be a competitive equilibrium.

Suppose now that there is a fixed world price *p* at which the final product can be obtained in exchange for the raw material. How will the competitive equilibrium be affected? To solve this problem we need to use Figure 10.3 which is constructed as follows. For any given level of final output, as specified by an isoquant in Figure 10.2, what is the maximum *net* output of the raw material that is feasible i.e. after requirements for the production of the fixed quantity of the final good have been deducted? A little reflection shows that the answer is given by maximising the vertical distance between OR and the specified isoquant for the final good, which is when their slopes are equal as at point *b* on OR and *c* on the isoquant in Figure 10.2. The distance between *b* and *c* is thus the maximum net output of the raw material consistent with output of the final good being at the specified level. Carrying out this exercise for all possible output levels of the final good up to the maximum at point *a* in Figure 10.2 generates the transformation curve VF in Figure 10.3. The distance OV on the vertical axis indicates the maximum amount of the raw material that the economy could produce, i.e. when the entire labour force is in that sector, while OF corresponds to the level of final good output at *a* in Figure 10.2 with all the raw material production used up in domestic industry.

The tangent to VF at point *q*, with slope equal to the relative price of the two goods in the world market, determines the free trade equilibrium. Domestic production of the final good is equal to Of, exports of the raw material to qf, imports of the final good to ff′ and

Figure 10.3:   Exchange of Raw Material for Final Goods

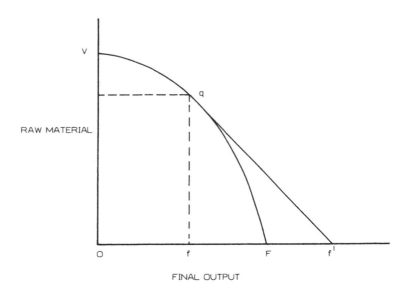

consumption of the final good to Of'. The distance Ff' is a direct physical measure of the gain from trade in terms of the additional consumption of the sole final good. The effects of tariffs on the final good and export taxes on the primary sector can be readily worked out. The analysis can also be extended to cover import of the raw material for domestic manufacture. The same technique applies, only we now have to *minimise* the vertical distance between OR and the specified isoquant in constructing the transformation curve between the final good and the net output (now negative) of the raw material.

The notion in much of the development literature is that resource-based industrialisation is a 'good thing'. Like everything else, however, it is only good up to a point, specifically point q in Figure 10.3. Thus suppose the country initially did not have the technology for resource-based manufacturing. It would then specialise at point V and trade at the world price p to obtain consumption of the final product. Acquiring the technology and producing at point q would then be superior, the lower output and export of the primary good, and hence imports of the final good, being more than compensated by additional domestic production of manufactures. Pushing resource-based industrialisation beyond q, however, by tariffs or export duties would be inefficient and reduce domestic consumption of the final good, and hence welfare.

Improvements in the terms of trade will clearly reduce the extent of resource-based manufacturing, in typical 'Dutch Disease' fashion. It is not clear, however, why the phenomenon should be referred to as a 'disease'. Relative price shifts always help some sectors and harm others. What matters for overall national welfare is whether the country is a net exporter or importer of the good that experience a rise in its relative price.

Before concluding the paper, which has been devoted exclusively to theory, I would like to say that the recent evidence on primary exports as an 'engine of growth' has been very encouraging indeed. Thailand and Malaysia have been remarkably successful with primary exports, though labour-intensive manufactured exports are growing in importance as capital accumulates rapidly. The advantage of Thailand is that its primary producers for the most part are independent owner-cultivators, so that the benefits of export expansion are widely diffused and stimulate further increases in productivity. Malaysia, with its mines and plantations, is more like the classic 'enclave' economy but even here the control and taxation of these enterprises by a national government has meant substantial contribution to the rest of the economy. The less favourable experience of many primary exporters may be due more to domestic policy failures than any intrinsic problem with this mode of development, to which Sweden is an impressive testimonial.

Notes

1. Findlay (1974).
2. Maneschi (1983).
3. Pasinetti (1960).
4. Casarosa (1978).
5. Myint (1958).
6. Caves (1965).
7. Baldwin (1956), (1963).
8. Hansen (1979).
9. Corden (1982).
10. Lewis (1954).
11. Jones (1971).
12. Findlay (1973), Ch. 5.
13. Findlay (1981), (1984).

14. Findlay (1980).
15. Roemer (1979).

Bibliography

Baldwin, R.E. 'Patterns of Development in Newly Settled Regions', *Manchester School*, Vol. 24 (1956).
____, 'Export Technology and Development from a Subsistence Level', *Economic Journal*, vol. 73 (1963).
Casarosa, C. 'A New Formulation of the Ricardian System', *Oxford Economic Papers*, vol. 30 (1978).
Caves, R.E. 'Vent for Surplus Models of Trade and Growth' in R.E. Baldwin *et al.* (eds.) *Trade, Growth and the Balance of Payments* (Rand McNally, Chicago, 1965).
Corden, W.M. 'Booming Sector and Dutch Disease Economics; A Survey', Working Paper No. 79, Australian National University, November (1973).
Findlay, R. *International Trade and Development Theory* (Columbia University Press, New York, 1973).
____, 'Relative Prices, Growth and Trade in a Simple Ricardian System', *Economica*, N.S. vol. 41 (1974).
____, 'The Terms of Trade and Equilibrium Growth in the World Economy', *American Economic Review*, vol. 70 (1980).
____, 'The Fundamental Determinants of the Terms of Trade', in S. Grassman and E. Lundberg (eds.) *The World Economic Order: Past and Prospects* (Macmillan, London and Basingstoke, 1981).
____, 'Growth and Development in Trade Models', Ch. 4 of R.W. Jones and P.B. Kenen (eds.) *Handbook of International Economics*, vol. 1 (North Holland, Amsterdam, 1984).
Hansen, B. 'Colonial Economic Development with Unlimited Supply of Land; A Ricardian Case', *Economic Development and Cultural Change*, vol. 27 (1979).
Jones, R.W. 'A Three-Factor Model in Theory, Trade and History', in J.N. Bhagwati *et al.* (eds.) *Growth, Trade and the Balance of Payments* (North Holland, Amsterdam, 1971).
Lewis, W.A. 'Economic Development with Unlimited Supplies of Labour', *Manchester School*, vol. 22 (1954).
Maneschi, A. 'Dynamic Aspects of Ricardo's International Trade Theory', *Oxford Economic Papers*, vol. 35 (1983).
Myint, H. 'The Classical Theory of International Trade and the Underdeveloped Countries', *Economic Journal*, vol. 68 (1958).
Pasinetti, L. 'A Mathematical Reformulation of the Ricardian System', *Review of Economic Studies*, vol. 27 (1960).
Roemer, M. 'Resource-Based Industrialisation: A Survey', *Journal of Development Economics*, vol. 6 (1979).

11 DUTCH DISEASE IN DEVELOPING COUNTRIES: SWALLOWING BITTER MEDICINE

Michael Roemer*

The debate of the 1950s and 1960s over primary exports as an engine of growth raised several questions about primary exports: (1) Will world demand for primary products be sufficient to propel growth in exporting countries? (2) Will adverse terms of trade siphon potential gains from LDC exporters to industrial country importers? (3) Can rapidly growing primary export industries transmit growth to the rest of the economy? The answer to all these questions is that it depends, on the product, the country, and the time period. Under some circumstances the case for primary-export-led growth is strong, and the literature has failed to establish a presumption against the use of primary exports to help stimulate development.

The 1970s provided an experiment of sorts, in which the first two questions were answered favourably for primary exporters. Boom conditions prevailed in the markets for several primary commodities. Little has to be said about the boom in petroleum, the price of which rose by a factor of 22 from 1970 to 1980. But several other commodity prices also soared, as Table 11.1 shows. Exporters of these commodities should have enjoyed rising income — if not net barter — terms of trade and buoyant export revenues. Several countries that export one or more of these commodities are shown in Table 11.2. For all but three of the nineteen listed, the dollar value of exports grew significantly faster than average LDC import prices.

If primary export sectors can transmit growth to the rest of the economy, then those countries experiencing export booms during the 1970s should have enjoyed sustained, rapid GDP growth. Many did: Indonesia, Saudi Arabia, Mexico, Brazil, Dominican Republic, Kenya, Malaysia, and Thailand all grew at more than 6.5 per cent a year for the decade, and over half the countries in Table 11.2 grew

* I would like to thank Hollis Chenery, Ronald Findlay, Andrew Kamarck, Markos Mamalakis, Malcolm McPherson, Rahman Soban, Bo Södersten, Richard Weckstein, and members of the seminars at Harvard Institute for International Development, the Yale Growth Center, and the Bangladesh Institute of Development Studies for their comments and suggestions.

Table 11.1: Price Indexes for Booming Commodities, 1970–80

Commodity	Index (1970 = 100) for	
	1975	1980ᶜ
Aluminum	141	306
Cacao	192	363
		(623 in 1977)
Coconut oil	124	219
		(328 in 1979)
Coffee	143	298
		(453 in1977)
Logs	156	447
Petroleum	826	2210
Pulp	287	412
Rice	251	301
		(376 in 1974)
Rubber	142	348
Sisal	381	503
Sugar	408	245
Tin	189	466
For comparison:[a]		
US Wholesale Prices	159	243
LDC Import Unit Values	217	373
All primary commodities[b]	173	288

a. IMF indexes.
b. Excludes petroleum.
c. Figures in parentheses give high levels for the decade if different from the 1980 level.
Source: International Monetary Fund (1982), pp. 82–5.

significantly faster than the average middle-income country during the 1970s. But there are blemishes: Ghana and Jamaica failed to grow at all, while Kuwait, Nigeria, Venezuela, Bolivia, and Tanzania were below-average performers. Indeed, those countries with the richest resource endowments — the middle- and high-income oil exporters — grew slightly slower than the average for all other middle-income LDCs. And the middle-income petroleum exporters grew more slowly during the 1970s, when their prices reached unprecedented levels, than during the previous decade of low oil prices.

The 1980s have added doubts. The world-wide recession punctured the commodity boom, and several of the high flyers of the 1970s — all the oil exporters plus Brazil, Kenya, and the Philippines — face economic retrenchment in the mid-1980s. For many of the countries listed in Table 11.2, it has become clear that a relatively long period of buoyant export revenues was not enough to stimulate

Table 11.2:   Selected Export Boom Countries, 1970–80

Country	Booming Commodity Exports	Growth (% p.a.) 1970–80 Dollar Revenue from Exports[a]	GDP[b]
Indonesia	Petroleum, wood, rubber	34	7.9
Kuwait	Petroleum	21	2.3
Mexico	Petroleum	28	6.6
Nigeria	Petroleum	35	5.3
Saudi Arabia	Petroleum	47	11.0
Venezuela	Petroleum	22	4.2
Bolivia	Tin, natural gas	17	4.5
Brazil	Coffee, sugar	22	8.6
Colombia	Coffee	18	5.8
Dominican Republic	Sugar	16	6.9
Ghana	Cacao, wood	11	0.2
Guatemala	Coffee, sugar	18	5.6
Ivory Coast	Coffee, cacao, wood	20	6.2
Jamaica	Bauxite, alumina	11	−0.7
Kenya	Coffee	16	7.6
Malaysia	Rubber, tin	23	7.8
Philippines	Coconut prods., sugar, wood	18	6.2
Tanzania	Coffee, sisal	8	4.4
Thailand	Rice, rubber, tin	25	6.9
For comparison:			
Growth of LDC import price index:		14	
GDP growth of middle-income countries:			5.6

a. Merchandise exports, current dollar values.
b. At market prices.
Sources: World Bank (1983): all data except line 1 (IMF, 1982) and line 2 (World Bank, 1982).

the kinds of structural change in the rest of the economy that might sustain growth after the export boom.

Diagnosing Dutch Disease

The important observation from the 1970s has been that export booms set up complex effects that actually retard growth in other parts of the economy. This phenomenon has been termed 'Dutch disease' because of the observed impact of North Sea gas production on the Dutch economy. With strong export revenues from gas, the guilder appreciated against other currencies, exposing Dutch industries to more intense foreign competition and causing unemployment.

As its name implies, this phenomenon is not confined to developing countries. Nor is it confined to petroleum or even to primary exports. What is true of petroleum exports has also been observed in the exports of copper from Zambia and cocoa from Ghana. Symptoms of Dutch disease may also result from large capital inflows, and might be observed in Egypt or Bangladesh as a consequence of large foreign aid receipts in the past few years; in the United States of 1982–4, as foreign private investors seek safe haven and high interest rates; in 1920s France, the recipient of German reparations; or, perhaps the outstanding historical case, in sixteenth century Spain as the gold flowed in from South America. Even resource-poor, labour surplus countries like Bangladesh, Turkey, or Egypt become infected by income remittances from their overseas migrant workers. When related to primary exports, the disease can occur because of a major world price increase, technological change that makes it much cheaper to produce an existing export, or a major resource discovery.[1]

The pathology of Dutch disease has been explored by Corden and others who have developed a three-sector model to trace its impacts.[2] In Corden's survey article, he defines the sectors as (1) the 'booming' sector which could be the oil or any other primary exporting industry during a period of rising prices, exploitation of a major resource discovery, or cost-reducing technological change; (2) other tradeables or the 'lagging' sector, which would include other exports and import substitutes in both manufacturing and agriculture; and (3) non-tradeables, including services, utilities, transportation, and so forth. Corden begins his analysis with a 'core model' which covers the medium term. Only one factor, labour, is mobile; other factors of production are specific to each of the three sectors. Capital is also immobile internationally, and the stocks of all factors are fixed, but factor prices are flexible.[3]

Growth in the booming sector has two separate impacts: a spending effect and a resource movement effect. Spending on the non-tradeable sector raises prices of non-tradeables in the short run, which causes a real appreciation of the domestic currency. (That is, the real exchange rate — defined as the nominal price of foreign currency deflated by an index of domestic costs — falls.) Although export boom revenues are also spent in the lagging sector, they do not lead to a rise in prices of tradeables, whose prices are determined in world markets; excess demand for tradeables is met through additional imports. As the price of the non-tradeables rises, labour is attracted from the lagging sector into the non-tradeables sector, causing a decline in output of the lagging sector.

The resource movement effect is activated when the increase in prices of booming sector exports raises the marginal product of labour in that sector, causing labour to move from both the lagging and non-tradeable sectors into the booming sector. Both the spending and resource movement effects pull labour out of the lagging sector. In industrial economies, where other tradeables are generally manufactures, the movement of labour from the lagging sector to the booming sector is called 'direct de-industrialisation'. The flow of labour out of non-tradeables, together with the spending effect that increases the demand for goods from that sector, causes a further movement of labour from the lagging sector to non-tradeables, and Corden calls this 'indirect de-industrialisation'. Although there is an unambiguous decline in the output of the lagging sector, the impact on non-tradeables output is uncertain: the spending effect tends to increase non-tradeables output, but the resource movement effect tends to decrease it.

When the booming sector is the petroleum industry, it may employ only small quantities of the mobile factor, eliminating the resource movement effect. In that case, the only change is a real appreciation of the currency, which causes a drop in the output of the lagging sector and an increase in the output of the non-tradeables sector.[4] In a developing country, the lagging sector is likely to include agricultural exports, import-competing food production, and manufactured import substitutes. Then the export boom may cause both de-industrialisation and 'de-agriculturalisation,' as has occurred to some extent in Indonesia, Mexico, Venezuela, and especially Nigeria.

If the three-sector analysis is extended to the long run, many other results are possible. In the long run all factors except land are mobile. If, for example, labour shifts out of the lagging and non-tradeable sectors into the booming sector, while capital can be shifted only between the lagging and non-tradeables sectors, either of these two sectors might suffer a decline in output: the outcome depends on the relative factor intensity of the two sectors. Even though the spending effect works through currency appreciation to lower the output of the lagging sector, if that sector happens to be more capital intensive, the net result could be an increase in output. If, however, the non-tradeables sector is more capital intensive, the movement of factors would reinforce the increase in non-tradeables.

Output of non-tradeables could rise so much that their price will eventually fall, causing a real exchange rate depreciation, contrary to the normal case. And when capital is mobile among all sectors, any outcome might occur; there is no presumption that any particular sector will have a rise or fall in output.[5]

As we discuss the policy impacts of Dutch disease, it is useful to keep this long-run analysis in mind. Most of the literature on the problems of mineral-rich developing countries is firmly (if implicitly) rooted in Corden's medium-term, three-sector analysis. The familiar catalogue of woes, including exchange-rate overvaluation and a decline in agricultural production, all depend on the factor immobility assumptions of Corden's medium-term model. In many cases, given the structural rigidities of developing countries, these may be quite valid assumptions for a wide range of policy decisions. Nevertheless, one must keep in mind that they are not valid for the long run in which development takes place.

Dutch Disease in Developing Countries

Corden's three-sector analysis is a helpful framework for understanding why export abundance leads to problems in developing countries. However, translation of the analysis into the LDC environment raises four questions about outcomes. First, the models reviewed by Corden assume full employment. If a developing country has substantial underemployment, either because many are engaged in low-productivity subsistence agriculture or because there are many underemployed urban job-seekers, then neither the resource movement nor the spending effects need occur, even in the medium term. One can imagine, in Corden's core model, a chain of events beginning like those he describes, but continuing as underemployed workers are absorbed into both the lagging and non-tradeables sectors (probably into cash crop agriculture, unskilled jobs in manufacturing and petty services). As non-tradeable prices rise due to the initial spending effect, workers would be drawn into those industries to increase supply and moderate the price increase, tempering or even eliminating real exchange rate appreciation. And the resource movement effect could be compensated by an infusion from the pool or surplus labour with little loss in output. However, the concept of a surplus labour pool is itself suspect; virtually no one argues any longer that LDCs contain large groups of underemployed with marginal products close to zero. In fact, oil-exporting LDCs that might have been described as labour surplus, such as Nigeria and Indonesia, did experience spending and resource movement effects, as we shall see.

The labour surplus argument can be extended internationally, with interesting implications. Several Middle Eastern oil exporters have welcomed large numbers of migrant workers from the Middle East and Asia. Like domestic surplus labour, such migrants should moderate the resource movement effect. To the extent that migrants remit incomes home or consume imported goods, labour and, by implication, many service industries, take on the characteristics of traded goods, dampening the spending effect and reducing real exchange rate appreciation. As dependence on migrant labour grows, more service industries can be treated like other traded goods. Eventually, the three-sector model collapses into a traditional two-sector model with an expanding production frontier due to additional supplies of labour. With oil the capital-intensive sector, the outcome could easily be an expansion of the other traded goods sector, rather than de-industrialisation, even in the medium term.

The third question involves the long run, when any outcome is possible depending on the relative capital intensity of the two non-booming sectors. In developing countries, it is not even possible to say whether the lagging or non-tradeables sector is more capital-intensive, because each is composed of subsectors with very different production characteristics. The lagging sector includes export agriculture and food production, both of which can be quite labour-intensive, along with import-substituting manufacturing, probably capital-intensive. Non-tradeables include capital-intensive utilities and transport services, as well as household and personal services and petty trading, probably the most labour-intensive pursuits in any economy. Under these conditions one cannot generalise about long-run Dutch disease impacts.

Fourth, the identification of traded and non-traded goods may be obscure even in the absence of imported labour. Many developing countries have so protected their fledgling industries through prohibitive tariffs and import quotas, that otherwise importable goods have been rendered non-tradeable; the prices of such goods bear no relation to world prices. The same may be true for some basic foods. These sectors may behave like non-tradeable services during an export boom.

A growing literature on Dutch disease in developing countries includes three recent contributions utilising models different from Corden's, that try to estimate the impacts of export booms. Harberger uses a three-sector model, but one in which output depends on relative prices; hence the resource movement effect is implicit rather than explicit in the model.[6] For a range of reasonable price and income elasticities, Harberger shows that an oil shock equal to 10 per cent of national income can lead to real exchange rate appreciation of 2.6 to 16 per cent. But the shift in income from the lagging sector to non-tradeables is modest: only 2 per cent of national product in the extreme case, possibly as low as 0.4 per cent. Consistent with Corden, Harberger's model generates its greatest exchange rate appreciation and shifts in output when the income elasticity of demand for home goods is highest (his highest level is one).

Timmer has analysed the impact of energy prices on agriculture for seven countries, including both oil exporters (Indonesia, Malaysia, and Mexico) and importers (Korea, Philippines, Sri Lanka, and Thailand).[7] Timmer develops a simultaneous equation simulation model in which a change in oil prices works its way through the economy via mechanisms that include changes in *per capita* income, exchange rate appreciation, and the rural–urban terms of trade. Based on the structures and experience (from 1960 to 1980) of these seven countries, Timmer simulates a sudden and sustained rise in the petroleum export share of GDP from 2 to 4 per cent. Five years after this boom has begun, agricultural value added *per capita* is about 15 per cent below what it would have been without the boom. Note the much greater output decline than in Harberger's estimate, despite the much smaller oil shock modelled by Timmer. Should the government control domestic inflation or devalue the exchange rate to maintain its real pre-boom level, agricultural GDP *per capita* is virtually the same, five years after the boom begins, as it would have been in the absence of the price rise. Conversely, petroleum importers suffering from the same oil shock (oil imports' share of GDP doubles to 4 per cent) who devalue by 25 per cent after the shock, can *increase* their agricultural value added *per capita* by over 10 per cent after five years, compared to the simulated value in the absence of shock. Timmer's model, though it uses a different production function, is consistent with Corden's medium-term results in that agriculture, the lagging sector, does suffer a drop in output, one that can be corrected by an appropriate policy response.

Pertinent data are collected in Table 11.3 for six petroleum exporters representing different parts of the world and different structural characteristics. All countries in the table except Mexico 'suffered' two oil shocks, each much larger than those modelled by Harberger and Timmer. Mexico's relatively modest shock came with the second oil price increase of 1979–80. In all countries except Mexico, the real exchange rate appreciated significantly from 1970 to 1981. Saudi Arabia and Kuwait experienced appreciations of a third or more in both oil shocks, as did Nigeria, Mexico and Venezuela during the second price rise. Indonesia devalued in 1978 to counteract its real appreciation.

In the context of growing economies, 'de-industrialisation' and 'de-agriculturalisation' must mean slower-than-normal growth, rather than absolute decline. Timmer treats the issue this way in his model. In the absence of a commodity boom, we would expect manufacturing to grow faster than other sectors, agriculture slower, and non-tradeables in between. During the period from 1960 to 1981, in both the developing countries as a group and the middle-income developing countries, manufacturing value added grew at more than twice the rate for agriculture. Using these rough guidelines, one can identify four clear cases of lagging sectors from the sectoral growth rates in Table 11.3. In Saudi Arabia, although agriculture and manufacturing grew briskly, both fell far behind non-tradeables, which grew at 16 per cent a year from 1970 to 1981. In Indonesia, agricultural value added growth was only 40 per cent of non-tradeables growth, and in Nigeria agriculture actually declined over eleven years.

However, in Kuwait, Nigeria, Indonesia and Mexico, manufacturing growth matched or exceeded that of non-tradeables. The explanation may well lie in heavy protection: prohibitive tariffs and quotas may have converted many manufactures from tradeables into non-tradeables. In Venezuela, all sectors grew slowly, especially considering the export boom, and in that sense both agriculture and industry may be characterised as lagging sectors. But with non-tradeables growing at only 5.5 per cent a year, these are not typical Dutch disease symptoms.

Lewis catalogues some ill effects of a booming traditional export sector in developing countries, effects that are not captured by the models.[8] First, there is a general relaxation of discipline by the ministry of finance over all fiscal matters as a consequence of mineral wealth. Second, and closely related, government officials,

Table 11.3: Dutch Disease Indicators

Country	Oil Shock (%)[a]		Real Exchange Rate[b]				Sectoral Growth Rates, 1970–81 (% p.a.)		
	1970–5	1975–80	1970	1975	1978	1981	Agriculture	Manufacturing	Non-tradeables[c]
Kuwait	183	71	167	100	119	86[d]	6.1	9.5	9.7[e]
Saudi Arabia	544	168	292	100	104	69[f]	5.3	6.7	15.8
Nigeria	73	46	117	100	121	89	–0.3	11.7	9.1
Indonesia	146	60	118	101	86/117[g]	106	4.0	13.4	10.1
Mexico	1	20	83	100	124	89	3.7	7.1	6.9
Venezuela	48	34	97	100	103	76	2.7	4.7	5.5

a. Increment in nominal value of petroleum exports divided by GDP at beginning of each period.
b. Index of local currency-to-dollar rate divided by the implicit GDP deflator and multiplied by an index of import prices. A decrease in the index represents a real appreciation.
c. Construction, utilities, transport and communication, public administration and defence, and other services.
d. 1980.
e. 1970–80.
f. Year ending June 30, 1981.
g. 1977 and 1979 values to show effect of 1978 devaluation.
Source: World Bank (1983).

attempting to utilise the additional resources productivity, move increasingly toward large-scale, capital-intensive, long-gestation projects which utilise large lumps of available capital. Third, the push to spend resources, coupled with the limited capacity of governments in most developing countries to manage large programmes, often leads to wasteful and poorly conceived projects. Fourth, because government is unable to absorb enough of the new surplus in public sector projects, it must attempt to channel resources to the private sector, yet the government is ill-suited to serve as a financial intermediary. Fifth, as Ul Haque observes, the private sector is less able to respond because government's own growth has crowded out private firms' access to scarce managerial and technical skills. Sixth, to make matters worse, private investors become infected with a rentier ethos, demanding quick, high returns on investment and concentrating in trade and urban property.[9] These six extensions of Corden's spending effect cause the newly generated capital to be invested inefficiently, so the amount of future growth promised by a given investment falls substantially.

Seventh, Lewis observes that large numbers of expatriates are required to manage the expanded investment programmes. Not only do expatriates earn a substantial fraction of the revenue generated by the projects, but they also set up an intensified demonstration effect that leads to demands by citizens for wages and consumption patterns similar to those of expatriates. Eighth, Lewis highlights the classic dual economy problem of wage followership. In the highly capital-intensive mineral sector, labour has a high marginal revenue product. Taking advantage of this, mining companies pay high wages to obtain the best workers. Both unions and government then use the mineral sector as a standard toward which all wages should move. Consequently, wages in the formal sector are well above the marginal revenue product of abundant labour in the informal sector, and investors have an incentive to favour more capital-intensive technologies. Wage followership leads to an entrenched high-wage labour aristocracy and growing underemployment among those not able to find jobs in the modern sector. Finally, Lewis notes that the booming mining sector, which dominates a small developing economy, has cyclical price and revenue patterns. With so much now dependent on mineral sector revenues and the fiscal linkage, any instability in mineral prices is transmitted immediately and in forceful ways to the rest of the economy.[10]

Although Dutch disease is generally associated with mineral

wealth, a similar malady afflicts countries whose agricultural exports suddenly boom. Indeed, within the medium-term Corden core model the effects of an export boom could be more severe. Agricultural exports such as coffee, cocoa, tea, palm oil, cotton, sisal, rubber, and others are far more labour-intensive than mining or petroleum. An equivalent expansion of output from a booming, labour-intensive agriculture would draw more heavily on the mobile resource, labour, than would an expansion of mineral exports. This suggests a greater resource movement effect, from both other tradeables (the lagging sector) and non-tradeables. The impact would be temporised if a pool of underemployed labour were available to supply the export sector directly or to replace the labour it draws from other sectors. Agricultural labourers and small farmers may spend a higher fraction of their additional incomes on tradeables, especially food and clothing, than would mine owners, large farmers or civil servants, reducing somewhat the spending effect.[11] But the differential impact would not be sufficient to avoid real exchange rate appreciation altogether. Hence in the medium term the economy would undergo de-industrialisation and de-agriculturalisation, possibly as severe as for a mineral exporter.

However, a recent study of three agricultural exporters questions these expectations.[12] Dick *et al.* use computable general equilibrium models for Colombia, Ivory Coast and Kenya to measure the short-term (two-year) impact of 10 per cent price increases in coffee, cocoa and tea. When the real exchange rate appreciates sufficiently to reestablish external balance, they find the services sector enjoys the most growth, from 1.0 per cent in Colombia to 2.3 per cent in Kenya, consistent with Corden. Most manufacturing sectors, with the exception of textiles in Kenya, show little growth or decline. But surprisingly, in Ivory Coast and Kenya, non-booming agricultural products grow by from 0.9 to 1.9 per cent: no de-agriculturalisation here. And the two-year shifts in output, though larger than Harberger's, are significantly smaller than those observed by Timmer, even allowing for Timmer's longer period. (The size of the shock modelled by Timmer is roughly comparable to that of Dick *et al.*)

Mineral export enclaves typically have few important backward or forward product linkages with other sectors. But export agriculture can have linkages: backward, to fertiliser, farm implements and fuel suppliers; and forward, to food processors, textiles, leather goods and certain chemicals. Agricultural export booms encourage backward-linked industries, but discourage forward-linked manufacturers, whose input costs rise. The net effect of product linkages on lagging industries is thus indeterminate, but seems unlikely to compensate much for the other effects of Dutch disease.

Why Treat the Disease?

In his article for this volume, Findlay asks why Dutch disease is a disease: any shift in the terms of trade favours some sectors over others. And why should the lagging sector should be protected at the expense of non-tradeables? The answer to both questions is obvious if the export industry is a cyclical one, such as cocoa, coffee, rubber, sisal, copper or tin. If the boom is expected to be short-lived, it is important to protect the rest of the economy from both the relative price and resource movement impacts. Both diversification and the realisation of linkages from the export sector are served by steady, long-term price signals to potential investors. This suggests a large stabilising role for government. Government may also wish to diversify the country's investment in assets simply to reduce the variance in income, whatever the effects on long-term growth.

Even if the export industry promises sustained long-run growth, governments may wish to diversify if the export sector is capital-intensive and does not promise substantial job creation, as is true for most mineral industries, especially oil. Whatever the arguments about maximising income growth and using transfers to distribute that income, most people and their governments consider employment to be an end in itself and cannot long contemplate the possibility of rising unemployment, even coupled with substantial income transfers to the unemployed. Governments placing a high value on equity will also find it tempting to protect the lagging sector, which is likely to employ a large share of low-income workers, especially in small-scale farming and labour-intensive manufacturing. However, protecting the lagging sector would stifle the growth of non-tradeables, including several low-wage, labour-intensive industries — especially petty trades, household and personal services. Most governments would choose to protect employment in manufacturing and agriculture rather than in services, but the costs of protection could cancel its advantages. Van Wijnbergen offers a more compelling reason to protect the lagging sector: if technological change, especially from learning by doing, is more rapid in the traded goods sectors, as seems likely, then any temporary reduction in the growth of traded goods output could lead to lower average productivity and hence lower national income in the future, even if primary exports continue to boom.[13]

When the exportable natural resource is in limited supply and expected to run out in the foreseeable future, as is petroleum in Venezuela and Nigeria, there is an obvious imperative to diversify into other tradeable production that can sustain economic development when the resource runs out. In this situation, the foregone growth of non-tradeables is of less concern, because without other goods to offer on world markets the country faces an eventual slide towards autarchy and reduced income.[14] These countries face a mammoth task in trying to transform the economy away from its natural resource base toward a more diversified productive base in a short period of time. Van Wijnbergen shows that, in a two-sector model of optimal capital accumulation and perfect foresight, price signals would lead private agents to invest in the lagging, traded goods sector before the natural resource is exhausted. But he doubts that any developing countries have the capital markets needed to transmit such price signals to investors, and in their absence government intervention is required.[15] Even when government and private agents have similar information on resource depletion, intervention may be required for all the reasons that shadow prices differ from market prices in developing countries. Indeed, one of the characteristics of mineral-rich economies (and of economies with cyclically booming commodity exports) that makes Dutch disease so virulent is the need for government intervention to capture the potential benefits of export booms.

Swallowing Bitter Medicine

Several policy instruments are available to protect the lagging sector, but each has serious drawbacks rooted in the political economy of development. Perhaps the most obvious antidote to Dutch disease is to sterilise the rapidly growing revenues of the booming sector. Government would have to accumulate foreign reserves, match those with additional savings, either a surplus on its own current account or through the private sector, and also prevent the additional reserves from becoming monetised in the domestic economy. Corden calls this 'exchange rate protection' because it avoids or reduces the real appreciation of the currency as a result of the expenditure effect.[16] Hence, the lagging sector is not disadvantaged by facing an appreciated exchange rate, though potential growth of the non-tradeables sector is sacrificed. By not spending all the revenues from its export sector, government reduces the problems of absorptive capacity noted by Lewis. Reserve accumulation and sterilisation is also an appropriate policy when a government expects a boom to be short-lived or expects export revenues to have marked cyclical behaviour. But reserve swings may have to be large: Dick *et al.* estimate that, to insulate their economies from 95 per cent of the variance in coffee, cocoa and tea prices (based on a three-year moving average), Colombia, Ivory Coast and Kenya would have to accept reserve changes of 50 to 100 per cent of their typical levels.[17]

But the prospects for successful sterilisation are not very bright. Everyone recognises that limited resources — government revenues, private saving, foreign exchange — give government a legitimate reason to resist the demands of a variety of constituencies for increased expenditures. Export booms remove this restraint, both actually and in the mind of the public. Whether the motive is humanitarian, such as the relief of poverty; developmental, such as the extension of infrastructure; or political, such as buying off both constituents and opponents with projects or other largesse, the demands become much more difficult to resist as it is generally known that revenues are flowing into the country at unprecedented rates. The finance minister who attempts under these circumstances to save export revenues and sterilise reserves is fighting a strong countertrend, and probably risking his job. (Davis recounts the stabilisation experience of several coffee exporters during the short-lived boom of the mid-1970s.[18])

The short horizon of many governments exacerbates this problem. Whether democratic or totalitarian, a government's concern about public opinion and political stability tends to focus on periods measured in months or, at most, a couple of years. Whatever troubles may lie three to five years ahead, it is tempting for governments to spend their way towards short-term political stability by using newly-found export revenues. The most striking recent example is probably that of Mexico under López Portillo, whose administration, limited to one term of six years, not only spent its current oil revenues, but borrowed against future revenues to an unsustainable extent. Revenue sterilisation requires a longer policy horizon than many governments have, or feel they can afford. This short horizon also helps to explain why the seemingly more tractable problems of cyclical exports are almost as difficult to solve as those of the more sustained booms in products like oil and diamonds.

In the absence of revenue sterilisation, government may still avoid the exchange rate impact of a booming export sector through two alternative but closely related measures. The first would be to manage a dual exchange rate, paying an appreciated rate to the booming export sector but maintaining a devalued rate for all other traded goods. Dual exchange rates were very common in Latin America after World War II as a means of protecting the non-traditional export and import substitution sectors. Although dual rates may be manageable for a short period, they set up large incentives to circumvent the dual system and over the long run may be very difficult to maintain.

The equivalent of a dual rate can be achieved by taxing the booming export sector and transferring these taxes as subsidies to all other traded goods. Subsidisation is the optimal policy if government's main concern is that firms in the lagging sector capture the external benefits of learning by doing, and hence continue to expand and further contribute to productivity increases. Taxation of a natural resource base has been widely practised and seems a perfectly feasible policy. The problem lies with subsidies to the lagging sectors. There are many technical questions about subsidies, including the issue of whether industries or factors of production ought to be subsidised. But bureaucratic problems are crucial. In governments with limited management and administrative capacities, payments of subsidies have often been badly mishandled. In particular, manufacturers typically complain that export subsidies are paid only after enormous effort and documentation on their part, intercessions with the officers in charge of the subsidy programme, and long delays. The expected return on an investment in a subsidised industry falls, the longer the delays and the greater the uncertainties of ever receiving payment. Furthermore, the temptation to use subsidy schemes as political tools is very great. If political favourites are able to obtain subsidies more easily than others, then to some extent the incentive becomes one of political support rather than the manufacture of products serving economic needs.

A fourth instrument, tariff protection, might also be used to prevent de-industrialisation. Very high and generally uneven tariff protection has been employed by countries such as Venezuela and Zambia to promote industrialisation in the face of appreciated exchange rates from the petroleum and copper industries, respectively. The problems with the almost universal pattern of differentiated industrial protection have been documented extensively in the development literature.[19] The proliferation of entrenched, skewed protective systems across the third world testifies to their political strength.[20] The liberalising reforms of the 1970s, especially exchange regime reforms that include more uniform and modest protection, have been intended to escape these pernicious systems. But no ready constituency exists for uniform and modest protection, because the natural tendency of both manufacturers and governments is to push for higher tariffs for specific industries. And even with uniform tariffs, other tradeables, particularly non-traditional exports, are severely disadvantaged unless they are uniformly subsidised. Most import substitution regimes have been ineffectual in subsidising non-traditional exports.

The problems of wage followership and the consequential capital intensity of the formal sectors can be mitigated if government undertakes a determined incomes policy to contain wage growth. At the same time, it needs to liberalise financial markets so that the interest rates represent the scarcity of capital, and hence the incentives lie in the direction of labour-intensive production techniques. The need for wage restraint on grounds of both employment creation and economic stabilisation has been widely recognised by most governments. But political exigencies work most strongly against counterboom wage policies. The trouble is that the required policies challenge the interests of a group with one of the most articulated political positions in society. Not only is labour typically organised into unions that represent an important political force, but labourers tend to concentrate in cities where they can exert immediate — and raucous — political influence. Some of the most strongly held economic policies in developing countries are aimed already at mollifying wage labourers: the minimum wage, cheap (often subsidised) food, mandated social welfare payments, job protection schemes, etc.

No happy ending suggests itself. One lesson of this essay is how similar the problems of resource-rich countries are to those of countries less well endowed but depending on a few primary exports. In all these countries, the strong tendencies of political economy will continue to work against policies that might harness primary export sectors to sustained development. The best hope is that the story of the curse of wealth, if told repeatedly in volumes like this one, may begin to find an audience of developing-country policymakers. Something like that has happened with import substitution, which is no longer embraced with quite the fervour of the 1960s. One advantage economists have in combating Dutch disease is that the failures are so palpable — witness the near-disasters of Mexico and Nigeria — that sheer fright may force policymakers to heed the warnings. Having wielded that stick, economists can also hold out a carrot: in recent years, countries like Malaysia, Thailand, Colombia, Ivory Coast and Kenya have managed to grow handsomely on a diversified base of primary exports. It can be done, and there are no obvious alternatives for many developing countries to consider.

Notes

1. There is little new in the concept of Dutch disease, although it has been analysed in innovative ways in recent years. It would be an interesting task — but for another paper — to embed the recent concerns about Dutch disease in the older literatures on staple theory, enclaves and dualism, and the terms of trade debate.
2. Corden (1982); Corden and Neary (1982).
3. Corden (1982), pp. 5–12, summarised the 'core model.'
4. Dutch disease can then be modelled in a two-sector economy, with the booming sector treated as a pure resource transfer, as is done by van Wijnbergen (1982).
5. Corden (1982), pp. 13–14; Corden and Neary (1982), pp. 833–9.
6. Harberger (1983).
7. Timmer (1982).
8. Lewis (1984).
9. Ul Haque (1982), pp. 10–11.
10. Lewis (1984).
11. Different spending patterns from additional income may also affect the degree of real appreciation in economies with buoyant capital inflows, including foreign aid, or high remittances from migrant workers.
12. Dick, Gupta, Mayer and Vincent (1983).
13. van Wijnbergen (1984).
14. Bruton (1981), pp. 6–7 makes the same point in terms of vulnerability to changing conditions in foreign markets for both the booming export and the financial assets in which exporting countries invest their reserves.
15. van Wijnbergen (1982).
16. Corden (1982), p. 32.
17. Dick *et al*. (1983), p. 414.
18. Davis (1983).
19. Bruton (1970); Balassa (1971).
20. Hirschman (1968) has explored the mechanisms underlying this strength.

Bibliography

Balassa, Bela, *et al. The Structure of Protection in Developing Countries* (Baltimore, 1971).

Bruton, Henry, 'The Import Substitution Strategy of Economic Development.' *The Pakistan Development Review*, vol. 10 (1970).

____, 'Economic Development with Unlimited Supplies of Foreign Exchange.' Williams College Center for Development Studies, Research Memorandum Series RM83 (1981).

Corden, W. Max, 'Booming Sector and Dutch Disease Economics: A Survey.' Australian National University Faculty of Economics and Research, School of Social Sciences, Working Paper No. 079 (1982).

Corden, W. Max, and Neary, J. Peter, 'Booming Sector and Deindustrialisation in a Small Open Economy.' *Economic Journal*, vol. 92 (1982).

Davis, Jeffrey M. 'The Economic Effects of Windfall Gains in Export Earnings, 1975–8'. *World Development*, vol. 11 (1983).

Dick, Hermann; Gupta, Sanjeev; Mager, Thomas, and Vincent, David 'The Short-Run Impact of Fluctuating Primary Commodity Prices on Three Developing Economies: Colombia, Ivory Coast and Kenya'. *World Development*, vol. 11 (1983).

Harberger, Arnold C. 'Dutch Disease — How Much Sickness, How Much Boon?' *Resources and Energy*, vol. 5 (1983).

Hirschman, Albert O. 'The Political Economy of Import Substitution'. *Quarterly Journal of Economics*, vol. 82 (1968).

International Monetary Fund, *International Financial Statistics Yearbook 1982*. (Washington, D.C., 1982).

Lewis, Stephen R. 'Development Problems of the Mineral-Rich Countries'. in M. Syrquin, L. Taylor and L. Westphal, (eds.), *Economic Structure and Performance: Essays in Honor of H.B. Chenery* (New York, 1984).

Timmer, C. Peter, 'Energy and Agricultural Change in the Asia-Pacific Region: The Agricultural Sector'. Harvard Institute for International Development, Development Discussion Paper No. 140 (1982).

ul Haque, Irfan, 'The Oil Economy Syndrome: Analysis and Policies'. Energy Research Group, Cavendish Laboratory, Energy Discussion Paper No. 24 (1982).

van Wijnbergen, Sweder, 'Optimal Capital and the Allocation of Investment between Traded and Non-traded Sectors in Oil-Producing Countries'. Development Research Department, World Bank (1982).

____ 'The Dutch Disease: A Disease After All?' *Economic Journal* (1984).

World Bank *World Development Report 1982* (Washington, DC, 1982).

____ *World Tables*, Third Edition (Washington, DC, 1983).

12 MIGRATION AND EMIGRANTS' REMITTANCES: THEORY AND EVIDENCE FROM THE MIDDLE EAST

Frank Kirwan

The OPEC-ordained increase in the price of oil in 1973 and subsequent increases during that decade transformed the external financial position of the oil-exporting countries. Nowhere was this more apparent than in the Middle East. The new-found wealth of the Arab oil-producing states induced many to embark on ambitious development plans. The focus of this paper is on the migration and remittance flows which this accelerated development set in train and in particular on the impact of such flows on the economy of one of the neighbouring labour-exporting states, Jordan.

The major oil producers in the Middle East are in general sparsely populated. Implementation of their post-1978 development plans therefore required substantial imports not merely of capital but also of labour. Much of the induced demand for labour was satisfied by immigration from non-oil-exporting states in the region with Jordan, Egypt[1] and the two Yemens particularly to the fore. In contrast to much migration in the developed world, the induced flows in this case were from the more advanced countries in the region to their less industrialised, less well educated, but richer rentier neighbours. As a result the unemployment problems of some of the non-oil-producing states, such as Jordan, vanished in the latter half of the decade, to be replaced in effect by excess demand conditions in some sectors of the labour market. Such conditions in turn attracted flows of replacement migrants from as far afield as Bangladesh, Korea, Pakistan and China, and gave rise to an increased volume of seasonal and rural-to-urban migration within the region.

The majority of migrants, both Arab and non-Arab, are unlikely to settle permanently in the oil-producing states. Most do not have such an option. Consequently this trade in human capital has generated financial flows of remittances towards the labour-exporting states, flows which in some cases have exceeded earnings from commodity trade.[2] The resulting expansion in aggregate demand in these countries, unaccompanied in the short run by a comparable increase in domestic supply, has led to pressure on both the domestic price level and the current account of the balance of payments. Restrictions on interest rates and the inadequacy of domestic capital markets have militated against the optimal employment of emigrants' remittances. Rather than financing capital accumulation in productive sectors, the bulk of these funds appears to have been channelled into residential construction and land speculation.

None of these effects is well documented. Indeed, even the quantification of migrant flows into and out of Jordan, one of the major Arab labour exporters, is fraught with difficulty. The unstable political situation in the Middle East characterised by the recurrent Arab–Israeli conflicts of 1948, 1967 and 1973, by the Jordanian and Lebanese civil wars of 1970 and 1975 respectively, and by the Israeli–Lebanese strife of 1981–3 have generated large movements of refugees. Such refugee flows are not well documented, but have had profound effects on demographic and labour market variables in Jordan.

While considerable resources have been devoted to the attempted quantification of migrant flows,[3] much less attention appears to have been paid to the induced flows of emigrants' remittances to the labour-exporting countries. In part this reflects a paucity of data, in part the traditional focus of migration theorists, or at least of those with an economic bias, on the operation of the labour market. Existing literature in this area has focused almost exclusively on microeconomic studies of the use to which emigrants' remittances have been put by their recipients,[4] to the neglect of broader macroeconomic considerations.

This chapter attempts in small measure to begin to fill this gap in the literature, focusing in particular on the case of the Jordanian economy where emigrants' remittances exceeded earnings from merchandise exports during the period 1974–81. The chapter is in three distinct parts: The first provides a factual outline of labour exporting from Jordan. The second considers the welfare impact of migration and remittances in a stylised $2 \times 2 \times 2$ model and concludes that welfare in the labour-exporting country will fall even if remittances are sufficiently large to maintain source country nominal income at its pre-emigration level. The final part is documentary and attempts to trace the macroeconomic and sectoral impact of remittance flows on the Jordanian economy during the period 1974–81.

1. The Background

The Hashemite Kingdom of Jordan comprises land on both sides of the river Jordan. That on the West Bank, comprising only some 6 per cent of the total land area, but without doubt the most fertile part, has been under Israeli occupation since the war of 1967. The land on the East Bank consists primarily of desert and mountain. Only about 15 per cent of the total land area is cultivable and of this only one-sixteenth is irrigated.[5] Agriculture accounted for only 7 per cent of GDP in 1980. Natural resources are few, though oil has recently been discovered in quantities sufficient to supply domestic needs. From a balance of payments viewpoint the most important natural resources are vast phosphate deposits of which only a small fraction has been extracted to date. Nonetheless phosphates have accounted for over 20 per cent of export revenues in recent years. The economy is characterised by a dominant services sector, accounting for almost 70 per cent of GDP and a correspondingly weak manufacturing base whose contribution to output in 1980 barely exceeded that of construction. The population of the East Bank numbers just over 2 million, but a considerable part of the labour force, perhaps as much as one-third, is employed in neighbouring oil-producing states. It is difficult to be more specific because demographic and labour force data are far from adequate. No full population census was carried out between 1961 and 1979, while the actual recording of deaths, and to a lesser extent births, is seriously incomplete.[6] Estimates of migrant flows are therefore likely to be subject to a greater than usual degree of error.

Birks and Sinclair[7] estimated that in 1975 there were approximately 660,000 Jordanians living in other Arab States, of whom 150,000 were economically active. These figures serve as benchmarks of pre-1975 migration, both voluntary and enforced. Kirwan[8] estimated that net emigration of 116,000 workers from Jordan had taken place over the period 1975–9. This net outflow can be placed in perspective by noting that the Jordan Development Conference[9] forecast 147,000 new entrants to the Jordanian labour force over the period 1975–80. The net outflow of Jordanian manpower therefore amounted to over three-quarters of the natural increase in labour supply during this period.

Only fragmentary data are available on the characteristics of Jordanian emigrants over the period 1975–9. The Ministry of Labour operates a permit system for migrants to Saudi Arabia,

Libya and Kuwait. However the system is voluntary and the majority of migrants appear to bypass it. The permit serves primarily as a certification of skills, years of training and work experience and is therefore most attractive to skilled and semi-skilled workers. The net outflow of Jordanian labour appears to contain a significant educated component[10] — a reflection of the selectivity of migration, the relatively advanced educational system in Jordan and the built-in bias of the recording system to identify the more qualified migrants.

Emigration of Jordanian labour in the latter half of the 1970s was offset to some extent by significant inflows of migrant workers. Such replacement migrants came primarily from the surrounding Arab States and to a lesser extent from the Asian subcontinent, particularly from Pakistan. By far the most important source of immigrant workers was Egypt, which accounted for over 60 per cent of the recorded inflow in 1978 and 1979. The overall picture is one where Jordan exports labour to high-wage oil-producing states and imports low-wage labour from non-oil-producing neighbouring states. This somewhat circular process stems from the greater opportunities for Jordanian labour in the oil-producing states due to the high educational attainment of the Jordanian labour force and the political acceptability of Jordanian compared for example to Egyptian labour in the later years of the Sadat regime following the signing of the Camp David accord.[11]

The importation of low-wage labour and the exportation of high-wage manpower have generated significant net flows of emigrants' remittances[12] in favour of the Jordanian economy. Such flows are documented in Table 12.1. The value of remittances by Jordanian emigrants rose sharply in the years immediately following 1973 as the oil-producing states embarked on development plans and began attracting Jordanian manpower in large numbers. The rapid rise may also reflect a qualitative change in the composition of the Jordanian emigrant stream, with a shift towards a smaller proportion of highly qualified manpower and increased emphasis on short term migration. The propensity of skilled and semi-skilled emigrants to remit appears to be somewhat greater than that of highly qualified emigrants, reflecting the longer expected duration of migration of the latter group.[13] The concentration of Jordanian emigrants in the construction sector, and the downturn which occurred in that sector in Saudi Arabia in 1978/9, contributed to a fall in the real value of remittances to Jordan in those years.

Remittances outwith Jordan did not assume any significance in the years prior to 1976, but have risen significantly in recent years as a consequence of increased inflows of replacement migrants. The resultant outflow amounted to 15 per cent of the value of the remittance inflow in 1981.

Table 12.1: Workers' Remittances, Jordan (JD million, 1975 prices*)

	Credit	Debit	Net
1974	26.9	—	26.9
1975	53.3	—	53.3
1976	122.3	6.1	116.2
1977	121.2	11.8	109.4
1978	116.7	14.7	102.0
1979	115.0	15.4	99.6
1980	136.0	26.5	109.5
1981	177.0	27.1	149.9

* Deflated by the Cost of Living Index.
Source: Central Bank of Jordan, Monthly Statistical Bulletin.

Such significant net inflows of remittances notwithstanding, the Jordanian authorities have called repeatedly for the establishment of an International Labour Compensatory Facility to reimburse labour-exporting countries for any loss incurred through emigration. Opposition by labour-importing states to the creation of such a facility has rested in part on the significant inflows of remittances enjoyed by many source countries, which opponents claim is an automatic form of compensation. Though the literature on the impact of emigration on welfare in the source country is extensive, it appears to have ignored the role of remittances. The next section of this paper extends the model of Rivera-Batiz[14] to include emigrants' remittances and shows that the welfare impact is indeterminate in such circumstances.

Like much theoretical analysis, the model presented below is stylised rather than a true reflection of Jordanian conditions. Its value is as a tool to highlight the complexity of the problem. The analysis outlined here suggests that the Jordanian call for a compensatory facility cannot be dismissed *a priori*, but must rest on a comprehensive evaluation of fact and theory. The remaining sections of this paper attempt to contribute to such an evaluation.

2. Remittances and Economic Welfare in the Source Country

The analytical framework for this section is the Heckscher–Ohlin trade model in simple two-country, two-factor and two-good guise. The countries are the source and the host, the factors physical capital (K) and labour (L) and the goods manufactures (X_T) and services (X_N). Production functions are assumed to be linear homogeneous but those in the host country display a factor neutral, product neutral technical superiority. Both factors are assumed to be fully employed and there are no factor reversals. The two goods differ in factor intensities. Following Rivera-Batiz (1982) labour-intensive services are assumed to be non-traded while trade in manufactures is initially balanced. All persons are assumed to have identical tastes with unitary income elasticity of demand for all commodities.

The assumption that the labour-intensive good is not traded reflects the fact that emigrants from labour-exporting countries were typically engaged in the tertiary or subsistence agriculture sectors in the source country. As noted above, Jordanian emigrants are no exception to this pattern. Following Krauss[15] it is assumed that the migrant produces in the host country but consumes in the source country with remittances linking both activities. This assumption avoids the problem of differing populations when comparing levels of societal welfare.[16] Consider figure 12.1. T-E-N is the production possibility frontier in the source country prior to emigration taking place. The real exchange rate (ratio of non-traded to traded prices) is represented by P_0P_0. The pre-emigration equilibrium is at point E with balanced trade in manufactures. The pre-emigration level of societal welfare in the source country is U_0. Migrants are assumed to own no capital. Holding product prices constant, the effect of emigration therefore follows straightforwardly from the Rybczynski theorem. Outward migration of labour reduces output of non-tradeables and increases output of tradeables. The production possibility frontier of the non-migrant remainder of the source country labour force can be represented[17] as T'N'. Given the assumption of unitary income elasticity of demand for all commodities emigration leads to excess demand for non-tradeables in the source country, to a rise in their relative price and thus to an appreciation of the real exchange rate. In the absence of emigrants' remittances societal welfare unambiguously falls.[18]

Figure 12.1:   The Effects of Remittances on Welfare in the Source Country

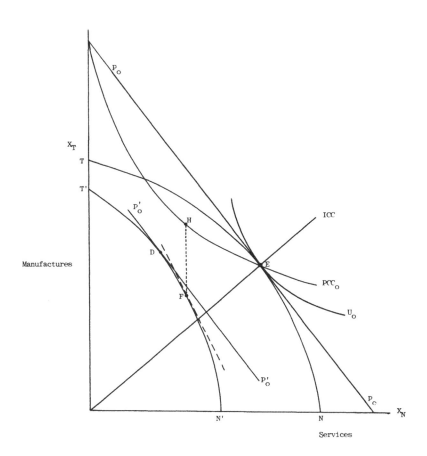

Now consider the case where remittances do occur. The simplest case to analyse is that where remittances maintain nominal income in the source country at the pre-emigration level. At the original set of commodity prices the source country budget constraint given such remittances is P_0P_0. Domestically generated income at the original product prices is $P_0'P_0'$ with remittances constrained to equal the vertical distance between P_0P_0 and $P_0'P_0'$. Emigration leads to excess demand for non-tradeables and thus to a rise in their relative price. Remittances accentuate this tendency. The composition of domestic production alters in response to the change in relative prices with the new production equilibrium to the right of D along T′N′. Changes in relative prices also provoke changes in patterns of consumption. The new consumption equilibrium must lie to the left of E along the price consumption curve PCC_0 (PCC_0 is the locus of points of tangency between budget line and indiference curve as P_0P_0 pivots about its vertical intercept). Given the fact that the labour intensive good is non-traded, the consumption equilibrium (H) must lie vertically above the production equilibrium (F). The consequent deficit on trade in manufactures is covered by the inflow of emigrants' remittances.

Notwithstanding the fact that emigrants' remittances maintain source country nominal income at pre-emigration levels, societal welfare still falls in this case. The final consumption equilibrium with remittances lies to the left of E along PCC_0 and therefore represents a lower level of welfare than prior to emigration. *A fortiori*, societal welfare will also be lower if emigration is accompanied by remittances which are less than the value of output foregone through emigration.

Where remittances cause source country income to rise the direction of the migration-and remittance-induced change in welfare is indeterminate. Figure 12.1 needs to be modified in such a case by the displacement of the price consumption curve to the right along the income consumption curve (ICC) (ICC is the locus of points of tangency between budget line and indiference curve as P_0P_0 is shifted parallel to itself) through E. The starting point for the effect of relative price changes on consumption in this case is to the right of E along ICC. The final equilibrium may lie on an indiference curve which is higher or lower than U_0, or indeed on U_0 itself, depending on the magnitude of remittances. There can therefore be no presumption in this model that societal welfare in the source country is increased through emigration merely because the associated remittances exceed the loss of domestically generated nominal income. Such an outcome may occur but is not guaranteed.

The outcome will obviously be somewhat different if unemployed resources exist in the source country throughout the period under consideration. So long as the outflow of labour does not exceed the original level of unemployment, no output will be foregone through emigration and any induced flow of remittances will act to increase the level of societal welfare. This particular case corresponds to that of the Jordanian economy in the early part of the 1970s when neighbouring oil producers were embarking on development plans. As documented below, later years saw a significant outflow of labour from a Jordanian economy effectively at full employment. This outflow of labour seems to have been offset in whole or in part by inflows of replacement migrants to Jordan. The opportunity cost of migration in terms of lost output is thus likely to have been small and certainly dwarfed by the scale of net remittances to Jordan from its expatriates. The analysis of the stylised model would therefore seem to suggest that emigration on balance acted to raise the level of societal welfare in Jordan.

As noted at the outset all models are stylised, that presented here being no exception. One particular omission should be noted: section 1 suggests that considerable human capital is embodied in Jordanian emigrants, while little is embedded in their replacement counterparts. The possibility that the resulting reduction in the Jordanian stock of human capital might be sufficient to offset the beneficial effects of remittances cannot be discounted *a priori*. Such questions are however outside the scope of a chapter of this length.

The foregoing analysis serves to highlight the complexity of the problem. It is clear that there can be no presumption on theoretical grounds that emigration has on balance harmed or benefited the Jordanian economy. The final section therefore adopts a more factual approach and attempts to identify the actual impact of emigration and remittances on the Jordanian macroeconomy and on the subsectors of agriculture and construction.

3. Macroeconomic Impact of Migrant and Remittance Flows

As noted in section 1, remittances loom large in the Jordanian economy, accounting for almost 25 per cent of GNP in 1976, thereafter declining in relative importance till 1979, but rising to almost 30 per cent of GNP in 1981. During the period 1974–81 their contribution to the Jordanian balance of payments exceeded that of merchandise exports.

In order to assess the macroeconomic impact of such a scale of remittances consider first the circumstances of the Jordanian economy in the early years of the 1970s and prior to the rapid growth in labour demand by oil-producing states which characterised the later years of the decade. The World Bank[19] estimated that over 14 per cent of the labour force were unemployed at that time. The state of the economy was one of aggregate demand deficiency, with the demand for labour services falling short of the supply forthcoming at the going real wage. In such circumstances employers have no incentive to increase employment even if the real wage falls as there would be no demand for the associated increment to output. Indeed, real wage reductions might, in the short run, further depress the level of aggregate demand and induce an additional decline in employment. In such circumstances the demand for labour becomes in effect totally unresponsive to changes in the real wage.[20]

Surplus labour may remain unemployed domestically or may migrate. But migration presupposes the existence of employment opportunities elsewhere for which the migrant is appropriately qualified. The geographic area over which migrants search, and to which it is within their financial capabilities to migrate, appears to be positively related to the educational attainment of the migrant.[21] The more highly educated are generally aware of employment opportunities over a greater area than their less well educated counterparts, while education also fits them both temperamentally and financially to avail themselves of such opportunities. Such factors can explain patterns of Jordanian migration prior to 1973. The educated became migrants, primarily outwith the Arab states, with Jordan having the highest rate of emigration of scientists and engineers to the US amongst the Arab states.[22] By contrast the less well educated remained to a large extent unemployed within the Jordanian economy due to a lack of job opportunities in their geographically narrower labour market prior to 1973.

Post-1973 this situation changed fundamentally. The accelerating pace of development in oil-producing neighbouring states, and in Saudi Arabia, Libya and Bahrain in particular, generated employment opportunities for all types of labour on a hitherto unprecedented scale. The resulting emigration and consequent inflows of remittances were such that by the later years of the decade the Jordanian economy was effectively at full employment. Since at the outset Jordanian employers were demand constrained, and the labour market was characterised by unemployment, the upsurge in emigration exerted no initial pressure on the real wage or on the level of output in Jordan. Emigration served simply to absorb the excess labour supply hitherto present in the Jordanian labour market with a resulting fall in unemployment. Given the subsequent scale of homeward remittances, emigration tended on balance to raise rather than depress the level of aggregate demand in Jordan. Thus emigration both directly absorbed unemployed Jordanian manpower and, with a brief lag indirectly generated increased domestic demand for labour as emigrants' remittances were reflected in consumer spending. In view of the fact that there were unemployed labour resources in Jordan at the outset, the initial opportunity cost of emigration in terms of output foregone was zero, while the effect on the Jordanian balance of payments was favourable, varying inversely with the proportion of emigrants' remittances spent on imports.

The effects on the labour market were such that by 1975 the level of unemployment in Jordan appeared to have fallen[23] to 2 per cent from a rate of 14 per cent in 1970. Subsequent years saw the beginnings of the phenomenon of replacement migration as immigrant workers were attracted to Jordan in increasing numbers, not only to fill jobs created by the emigration of their indigenous counterparts, but also to accommodate the rise in the domestic demand for labour, particularly in the construction sector, fuelled by the rapidly rising volume of emigrants' remittances. In real terms GDP increased by 79 per cent over the period 1970-9, while total employment grew from 301,000 to 393,000 over the years 1970-8, an increase of 30 per cent.

It is difficult to substantiate the hypothesis that labour shortages are, or have been, a significant constraint on economic development in Jordan, though specific skill shortages have undoubtedly appeared. Jordan, while enjoying full employment in its domestic labour market, also enjoys access to substantial reserves of labour in neighbouring non-oil-producing Arab states. Indeed as an indirect consequence of the Camp David accord, Jordan appeared to be the most important Arab destination for Egyptian migrant workers[24] during the years 1979-81.

It would appear therefore that emigrants' remittances played a crucial role in mobilising resources in the Jordanian economy. The exportation of labour provided Jordan with a highly lucrative source of foreign exchange, while at the same time any resulting constraint on labour availability was significantly eased by the importation of labour from neighbouring states. However, the foregoing macroeconomic analysis does not tell the complete story. A more disaggregated approach would suggest that the impact of remittances on the economy was highly uneven, being concentrated on the construction sector. Some evidence to support this assertion is presented below, and for purposes of contrast the impact on the agricultural sector is also explored.

The Impact on the Construction Sector

Table 12.2 gives an indication of developments in the construction sector. Construction accounts for almost two-thirds of gross domestic fixed capital formation in Jordan. Within this sector one-third of activity is residential. Construction output rose markedly in the latter part of the 1970s and if trends in the number of building permits issued are any guide to recent levels of activity, the pace of expansion has not slackened in more recent years.

The rising volume of activity in the construction sector was not accompanied by a similar expansion in the domestic production of building materials. Production of iron and cement both lagged behind the volume of construction activity. The result was upward pressure on the prices of such materials, which outstripped all other components of the wholesale price index with the exception of certain food products. The remaining excess demand for materials was accommodated by imports, particularly of cement, which increased fivefold during the period 1976–9.

Table 12.2: Construction Sector Indicators 1975 = 100

| | Construction Output | | Wholesale Price | | | Real |
	Residential*	Non-residential*	Construct. Material	Total	Dom Prod Cement	Wages Con**
1975	100	100	100	100	100	100
1976	128	149	124	114	102	123
1977	144	150	131	122	94	143
1978	153	165	141	128	96	153
1979	168	185	155	136	108	142
1980			189	156	158	142

* Sectoral Gross Domestic Fixed Capital Formation deflated by the Wholesale Price Index for Construction Materials.
** Deflated by the Cost of Living Index.
Sources: Hashemite Kingdom of Jordan National Accounts Statistical Yearbook; Central Bank Monthly Statistical Bulletin

The upsurge of activity in the construction sector appears to have had a significant effect on the labour market, though once again available data are fragmentary. It is in this sector that the phenomenon of replacement migration has been most pronounced as there has been a significant outflow of labour from the Jordanian construction sector to the oil-producing states. Indeed, Shaw[25] estimates that over 40 per cent of all Jordanian emigrants are employed in this sector at their destination. This outflow of skilled and semi-skilled labour has been partially accommodated by an inflow of Egyptian and Syrian migrants, over 60 per cent of whom are engaged in construction activity. The net result appears to have been a significant rise in the level of real wages in this sector. The ILO[26] suggest that wages in construction rose by 42 per cent in real terms over the period 1975–80. By contrast real wages in the non-agricultural sector as a whole appear to have risen by only 15 per cent over the same period. Thus to the extent that emigrants' remittances have underpinned the construction boom they have contributed to a significant shift of sectoral labour costs in Jordan.

A word of warning may be in order at this point. The correlation between construction activity and emigrants' remittances does not prove a causal link between the two. However, there is micro-economic evidence[27] from other studies, that a disproportionate share of emigrants' remittances to the Arab states is invested in land and buildings. This mirrors patterns observed in the case of European migrants.[28] Though the multiplier effect is large during construction phase, there is little further impact on the economy once the project is completed. The share of gross domestic fixed capital formation going to plant and equipment has increased only marginally since 1974. The absorption of a large part of remittances by the residential construction sector would not appear to be to the long term benefit of the Jordanian economy.

The Impact on the Agricultural Sector

World Bank[29] estimates suggest that employment in agriculture fell from 115,000 to 78,000 over the period 1970–5. This contraction appears to have continued in recent years. Table 12.3 sets out some salient features of the agricultural sector.

Table 12.3: The Agricultural Sector

	Index of Ag. Production (1969/70 = 100)	Irrigated Area (000 ha)	Tractors in Use	Number of Land Sales (ex. Amman)
1974	134	70	3547	14137
1975	86		3748	20851
1976	95		3914	23306
1977	97	83	4074	15608
1978	111		4223	17132
1979	81		4370	
1980	135	85	4520	

Sources: FAO Production Yearbook; Hashemite Kingdom of Jordan Statistical Yearbook

The total acreage under cultivation[30] appears to have changed little since 1974. However, with the exception of 1978 and 1980 agricultural output has been well below 1974 levels. A variety of factors underlie this output trend amongst which are the low average level of rainfall in recent years, and the rundown of agricultural holdings bordering the ceasefire line with Israel. The contraction of the agricultural labour force may also have been a contributory factor, but data do not exist to substantiate this hypothesis.

Egyptian immigrant workers[31] formed a significant part of the agricultural labour force in the Jordan Valley in 1975 while by 1979 the UNFPA[32] estimated that there were 18,000 immigrant workers engaged in this sector. It seems plausible to suggest that Jordan faces a highly elastic supply curve of unskilled labour to its agricultural sector, the source of these workers being the neighbouring states of Egypt and Syria. Consequently it seems unlikely that labour shortages have been an important contributing factor to the disappointing performance of this sector in recent years. Localised and short-term labour deficiencies may have arisen, but there is no evidence that they have been widespread.

On the important question of whether emigrants' remittances have been used to any extent to restructure and modernise the agricultural sector, the available evidence is limited, ambiguous and indeed sometimes contradictory. Jordanian data suggest that the number of tractors[33] sold has declined continuously since 1974, while a similar pattern is evident in the sales of other agricultural implements such as reapers, harrows, cultivators and disc drillers. However the FAO[34] estimates that the number of tractors in use has increased by a quarter between 1974 and 1980. Jordanian data are consistent with emigrants' remittances resulting in increased mechanisation of agriculture, while the FAO data suggest the opposite.

Another potential outlet for emigrants' remittances is the consolidation of existing agricultural holdings. One indicator of trends in this respect is the number of sales of agricultural land. However, the only data series available refers to all sales of land, both agricultural and non-agricultural. The best that can be done is to attempt to remove the major non-agricultural component by excluding the governorate of Amman from the series. Apart from a pronounced increase in activity in 1975 and 1976 (the years in which remittances were rising most rapidly), the number of land sales showed only a small increase over the period 1973–8.

One aspect of the agricultural sector which has however undergone significant development in recent years, perhaps as a consequence of emigrants' remittances, is irrigation. The area irrigated by artesian wells has increased substantially. However, similar data do not exist for the East Bank prior to 1973, so it is impossible to ascertain whether the rate of expansion of irrigated land has accelerated over the period since emigrants' remittances became significant.

It seems unlikely that the migration of Jordanian labour has had a significant depressing effect on the volume of agricultural output as the supply of replacement migrants appears to be highly elastic. Any initial outflow of labour from the rural sector probably consisted largely of the agriculturally under-employed whose marginal product was insignificantly different from zero. However, it is equally difficult, given existing data, to isolate any significant beneficial effect of emigrants' remittances on this sector. Swanson's[35] conclusions concerning the impact of such remittances on three villages in the Yemen Arab Republic may be equally appropriate to Jordan. He found a dearth of investment opportunities in rural areas with a resulting inflation of land prices and little evidence of consolidation of holdings. Given the fragmented nature of existing units, modern technology is inappropriate and does not represent an attractive investment outlet for emigrants' remittances.[36]

Conclusions

It is clear that the post-1973 upsurge in Jordanian emigration to neighbouring states and associated inflows of remittances wrought two important changes in the Jordanian economy. The hitherto high level of unemployment rapidly vanished, partly through emigration, partly through increased domestic demand for labour. At the same time any foreign exchange constraint on Jordanian development was relaxed, and the economy entered a period of rapid growth. This growth was underpinned not only by a rising volume of emigrants' remittances but also by a substantial increase in budgetary support to the Jordanian government from neighbouring oil-rich states. The outflow of labour was of such proportions that inward flows of replacement migrants were generated and significant remittances outwith Jordan began to emerge. In more recent years Jordan may actually have been a net importer rather than a net exporter of labour.

Jordan has been amongst the most rapidly growing of the non-oil-exporting states in the region. Growth in the last ten years has been markedly more rapid than in the decade immediately prior to 1973. Emigration-induced inflows of remittances have significantly raised nominal and real incomes. While the theoretical analysis of section 2 cautions against firm conclusions on the welfare impact of emigration on the source country, assertions that the massive outflow of labour from Jordan has adversely affected the economy are difficult to substantiate.

Labour migration is likely to remain an extremely important feature of the Jordanian economy in the medium term even though the direction and composition of migrant flows may alter over time[37] as the nature of the oil-exporting states development process matures and to some extent decelerates. In particular, future years are likely to see a decline in the relative importance of construction activity and a consequent decline in the demand for such labour. However, the utilisation of the facilities constructed in the early stages is still likely to require a substantial immigrant presence — though to what extent the immigrant labour force will continue to be Arab dominated remains uncertain.

Further inflows of remittances to Jordan are therefore somewhat uncertain and are likely to fluctuate markedly from year to year, as they have done in the past. The extent to which such instability will prove a constraint on development in later years is now much reduced, at least in the short term, as such fluctuations are now eligible for compensatory financing under the IMF's facility[38].

Notes

1. Commercial quantities of low-sulphur oil have in fact been discovered in Jordan's eastern desert, while Egypt recently regained possession of the Sinai oilfields. Neither country exports oil however.
2. See Ecevit (1979) for comparative data on the relative importance of emigrants' remittances in twelve labour-exporting countries.
3. Birks and Sinclair (1980).
4. See Oberai and Singh (1980); Rempell and Lobdell (1977); and Stark (1980).
5. FAO Production Yearbook (1981).
6. Abu Jaber (1980).
7. Birks and Sinclair (1980).
8. Kirwan (1981).
9. National Planning Council (1976).
10. Fechter (1980).
11. See Dessouki (1982); Socknat (1979); and Birks and Sinclair (1979).

12. Defined here, following the IMF (1977), as private transfers from workers residing abroad for more than a year.
13. Oberai and Singh (1980).
14. Rivera-Batiz (1982).
15. Krauss (1976).
16. See Kenen (1971).
17. See Bhagwati and Brecher (1980).
18. See Rivera-Batiz (1982) for an extended discussion.
19. World Bank (1976).
20. Barro and Grossman (1976).
21. Schwartz (1976).
22. Fechter (1980).
23. World Bank (1976).
24. Dessouki (1982).
25. Shaw (1978).
26. ILO Yearbook of Labour Statistics 1982.
27. See Swanson (1979); Birks and Sinclair (1979).
28. See Cerase (1974) and Rhoades (1978) for example.
29. World Bank (1976).
30. FAO Production Yearbook (1981).
31. Birks and Sinclair (1980).
32. UNFPA (1976).
33. Hashemite Kingdom of Jordan, Statistical Yearbook.
34. FAO Production Yearbook (1981).
35. Swanson (1979).
36. Though Rhoades (1978) found nonetheless that remittances from Spanish workers in Germany were used to purchase inappropriate agricultural machinery on their return to rural Spain.
37. Serageldin and Socknat (1980).
38. Goreux (1980).

Bibliography

Abu Jaber, Kamul, 'Levels and Trends of Fertility and Mortality in Jordan', in Abu Jaber, K. (ed.). *Levels and Trends of Fertility and Mortality in Selected Arab Countries of Western Asia.* Population Studies Programme, University of Jordan (1980).
Barro, R.J. & Grossman H. *Money, Employment and Inflation* (Cambridge University Press, London, 1976).
Bhagwati, J.N. and Brecher R.A. 'National Welfare in an Open Economy in the Presence of Foreign-owned Factors of Production'. *Journal of International Economics*, vol. 10 (1980).
Birks, J.S. and Sinclair C.A. 'Egypt: A Frustrated Labour Exporter? *Middle East Journal*, vol. 33 (1979).
____, *International Migration and Development in the Arab Region* (ILO, Geneva, 1980).
Cerase, F.P. 'Expectations and Reality: A Case Study of Return Migration from the United States to Italy'. *International Migration Review*, vol. 8 (1974).
Dessouki, A.E.H. 'The Shift in Egypt's Migration Policy 1952-78'. Middle East Studies vol. 18 (1982).
Ecevit, Z.H. 'International Labour Migration in the Middle East and North Africa: Trends, Effects and Policies'. Paper presented at the Rockefeller Conference on

International Migration, Bellagio, Italy, June 1979.

Fechter, Alan, 'Arab Scientific Manpower in the US'. Paper presented at the ECWA Seminar on the Arab Brain Drain, Beirut, 4–8 February, 1980.

Goreux, L.M. *Compensatory Financing Facility* (International Monetary Fund, Washington. DC, 1980).

IMF *Balance of Payments Handbook* (Washington DC, 1977).

Kenen, P.B. 'Migration, the Terms of Trade and Economic Welfare in the Source Country'. In Bhagwati, J.N. *et al.*, (eds.) *Trade, Balance of Payments and Growth* (North Holland, Amsterdam, 1971).

Kirwan, F.X. 'The Impact of Labour Migration on the Jordanian Economy'. *International Migration Review*, vol. 15 (1981).

Krauss, M.B. 'The Economics of the Guest Worker Problem: A Neo Heckscher-Ohlin Approach' *Scandinavian Journal of Economics*, vol. 78 (1976).

National Planning Council, Report of the Jordan Development Conference, Amman (1976).

Oberai, A.S. & Singh H.K.M. 'Migration, Remittances and Rural Development'. *International Labour Review*, vol. 119 (1980).

Rempel, H. & Lobdell R.A. 'The Role of Urban to Rural Remittances in Rural Development'. *Journal of Development Studies*, vol. 14 (1977).

Rivera-Batiz, F. 'International Trade, Non-traded Goods and Economic Welfare in the Source Country'. *Journal of Development Economics*, vol. 11 (1982).

Rhoades, R. 'Intra-European Return Migration and Rural Development'. *Human Organisation*, vol. 37 (1978).

Schwartz, A. 'Migration, Age and Education'. *Journal of Political Economy*, vol. 84 (1976).

Serageldin, I. & Socknat J. Manpower and Migration Needs in the Middle East and North Africa 1975–85'. *Finance and Development*, vol. 17 (1980).

Shaw, R.P. 'Migration and Employment in the Arab World: Construction as a Key Policy Variable'. *International Labour Review*, vol. 118 (1978).

Socknat, J.A. 'The Potential Relationship of International Migration for Employment and a Middle East Peace Settlement — An Assessment'. *Middle East Review*, vol. XI (1979).

Stark, O. 'On the Role of Urban to Rural Remittances in Rural Development'. *Journal of Development Studies*, vol. 16 (1980).

Swanson, J.C. 'Some Consequences of Emigration for Rural Development in the Yemen Arab Republic'. *Middle East Journal*, vol. 33 (1979).

UN Fund for Population Activities. Jordan — Report of Mission on Needs Assessment for Population Assistance, New York (1979).

World Bank Country Economic Memorandum on Jordan. Report No. 1738-JO, New York (1976).

PART FOUR
GENERATING CHANGE

13 DYNAMIC ASPECTS OF AGRICULTURAL POLICY: INTERVENTION OR REGULATION?

Ian G. Simpson

Introduction

Government policy for an economic sector such as agriculture can be of an interventionist nature, changing product and factor prices and establishing new institutions for production and distribution. Such interventionist policies have specific objectives. In contrast, regulatory policies seek to create the conditions which will facilitate endogenous change and avoid the less desired consequences of such change. The objectives will be general rather than specific.

Dr Eric Ojala, a New Zealander who was to have a distinguished career in FAO, in his innovative book *Agriculture and Economic Progress* (1952) recognises that agriculture's proportionate contribution to economic welfare and to national income must diminish if general economic progress is to be achieved. He goes on to state that his most important general conclusion is that economic progress calls for flexibility in the organisation of production. He continues: 'It should be possible to harness, husband and direct the economic forces to some degree in the interests of human welfare, but only chaos can result from attempts to frustrate them. A basic problem of national and international agricultural policies in the future will be how to achieve a satisfactory degree of farm income stability, while retaining a satisfactory degree of flexibility, in agriculture and in the economy as a whole.'[1]

The argument in this paper is that although in the developing countries government intervention in the agriculture sector has become far-reaching, operating through a whole range of policy instruments, the requirements of stability and flexibility have not generally been attained. Government intervention often hinders the necessary change and adjustment in the agricultural sector required for economic development. Policies have unduly emphasised price intervention, service provision and externally derived change in the units of organisation but given insufficient attention to the achievement of stable economic, social and ecological conditions under which individual farmers and other agents can respond flexibly to changing market conditions.

In the following section the wide scope of interventionist policies in agriculture is briefly reviewed. Certain of the general hazards arising from such policies are then examined followed by a discussion of the shortcomings of specific types of intervention. Some examples are included but the length of the paper restricts the numbers which can be quoted. Knowledge of the literature, however, will confirm that these are not isolated but reflect experience in many parts of the world. In turning to regulatory policy, a particular emphasis is given to issues in the utilisation of agricultural land and associated natural resources and to the lessening of price uncertainty. Problems in facilitating market adjustment while maintaining a sufficient degree of stability are referred to.

The Scope of Government Policies for Agriculture

Although the involvement of governments with agriculture can be traced back for 5000 years or so to the irrigated agriculture of Sumeria, the first to produce a surplus over and above the subsistence needs of producers, it is in the twentieth century consequent upon the great depression of the 1930s and World War II that such involvement has become all-pervasive. Governments are not content to let agricultural product prices be determined by competitive markets. Rather these are set on the basis of political decisions with complex systems for their administration and the use of production quotas when budgetary costs became excessive. Agricultural research programmes in developed countries are state funded at levels equivalent to one to two per cent of the sectoral value added and large numbers of extension workers are employed to diffuse the results to farmers. Subsidised credit is frequently provided to farmers through specialised agencies and the subsidisation of farm inputs such as fertiliser and machinery is widespread. Governments are concerned with the institutions and organisations which control production. Such concern has led in many developing countries to land reforms of either a distributivist or collectivist type. In the wealthier countries attempts have been made through structural policy to hasten the disappearance of what are regarded as subeconomic farms or in a few instances to impose limits on the upper size of farm. Systems of taxation may have profound effects on the types of production unit. Governments, often with the support of the international agencies, are concerned with direct investment in agricultural projects. Frequently such projects require the establishment of new agencies to administer schemes for settlement, irrigation or other forms of development.

It is not surprising that governments involve themselves so deeply in the functioning of the agricultural sector. Food is an essential need. The agricultural population is numerically dominant in the poorer developing countries and even when, as in the wealthier countries, agriculturalists represent only a small fraction of the labour force, there are many others who retain interests in agriculture through backward and forward linkages, through the continued ownership of agricultural land or from recent family connections. Governments cannot ignore the interests of these people.

Some Hazards of Intervention

1. *Errors from Inadequate Knowledge*

Agricultural policies as implemented tend to be based on short-term considerations without clear definition of long-term objectives, or with such conflicting objectives as those of providing both rising farm incomes and lower consumer prices.[2] Even when objectives are clear policies are too often formulated with a totally inadequate knowledge of relationships involved. For instance, Hill, in arguing strongly for the application of what she refers to as 'indigenous economics', based on extensive field experience of the problems of the rural sectors of developing countries states: 'we are so ignorant of the economic condition of men in rural tropical areas that we do not know how ignorant we are'. She, like others, gives little credibility to the official statistics which form the basis for agricultural planning in India and elsewhere in the developing world.[3] While she expresses the hope that the findings of indigenous economists may be digested to give these a wider comprehensibility and appeal, her approach to the study of rural problems is unlikely to be widely replicated. While data deficiencies are most glaring in developing countries, there are still many inadequately documented aspects of agriculture in developed countries with relatively little information available for policy formulation on, for instance, the distribution of land ownership, the size of farmers' non-farm sources of income, or on the operations of the larger agricultural and agri-business firms.

2. *Government Actions Increasing Uncertainty*

Government intervention in price policy may aim at the reduction of market uncertainty but as MacLaren points out policy uncertainty can lead to an equally serious loss of welfare when decisions are delayed beyond the times at which farmers must take production decisions. He cites the actions of the EEC ministers in delaying price decisions through political wrangling.[4] Similar situations are common in the developing world. Sako and Cotterill, for instance, note that in Mali official prices for millet which is planted are June are not announced until the following December.[5] Governments pursue policies which in time become insupportable due to excessive budgetary costs. Enforced abrupt departures from such policies can be more damaging than the market uncertainties that they were introduced to mitigate.

Governments in numerous developing countries have established monopoly agencies for the distribution of farm input supplies but often these are unable to supply the right quantities at the right time. Such discontinuity of supply increases uncertainty and reduces the incentives to adoption. Similar problems arise when purchasing agencies are unable to take in supplies or to make speedy payments for those that have been received.[6]

3. *Excessive Institutional Longevity*

Government policies frequently involve the establishment of new agencies such as marketing or intervention boards, rural development agencies, agricultural credit banks and the like. Such agencies tend to have an enduring viability even though the circumstances which prompted them may have changed or their record indicates an inadequate fulfilment of the objectives. A frequent consequence is the existence of a number of agencies concerned with the rural sector with overlapping functions.[7] Similarly, organisational forms appropriate to the early stages of smallholder agriculture, set up following a land reform or in land settlement, can become a hindrance to continued development as the schemes reach a more mature stage. The Mexican ejido, the post-land-reform collective village organisation, has been criticised, for instance, for a lack of adaptation to either population growth or to the change from subsistence oriented to more commercial agriculture. In the Sudan, the very large Gezira irrigation scheme which was started in 1926 inherited a small tenant crop-sharing system in which no fundamental change was made until 1981, in spite of a large expansion in its size, major shifts in the cropping system and radical changes in the perceptions of the farm labour force as education and migration opportunities increased.[8]

Often institutional innovations are brought in at times of crisis when there is no opportunity to study alternatives or to consider possible long-term outcomes. For example, the United States Agricultural Adjustment Act of 1933 passed Congress within four months of the Roosevelt administration attaining power at a time when farm incomes were only one-third of 1929 level and over 25 per cent of Americans were still dependent on such incomes. The policies introduced through the Act, such as land retirement and the Commodity Credit Corporation as a support agency, are still to the fore fifty years later. Similarly in the EEC the main elements of the present Common Agricultural Policy were the result of intense political discussion at the end of 1961 and into 1962 (with the clock stopped at midnight on December 31st!). Post-revolutionary governments are under even more intense pressure for action. Carr and Davies note for the Soviet Union that in spite of intensive discussion of the agrarian problem during the 1920s, 'in the last weeks of 1929 the decision was taken suddenly without apparent debate to collectivise the mass of peasantry by force and to liquidate the Kulaks'.[9] The consequences continue to be profound. Many newly independent African governments have had to hastily put together policies for the settlement of land vacated by European farmers. In the most recent case, that of Zimbabwe, as elsewhere policies have been introduced without an adequate understanding of the problems of the African rural population.[10] The effects will doubtless be apparent for many years.

Limitations of Specific Forms of Intervention

1. Price Intervention

Consequent upon major shifts in policy of the kinds mentioned above, emphasis is usually put on price manipulation to achieve short-term adjustment and on research, extension and other service programmes linked with project investment and in some cases structural change for longer-term change. Even freed from the stress of crises, it is difficult to develop effective policies in these areas given our still deficient understanding of farmers' responses to external stimuli. There can be no rational price intervention unless the elasticities of supply have been determined.

In relation to price policy, agricultural economists have used two principal forecasting tools — historically derived price-supply elasticities and normative linear programming and related models. Both have severe limitations. Askari and Cummings tabulate the supply elasticities for various agricultural commodities as derived from around 700 studies using the Nerlove approach. They conclude: 'A glance at these tables reveals both the diversity of the supply responsiveness studies available and the wide range of elasticities that have been estimated. These results though useful to policy makers, cannot in themselves dictate policy decisions. Still unexplained is why, if these results reasonably reflect the responsiveness of the cultivators concerned, considerable differences in elasticity exist for the same crop in various regions or why in the same country, the degree of supply responsiveness may vary widely from crop to crop'.[11] Even if more consistent results had been obtained aggregate supply responses are of more value for policy than those for single commodities, but as Krishna reminds us, estimates of these are surprisingly few.[12] The reversibility of supply functions has been questioned and it would indeed seem naïve to expect that, given the acquisition of resources with low salvage values needed for expansion, a corresponding contraction would follow from an equivalent reduction in price.

In developing country situations with production for subsistence still important, the existence of perverse supply response has yet to be totally dismissed. For instance, Barnum and Squire, in their model of an agricultural household related to rice production in West Malaysia show that marketed rice output may have a negative elasticity to its price, given the interaction between leisure preferences and supplementary wage employment for farmers.[13] Ellis highlights our lack of knowledge of supply response in an African context.[14] Even in an EEC context, Capstick points out that squeezes in the real prices of milk and cereals since 1975 have not generated much in the way of checks on production and raises the question of perverse supply although also stressing the role of underlying technological change which is insensitive to small movements in prices.[15]

As an alternative to the use of time series regression, programming models of representative farms or of regions as an entity have been used to obtain normative predictions of supply response. These are demanding both of data and of analytical skills. Poorly specified models which do not correctly represent farmers' objective functions, constraints and activity range and which incorporate inaccurate data can be worse than useless. Aggregation bias — the extent to which applications to representative farms provide results which can be used to indicate aggregate response without misrepresentation — is a continuing problem.

Neither regression nor programming models indicate the long-term effects of higher prices on agricultural land values or on the acquisition of farm assets with low salvage values which will be kept in production even if prices subsequently fall. Given that the cost of new capital is determined outside the agricultural sector and that farm wages are based either on a subsistence minimum or after what Fei and Ranis refer to as 'the turning point', terminating the labour surplus condition, linked to non-agricultural wages, additional revenue from higher prices will be capitalised in land values.[16] Clark puts it succinctly: 'When agriculture is subsidised or given six concessions or helped in any other way, the benefit accrues in the form of a rise in the price of land rather than in the income of the farmer as such'.[17] There have been some studies documenting this for the USA and the UK, while in many countries agricultural land values have risen in real terms. With these increases land is an excellent security on which to borrow and those fortunate enough to own land are well placed to expand the scale of their activities so widening the distribution of farm size — not in many instances a desired policy objective.

Our ability to predict the consequences of using administered prices for policy ends seems still so limited that it would seem preferable to pursue non-interference, other than taking measures to ensure competitive behaviour such as providing free access to market information (transparency) and to smooth out some of the more abrupt fluctuations in international markets.[18]

2. Service Programmes

Substantial assistance to agriculture by means of government-funded support programmes can be seen as justified, given the small size and limited resources of the majority of farm production units. The funding of agricultural research programmes is accompanied by the building up of an extension service; credit and marketing programmes need the recruitment of administrative cadres, and irrigation, settlement and other special schemes have their own needs for government-funded personnel. Total expenditures can be of significance relative to agriculture's contribution to GDP.

Agricultural research can be regarded as an investment activity on which inputed high economic rates of return have been recorded in numerous studies. However, a World Bank paper gives reasons for suspecting an upward bias in these studies.[19] There have not, to my knowledge, been any comparisons between the imputed rates of return on publicly funded research as against those for privately financed research. However, the latter is important for the development of chemical products, mechanisation and to some extent in plant breeding. In spite of the studies referred to, there is sufficient evidence to suggest that there are often considerable inefficiences in research establishments.[20] These are likely to be associated with factors such as a reward system to staff which leads to X-inefficiency, incentives to maximise budgets and a poor perception of farmers' objectives and effective constraints. Moreover, if agricultural output and input prices are not at efficiency levels, scientists will be unable to identify the innovations that will raise the economic efficiency of the sector through the processes of induced innovation. Agricultural research is indeed essential for agricultural progress but government support of it needs to be selective.

The causes of inefficiency in research establishments also apply for field services such as extension and supply provision. Indeed with the inevitable wide spatial dispersion of staff, X-inefficiency is likely to be greater. I have commented on the weaknesses of the 'agro-bureaucracy' elsewhere, drawing attention to the frequent inability of extension workers to advise on innovations that farmers perceive as rewarding and with low risk, the bias towards the more wealthy farmers, some of whom re-lend money borrowed at cheap rates from public agencies and the marketing failures of cooperatives managed by ill-informed and inexperienced managers.[21] I concluded: 'The contribution to agricultural and rural development of this agrobureaucracy in most instances is unlikely to be fully commensurate with the costs involved in its upkeep particularly having regard to the alternative uses of funds'. Possibly this is an over-bold statement but many references can be called in support. For instance in reference to North East Brazil: 'There has been a massive growth in the bureaucracies servicing rural areas over the past thirty years without any apparent benefit to the peasant population and with less than one per cent of the rural population being effectively serviced by state and federal government agencies'[22]. Or in Mexico:

The weakest aspect of public agricultural activity has traditionally been the extension service. Before 1970 many states of Mexico had only a handful of extension agents who enjoyed talking with their friends in their offices and occasionally set up demonstrations with a limited clientele. The production increases in the Green Revolution occurred not through public extension activities but rather because more progressive farmers adopted new seeds and practices on their own initiative.[23]

Agrobureaucracies too often in both developed and developing countries attempt to undertake tasks which either farmers or supporting commercial agencies can do as effectively and without the rigidities and inefficiencies inherent in publicly funded agencies. Given this premise, government policies should emphasise better management of the existing agencies rather than their expansion.

3. *Government Project Investment*

Direct government investment assisted by international lending is of particular importance in developing countries. This is essential for meeting infrastructural needs such as the construction of large-scale irrigation facilities or the transport networks without which agricultural development will not proceed far. Nevertheless, it has to be recognised that errors in identification of necessary projects are common and their planning is often at fault.[24] Governments frequently find it politically impossible to recoup their expenditures through economic charges for facilities such as the use of irrigation water with the consequence that loan repayments and sometimes even operating expenditures become a charge against the general budget pre-empting other desirable expenditure. World Bank evaluations show that the majority of its agricultural projects have given acceptable economic rates of return but these are probably among the better prepared projects. The evaluations are made relatively early in the implementation phase and do not reflect all the longer term consequences.[25] In some areas, such as those where rural poverty is particularly apparent, competition between international and national donors has resulted in the approval of projects with little real prospect of success. Rural development projects lacking significant infrastructural components need particularly careful appraisal.

4. *Structural Change*

The pressures for structural change through land reforms and similar measures are political in the first place although they are likely to reflect acute social and economic imbalances in the rural areas. As Worsley notes: 'a particularly dangerous situation exists where millions of people lack access to any land at all'.[26] However, it is in the establishment of the post-reform structures that politicians are prone to rush in with little regard to past historical experience and with an unawareness of the real situation in the countryside.

There now seem to be few if any examples of *generalised* collective systems which can be regarded as successful in terms of *both* equity and efficiency. The introduction of the 'responsibility system' in Chinese agriculture from 1979 is perhaps the most significant recognition of the limitations of collectivism.[27] The distribution of land into individual holdings usually of a standard size also rarely achieves the desired objectives especially as it disregards the varying availability of non-land resources possessed by households. Frequently, large fractions of the rural population are excluded from the land distribution. The official parcelling is soon circumvented by unrecorded transactions and differentiation between households reappears.

Golabian writes of the Iranian land reform which was initiated in 1962 that, 'The traditional fluid pattern of organic composition of production factors which in spite of its backwardness had some very progressive characteristics that could be used for further development was converted into a rigid system of smallholdings'; this rigid system was unlikely to be viable over any extended period of time.[28] Radwan is clear on the limitations of distributivist reforms. 'The basic policy conclusion that this study arrives at is this. The Egyptian experience of agrarian reform has been more successful than many others. Recent trends, however, indicate that these reforms have spent their force and we are back to square one.'[29]

As I shall argue shortly, governments cannot avoid some responsibility for the allocation of ownership and use of agricultural land but legislative measures aimed at a general redistribution are unlikely to achieve the objectives sought.

Regulatory Policies for Stability

The aspects of policy discussed so far represent primarily the interventionist role of governments. I turn now to the regulatory role, the purpose of which can be taken as that of creating a sufficient degree of stability for individual farm producers and others associated with the agricultural sector to be able to respond flexibly to emerging trends. Market forces can act as a spur to appropriate decision-making by producers provided that there is a sufficient degree of regulation to prevent monopoly profits, to offset incentives for short-term resource exploitation and to mitigate the shock of short-term price fluctuations particularly those attributable to external factors.

Regulation of Agricultural Land Markets

State regulation in some form is necessary in respect of the use of ownership of agricultural land. Such land unlike other factors is in finite supply and commands rents. These can be expected to appropriate the agricultural surplus after labour and capital have been remunerated in terms of their opportunity costs. Those who possess agricultural land, whether as landlords or as owner farmers, are in a privileged position, not simply in terms of obtaining property income but also in access to outside capital for the intensification and extension of their activities, land being, of course, the ideal collateral. With the scope for bringing new land into production becoming increasingly limited, intensified land use is necessary to meet the rising demand for agricultural products in consequence of rapid population and income growth. The ability of those already holding land to intensify leads to increased differentiation among the members of the rural population with social instability eventually becoming a threat to further investment. As noted earlier neither collectivisation nor redistribution policies offer effective solutions. They lack the elements of flexibility to permit adaptive change as becomes necessary, for instance, when the size of the agricultural population starts to fall absolutely as well as proportionately. There needs to be scope for land transactions so that household resources in respect of capital and labour can be matched with appropriate areas of land. Attempts to prohibit such exchange are in practice usually circumvented by informal but insecure transactions. There are many examples of nominal occupiers subletting, often on an annual sharecropping basis. The writer has observed this in irrigation schemes in the Sudan, Sri Lanka and Iraq while Yates and others have commented on its frequency on the Mexican ejidos.[30] In theory, land taxation at a level which expropriated the greater part of economic rent would act against the accumulation of large land areas by single individuals and yet retain the element of flexibility needed for change. Although agricultural land taxation has a long history it is unrealistic to anticipate the widespread introduction of new systems. Governments are unlikely to risk the stirring up of farmer opposition. Land taxation cannot be effective unless based on detailed cadastral survey. Such a survey can take many years to complete, extending well beyond most politicians' periods of reference. Without some discretion in collection to allow for periodic shortfalls in earnings, land taxation can result, as in nineteenth century India, in widespread farmer indebtedness, but such discretion is very difficult to achieve within a bureaucratic framework.

In the absence of effective land taxation, the use of administrative regulation of land would seem unavoidable. Such regulation should be aimed at modifying the pattern of change rather than directing it as in interventionist structural change policies exemplified by land reforms. Both excessive accumulation of land and its overfragmentation should be prevented. Devolved administration and control is preferable to centralised procedures but clearly the centre has a responsibility to avoid dominance by local elites.

It may be necessary for the state to acquire ownership to prevent this occurring but the approach will depend on the circumstances. Clearly no single solution will apply to situations varying from those with traditional allocation of usufructuary rights still persisting under conditions of low pressure on land, to those where freehold rights are long established as in densely cropped zones surrounding large cities. In the first type of situation a government might declare its ownership in advance of scarcity raising land values above nominal levels and thereafter offer extended and secure leases to individual farmers. In the second type government could exercise prior rights of purchase for the purpose of reallocating land from large holders to small farmers probably on a similar leasehold basis. Whatever the precise arrangements, farmers should have both secure tenure and the right to dispose of the lease to others at values which can be expected to equate with the capitalised difference between the true economic rent and that collected by government. With selective purchases, the assessment of land values becomes feasible in contrast to the comprehensive valuations needed for land taxation. Some degree of undervaluation will both ease collection problems and provide sufficient incentive for market transactions to occur.[31] Selective action will be less likely to arouse political opposition.

Stabilisation of Agricultural Prices

The short-run price inelasticity of the supply and demand for the majority of agricultural commodities results in large price fluctuations which add to the uncertainties arising from the effects of natural causes on production. Consequently as Bigman states, after quoting work by Sandmo and by Leland on the expected utility of profits, 'a strong case for price stabilisation exists in cases where producers are risk-averse'.[32] It is a well founded assumption that the majority of small agricultural producers in developing countries are risk-averse. To quote Bigman further: 'a reduction of risk by stabilising the price is likely to lead to a more efficient allocation of resources, a choice of more efficient techniques, and an allocation of more resources for production and hence more output and lower price'.

Price stability can, in the face of production instability, accentuate the variability of aggregate revenue in instances where demand is very inelastic but to the individual producer, the easing of one risk element should be a stimulus to output expansion.[33] Of course, if markets are open to international trade, price movements need bear no relationship to the level of domestic production. It can be argued on efficiency grounds that domestic producer prices should be kept in line with world prices as these apply at the nation's border but there can be no gain in attempting to follow every shift in these. The problem for government or its agency is how to achieve a degree of price stabilisation while not departing from long-term movements in external prices. It is not appropriate to discuss here the many technical problems involved in the use of buffer stocks or smoothing formulae.

Regulation to Preserve the Resource Base

Ecological stability involving the preservation of the natural resource base is clearly a responsibility of government as guardian of continuing existence of the state, yet it is often given insufficient attention. Reports are widespread of careless deforestation as cropping extends to slopes where erosion is unavoidable or areas in the humid tropics are cleared for grazing with a rapid fall in soil fertility levels; of water levels in aquifers falling as a consequence of overpumping for irrigation and of the degradation of natural pastures due to overstocking. Such occurrences are found in socialist as well as mixed economies. In fact the misuse of resources can be greater when occupation rights are poorly defined and the absence of resource prices may lead to decisions which ignore the cost of future losses. There is some evidence that colonial regimes in the later periods had a greater concern for the preservation of the resource base than the successor national governments.[34] A greater emphasis on establishing and upholding legal rights to permanent occupation but not necessarily the ownership of agricultural land by individuals or small groups should lessen the pressure for short-term exploitation but in certain circumstances statutory conservation measures, properly enforced, will be appropriate. More studies are needed on the practical means of ensuring the conservation of natural resources for future production.

Conclusion

Agricultural development depends primarily on the initiatives and responses of individual farmers and of other supporting agents to changes in factor and product prices. The ability of governments even when, as is by no means always the case, their actions are based on economic analysis, to intervene usefully to alter the direction and rate of such development is much more limited than is often supposed. The responses of agricultural producers and, perhaps equally important, of agricultural support institutions, remain insufficiently predictable for the straightforward equating of means and ends. Governments through their interventions often create additional uncertainties which are detrimental to progress. It is recognised, however, that alternative funding is unlikely for the provision of certain types of agricultural research and for infrastructure especially in the form of roads and major irrigation works. Governments clearly must provide support for these. In other areas there would seem to be much to be said for government actions being primarily limited to those required to establish the conditions of comparative stability necessary for effective individual responses, and for preserving the resource base through regulatory rather than interventionist policies.

Notes

1. Ojala (1952), p. 183.
2. For example the Agricultural Prices Commission in India is enjoined to provide remunerative and incentive prices to farmers *and* to ensure that the issue price is

not too high for poorer consumers. This may be compared with article 39 of the Treaty of Rome which refers to ensuring both reasonable prices to consumers *and* increasing the individual earnings of persons engaged in agriculture.

3. Examples of similar comments: Wade (1982), p. 69, writing of irrigation in South Korea notes that records of the area under different paddy varieties (especially HYV and non-HYV) are provided by local villagers and are likely to be unreliable — 'which matters because these figures are sent to the Ministry of Agriculture to become part of the official national figures'; Shepherd (1983) p. 303, on the development of Sudanese agriculture states on the central clay plains: 'There is thus a complex and crucial regional setting for the development of mechanised farming which contains dynamics and interactions about which little is known by national or international policymakers'.

4. MacLaren (1980), pp. 400, 401.

5. Sako and Cotterill (1981), p. 30.

6. Saadat and Van Gigh (1981), p. 39 writing of World Bank projects in West Africa illustrate this point. 'In most of West Africa, for instance, farm inputs including fertilisers and seeds are rarely supplied by the commercial sector, and the state monopolies that handle such inputs are seldom efficient. The resulting long delays in the delivery of inputs to farmers and the high costs to the Treasury mean that farmers willing to innovate cannot implement the agronomical recommendations on which development depends.' In the same paper the authors point out: 'The unpredictability of prices is complicated by government intervention in agricultural pricing'.

7. Etienne (1982) p. 70 quotes M. Bhattacharya on India: 'At the field level . . . multiplicity of functional departments and agencies has led to virtual balkanisation of the field'.

8. Simpson (1980).

9. Carr and Davies (1969), p. 270.

10. Kinsey (1982), writes: 'Settlement schemes are currently being designed under great time pressure — there seems to be a pronounced inability and or unwillingness to take the time to learn either from others' experience with resettlement or from the lessons which are beginning to emerge from Zimbabwe's own programmes.'

11. Askari and Cummings (1977), p. 263.

12. Krishna (1982), p. 234.

13. Barnum and Squire (1979), p. 95.

14. Ellis (1981).

15. Capstick (1983), pp. 271, 272.

16. Fei and Ranis (1975).

17. Clark (1973), p. viii.

18. Tolley, Thomas and Wong (1982), p. 232, conclude an analysis of price intervention in four developing countries: 'Time after time, price programmes have gone awry not necessarily from lack of good objectives, but more because their effects have been imperfectly understood. Usually policies have a variety of consequences, unforeseen by policymakers, owing to the responses of producers and consumers to price changes.'

19. World Bank (1981), p. 19.

20. The newly appointed director of a major British research institute was reported in the farming press in April 1973: 'Given the wealth of our facilities, the huge number of staff and the knowledge that we spend near £4 million a year, can we honestly claim that we are earning our keep? I think not.'

21. Simpson (1982).

22. Dias (1981).

23. Sanders (1979), p. 34.

24. For instance, see criticisms of West African agricultural projects by Wallace (1980); D'Silva and Raza (1980); and Apeldoorn (1981).

25. A.W. Clausen, World Bank President at the annual meetings of the World Bank and its affiliates in 1981 reported 49 agricultural projects reviewed had an average economic rate or return of 19.5 per cent (quoted in *Finance and Development*, vol. 18, no. 4 (1981) p. 9.).

26. Worsley (1981), p. 283.

27. For a discussion of the responsibility system see Watson (1983).

28. Golabian (1977), p. 104.

29. Radwan (1977) p. 82.

30. Yates (1981), p. 148: 'It is true (and especially in the irrigation districts), many ejidatarios, in some districts more than half of them, rent their parcelas illegally to private farmers and live off their rents.' See also Finkler (1978).

31. The arguments of this section link to those in an editorial of the Beijing *Renmin Ribao* of 20 January 1984 (as reported in 'Daily Report China' from the Foreign Broadcast Information Service in the USA) 'Land is the most fundamental means of production in agriculture and is also the basic condition on which the peasant's survival depends. Once the land contract system is sound, the system of contracted responsibilities with payment linked to output will have a firm foundation. In order to make the land contract system sound we must first stabilise the right to land. Generally speaking, the contracted period for land should be more than 15 years . . . What is more important is that with the shift of rural labour power to non-agricultural departments, we may encourage the gradual concentration of land for peasants especially good at farming by means of collective unified readjustment *or transfers through individual negotiations.*' (author's italics).

32. Bigman (1982), p. 57.

33. Anderson and Just are reported to have evidence that farmers in industrialised Western countries do take account of yield and price correlations whereas farmers in developing countries do not. They suggest that the government could attempt to reduce and eliminate risks from the market through price stabilisation schemes. 'This approach has the advantage of exploiting opportunity for pooling risks over space and time thereby increasing the socially desired output of risky commodities.' *World Bank Research News* (1980) vol. 1, no. 3, pp. 16–17.

34. The considerable emphasis on soil conservation during the late colonial period in Southern Africa is discussed by Beinart (1983).

Bibliography

Apeldoorn, G. Jan Van. *Perspectives on Drought and Famine in Nigeria* (London, 1981).

Askari, H. and Cummings, J.T. 'Estimating Agricultural Supply Response with the Nerlove Model: A Survey' *International Economic Review*, vol. 18 (1977).

Barnum, H.M. and Squire, L. *A Model of an Agricultural Household — Theory and Evidence.* (Baltimore and London, 1979).

Beinart. W. 'Soil Erosion, Conservationism and Ideas about Development: a Southern African Exploration, 1920–60.' Unpublished paper to Development Studies Association Conference, Brighton (1983).

Bigman, D. *Coping with Hunger: Toward a System of Food Security and Price Stabilisation* (Cambridge, Mass., 1982).

Capstick, C.W. 'Presidential Agricultural Policy Issues and Economic Analysis,' *Journal of Agricultural Economics*, vol. 34 (1983).

Carr, E.H. and Davies, R.W. *Foundations of a Planned Economy, 1926-9* (London, 1969).
Clark, C. *The Value of Agricultural Land* (Oxford, 1973).
Day, R.H. and Singh, I. *Economic Development as an Adaptive Process: the Green Revolution in the Indian Punjab* (Cambridge, 1977).
Dias, G.M. 'The Impact of Public Service Agencies in Subsistence Agriculture in North Eastern Brazil: a Preliminary Evaluation, in Crouch, B.R. and Chamala, S. (eds.) *Extension, Education and Rural Development*, vol. 2. (Chichester, 1981).
D'Silva, B.C.D. and Razaa, M.R. 'Integrated Rural Development in Nigeria — The Funtua Project'. *Food Policy*, vol. 5 (1980).
Fei J.C.H. and Ranis G. 'A Model of Growth and Employment in the Open Dualistic Economy — the Cases of Korea and Taiwan'. *Journal of Development Studies*, vol. 11 (1975).
Finkler, K. 'From Sharecroppers to Entrepreneurs — Peasant Household Production Strategies under the Ejido System of Mexico' *Economic Development and Cultural Change*, vol. 27 (1978).
Golabian, H. *An Analysis of the Underdeveloped Rural and Nomadic Areas of Iran* (Stockholm, 1977).
Hill, P. *Studies in Rural Capitalism in West Africa* (Cambridge, 1970).
____, *Dry Grain Farming Families: Hausaland (Nigeria) and Karnatka (India) Compared* (Cambridge, 1982).
Kinsey, B.H. 'Emerging Policy Issues in Zimbabwe's Land Resettlement Programmes', *Development Policy Review*, vol. 1 (1983).
Krishna, R. 'Some Aspects of Agricultural Growth, Price Policy and Equity in Developing Countries'. *Food Research Institute Studies*, vol. 18 (1982).
MacLaren, D. 'Agricultural Price Policy Uncertainty and the Risk Averse Firm'. *European Review of Agricultural Economics*, vol. 7 (1980).
Norton R.D. and Solis L.M. *The Book of CHAC — Programming Studies for Mexican Agriculture* (Baltimore and London, 1983).
Ojala, E.M. *Agriculture and Economic Progress* (London, 1952).
Radwan, S. *Agrarian Reform and Rural Poverty* (Geneva, 1977).
Rosine, J. and Helmberger, P.A. 'Neoclassical Analysis of the US Farm Sector', *American Journal of Agricultural Economics*, vol. 56 (1974).
Saadat, O. and van Gigh, F. 'Lessons from the Field: Rural Development in West Africa', *Finance and Development*, vol. 18 (1981).
Sako B, and Cotterill, R.W. 'An Econometric Analysis of Supply Responsiveness in Traditional Agriculture Millet, Sorghum and Rice Farmers in Mali'. Michigan State University, Department of Agricultural Economics. African Rural Economy Program Working Paper no. 36 (1981).
Sanders, T.G. 'The Plight of Mexican Agriculture', in Huddleston B. and McLin, J. (eds.) *Political Investments in Food Production* (Bloomington, 1979).
Shepherd, A. 'Capitalist Agriculture in the Sudan's Dura Prairies'. *Development and Change*, vol. 29 (1983).
Simpson, I.G. 'Institutional Constraints to Agricultural Development in the Sudan' in Centre for African Studies, *Post Independence Sudan* (Edinburgh, 1980).
____ 'Are Agrobureaucracies Essential? The Need for Direct Farmer Research Links', *Agricultural Administration*, vol. 9 (1982).
Tolley, G.S., Thomas, V. and Wong, C.M. *Agricultural Price Policies and the Developing Countries* (Baltimore, 1982).
Traill, W.B. 'An Empirical Model of the UK Land Market and the Impact of Price Policy on Land Values and Rents'. *European Review of Agricultural Economics*, vol. 6 (1979).
Wallace, T. 'Agricultural Projects and Land in Northern Nigeria'. *Review of African Political Economy*, vol. 17 (1980).
Watson, A. 'Agriculture Looks for "Shoes That Fit"': The Production Responsibility

System and its Implications'. *World Development*, vol. 11 (1983).
World Bank, *Agricultural Research: Sector Policy Paper* (Washington DC, 1981).
Worsley, P. 'Paradigms of Agricultural Development'. *Sociologica Ruralis*, vol. 26 (1981).
Yates, P.L. *Mexico's Agricultural Dilemma* (Tucson, 1981).

14   PERU — 20 YEARS OF AGRARIAN REFORM

Tom Alberts

1. Introduction

In the 1950s agrarian reform was generally neglected by economists. The interest in agrarian reform grew in the 1960s and culminated in the 1970s with a large number of books and studies. In the middle of the 1960s most Latin American countries had agrarian reform programmes, but today Peru remains the most important enduring Latin American example of a planned major reform without a revolution. Was the Peruvian agrarian reform successful and what can be learnt from it?

The agrarian reform efforts in Peru gained momentum after rural guerrilla movements, US pressure for land reform during the Kennedy regime, and a growing consensus in Peru that something had to be done about the 'agrarian problem'. The first agrarian reform law was passed in 1962. Little was done, however, until 1969 when a military government launched an ambitious reform programme. This included a radical agrarian reform.

In terms of numbers it was impressive. Within a period of ten years, about 10 million hectares were expropriated and handed over to about 400,000 families. Practically all big farms were expropriated, and the Peruvian landed obligarchy was eliminated. Today almost 50 per cent of agricultural output comes from land that was expropriated during the agrarian reform.

The reform had two basic objectives: namely, social justice and an increase in the rate of agricultural growth. This chapter will argue that the Peruvian agrarian reform was not successful in meeting these two central development objectives. The chapter will be organized in the following way. In the next section we will give an account of the 'agrarian problem'* in Peru. In section 3 we will discuss the causes of agricultural stagnation. Thereafter, we will discuss if agricultural growth was affected by the reform and if so,

---

* Unless otherwise stated, the material in this chapter is based on my book *Agrarian Reform and Rural Poverty. — A Case Study of Peru.*

to what extent. In section 5 we will give an overview of income distribution in Peru. In the section which follows we will discuss the effects of the agrarian reform on rural poverty. In the last section we will summarise our main findings.

We will, in this paper, divide the Peruvian agrarian reform into four phases. The criterion used is based on the land transfer process. In the initial phase, 1962–8, little expropriation and adjudication (transferring land to the beneficiaries) was accomplished. In the second phase, 1969–76, massive expropriations and adjudications took place. In the third phase, 1977–80, the land transfer process was concluded and few new expropriations were carried out. At the end of this period most of the land involved in the reform had been transferred to the beneficiaries of the agrarian reform. Consequently, as of 1981 Peru entered into what can be called the post-reform era.

2. The Agrarian Problem

Peru has undergone profound changes since 1950. The population has grown from 8 million to over 19 million people, in 1983 (Table 14.1). While in the 1950s the urban population was about one-third of the total population it is now two-thirds. However, the rural population has not yet started to decline in absolute numbers as it has in some other Latin American countries. The *Costa*, a narrow coastal strip of desert interrupted by some 52 rivers which carry water a few months of the year, today contains about half of the population while a few decades ago it had less than one-third. The *Sierra*, made up of three Andean ranges at heights above 2,000 metres, contained two-thirds of the population in 1950 and today has some 40 per cent. The *Selva*, the jungle area in the east, has slowly increased its population to a little more than 10 per cent of the total.

Peru has been favoured with a great variety of natural resources. Although the export booms (guano, rubber, copper and fish, to mention a few of the products) had only one commodity as the principal source for economic growth, Peru never depended on any single export good. The economic performance was impressive in earlier decades. *Per capita* gross domestic product (GDP) grew 2.7 per cent per year in the 1950–60 period and 2.5 per cent in the 1960–70 period, while in the following ten-year period (1970–80) it dropped to 0.6 per cent per year (Table 14.1).

Agricultural production statistics are of low quality. What is available suggests that agricultural growth has been much less impressive. On a *per capita* basis, it grew by 1.9 per cent yearly in the 1950-60 period, 0.4 per cent in the 1960-70 period, and in the 1970-80 period the growth rate became negative, −1.3 per cent. In these 30 years agriculture completely lost its importance for the economic growth of Peru. Its contribution to GDP decreased from over 20 per cent in 1950 to 13 per cent at the beginning of the 1980s (Table 14.1). In 1951 agriculture's share in total exports was 54 per cent and in 1981 it had dropped to 5 per cent.[1] Agricultural imports have increased, but their share in total imports shows no definite trend. As was mentioned above, the rural population is nowadays a minority.

The agricultural sector has increasingly become a bottleneck for overall economic growth. This was becoming evident at the beginning of the 1960s. Peruvian policy makers then realised that something had to be done. The agrarian problem was not only a question of growth, but also of distribution. Land-ownership was extremely skewed. The first agricultural census in 1961 revealed that 3,600 farms had three-quarters of the agricultural land. At the other extreme, the *minifundios*, some 700,000 farms, had less than 6 per cent of agricultural land (Table 14.2). The land of a great many of these small farms was fragmented into many small tracts, the continuous subdivision of which was a serious problem. Historically, the *latifundios* had secured cheap labour by monopolising land and alternative employment opportunities. Particularly in the Sierra technological progress was almost absent; the landowners were satisfied by squeezing wages to obtain profits.

The basic objectives of the agrarian reform were to increase the rate of agricultural growth, and to redistribute rural income through land redistribution. The latter objective was given varying degrees of priority during the 20-year period 1962-82.

3. Causes of Stagnation

There are several reasons for the tendency of agriculture to stagnate in Peru. We will discuss a few of the most important ones such as the weak resource base, government policies towards agricultural growth, and the land tenure system.

Peru is a large country, more than twice the size of France. One

Table 14.1: Peru: Gross Domestic Product (Million 1970 Soles)

	1950	1955	1960	1961	1962	1963	1964	1965	1966	1967	1968
(1) Agriculture	17104	21774	26047	26818	27456	27862	29236	29830	31429	32652	31542
(2) Fisheries	311	648	1972	2782	3595	3747	4832	4002	4725	5399	5496
(3) Mining	3440	5190	14618	15748	14825	15611	16257	16456	17792	17963	18886
(4) Manufacturing	10286	14946	28072	30846	34057	36499	39747	43066	47295	49660	50852
(5) Constructing	3892	6262	7022	8623	9408	8125	8987	10156	11057	9884	8259
(6) Electricity, gas and water	424	490	1185	1472	1534	1630	1744	1857	2057	2247	2374
(7) Housing	6624	7363	7598	7834	8076	8327	8585	8852	9126	9409	9701
(8) Government	6678	8147	11183	12637	13538	14541	15369	16225	17213	17797	18206
(9) Others	27043	36490	42941	45722	53756	56667	60612	63933	67418	70413	70047
(10) GDP	75802	101 310	140 638	152 482	166 245	173 009	185 369	194 407	208 112	215 424	213 363
(11) POPULATION (THOUSAND)	8069	8891	10162	10457	10760	11072	11393	11723	12058	12404	12760
(12) GDP/POPULATION	9394	11395	13840	14582	15450	15626	16270	16583	17259	17367	16878
(13) GDP AGR./POPULATION	2120	2449	2563	2565	2552	2516	2566	2544	2606	2632	2472
(14) GDP AGR./GDP IN PER CENT	22.56	21.49	18.52	17.59	16.52	16.10	15.77	15.34	15.10	15.16	14.65

	1969	1970	1971	1972	1973	1974	1975	1976	1977	1978	1979	1980	1981	1982	1983
(1)	33624	36247	37334	37633	38536	39422	39816	41130	41130	39896	41125	38865	43861	45177	41227
(2)	4941	6576	5682	2960	2276	3093	2623	3145	2972	3867	4235	4116	3523	3452	1912
(3)	18735	19840	19046	20398	20276	21026	18734	20401	25952	29871	32948	32025	30616	32116	29754
(4)	51586	57223	62140	66662	71595	76965	80582	83966	78503	75682	78634	84080	82802	80898	68413
(5)	8812	10010	11061	12433	13055	15927	18603	18082	16690	14003	14521	17145	19156	19731	14698
(6)	2493	2608	2806	2966											
(7)	10002	9802	10243	10714											
(8)	18570	19368	20627	22071	22557	23076	24114	24596	25285	25159	25033	25408	26015	26535	26535
(9)	75509	78992	84075	91945	116 089	124 370	129 557	132 239	129 192	125 505	129 342	134 214	140 312	140 876	123 954
(10)	224 272	240 666	253 014	267 782	284 384	303 879	314 029	323 559	319 724	313 983	325 838	335 853	346 285	348 785	306 493
(11)	13127	13447	13830	14224	14628	15044	15470	15908	16358	16819	17293	17760	18239	18732	19238
(12)	17085	17897	18295	18826	19441	20199	20299	20339	19545	18668	18842	18911	18986	18620	15932
(13)	2561	2696	2699	2646	2634	2620	2574	2585	2514	2372	2378	2188	2405	2412	2143
(14)	14.99	15.06	14.76	14.05	13.55	12.97	12.68	12.71	12.86	12.71	12.62	11.57	12.67	12.95	13.45

Sources: GDP 1950–72, BCR (1968) and Brundenius (1976).
1973–80, BCR, Memoria (1980), p. 127.
1981–3, Republic of Peru, 1983, p. 5.
Population: 1950–5 BCR (1968), p. 11.
1960–9, IBRD, World Tables, 1980, pp. 160–161.
1970–83, IBRD, Peru (1981), pp. 27 and 134.
Note: Growth rate estimates in the text are based on fitted curves.

Table 14.2: Land Tenure in Peru 1961 and 1972

Size (hectares)	Production Units 1961		1972		Area covered 1961		1972	
	Number	%	Number	%	Hectares	%	Hectares	%
<1	292 920	34.7	483 350	34.8	129 092	0.7	185 132	0.8
1– 5	406 507	48.2	600 425	43.2	907 096	5.1	1 375 316	5.8
5– 20	107 853	12.8	231 840	16.7	887 574	5.0	2 036 421	8.6
20– 100	24 638	2.9	59 592	4.3	953 307	5.4	2 182 599	9.3
100– 500	7 684	0.9	11 279	0.8	1 551 039	8.8	2 150 668	9.1
500–2,500	2 612	0.3	2 785	0.2	2 642 106	14.9	2 824 225	12.0
2,500–	1 026	0.1	1 017	0.1	10 651 831	60.1	12 790 788	54.3
TOTAL	843 240	99.9	1 390 288	100.1	17 722 045	100.0	23 545 149	99.9

Average area per production
unit
(hectares)

1961   21.0
1972   16.9

Source: Alberts, 1983, p. 137.

could, therefore, believe the country to have an abundance of agricultural land. On the contrary, it can be shown that the agricultural resource base is quite limited. The total cultivated area has increased, but on a *per capita* basis it has decreased. On an index basis it dropped from 100 in 1929 to 77 in 1961, and to 64 in 1972. In 1971, Peru had 0.18 hectares of arable land *per capita*, while a country which is considered to be overpopulated — India — had 0.2.[2]

Land has become increasingly scarce in Peru and marginal land has been brought into production. Land destruction, soil erosion and the salinisation of irrigated land are taking place as a result of the pressure for new land. For many decades governments have carried out irrigation schemes on the coast to increase agricultural land. This was a successful strategy during the first half of this century. Since then, the construction costs per hectare have risen rapidly, because the most profitable projects have already been implemented. The development potential of the *Selva* is still an open question and government sponsored colonisation schemes have been costly and have had only little impact on agricultural development.

In the period 1950–80 Peru attempted a rapid industrialisation of the country by following the strategy of import substitution. The basic elements of the strategy of import substitution have been: (a) raised tariffs on imported manufactured goods; (b) stimulation of industrial investments. The latter was accomplished by favourable financial treatment — low taxes; low rates of interest charged on loans from the public sector; special, favourable conditions for imports of capital goods; and to some extent for intermediary inputs too. This kind of import substitution has an inherent bias against agriculture.

Import substitution generally leads to an overvalued currency and this happened in Peru as well. Exporters received less in domestic currency than they would have done had the currency been in equilibrium. Since agriculture accounted for more than half of exports, agriculture was particularly hit. As a result, the share of agricultural exports decreased rapidly and was about 5 per cent in 1981.

Thorp and Bertram have concluded that for the period 1930–77 the terms of trade moved against the agricultural sector:

> In addition to the long-standing role of export agriculture as a net supplier of funds for investments in other sectors agriculture in general (including the traditional sector) had been subjected over

the long term to a steady squeeze on its surplus as the terms of trade shifted in favour of urban sectors.[3]

Furthermore, governments' policies were aimed at keeping food prices low. Different governments have intervened directly and indirectly in the price system. The most common practice has been to fix legal maximum retail prices and at times minimum retail prices. Food subsidies have been common.

These factors taken together obviously made the return on investments in agriculture less profitable than otherwise, and government policy had made it relatively profitable to invest outside agriculture.

In addition to these objective factors we should also consider the expectations of investors. The Cuban revolution in 1959; the emphasis of the Alliance for Progress, initiated during the Kennedy era by the United States, on agrarian reform; rural unrest at the beginning of the 1960s, and the pressures for agrarian reform in Peru were all important factors and probably all lowered the expected rate of return on investments in agriculture *vis-à-vis* other sectors.

As a result of these factors private investments in agriculture were very low before the radical reform in 1969. There are no data to prove this point but a few examples suggest this to be true. The value of machinery and equipment represented only a small fraction of the total value of expropriated farms. Although massive slaughtering did not take place in Peru during the reform, the herds of the large farms had decreased between 1961 and 1972. The commercial banks' credit to agriculture is also indicative. Since 1955 outstanding credit (in constant prices) remained practically constant until the agrarian reform in 1969 when it then decreased rapidly.

Because the private sector shifted its interest from agriculture to other economic sectors it became necessary for the public sector to engage itself more actively. In 1950 public sector receipts from agriculture were ten times higher than expenditures in the sector. By 1970 the situation was in balance. In 1950, 36 per cent of institutional credit to agriculture came from the public sector, and the balance from commercial banks. By 1980, the public sector accounted for 97 per cent, the commercial banks hardly playing any role whatsoever.[4]

4. Agrarian Reform and Stagnation

To break the trend towards agricultural stagnation, important changes in economic policy would have been needed. In particular it would have been necessary to increase investments in agriculture. Such a change would have required Peruvian policy makers to be aware of the basic causes for agricultural stagnation. This was not the case, and Peruvian policy makers had a great belief in the potential for agricultural growth. One current belief among the military was that once the oppression of the *latifundios* had been eliminated, growth would be almost automatic. But, as we have discussed earlier, agricultural stagnation had several causes.

To reap the benefits of structural reforms, of new investments and of new economic policies, takes time. The proper timing of the introduction of necessary measures is of crucial importance. A long run strategy to increase the rate of agricultural growth would have been to increase the area under production, particularly with new irrigation schemes. However, as was noted in the previous section, the new schemes tend to be capital intensive, have a long gestation period and many have a low economic return. It would, therefore, seem logical first to concentrate government efforts on carrying out the reform and on improving the use of the available resources, before embarking on new major irrigation schemes. This was particularly true at the time, because major undertakings require administrative personnel who became scarce during the reform. Another factor to consider is that investments in improving and maintaining the existing irrigation systems had a high economic return.

During the period 1969–76, a period of major reform activities, there was initially little new investment in irrigation to expand agricultural land. But only a few years after 1969, investments in irrigation increased rapidly.[5] Thus, during these years of massive transfers of land, the government initiated major new investments in irrigated land. Little was invested, however, in maintaining the existing system. The level of investment in agriculture was probably very low during the reform process and the share of long-term credit in the total yearly credit of the Agricultural Development Bank dropped to one-half of the level in the 1950s.

One of the keys to increasing the rate of growth of agricultural production would have been a rapid rate of growth in investments in the new enterprises emerging from the reform. However, most public investments were channelled into non-agricultural projects and most of the investments that were made in agriculture became earmarked for irrigation projects. Moreover, since most of the administrative capacity of the extension services was transferred to the administration of the agrarian reform one instrument for inducing technological advances virtually disappeared. Another factor during the reform process was that medium sized farmers, though not particularly important in total production, felt great uncertainty with respect to their landholdings and invested little, if anything at all. The small farmers were virtually abandoned during the reform.

Curiously enough, in spite of the government's willingness to change the agrarian structure completely and risk the possibility of a drastic decline in agricultural production, its economic policies towards the agricultural sector were extremely biased in favour of the urban consumer until the end of the 1970s. Government intervention in the markets increased significantly; food subsidies increased rapidly, and the overvalued currency discriminated against agricultural exports while it induced food imports.

Peruvian policy makers were influenced by policies proposed by the UN Economic Commission for Latin America, FAO and academics. Many arguments for the positive effects of agrarian reform on production can be found. Few, if any, would, however, argue that an automatic relation exists between agrarian reform and increases in production. Still, the economic policies in Peru during and after the reform, and the planned high rates of growth for agriculture suggest that Peruvian policy makers believed that agrarian reform was not only a necessary condition, but also a sufficient condition for increasing agricultural growth.

The combination of a weak resource base, discriminatory economic policies, and lack of investments and capital suggest that agricultural growth will be sluggish for the rest of this century.

5. Income Distribution

In 1960 the income distribution in Peru was one of the most skewed in the whole world. While the 20 per cent poorest received 2.5 per cent of the personal income, the richest 5 per cent received 39 per cent. The average for middle income countries was 4.6 (for the poorest) and 24.2 per cent (for the richest) respectively for that year.[6]

One important reason was the low level of agricultural development which exerted a downward pressure on wages. Urban incomes were significantly higher than rural ones. Thus, in 1972 urban household incomes were 3.3 times higher than rural ones.[7] Given the very uneven distribution of income in Peru, it is noteworthy that rural incomes were even more skewed than urban ones. One reason for this was that agricultural land ownership was extremely uneven. This meant that rural incomes were very low and economic growth in the urban areas attracted waves of migrants to the cities in search of a better income. The rapid growth of urban centres is a testimony to this.

Prior to the agrarian reform in 1961, there were some 840,000 production units in Peru, covering an area of 18 million hectares. 3,600 farms (0.4 per cent of the total) had no less than 76 per cent of the land. On the other end of the spectrum 700,000 farms (73 per cent of the total) had about 7 per cent of agricultural land. Part of this land was leased from the big landowners. (For statistical details see Table 14.2.) Poverty was particularly widespread in the *Sierra*. Such a skewed distribution of land has few parallels in the world. A programme of economic development would have to include an agrarian reform, and it was long overdue when it came in 1969.

The potential impact of agrarian reform on rural income distribution can be illustrated with the following example. Redistributing only one-fifth of the income, from the richest 5 per cent in the rural sector to the poorest 30 per cent, would double the income of the latter group.[8] Such a measure would, if not eliminate, at least radically reduce rural poverty.

6. Agrarian Reform and Rural Poverty

During the period 1962–68 little progress was made in agrarian reform. About 550 farms and 1 million hectares were expropriated. Only 14,000 families benefited, and they received 400,000 hectares. The impact on land tenure was minimal in relation to the total number of rural families at this time, about 900,000, or the total amount of agricultural land, about 18 million hectares.[9]

After the military coup in October 1968, the agrarian question was much debated within the military regime. Two distinct approaches can be identified. The more conservative emphasised the need to increase the growth rate, and wished to minimise the possible disruptive effects of the agrarian reform on production. Hence, expropriations were to be limited to a minimum and mainly under-cultivated land was to be expropriated. Obviously this approach had great support from the traditional landowning classes. The other approach, the radical, wished to eliminate once and for all the Peruvian landed oligarchy. The question of social justice was a prime objective and this group was even willing to sacrifice production to achieve social justice.

In February 1969 the Minister of Agriculture presented an agrarian reform proposal, modelled on the conservative ideas, to the military government. After intensive infighting among the military the minister was forced to resign, and a radical reform law was passed in June 1969. The law itself would have permitted the military to expropriate practically anything it desired. Obviously, the law could also be changed by military decree. What was more interesting was the subsequent actual implementation of the law. In this respect the government quickly demonstrated its determination to carry out a radical reform. A few days after the promulgation of the law, the military occupied the economically important sugar estates on the Coast. Foreign economic interest in these were important and their expropriation had a dual significance: a show of force; and the underlining of the nationalistic fervour of the government. This move by the government ensured that, from then on, rapid and massive expropriation could take place practically without any violence.

In the period 1969–80 about 16,000 farms and 9 million hectares were expropriated. Close to 400,000 families benefited by the reform.[10] Adding the results from the preceding period (1962–68), more than half of the irrigated land and about 43 per cent of dry land had been expropriated for the agrarian reform in Peru. The reform had affected close to half of the total agricultural production.

The beneficiaries of the reform did not receive the land, capital and other assets free of charge. If the repayment obligation had been great the effects on income distribution would have been very small. The repayment obligation was quite modest for two reasons. The first is that the valuation of the assets to be expropriated was based on the landowners' earlier assessment of their value. The landowners had had an interest in declaring low values so as to evade taxes. Moreover, these values had not been adjusted and, during the reform, were not adjusted for inflation. The rate of inflation accelerated in the 1970s so that the value of 100 Soles in 1969 prices was, for example, only 11 Soles in 1979.[11] The beneficiaries did not have to start repaying for three to five years, and the repayments were to be made during some 20 years. The rate of interest charged on the outstanding debt was significantly lower than the rate of inflation. Obviously it cannot be claimed that the repayment burden on the beneficiaries was excessive.

The former landowners were only paid a small amount in cash and the rest in non-transferable bonds. Was this compensation just? As Dorner has pointed out,

> . . . whether payments for land are indeed 'unreasonable' is a matter to be judged in terms of historical circumstances. Present owners or their ancestors often gained access and ownership to the land by reason of their favoured power position. In many cases present market value reflects investments in infrastructure, much of it created either by the underpaid labourers who are the reform's intended beneficiaries, or through government investments financed by general tax revenues only part of which were collected from present landowners.[12]

The idea that an agrarian reform is costly and will produce inflation was also expounded in Peru. Facts do not bear out this assertion. It is true that both the national budget deficit and the rate of inflation grew after 1969. The cause for this, however, was not the agrarian reform. The reasons are as follows. Only a minor part of the compensation payments to the expropriated owners was paid in cash. The major part was paid in non-transferable bonds. The nominal rate of interest on these bonds was low (4–6 per cent) while the rate of inflation was accelerating; the redemption period was long (20–30 years) and they were not adjusted for inflation. Consequently, even during the period of massive expropriations, 1969–76, compensation payments for expropriations, minus the beneficiaries' payments to the government, represented only about 0.3 per cent of government expenditure. The national budget was hardly affected by the reform. Therefore, an agrarian reform does not necessarily produce inflation, nor has it to be costly.

All these factors mentioned above may at first sight suggest that the reform was an outstanding success in terms of the objective to redistribute income. This was not the case, however. The basic question which has to be answered is: who reaped the benefits of the reform? Before proceeding, it is useful to recall some of the prevailing lines of thought in Peru.

One dominant feature of land tenure in Latin America has been the presence of large landowners who exploit cheap labour. Technological improvements were rare in these latifundios. At the same time, modern agriculture developed both on large and smaller farms. At the other end of the spectrum we find millions of peasants scraping out a meagre subsistence income because of lack of access to the basic means of production, particularly land. Attempts at modifying the prevailing structure of ownership of land by peaceful means have not been successful in Latin America. Changes in agrarian structure have usually been accompanied by revolutions as in Mexico, Bolivia, Cuba, and more recently in Nicaragua. Therefore, advocates of agrarian reform in Latin America have concentrated their efforts on attacking the prevailing ownership of land, with little immediate concern about who would benefit from the reform, and how they were to benefit.

The same was also true in Peru. The slogan — *La tierra para quien la trabaja* — the land to the tiller, focused on the exploitative nature of the worker–owner relationship, while stressing that large rents were extracted from the peasants. One of the slogans of the Peruvian reform after 1969 — *El patrón nunca más comerá tu pobreza* — the landlord will never again eat of your poverty, expressed the same view of exploited workers. The Marxists were obviously one of the more important groups to criticise the land tenure. The Marxist conceptual framework is that of exploitation. It was, therefore, logical to concentrate criticism on the exploitative nature of the landlord–worker relationship.

One idea which gained acceptance in Peru as early as the 1950s, was that leasing land to the peasant families had to be regulated, if not prohibited. Therefore, as landowners at the end of the 1950s realised that leasing land to the peasants was becoming a dangerous venture, they started to rearrange tenant arrangements by means ranging from selling land to simply evicting the peasants.

One of the more basic problems in Peru was, however, that hundreds of thousands of peasants simply had marginal access to land. Therefore, a mere redistribution of land to the permanent workers on the estates and to the tenants would leave the poorest segments of the rural population — the seasonal workers and the *minifundistas* — without any benefits from the reform.

The above-mentioned factors, the necessity to concentrate efforts on breaking the power of the landed obligarchy, and the notion of exploitation of the workers, were decisive in shaping the course of the Peruvian reform. Another set of factors was also important, namely, a belief in economies of scale in agricultural enterprises and the need to reduce the danger of any great disruption in production. Viewed in retrospect there was an odd alliance of a variety of political forces who agreed on the need to form collective forms of enterprises: the military (economies of scale, discipline and the desire to control the process); progressive forces within the Catholic Church (with strong inclinations towards non-capitalist associative forms of human co-operation); and the Marxists.

Therefore, the Peruvian agrarian reform primarily involved the permanent workers of the expropriated estates, and tended to benefit the richer 20 per cent stratum of the rural population. Only a fraction of the land was awarded to individual families, 2 per cent, and the rest went to different collective forms of production.[13] In total, some 400,000 families benefited from the agrarian reform.

When the drought, which was affecting Peruvian agriculture at the end of the 1960s, gave way, production levels rapidly returned to normal. In addition favourable export prices for agricultural goods, mainly sugar, permitted a very rapid rise in wages on many reform enterprises. Pressures for incorporating peasants from outside the reformed sector were strong during the reform period. The government did, however, decide to limit the scope of the reform, and already in 1971 the pattern was clear. As of 1977, the rate of expropriation (area and number of farms) decreased and it almost ceased as of 1979.[14]

The rural poor did not benefit by the agrarian reform. In 1961 there were about 700,000 families who had less than 5 hectares. In 1972 this figure had risen to 1.1 million and hardly any of these received land during the reform process.[15] Moreover, even though the rural poor have neither received much assistance from the extension services nor much institutional credit, during the reform these services virtually disappeared for the rural poor because the reform absorbed most of these resources. Public investments were directed towards large scale irrigation projects on the coast. These projects can only marginally improve the economic situation of the rural poor because there is not enough land to distribute. Moreover, the rural poor are concentrated in the Sierra which for many decades has received only very little support for development.

Today there are some 1,600 reform enterprises, excluding Indian communities.[16] Traditionally these farms have employed seasonal labour from the outside. Modernisation on such enterprises almost inevitably means mechanisation and, if so, an important source of income of the rural poor will be cut off.

In summary, the prospects are not very bright for the Peruvian peasants today. At the beginning of the 1960s rural guerrilla movements threatened the regime. One of the military's most important reasons for carrying out the agrarian reform was the conviction that Peruvian national security ultimately depended on social stability and national integration. Agrarian reform was, among other things, to appease the peasants. This was not successful, and, at the beginning of the 1980s, the rural guerrilla movement has again gained momentum in Peru.

7. Summary and Conclusions

The Peruvian agrarian reform is important. It is almost the only enduring Latin American example of a planned major reform without any revolution. The agrarian reform had two central objectives, namely, to increase agricultural growth and to improve the standard of living of the rural population. The first agrarian reform law was passed in 1962. Little was accomplished until 1969 when a military government passed a new reform law and rapidly and effectively commenced expropriating agricultural land. At the end of the 1970s, 16,000 farms, about half of the agricultural land, had been expropriated, and 400,000 rural families had received about 10 million hectares. In terms of numbers, the reform was a success. In this chapter we have argued that the Peruvian agrarian reform did not meet its objectives.

The growth rate of Peruvian agriculture had been stagnating since the 1950s at least. There were several reasons for this. One was that agricultural land had become increasingly scarce. Another cause was that economic policies favoured industrialisation and urban growth. Investments in industry were stimulated thus making investments in agriculture relatively less profitable. In addition, agrarian reform was becoming accepted as being a necessary reform, thus making investments in agriculture even more risky. During the reform process 1962–81, the same discriminatory economic policies were continued, if not accentuated, until the end of the 1970s. The government intervened frequently to keep agricultural prices low. Interference in the marketing system also became frequent. As a result agricultural growth rates declined.

The rapid economic growth in the period 1950–70 did not benefit the poorer strata in Peru. The rural income distribution was extremely skewed prior to the agrarian reform, because of the very uneven distribution of land. An agrarian reform could have had an enormous impact in eradicating rural poverty. However, the 400,000 rural families who benefited from the reform belonged in general to the 20 per cent relatively richer stratum. Today, there are over one million poor peasant families who are no better off than before the reform. Rural poverty continues to be acute in many areas of Peru.

After 20 years of agrarian reform efforts in Peru, agricultural growth continues to be below that of the population. The rural poor did not benefit from the agrarian reform. At the beginning of the 1960s rural social unrest and guerrilla movements were spreading. Now, twenty years later, they are active again.

Notes

1. Alberts (1983), p. 14; BCR (1982), p. 67.
2. Alberts (1983), pp. 212–3.
3. Thorp and Bertram (1978), p. 278.
4. Alberts (1983), p. 253; BCR Boletín (March 1982), pp. 31 and 33.
5. Alberts (1983), p. 226; IBRD (1981), p. 50.
6. IBRD (1980), pp. 460–3.
7. Alberts (1983), p. 81.
8. Ibid., p. 90.
9. Ibid., p. 193.
10. Matos Mar and Mejía (1980), p. 179; Alberts (1983), pp. 138–42.
11. Alberts (1983), p. 251.
12. Dorner (1972), pp. 47–8.
13. Matos Mar and Mejía (1980), p. 179.
14. Ibid. p. 171.
15. Table 14.2 and Alberts (1983), Ch. 5.
16. Matos Mar and Mejía (1980), p. 190.

Bibliography

Alberts, Tom, *Agrarian Reform and Rural Poverty. — A Case Study of Peru* (Westview Press, Boulder, Colorado, 1983).
BCR, Banco Central de Reserva del Perú. *Cuentas Nacionales del Perú 1950–67.* (Lima, Peru, 1968).
____ *Memoria.* Various years.
____*Boletín.* March (1982).
Dorner, Peter, *Land Reform and Economic Development* (Penguin Modern Economic Texts, 1972).

IBRD, International Bank for Reconstruction and Development. *PERU Major Development Policy Issues and Recommendations* (Washington DC, 1981).

_____ *World Tables 1980* (John Hopkins University Press, Baltimore and London, 1980).

Matos Mar, José and Mejía, José Manuel, *La Reforma Agraria en el Perú* (Instituto de Estudios Peruanos, Lima, 1980).

Republic of Peru, *1983 — External Financing Program. Statistical Information* (Lima, 1983).

Thorp, Rosemary and Bertram, Geoffrey, *Peru 1890–1977. Growth and Policy in an Open Economy* (Macmillan, London and Basingstoke, 1978).

15 THE INTERACTION OF RESEARCH AND TRAINING IN AGRICULTURAL DEVELOPMENT *

A. Steven Englander

Over the past twenty-five years evidence has accumulated to suggest that agricultural research is highly productive in both developed and less developed countries. The estimated real rates of return are extremely high, much higher than the returns from any safe financial asset and probably higher than the returns to many alternative LDC projects, although the evidence is less solid here.[1] Moreover, while the range of estimated returns is quite large, few studies report real rates of return below 15 per cent, suggesting that risk of failure is not an important factor inhibiting investment in research.

At the same time, technology transfer has assumed a prominent role in the agricultural development literature. In part, this has occurred because of the tremendous success of the 'Green Revolution' wheat and rice varieties. The wheat varieties, developed by the International Wheat and Maize Improvement Centre (CIMMYT), have spread through North Africa, the Middle East, Pakistan, India, and other regions. The rice varieties of the International Rice Research Institute (IRRI) achieved similar success in many rice growing regions of Asia.

The potential for technology transfer, so apparent from the 'Green Revolution' varieties, gave some early hope that the problem of creating agricultural technology for developing countries had been solved. These expectations were no doubt raised by the enthusiasm of farmers in adopting the new varieties. But the importance of domestic research capabilities became appreciated as more insight was gained into the process by which agricultural technology is transferred among nations. Evidence quickly accumulated to show that local research greatly enhances the productivity of transferred

* I would like to thank Robert Evenson, Ronald Findlay, Gustav Ranis and Brian Wright for their comments and suggestions on various drafts. I would also like to thank Hyacinth Hamilton for fine and patient typing of several drafts of this paper. None of the above are responsible for any remaining errors. The opinions expressed are my own and not necessarily those of the Federal Reserve Bank of New York or the Federal Reserve System.

technology. A particularly striking case is that of India — despite the high yields of the CIMMYT varieties introduced in India in the mid-1960s, it took only about eight years for Indian reselections of these varieties or crosses of Indian and CIMMYT varieties to displace the directly transferred CIMMYT varieties almost completely.[2] Also, it gradually became apparent that some countries would not benefit greatly from these new varieties or would benefit only after a significant investment of resources in adapting the technology to their needs.

The bulk of the evidence now seems to suggest that domestic research and the transfer of agricultural technology are complements, rather than substitutes. To some degree this makes the development of a local research capacity a preferred strategy regardless of the potential for transferring technology. If a country grows its crops in an environment which is much different from that of other countries which grow the same crops, it must of necessity develop its own research capability. However, even those countries with growing environments which lie closer to the norm elsewhere for their groups generally find a high return to adapting and improving the varieties which they import. There are, of course, conditions under which 'free riding' on the technology of other countries may be optimal: for example, the case of a small, agriculturally homogeneous region adjacent to a larger, similar region in a country with a developed research infrastructure. Nevertheless, environments being as diverse as they are, there seem to be relatively few instances in which such an approach would be optimal.

With this evidence on the importance of domestic research, it seems appropriate to pay more attention to the process by which domestic research capacity is acquired. The very persistence of studies over 25 years, testifying to high returns to agricultural research, recommends a closer look at why there seems to be inadequate investment in research capacity. True, some analysts have criticised the methodology of these studies, while others have pointed to public goods problems as an explanation of the high returns. However, in addition to appealing to methodology and the public's demand for research, it is worthwhile to examine the supply side to see whether there are factors which constrain the ability of the system to invest optimally in research.

In this chapter I examine some aspects of the interaction of agricultural technology transfer, domestic research capacity and the development of agricultural research systems. The first section provides a model of agricultural research and technology transfer, indicating some circumstances when technology transfer is desirable and others when it is a sign of a weak research system. The second section estimates the inherent advantages of local varieties over foreign varieties and of local adaptations of improved foreign varieties over the foreign parents. The third section takes the importance of domestic research capacity as a given and examines some reasons for underinvestment in such capacity.

My conclusions are:

(a) Locally developed wheat varieties have a strong inherent advantage over foreign varieties of about 425 kilograms/hectare.
(b) An important technological advance abroad may give foreign varieties a temporary advantage, but competent adaptive research should quickly restore the advantage of local varieties.
(c) Problems in training and retaining skilled researchers may keep research systems understaffed as well as give the system a relatively unproductive long-run focus.

Domestic Research and Technology Transfer

This section models some of the factors which influence a research system's choice between adapting a foreign technology or developing a local technology. The model is highly idealised, although for concreteness I focus on how a region's research system decides its crop breeding strategy. By formalising some of the factors which affect the decision we may acquire some sense of where and why technology transfer becomes an attractive option. More importantly, perhaps, we will see why a domestic research capability remains desirable, if not essential, even when there is scope for technology transfer.

First of all, what is meant by local and foreign technology? I focus on crop breeding as a representative research activity because it has the advantage of making the distinction very clear. Most regions have traditional crop varieties which farmers use extensively and which are particularly well suited to the growing conditions of the region. In some cases, regions with a slow overall pace of technological advance gradually develop highly specialised varieties and technology closely tailored to the local environment.[3] The local research system may choose to emphasise improving these varieties, selecting and cross-breeding among them, and introducing only relatively minor characteristics from foreign varieties. When these are the emphases, the research system can be said to focus on developing local technology.

Alternatively, the research system may find in foreign varieties a package of characteristics which, adapted properly, are better suited to their region. In this case the building blocks of the region's future technology are the foreign varieties. However, I argue below that without modification, the foreign varieties are probably inferior to the domestic ones. Even where they are superior, the domestic research system is likely to be able to develop varieties based on the foreign varieties which are better than they are.

The reason for the superiority of domestic research is embedded in the objectives and constraints which guide research. Consider a breeder: When he crosses two varieties, he wishes to produce, for a region, a third variety with characteristics of greater value than either of the two parents. If it does not have better characteristics in terms of the region's needs, it will be discarded.[4] If the breeder makes many crosses, several of which produce improved plants, typically only the best few will be released.

The breeder not only knows the characteristics of the parents but also the expected characteristics of the crosses. The breeder is not nearly as concerned with the productivity or value of the *average* cross as with the expected value of the *best* cross.

Two properties of the statistics of extremes are relevant to agricultural research:[5]

(a) the more crosses, the better will the best cross be, and
(b) the marginal expected improvement from each additional cross is positive, but diminishing.

Using his knowledge of the parent varieties and the laws of genetics, the breeder has some prior idea of what any breeding programme is likely to accomplish. All of this is subject to chance, however. While the breeder has a set of outcomes in mind, the randomness inherent in breeding can produce far different results from those expected or desired. Figure 15.1 illustrates some of these considerations diagrammatically.

Figure 15.1 shows the relation between the goals of the breeding

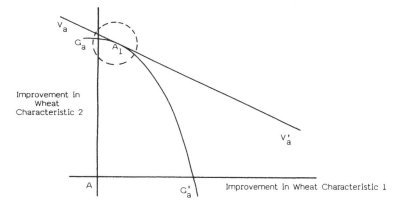

Figure 15.1:   The Goals of the Breeding Programme

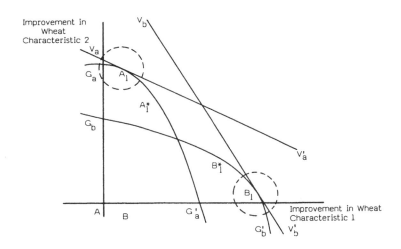

Figure 15.2:   The Goals of the Breeding Programme:
Two Regions

programme and the needs of the region. It also illustrates the probabilistic nature of the final outcome. $G_a G_a'$ describes the set of expected best genetic improvements from a research programme of a given size. The breeder can aim at any point along the curve, although there is no guarantee that he will achieve it. Where he aims is determined by the relative value which the region places on the research objectives. In Figure 15.1 the relative value is shown as the slope of $V_a V_a'$, and the point A_1 is the goal of the breeding programme. The effect of chance is illustrated by the dotted curve around A_1 — A_1 may be the target and the expected result, but the probability of falling within the dotted curve may be none the less quite small.

A second region can easily be introduced into this analysis. Consider Figure 15.2. Region A has the same goals and expected research possibilities as in Figure 15.1. Region B's priorities and expected possibilities are both somewhat different, and region B may be starting with varieties with somewhat different properties. Note that neither region would prefer the variety at which the other is aiming. The point A_1 is below $V_b V_b'$ while B_1 is below $V_a V_a'$.

Also, neither region could choose any point along its expected research possibility frontier which on average would produce a better variety for the other region than the other region's own research. That is to say, all points on $G_b G_b'$ lie below $V_a V_a'$ and all points on $G_a G_a'$ lie below $V_b V_b'$. While this is an assumption which Figure 15.2 purposefully depicts, it does correspond to the empirical generalisation that most regions are better suited to solving their own problems than those of other regions. In part, there is simply a tendency for each region to be the best natural laboratory for researching its own problems.

Note, however, there are also some possibilities for cooperation. If region A aimed at a goal somewhat to the right of A_1 and region B at a goal somewhat to the left of B_1, their likelihood of producing the 'best' variety for the other region would be enhanced without greatly diminishing the expected gains from their research to themselves. (One can see this by drawing lines parallel to $V_a V_a'$ and $V_b V_b'$ through A_1^*. A line parallel to $V_a V_a'$ is not much farther from $V_a V_a'$, but the one parallel to $V_b V_b'$ is much closer to $V_b V_b'$. Analogous conclusions hold for B_1^*.) In recent years some such regional cooperation in research has occurred, for example among the *Cono Sur* countries of Latin America.[6]

Even where regions do not cooperate, however, there still exists a possibility that a region will produce a variety which is particularly well suited to some other region. There are several ways by which this can occur. If there are two reasonably similar regions, of which one has a much larger research programme, then the varieties it develops may be well suited to a second region, even though the research takes only local priorities into account. For example, imagine that region B's expected research possibilities curve was condensed to one-fourth that depicted in Figure 15.2, as illustrated in Figure 15.3. Then if region A produced a variety such as A_1, it would be superior to any variety that region B could expect to produce. Region B might still maintain a research programme, however, because of the chance that it might produce a superior variety or region A an inferior one. Nevertheless, on average one would expect the region A varieties to dominate. Alternatively one region may produce a 'breakthrough' variety which is far better than expected. For example, region A may develop a variety which is well beyond its expected research possibilities frontier. In either case, region B is faced with region A having made much greater advances than it can expect to achieve on its own. How does it respond?

Whether or not region B attempts to exploit the advance in region A for itself depends on how well the advance can be adapted to the region. Three alternatives are illustrated in Figure 15.4. In the first, the variety with characteristics at point X is produced. Despite the advance, X is still much less preferred than the variety at B_1 which region B could produce on its own. While there may be some instances in which region B may yet find it worthwhile to incorporate variety X into its breeding programme, in many cases a variety such as X is too far removed to be considered useful.

A variety such as Y, however, usually presents a more difficult decision to the research system. On the one hand, it cannot compete directly against B_1, the best variety region B expects to produce for itself. On the other hand, it is close and has superb characteristics in at least one dimension. In many cases, the next round of research, particularly if conducted in region B, holds promise of repairing some of the variety's defects from region B's point of view. Since region A was not emphasising the improvement of the characteristic which region B valued relatively highly, there may be considerable room for such improvement. And if there is some possibility of crossing the B_1 and Y varieties, the resultant variety may be superior to either individually. By way of illustration, variety YB is depicted as possessing the sum of the improvements built individually into Y and B_1. It may be unrealistic to expect such a superior variety to

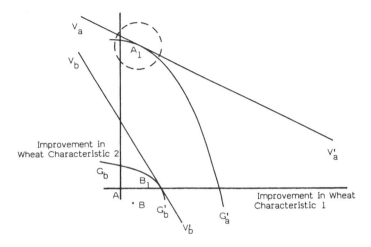

Figure 15.3:   Region A Superior to Region B

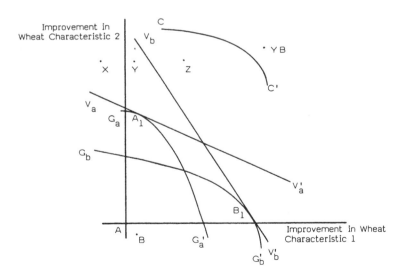

Figure 15.4:   The Response of Region B

emerge, but a curve such as CC′ may represent more realistic possibilities.

Yet another possibility is that region B may alter its environment somewhat so that it no longer places quite as much emphasis on the first characteristic, thus becoming able to exploit region A's advance. While this may seem far-fetched at first glance, recent experience suggests it is not so, especially when great advances have been made. For example, the great advantage to growing high yielding wheat varieties under a well regulated water supply probably encouraged the proliferation of tube wells and other irrigation methods in India. Were it not for these benefits, research in many regions of India would have emphasised drought resistance much more as a characteristic to breed into varieties.

Each of these possibilities suggests that there are at least some cases where a region may wish to reorient its research towards a foreign technology, even if the latter does not initially display clear signs of superiority. The process may be gradual, however, because the potential of the technology may be uncovered only in stages. Nevertheless, the perceived potential of the technology may be sufficiently large as to encourage the region to commit the resources for adaptation.

The third possibility is that region A develops a variety such as Z, which is immediately superior to anything that region B expects to produce. In this case, region B's farmers immediately adopt Z, the foreign variety. Here, as in the case discussed just above, there are reasons to expect that region B researchers may be able to greatly enhance the productivity of the new technology in their region. Even with the best intentions, the region A system is unlikely to produce just the right variety for region B. Whatever advance is made can probably be greatly augmented by the region B system.

One necessary reservation to the above analysis is that it does not deal directly with region B's independent research potential in the future. The system produced variety B_1 initially. What can it do subsequently on its own? Recent research suggests two possibilities.[7] If the underlying research base (the stock of basic or fundamental research) is unchanged, then research opportunities may become exhausted. Future breeding research may be less productive and improvements as great as moving from B to B_1 no longer obtainable in subsequent periods. It is in these circumstances that adaptive research becomes more and more attractive. And, indeed, if the independent research prospects are sufficiently depleted, then even a programme of combining B_1 with X may be pursued. Thus, a reliance on adaptive research may reflect underlying weakness rather than strength in a research programme.

In contrast, a research programme which has a strong scientific research base can replenish periodically the potential for applied research. In this case the varieties along CC′ may be less desirable than those based more on local research.

Thus, it seems that irrespective of which alternative emerges, there remains a large scope for domestic research. If another region's advance is entirely irrelevant to the region, the latter must depend on its own research while facing a stronger competitor. If the advance is somewhat relevant, the region may have to invest considerable resources to adapting it before benefiting at all from the advance. Even if the advance is dramatic for both regions, there is likely to be considerable scope for a domestic contribution. Implicitly, there is some unfairness here. Adaptive research seems most productive when the advance is already pretty well suited to the region. Indeed, the return to adaptive research in such cases is likely to be higher than the return to a similar region pursuing an independent research path.

The above analysis suggests the considerations which may guide the choice of research orientation. However, it is empty unless it is shown to have significant empirical content. In the next section we see that the magnitudes involved are very significant from an economic perspective.

Measuring the Benefits from Domestic Research

To assess the quantitative significance of the above discussion it is necessary to answer the following questions:

(1) How much better are local varieties than foreign varieties in general?
(2) Can advances in foreign technology ever outweigh the domestic advantage?
(3) How superior are the domestic adaptations of the foreign varieties?
(4) Is it the case that there are higher returns to adaptive research when the transferred technology is initially more suitable?

Below we provide answers to the first three questions. The fourth, while interesting and important, requires somewhat more extensive data than were available.

To answer the first three questions, I relate the productivity of wheat varieties to climate, fertiliser application, and varietal-technological factors. By productivity I mean yield in kilograms per hectare. While there is some controversy over whether this measure of productivity is most appropriate, it is commonly used by economists and agricultural researchers and probably provides a reasonable first order approximation to the economist's ideal measure of productivity.

The first question is answered simply by seeing whether locally developed varieties are more productive locally than are foreign varieties in 21 countries, holding constant all environmental and technological factors other than the country of origin.

The second question requires a judgement as to whether certain varieties embody a technological breakthrough. Fortunately a clear example of such an advance exists in the data. By most definitions the 'Green Revolution' wheat varieties produced by CIMMYT in Mexico represent a significant technical advance. We can compare their productivity with that of the *traditional* varieties of each country and see whether the breakthrough outweighs the local advantage.

Finally we note that after the CIMMYT varieties became available, many countries reselected the CIMMYT varieties locally or crossed the CIMMYT varieties with domestic varieties. To answer the third question, I therefore compare the productivity of these local adaptations with the productivity of the directly transferred CIMMYT varieties.

The short answers to the questions are as follows. The average advantage to a local variety, holding all other factors equal, is about 425 kilogram/hectare (kg/ha). Almost all countries show a positive local yield advantage. CIMMYT varieties from Mexico are estimated to outperform the traditional local varieties in 15 of 21 cases. (We exclude Syria which produced highly anomalous results.) Local reselections of, or crosses with, CIMMYT varieties are estimated to yield 430–479 kg/ha more than their traditional counterparts, surpassing the yield advantage of CIMMYT over local varieties in 9 of the 15 instances. For these 9, the yield advantage of their adaptive technology is about 240 kg/ha.[8]

The Role of Training and Personnel Policies

We have seen thus far that the domestic component of research is very important. However, while the productivity of research programmes is much studied and measured, the process by which research capacity is acquired is relatively neglected. Little attention has been paid to the training and retention of researchers. Consider two references to the subject which assign a much more important role to these factors.

. . . The Kenyan government failed to improve salaries and benefits for its maize breeders and so reduced the incentives for trained Kenyans to stay with the national program . . . Some 16 years of A.I.D. support of maize breeding, albeit on the regional level, produced only 3 Ph.D level Kenyan breeders — none of whom is now working in the country's maize research program. In the circumstance it is not surprising that the comprehensive breeding improvement program installed by US technicians is no longer operating in Kenya.[9]

The committee was highly critical of the existing [Brazilian circa 1970] research system. It pointed out . . . that the existing administrative structure inhibited the training and promotion of well-qualified personnel . . . that of the 1902 individuals considered to be formal researchers only 10 per cent could be considered professionals with some kind of graduate training in research . . . that the salary policy did not allow the government to compete in the professional labour market . . . Only about 3500 of the roughly 6700 employees of the old system were transferred to EMBRAPA [the new research organisation].[10]

Such comments are not atypical in descriptions of the research systems of many developing countries. At first glance, however, they seem to be slightly contradictory — the first quote deploring the inability to retain personnel, the second being rather deprecatory of the quality of the researchers that the system possesses. Of course, there is no real contradiction since, in the general exodus of researchers from a system, the first to leave are often the best, while lesser-skilled researchers may experience more difficulty in finding outside positions. Such anecdotes suggest, however, that personnel and training problems may place severe constraints on the construction of research systems.

Research systems in developing countries should be regarded as integrated research and training systems. In some cases the integration is formal, in others the research and training may be under different departments in the Ministry of Agriculture or even in separate ministries. Whatever the formal institutional arrangement, however, the long-term plan for building an agricultural research system must be consistent with the country's training capacity or ability to have researchers trained abroad. While some complementarities may exist between research and training, on the whole the two activities probably compete for one scarce but crucial resource, the researchers available to the system. It is highly trained professionals (PhD level in most cases) who form the backbone of both research and training systems. But a greater emphasis on one activity almost undoubtedly means less on the other.

In an earlier work, I provided a two-period model of an agricultural research system's choice between research and training.[11] The system allocated its stock of professionals between research and training new researchers to maintain or expand the system. Below I discuss the implications of this model for agricultural research policy.

It is easy to show that the current and future productivity of research, the productivity of training, the retirement rate of researchers and the availability of resources will affect the optimum division of resources. The availability of additional resources in the form of researchers in the initial period results in more research in both periods and more training. If the productivity of current research falls relative to future research then resources to current research are reduced and more training is undertaken.

If research in the future is expected to be less productive than current research, then the marginal product of training will have to be high. Resources will be diverted from research to training only when many researchers can be trained with a relatively low sacrifice of current research. On the other hand, if future research productivity is expected to be high, perhaps because of advances in basic science, then a lower initial productivity of training will be tolerated.

A rapid turnover of personnel can have as debilitating an effect on the system as low research or training productivity, however. The net result is a lower research output in both periods. However, a less obvious point is that if the research system is not considered as a whole, a high turnover system may be classed mistakenly as a highly productive system. Consider two systems which differ only in terms of the rate at which professionals quit after the initial period. The training capabilities and the functions which relate agricultural improvement to research activity are the same. If there are diminishing marginal returns to research, the high turnover region will assign fewer professionals to research in either period. But we would measure the corresponding marginal and average rates of return as being higher in both periods in the high turnover region. Yet when both research and training costs are considered, the low turnover system is clearly superior. In the long run, it produces both more research and more researchers.

A high turnover rate in the research system can put a good deal of pressure on the country's training capacity, and perhaps result in a greater than desirable proportion of resources devoted to training. Casual observation suggests that the professionals who leave the system do not remain in research in the private sector. Some become administrators, functionaries or businessmen. Others go abroad. From the point of view of efficiency, one would not worry if both publicly funded research and other career options paid salaries in proportion to the marginal value product of the employees. However, casual observation, buttressed by our second quotation, also suggests this is not the case, and that researchers are often undervalued by the public sector.

Other stumbling blocks may emerge from the need to have a steady stream of professionals to fill vacated positions. In the discussion above, we assumed that the supply of trainees was fixed — if we relax this assumption, the need for more professionals may cause more trainees as well as professionals to be involved in training. But the second tier of trainees admitted are likely to be less talented than the first, and less likely to emerge succcessfully from their training. The training programmes which evolve may then be overcrowded and of relatively poor quality. In trying to produce more researchers overall, the success rate of the training programme may plummet.

A training programme which produces a lot of fodder in the search for some jewels may be efficient from the research system's perspective, even if it has undesirable and perhaps wasteful social effects. Even so, however, there may be strict limits to the numbers of researchers who can be trained. The supply and quality of trainees depend not only on the salaries and potential of a research career, but also on the ability of the high schools and colleges to produce potential trainees. If the overall level of education is low, the potential trainees may have more attractive options than a career in research.

For countries in this position, a reliance on foreign researchers (a second weakening of our earlier assumptions) may emerge. Between 1964 and 1978 about two-thirds of the researchers employed by the Kenyan research system were foreigners,[12] and their average tenure was not much less than that of a native Kenyan. Note that from the point of view of maize breeding, the programme referred to in this section's first quotation was a success — its failure was that no Kenyan successor to the AID programme survived. Most countries can obtain foreign researchers to staff a few selected crop research programmes, perhaps even cheaply. But very few will find enough to provide adequate coverage for all relevant crops at both scientific and applied levels. Moreover, the experience which the imported researchers acquire in the course of their stay is lost for the most part when they depart.

A preferable alternative may be to rely on foreign training in the initial stages of building the research system. This option offers a number of advantages. In many developed countries there would be fairly good quality control both entering and leaving the programme. The domestic system would not be required to allocate many resources from research for training. The building up of training capacity could also proceed at a more relaxed pace, first entrenching programmes for training BA and MA level researchers and proceeding to the PhD level only when the supply of both professionals and potential PhD students is sufficient to insure an adequate programme.

Another implication of an inability to retain highly skilled researchers is that the overall orientation of the research system may shift to what may be less productive research in the long run. A system which cannot retain its skilled researchers for any length of time faces a chronic shortage of the advances in basic agricultural sciences that rejuvenate the productivity of the system. Recall that in the preceding section we discussed the exhaustion of applied research which occurs because the underlying scientific base is stagnant. In such cases where more intensive applied research is unproductive in the sense that additional efforts do not produce varieties which are significantly better over large regions, the response of the system may be to conduct more extensive research, perhaps focusing on selecting varieties and introducing minor improvements in varieties aimed at smaller regions. A geographical narrowing of the research focus may occur precisely because the underlying technology is stagnant. Even relatively minor improvements, applicable to limited areas, become attractive if replacement varieties are not expected to appear for some time. Such improvements would not be worth pursuing, however, if the research system is expected to produce a stream of major innovations or radically different varieties. Thus, an agricultural research system consisting of a diffuse network of small agricultural experimental stations with relatively unambitious research programmes is often symptomatic of an underlying malaise in the system. Such characteristics typify a number of agricultural research systems, the pre-1970s Brazilian system for one.[13] One of the reasons for retaining so few of the previous researchers when the system was upgraded in the 1970s is that a large number may have become superfluous. And, indeed, many of the old experimental stations were shut down at the time.

The most important policy prescription and the most obvious perhaps, is to reduce the turnover of skilled personnel unless there are good reasons for the turnover. Typically, though, the reasons are that agricultural research has low prestige and low salaries compared to outside work, funding levels are uncertain and the facilities inadequate. If so, the potential for successful research is undermined early on. With competitive salaries and stable funding, however, the system can retain a stable cadre of researchers, lessening the burden on the training system and producing a system better able to produce independent advances and take advantage of foreign advances.

Notes

1. Evenson *et al.* (1980) provides a good listing of rate of return estimates.
2. Dalrymple (1980) provides data on varieties and averages.
3. See Schultz (1964) for a careful elaboration of this argument.
4. For a more rigorous discussion see Melton and Ladd (1979) or Englander (1981).
5. From a statistical point of view this is a problem in the statistics of extremes analysed by Gumbel (1958) and others. Evenson and Kislev (1975) were the first to relate it to agricultural research.
6. For more discussion of regional cooperation and derivation of the optimality conditions which should be fulfilled, see Englander (1981).
7. Evenson and Kislev (1975); Evenson and Binswanger (1978).
8. More detail on the data and methodology are provided in Englander (1981).
9. Johnson *et al.* (1979).

10. Ruttan (1982).
11. Englander (1981).
12. Jamieson (1981).
13. For more discussion, see Evenson and Binswanger (1978); Evenson (1981).

Bibliography

Dalrymple, D.D. *Development and Spread of High Yielding Varieties of Wheat and Rice in Developing Nations* (U.S. Department of Agriculture in cooperation with the Agency for International Development, Washington, DC 1980).

Englander, A.S. 'Technology Development and Transfer in Agricultural Research Programs' unpublished PhD dissertation, Yale University, New Haven (1981).

Evenson R.E. 'Comments on the Brazilian Agricultural Research System circa 1981', (mimeograph, University of Sao Paulo, 1981).

Evenson, R.E. and Binswanger H.P. 'Technology Transfer and Research Resource Allocation', ch. 6 in Binswanger H.P. and Ruttan V.W. (eds.), *Induced Innovation: Technology, Institutions and Development* (Johns Hopkins University Press, Baltimore, 1978).

Evenson, R.E. and Kislev, Y. *Agricultural Research and Productivity* (Yale University Press, New Haven, 1975).

Gumbel, E.J. *Statistics of Extremes* (Columbia University Press, New York, 1958).

Jamieson, B. 'Resource Allocation to Agricultural Research in Kenya, 1963–1978' unpublished PhD dissertation, University of Toronto, Toronto (1979).

Johnson, C.W., Byero, K.M., Fleuret, P., Simmons, E. and Wasserman, G. 'Kitale Maize: The Limits of Success' (mimeograph, Agency for International Development, Washington, DC, 1979).

Melton, B. and Ladd, G.W. 'Economic Value of Genetic Shifts in the Production Function', *Applications of Economics in Plant and Animal Breeding*, Iowa State University Department of Economics, Discussion Paper no. 98 (1979).

Ruttan, V.W. *Agricultural Research Policy* (University of Minnesota Press Minneapolis, 1982).

Schultz, T.W., *Transforming Traditional Agriculture* (Yale University Press, New Haven, 1964).

PART FIVE
THE SOCIALIST EXPERIENCE

16   ON THE SOCIALISATION OF LABOUR IN RURAL COOPERATION *

Stefan Hedlund

The purpose of this paper is to address one of the perhaps most central issues in the debate on rural cooperation, namely that of the socialisation of labour. By socialised labour we shall understand the joint sharing of rewards from jointly performed operations, i.e. the absence of a direct link between individual effort and individual rewards, and in pursuing our objective we shall, on the one hand, review some recent writings on the subject and, on the other, introduce empirical evidence from three countries where rural cooperation featuring socialised labour has been attempted on a wide scale. Our general purpose is to show that much of the formal work done has served to cloud the crucial issue, namely the quality aspect of socialised labour. Empirical evidence will be used to substantiate this claim.

The argument will proceed in three steps, investigating in turn three different modes of cooperation that feature different degrees of socialised labour. The aim is to show the crucial role of incentive systems, a role that has been partly lost in the literature. In the final section, we will then draw together the evidence presented, in order to issue a warning against a reliance on socialised labour in a comprehensive development strategy. First, however, let us briefly review the case for cooperation.

The Case for Cooperation

One very important general reason for the formation of cooperatives will obviously be of an ideological nature; the joining together in groups, either for the realisation of common religious or ideological principles, or for purposes of mutual protection in times of economic or other hardship, has always held a great appeal for

* Research for this paper has in part been financed by a grant from SAREC. This is gratefully acknowledged.

certain people. While it must be pointed out that such cooperatives, far from forming the basis of the development strategy with which we are concerned here, have with few exceptions been isolated occurrences, we note that the ideological principle is important as a driving force and we shall return to it below.

In the present context, our primary concern is cooperatives that are formed for material gain, where the pooling of land, labour and other resources is intended to lead to higher production as well as higher peasant income. Here, economies of scale will obviously be of major importance, particularly those that may be termed 'external', i.e. those that pertain to activities such as purchasing, marketing and extension. Their existence is generally admitted; as Michael Lipton notes 'Scale economies in product distribution . . . and storage, and in obtaining inputs, are unquestioned, as are the higher per-acre costs of administration and extension for small farmers.'[1] Louis Putterman would also seem to be in agreement with this statement: 'The latter (external) type of economies are rather widely admitted'; moreover, he also makes the further important remark that 'it is frequently supposed that they can be captured through cooperation of otherwise distinct farm units'.[2] We shall return to this important point below.

A more controversial point with regard to cooperation is the existence of 'internal' economies of scale, i.e. of a relation between productivity and the size of the farm. Here Putterman notes that 'it is often quite flatly claimed that these (internal economies) do not exist in agriculture'.[3] The classical case against such economies is that of Nicolas Georgescu-Roegen,[4] who emphasises the 'unflinching rhythm of life', and points out that biologically determined gestation periods, climatically determined conditions for production, the sequential nature of production tasks, etc., all combine to place severe limitations on the scope for division of labour in agricultural production.

We shall not venture further into that debate — which extends back to Marxian and Soviet concepts of farms as 'rural factories' — but instead deal with Putterman's reservation that 'the evidence on size-productivity relationships does not at all prove that agricultural returns to scale are constant or decreasing'.[5] If this reservation is limited to private agriculture, then it may be debatable, but if it is extended to cooperatives featuring socialised labour, then it will be our contention that it is mistaken.

Our discussion in relation to the evidence that will be presented below will consequently centre on two issues; firstly, the role of incentives in cooperatives and secondly the relation between these incentives and the size of the cooperative. What we are hoping to demonstrate is that successful socialisation hinges critically on the existence of an ideological motivation that is not likely to be present in large scale applications and further that the problem of the insufficiency of non-material incentives is aggravated by the growth in size of the cooperative. Let us now proceed to investigate the evidence.

Modes of Cooperation[6]

Our choice of examples has been made according to two criteria; firstly, a wish to explore the link between the remunerative system and labour participation, i.e. the role of material incentives; and, secondly, to discuss the feasibility of various forms of cooperation as a basis for a comprehensive rural development strategy.

For the first purpose, we shall identify three different modes of cooperation; a pure *commune*, with full socialisation of labour and with equal distribution of the proceeds; a *collective*, with only partial socialisation (i.e. with competing 'private plots') and with different systems of distribution; and, finally, an *association*, with no socialisation but realising the full benefits of 'external' economies of scale. These three models will be referred to as Modes A, B and C, respectively.

For the second purpose, examples will be chosen according to three requirements; (a) cooperation must form part of official policy on agriculture; (b) cooperatives must account for the bulk of agricultural production (or at least be intended to do so); and (c) cooperatives must play an important role in the general development process. These requirements are necessary in order to rule out such cases as those where the cooperatives have emerged on a voluntary basis, founded by pioneers and with a good track-record of their own, but of little overall economic significance.

What we need are cooperatives that are the result of a decisive and all-embracing government policy to promote cooperation as the basis of agricultural production. With this purpose in mind, we have chosen to draw evidence from Israel, from the Soviet Union and from Tanzania. All three cases satisfy the three criteria outlined above. Examples that have been ruled out are, for example, the

Hutterian Brethren of the Great Plains in the United States and Canada, and the French GAEC. While both pose interesting problems and also show records of success, they fall outside the scope of our paper; in the first case, religiously motivated communities have isolated themselves from the rest of society while in the latter cooperation was introduced into an already developed economy.[7] Table 16.1 summarises the evidence to be presented.

Table 16.1: Modes of Cooperation

	Mode A	Mode B	Mode C
Israel:	Kibbutz	Moshav Shitufi	Moshav Ovdim
Soviet Union:	Kommuna	Kolkhoz	Zveno
Tanzania: *	Ujamaa	Ujamaa	Block Farms

* Note that there is no terminological difference between Modes A and B in Tanzania; it is intended that Mode B should be a transitional stage, leading to Mode A.

Let us now proceed to look at these different forms of cooperation, starting with Mode A.

Mode A: Commune

The pure commune is the most 'demanding' form of cooperation. It exhibits full socialisation of labour as well as of the other means of production. Even consumption may be fully socialised, with equal distribution, joint living quarters and joint meals in canteens. Distribution of the proceeds of the commune among its members is supposed to be either fully equal (one share per member) or on a 'needs' basis. For our purpose, however, the important point is that the link between effort and reward is removed. Incentives to work in the commune are entirely non-material; on the one hand there is a 'carrot', in terms of working for the common good, and on the other there is a 'stick', in terms of social pressure on shirkers. Nowhere, however, is there any direct material loss to the individual who does not pull his weight. That this form of cooperation places high demands on its members is also reflected in the evidence.

The *Tanzanian* perception of this difficulty is probably best reflected in a statement by President Julius Nyerere, writing on the development of Tanzanian socialism and rural cooperation:[8]

The people would keep their individual plots; the community farm would be an extra effort instead of each family trying to expand its own acreage . . . the final stage would come when the people have enough confidence in the community farm, so that they are willing to invest all their effort in it, simply keeping gardens around their houses for special vegetables, etc.

Thus, for President Nyerere the establishment of pure communes is not even a policy goal — other than in the long run.

Soviet experience probably accounts for much of the generally negative attitude to communes. The *kommuna*, being the first of Soviet cooperatives to emerge, was originally set up by demobilised soldiers returning from World War I only to find their villages in a shambles.[9] Initially this new form of agriculture was given heavy government support and preferential treatment in the allocation of land and livestock from the expropriated estates. The kommuna was hailed as the true form of communist production but very soon this attitude changed. By the end of 1918, Bukharin wrote that the kommuna could only be accepted as a step toward the state farm, the *sovkhoz*,[10] and by early 1919 Lenin himself attacked it, saying that 'artificial false communes are the most dangerous of all' and that it was 'harmful, even fatal for communism to try to put in effect prematurely, purely and narrowly communistic ideals'.[11] The obvious explanation is that it rapidly became clear to the leading Bolsheviks that the kommuna — with its absence of a link between individual effort and rewards — held a great attraction for the poor peasants, who joined in the anticipation of a 'free lunch', but less so for the better-off peasants who preferred to enjoy in private the fruits of their labour.[12] Thus, once the supply of 'communistic' pioneers was exhausted, the kommuna rapidly degenerated into a welfare institution, making larger and larger claims on the state budget and finally it had to be abolished altogether.[13] Future Soviet experiments with cooperation would establish very clearly the link between work and subsistence.

The example that stands out with respect to Mode A cooperation is the *Israeli* kibbutz which, in spite of exhibiting many of the same organisational and remunerative characteristics as the Soviet kommuna[14] and in spite of being the mainstay of agricultural development, at least up until the formation of the State of Israel in 1948,[15] has not run into any of the problems mentioned above. Consideration can be given to two highly important and interrelated explanations.

The first concerns recruitment. As we have seen above, the really crucial feature of the commune is the lack of material incentives to work; with the admission of members who lack the 'right' ideological mental framework, shirking is bound to grow to such proportions that the social fabric of the commune is destroyed, with a resultant breakdown of production. The kibbutz movement has always been very conscious of this fact and consequently has been very restrictive in recruitment, even to the point of coming into conflict with the Israeli government over the absorption of new immigrants. The main source of recruitment has always been via Zionist youth organisations abroad, where training has been given not only in basic ideology but also in agricultural matters; even then, however, new members have only been admitted after a year of candidacy. Hence, the kibbutz has always been an elitist organisation, which brings us to our second explanation.

Due to the very high level of productivity, that is a result of not only the substantial level of investment, but also the high educational standards and level of motivation of the workforce, the kibbutz has never been a burden to the state budget in the way of the Soviet kommuna. On the contrary, it has always been a highly dynamic element in development, supplying more than its share of production as well as of political and other leadership. This has given the kibbutzniks a prominent status in society which in turn has helped improve the 'carrot' of non-material incentives to work. Furthermore, the high educational standards and ideological homogeneity of the kibbutz has made the 'stick' of social pressure on shirkers rather potent.[16]

In conclusion, the success of communes can be seen to depend crucially on the recruitment of members with similar ideological frameworks. In all our cases, the success of early settlements derives from precisely this factor.[17] The pioneers have been permeated with socialist ideals (in the Israeli case combined with the Zionist dream) and have been quite prepared to make personal sacrifices for the common good.[18] Material incentives become quite unnecessary; peer control and a strong sense of solidarity remove all problems of free-riding.

The problems start when cooperation becomes part of official policy. In order to expand the cooperative movement, more peasants will have to be recruited and those who have not joined already — on a voluntary basis — must be given incentives to do so (barring compulsion, which we will return to below) and these incentives will necessarily be of a material nature. Thus we have

introduced a contradiction with the very basis for Mode A cooperation; the new recruits will join for material gain and will soon dis-
cover that there is no compulsion to work for subsistence. As a
result, the government will have to give the communes increasingly
preferential treatment, in order to attract new members, whereas the
contribution from these new members will fall rapidly. This is the
fate that befell the Soviet kommuna and under a comprehensive
development strategy which builds on communes, there appears to
be no way of avoiding these 'scissors'. The essence of the problem is
captured by Alec Nove:[19]

> If one assumes that the 'new man' . . . will require no incentives,
> problems of discipline and motivation vanish. If it is assumed
> that all will identify with the clearly visible general good, then the
> conflict between general and partial interest . . . can be assumed
> out of existence.

As long as these 'new men' are not forthcoming in sufficient numbers, however, Mode A cooperation would seem to be a dead end,
and the success of the kibbutz a special case of a favourable
hothouse atmosphere, unlikely to be reproduced elsewhere.

Mode B: Collective

The collective is a hybrid form, featuring both private and communal production. Each member household has a 'private plot', which
is cultivated by household labour and with tools and implements
owned by or at the exclusive disposal of the household. Parallel with
this private sector there are also communal fields where joint production takes place, where the means of production are owned
jointly and where the joint proceeds are distributed according to
some principle to be specified below.

Several aspects of this mode of production have been dealt with in
the literature regarding the 'theory of the kolkhoz'. The initial contributors viewed the collective as a labour managed firm and discussed adjustment to changes in such variables as product prices and
land rent,[20] and in a second step the division into a 'private' and a
'socialised' sector was explicitly recognised.[21] Of chief interest for
our purposes, however, are the more recent contributions, which
take into consideration individual incentives to supply labour for
the purpose of joint production.[22] As we have seen above, the vulnerability of the commune derives largely from its susceptibility to

shirking and as we shall see below, many of the same problems apply to the collective. Our main interest will thus lie with the role of the system of remuneration in creating incentives for the individual to participate actively in joint production.

On this point, a cursory reading of the literature would not seem to lend any support for our pessimistic view. John Bonin, for example, writes that: 'we show that policies similar to those employed by Stalin, e.g. increasing fixed charges and crop quotas on the collective plot, generate positive work incentives on both plots (collective and private) at the expense of leisure'.[23] The same conclusion is reached by Dwight Israelsen: 'the findings of this paper can be applied to two major criticisms of Soviet and other collective farms — that collective organisations are inherently inferior to others in providing individual economic incentives, and that the large size of some of the collectives exacerbates this problem. We have demonstrated that both criticisms are misdirected.'[24] Israelsen also finds that: 'assuming that the goals of Soviet planners include extracting the maximum amount of labour from agricultural workers for a given level of income, our analysis suggests that they should retain the collective type of organisation rather than moving toward a more communal or a more 'capitalistic' form'.[25]

While the above observations apply primarily to the Soviet kolkhoz, Putterman makes similar points with regard to Chinese and Tanzanian agricultural cooperation: 'within the limited scope of our model we have found nothing inconsistent in the notion that collective cultivation may be popularly embraced by a self-interested peasantry',[26] and 'it is also possible that social and psychological aspects of participation, democracy and identification with the enterprise may produce even better incentives in cooperatives than in their conventional counterparts'.[27]

If we now return briefly to our initial query, whether agricultural cooperation can be recommended as a basis for a rural development strategy, the answer would seem to be in the positive. Empirical evidence from attempts at doing so, however, stands at loggerheads with these contentions, and in our view this represents a manifestation of some of the dangers inherent in abstract modelling.

As possible explanation for the failure of the models to agree with observed reality might be that the models as such are 'good' but that other elements have interfered to distort the predicted results. Bonin goes part of this way — with respect to the Soviet kolkhoz — by noting that: 'An important disincentive to work on the collective plot for the Russian peasant was his intense aversion to the collective form of agriculture'.[28] Bonin's conclusion, however, is simply that this necessitated the introduction of compulsory work quotas and the above-cited contentions are still seen to hold. The question that one is immediately led to ask, is whence this aversion came, if not from the very *system* of the kolkhoz? Aversion during Stalin's rule can be explained by compulsion and wholesale violence, but surely this does not apply to today's generation of kolkhozniks, who are able to leave at will. The aversion, however, remains, and the kolkhozniks are increasingly exercising their right to leave. As an explanation, we shall instead argue that there are some *general* characteristics of the proposed models that should lead us to predict results that actually agree very well with observed performance, and this brings us back to our interest in the system of remuneration.

Remuneration for work in the collective will be either according to *need* or according to *work*.[29] In the former case, we are back to the commune (with respect to the socialised sector), with an absence of direct material incentives to perform collective work. On this point there would also seem to be a consensus of opinion that (in the absence of altruistic motives) this form of remuneration creates an inferior incentive. Israelsen for example, notes that 'the work incentives on the collective (other things equal) are much greater than those on the commune'.[30] We shall thus focus on remuneration based on work performed.

In the 'traditional' formulation of the problem,[31] the individual member is paid the average product of labour (VAP) in the collective. This will fully exhaust the surplus of the collective over non-labour cost, and it also agrees well with the principles of producer cooperation.[32] This model, however, is based on equal *per capita* distribution and in order to study individual incentives, we need a yardstick that is related to work. The one that is most commonly used here, is the number of hours contributed per member, where hours are homogeneous in terms of output. The share of the individual in the surplus of the collective will thus be determined by his share in the total number of hours performed. From this it can be shown that the incentive to perform extra hours of work (defined as the marginal addition to income that derives from an extra hour of work) will be a convex combination of the marginal and average products of labour — VMP and VAP respectively.[33] The return to the individual will on the one hand be a *share in the addition* to output (represented by the VMP) and on the other an *extra share* in the previous total (represented by the VAP).

This formulation leads to Israelsen's above-cited conclusions; firstly, that work incentives are greater in collectives than in other modes of production (since members are paid a combination of VMP and VAP, which will be greater than VMP in the normal production range where VMP is falling) and secondly, that the strength of these incentives increases with the size of the collective (since the increased membership size will increase the weight on VAP).

It is at this point that we have our major disagreement with the models referred to above. Given the mode of joint production and the sequential nature of agricultural production in particular, the individual peasant will be given work assignments that vary from day to day and the connection between his performance and his rewards will necessarily be very weak. Should he decide to shirk his communal obligations, then this will obviously reduce the surplus of the collective as a whole, but for the individual concerned the cost will be negligible, since it will be spread out evenly over all members, or rather, over all labour hours contributed. Since all members face the same situation,[34] this may well give rise to a Prisoner's Dilemma situation, where all members decide to shirk.

If we take one step further, and acknowledge the existence of private plots, then another dimension will be added.[35] If it is the case that the private plot is more profitable than communal work, then the Prisoner's Dilemma will not materialise. Not even by cooperating will the peasants be able to improve their situation compared to just working the plot. Should the plot be less profitable, then the peasant will have an incentive to put in a number of *hours* of collective work on the margin, but not to be concerned with the *quality* of his work. By expending as little energy as possible in carrying out his collective work assignment, effort will be conserved that can later be converted into cash by working the plot, all the while preserving collective pay intact, since this is based on *hours*. If all members should decide to behave in this same way, then the effect on the individual's pay will of course no longer be negligible. Instead we get cumulative causation, where deteriorating performance leads to more shirking and we have a vicious downward spiral, with no immediately stabilising factors.

One seemingly simple solution would be to do away with the plots altogether, thus reducing the opportunity cost to the individual of providing collective labour. In part, Bonin goes along with this proposal suggesting that: 'if the state desires to divert more labour to the collective plot, the price of the private plot output should be decreased'.[36] On the other hand, however, he then goes on to argue that: 'contrary to popular belief, the collective farm need not be inefficient nor provide poor work incentives to peasant households. The poor work incentives attributed to Soviet collective farms from observations on aggregate agricultural performance may be due more to the adverse reaction of the Soviet peasant to the suppression of private enterprise in the countryside.'[37]

Bonin's own qualification confirms that his first recommendation is wide of the mark. This, however, is understandable only in terms of the *quality* of work. By suppressing the private sector, it will surely be possible to make the peasants contribute more hours, in order to compensate for the loss of income from the plot, but there is nothing to say that they will contribute any effort. On the contrary, we would be led to believe that there would be a further deterioration in work discipline, adding to the vicious spiral of lacking incentives to perform collective work.

In summary, we can only agree with Hans Aage in noting that 'probably (the models) are realistic in the sense that they describe an incentive, not to work efficiently but only to put in long hours'.[38] Long hours at low productivity, however, can hardly be a desirable outcome and especially not if they are at the expense of productive private plot activities.

If we now return to the empirical evidence, the best known case is probably that of the *Soviet Union*. Following the collapse of the kommuna the search for a new policy lasted throughout the 1920s, and it was not until Stalin embarked on the policy of mass collectivisation, in 1929, that the kolkhoz emerged as an important form of rural cooperation.[39] Two very important facts should be observed at this point. Firstly, while there was still an element of free choice for the peasantry, the kolkhoz held a very weak appeal. Those peasants who did prefer cooperation — and they were precious few — largely chose other forms.[40] Hence, the carrying out of the programme for mass collectivisation had, to an unprecedented extent, to include compulsion and violence.[41] Secondly, the system of remuneration that was introduced was in essence that of Ward and Domar, i.e. VAP, which meant that the peasants were reduced to a status of residual claimants, labour payments being made only after all other expenses had been met.[42] The obvious aim of the latter was to force the peasants to absorb the natural fluctuations inherent in agricultural production and there was nothing in the system to guarantee that any labour payments at all would be made (i.e. that VAP $\neq$ 0). As a *concession* to the forcefully collectivised peasants, a provision was made for tiny 'private plots' around the homesteads, and it was these plots that would later provide subsistence in times when collective pay was reduced to virtually nil. It is thus of paramount importance to note that the rather peculiar split into a 'private' and a 'socialised' sector was not an element of desired policy, but rather a forced retreat. In the state farm, the *sovkhoz*, for example, where there was a fixed monthly wage, there were originally no private plots.

In terms of agricultural production as such,[43] early Soviet agricultural policy can only be seen as an unmitigated disaster. The countryside was reduced to the state of an exploited colony and via a system of compulsory domestic passports — which were not generally issued to the peasants — the producers were tied to the land; the kolkhoz was simply feudal serfdom in socialist attire.

The most interesting point, however, is that following Stalin's departure, the kolkhoz has remained a major problem in spite of a long row of seemingly beneficial changes in policy.[44] Violence has ceased, peasant earnings more than doubled during the Brezhnev era and agricultural investment has reached unprecedented levels.[45] Finally, in 1975 the peasants were 'freed' a second time by being generally issued with passports and thus also formally allowed to leave the kolkhoz. Nevertheless, performance has not improved. Although the agricultural sector uses up a third of the total investment in the economy, a quarter of its whole-year labour force, an additional 15 million urban residents at harvest time and an ever increasing amount of scarce foreign exchange to import food, scarce food supplies still have to be rationed amongst the population.

One important explanation for this state of matters is found in the remuneration system discussed above. In the early stage, when pay was very low, the kolkhozniks would go to great lengths in order to avoid working for the kolkhoz and Michael Bradley quotes a Soviet source from 1965, saying that collective work was performed with the sole aim of maintaining the right to the private plot.[46] Over time, kolkhoz pay has increased substantially and today accounts for the bulk of household income.[47] This, however, has only produced the effect pointed out by Aage; peasants put in long *hours* but very little *effort*. Furthermore, this policy has been directly counterproductive in that it has produced strong income effects, manifested in the form of a reduced labour input on the private plot. Overall agricultural production has thus been affected negatively.

Another explanation for the poor performance concerns size. In Israelsen's formulation above it was seen that the incentives to work were strengthened as the collective grew in size. In practice, however, we observe the opposite. An extreme belief in the benefits of large scale has turned the kolkhozy into gigantic enterprises, some of which comprise well over 100,000 hectares of land, thousands of head of cattle and hundreds of member households.[48]

If we view this development in the light of the form of the remuneration system, where there is no direct link between the effort expended by the individual peasant and the rewards that accrue to him, then the conclusion becomes self-evident. Instead of Israelsen's situation, where the individual is urged to contribute more labour since the extra hour is paid more (VAP) than it contributes (VMP) and where this urge gets stronger as the membership grows (increased weight on VAP), we get a situation where the individual chooses to minimise the effort expended, as this will not influence his pay, and where his chances of doing so increase with the size of the cooperative. In the absence of a direct link between effort and reward, there are only two things that can make people work conscientiously: either a sense of solidarity coupled with peer control, or strict supervision coupled with sufficiently punitive measures.

It is obvious that a growing membership has eroded the former.[49] Instead, the hallmark of kolkhoz development has been that of supervision.[50] From the outset, Bolshevik agricultural policy was aimed at erecting an elaborate structure of supervision and control, from party committees at various levels down to the use of specialised manpower — such as agronomists — for the purpose of watching the work of, say, tractor drivers. Over time, this policy has not undergone any fundamental changes, merely refinement and expansion. The costs of running the control apparatus are substantial, particularly in the light of growing labour shortages. It should be noted, however, that control becomes imperative under an incentive system where shirking carries high private rewards.

The *Tanzanian* experience shows that these problems are not unique to the Soviet kolkhoz. A highly important ingredient in President Nyerere's programme for 'Tanzanian Socialism' was a restructuring of the countryside, the basis of which would be the joining together of peasants in *ujamaa* villages.[51] In a first stage, these villages would be cooperatives, exhibiting features similar to

Mode B cooperation, i.e. communal combined with private production, while the long-term goal was to achieve the full socialisation of
Mode A.[52]

Although the element of voluntariness was explicitly stated, Putterman notes that 'it is almost certainly the case that most collective
farming undertaken in Tanzania's villages was a response to governmental orders and initiatives'.[53] Faced with an uncooperative
peasantry, the government tried material incentives as well as
administrative coercion, but baulked at the use of Stalinist terror
and eventually shelved the whole project: '. . . by the same token,
the apparent abandonment or postponement, more recently, of the
attempt to introduce collective cultivation on a wide scale, was evidently the outcome of deliberations at high official levels'.[54]

A possible source of misunderstanding with regard to the
Tanzanian experience concerns the traditional form of African
agricultural production. As Putterman notes, 'experience in many
developing countries shows a preference for group work, for reasons of pacing and morale'.[55] While the performance of joint work
has always been a predominant feature, it is, however, important to
distinguish this from agricultural cooperation as we have understood it above. Within the group of family and relatives it has been
natural to work together and to share the proceeds of that work
equally. At this level, there has thus traditionally been full socialisation of labour and in Swahili this is referred to as *ujamaa*. Also
within the larger group, such as the village, it has been natural to
perform joint operations, particularly at harvest time or in times of
emergency. The basis for this form of cooperation, however, has
been very different. Proceeds from the operations have always
accrued to the owner/organiser, while remuneration for the labour
contributed has been via reciprocity and/or via providing a joint
meal after completion of the chores.[56] In Swahili, this latter form is
referred to as *ujima*.[57]

The basis of Nyerere's policy was an attempt to transfer the full
socialisation of the small group onto the larger group, which is also
implied by his calling the new cooperatives ujamaa. This is where the
policy has failed. While peasants have long been used to working
together, the notion of sharing the proceeds and of being dependent
on others — whom you do not know closely — has been viewed
with suspicion. Instead, they have chosen to retreat into private plot
activities and the collective sector has collapsed. Given the less strict
rules on labour participation — as compared to the Soviet

case — it has frequently been found that households that actually do provide labour for communal tasks tend to send their least productive members. The similarity between the Soviet and the Tanzanian models is found in the absence of private incentives to supply collective labour (or effort) and the difference is found in the fact that Nyerere is no Stalin; thus Tanzania has no collective farms and the predictions from above, regarding Mode B cooperation, seem to agree well with Putterman's observation that 'nearly all village land is cultivated by individual households for private subsistence and cash income'.[58]

Turning now to the *Israeli* case, we again find an exception. Mode B cooperation in Israel is represented by the *moshav shitufi*, which on the one hand has avoided the problems mentioned above but on the other has also remained a small enclave in the agricultural sector. Out of a total of 690 cooperative settlements in 1980, only 35 were of this type, while comparable figures for 1948 are 25 out of 356.[59] An important conclusion may be drawn as regards the attractiveness of this form of cooperation. Of the examples that we have chosen, Israel most closely exhibits a truly free choice of tenure. Here the vote has gone strongly against Mode B cooperation, with its peculiar mix of private and communal activities. Most of those farms that do exist have been founded by soldiers demobilised from the British army after World War II. To them, this form of cooperation was very similar to the type of military life they had grown used to.

Our experience with cooperation thus far seems rather sombre. Success in Mode A was seen to depend crucially on the recruitment of sufficient numbers of ideologically motivated members; failure on this point would lead to free-riding and to a breakdown of production. Mode B, on the other hand, was seen to depend crucially on the use of compulsion; in the absence of compulsion (the Tanzanian case) peasants would withdraw to their private plots and leave the communal sector to collapse, whereas even in the presence of compulsion (the Soviet case) it was seen to be possible only to elicit hours and not effort.

Evidence from Eastern Europe also clearly indicates what happens if compulsion is removed; in both Poland and Yugoslavia collective agriculture collapsed once the peasants were given a free choice. Furthermore, in the case of Mode B there does not even seem to be any hope of recruiting sufficient numbers of motivated pioneers; Israeli evidence indicates that these would opt for the 'true' cooperation of Mode A. Regarding both Modes, the exception

(Israel) can largely be explained by a highly selective recruitment of an ideologically homogeneous membership. Let us now change our framework slightly and look at Mode C cooperation which is characterised by the absence of socialised labour.

Mode C: Association

The most interesting illustration of Mode C cooperation is probably that of *Soviet* proposals for *zveno* production.[60] A zveno (roughly translated as 'link' or 'team') would consist of a small group of peasants (three to twelve people) who are given a plot of land to cultivate, have the necessary implements put at their disposal, and who will eventually be paid in accordance with what they produce.

At one stroke, all the above-mentioned problems would thus be removed. A clear and direct link would be established between effort and reward, since the same group of peasants would be responsible for the entire production cycle and their income directly dependent on the eventual outcome, something that is in stark contrast to the present kolkhoz practice, where the peasants are constantly shifted around between different tasks and with unclear responsibilities. Furthermore, the zveno would also be small enough to exercise effective peer control amongst its members, thus preventing the disciplinary problems that are all too common in the large kolkhoz brigades.

It is thus not surprising that highly positive results have been reported for zveno experiments — sometimes doubling or even trebling yields obtained by the use of socialised labour.[61] Nor is it surprising that Soviet authorities have been sceptical about the zveno — in spite of the highly positive results which have been reported — since this form of organisation would attack the very foundations of kolkhoz production. A kolkhoz where production takes place on separate plots of land that are cultivated by separate groups of peasants under self-determination and with pay according to results, would be reduced to a mere umbrella organisation, responsible for the purchase of inputs and the marketing of output.

In practice, however, it may well be the case that 'the more empirically minded Soviet experts and even party functionaries foresee this development of links as a quiet and relatively painless return to a form of functional private farming, without the reconversion of land into a private market commodity'.[62] The important thing to note is that all advantages of small scale private farming would be realised in this system, within the framework of a cooperative that offers the possibility of reaping important *external* economies of scale.[63]

Many of the same conclusions can also be drawn from *Tanzanian* experience. The present system of block farming features private production on individual plots of land, within the framework of village cooperatives that offer the possibility of improved purchasing, marketing and extension activities, i.e. the reaping of important *external* economies of scale. It is also important to note that 'the drive for villagisation has been a separable strand of policy from that of collectivisation *per se*. While the former goal, to gather the population into administrative, social, economic and political units, became obligatory by national policy in 1973, the latter aim, collective cultivation of village land, was to remain a matter of local discretion.'[64]

The acid test of the viability of Mode C cooperation, finally, is that of *Israel*, as represented by the *moshav ovdim*.[65] Via centralised marketing and purchasing organisations, it has been possible to achieve important cost reductions and via the joint employment of outside specialists (doctors, teachers, etc.) it has been possible to provide the members with some of the services available in the kibbutz, whilst preserving the essential nature of private farming, i.e. the link between effort and reward. It is also striking to observe the difference between kibbutz and moshav, in terms of the variety of housing and the existence of cars parked in private driveways in the latter. The general attraction of this mode of cooperation is also borne out by its rapid expansion. Between 1948 and 1980, the moshav ovdim outgrew the kibbutz quite substantially, as can be seen from Table 16.2.

Table 16.2: Relative Expansion of the Kibbutz and the Moshav Ovdim

	1948		1980	
	Kibbutz	Moshav	Kibbutz	Moshav
Settlements:	211	120	255	400
Population:	63,500	31,200	111,200	143,700

Source: Statistical Abstracts of Israel, 1948/9 and 1981, Table II/9.

The changing pattern is largely due to changing external circumstances. Prior to 1948, immigrants had very strong socialist-zionist convictions and this, in combination with difficult security conditions,[66] made the kibbutz an attractive form of settlement. After the establishment of the State of Israel, however, there was an improvement in the security situation as well as a gradual change in the character of immigration and, as a result, normal farming conditions became more important in deciding on the form of settlement. Here, the *moshav ovdim* proved superior. Thus, in all three examples quoted above, we find that when given a free choice, peasants will (in the absence of strong religious/ideological motivation) opt against socialised labour and, furthermore, if socialisation is carried out this will necessitate compulsion, which was seen to produce hours but not effort.

Conclusion

What conclusions then can be drawn from the evidence presented above? Here much will depend on the reasons for choosing cooperation. In Putterman's view, 'unlike capitalist farming, collective or cooperative farms would promote social and economic equality and justice'.[67] Such reasoning has quite clearly been important in Tanzania, where the ujamaa program has had more far-reaching goals than simply to stimulate production. By restructuring the countryside, Nyerere aimed at a radical change in society that would bring about a more egalitarian structure in general.

In the Soviet Union, on the other hand, we find the opposite situation. As Stalin himself expressed it:[68]

Only people who are ignorant of Marxism can maintain that the Russian Bolsheviks wish to gather all riches in one pile and then distribute it equally. That has nothing to do with Marxism.

Thus, the reasons for introducing the kolkhoz must be sought elsewhere and, as Arthur Wright puts it, collectivisation is perhaps better viewed as a 'sudden and desperate lunge to extricate the leadership from a deep economic and political crisis, a crisis which was largely of its own making'.[69]

If, however, the purpose of cooperation is to serve as a basis for a rural development strategy, then the policy maker will soon find himself in a dilemma. If collectivisation is to produce a tangible effect, then it must be comprehensive, i.e. it must encompass the bulk of the peasantry. This can be achieved either on a voluntary basis or by the use of force, and there would seem to be a consensus of opinion that the latter is not desirable. Voluntary collectivisation, however, must rest on the creation of viable incentives for the peasantry to join. Such incentives can be either material or non-material and it has been our ambition in this paper to show that voluntary collectivisation based on material incentives conflicts with the principle of socialised labour. Voluntary collectivisation based on non-material incentives, on the other hand, conflicts with the need for comprehensiveness; there would simply not be enough such 'new men' for the creation of more than a small enclave in the overall agricultural sector.

What remains then is collectivisation that aims at the reaping of such 'external' economies as are widely recognised to exist and in this context it might be of some interest to note that Lenin, in one of his last pamphlets, *On Cooperation*, sees cooperation as the joining together of peasants for the commercialisation of their produce. Joint production was not even mentioned.[70] Maybe the time has come to advocate a stricter adherence to pure Leninist principles in devising rural development strategy?

Notes

1. Lipton (1978), p. 325.
2. Putterman (1983), p. 81.
3. Ibid.
4. Georgescu-Roegen (1960), p. 5.
5. Putterman (1983), p. 81.
6. See Galeski (1977) for a more exhaustive classification of various forms of cooperation. Galeski, however, is chiefly concerned with the circumstances under which different forms of cooperation might arise and as our ambition is to discuss their development and viability, we have excluded some of his dimensions.
7. See further Bennett (1977); Raup (1977).
8. Nyerere (1968), p. 19.
9. See Wesson (1962) for an account of the rise and fall of these communes.
10. *Izvestia*, December 6, 1918.
11. Wesson (1962), p. 108.
12. Lewin (1968), p. 108.
13. See further Hedlund (1984), pp. 46 ff.
14. Many of the pioneers of the kibbutz movement were Russian revolutionaries who had become disillusioned with the prospects of realising important Jewish aims within the framework of a Russian revolution and thus chose to emigrate to Palestine. The first kibbutz — or kvutzah as they were then called — was set up in the Galilee in 1909. See further Weintraub (1969).
15. Of the 255 kibbutzim that exist today, 211 were formed before 1948. *Statistical Abstracts of Israel*, 1981, Table II/9.
16. According to a common Israeli saying, *gossip* is the kibbutz police force; if

somebody does not pull his weight, his social life will suffer. It should be pointed out, however, that there are precious few other means of control. Expulsion from the kibbutz is not as simple as it might seem, since this would mean — *inter alia* — evicting the person from his home, something that would come into conflict with Israeli housing laws. Nor will it be possible to withhold food or other basic necessities; once a member is admitted, the kibbutz has accepted a wide range of obligations towards him, most of which cannot be easily revoked. This of course explains the very firm stand on recruitment policy.

17. A case in point is the Ruvuma settlement in Tanzania, which emerged on a voluntary basis and was quite successful until it became part of the national ujamaa program. Coulson (1982), pp. 263 ff.

18. Even today a kibbutznik will look at you in bafflement when asked about kibbutz policy on issues such as absenteeism, shirking and drunkenness at work, problems that are all too common to the kolkhoz.

19. Nove (1983), p. 10.

20. Ward (1958); Domar (1966).

21. Oi and Clayton (1968).

22. Bradley (1971, 1973); Cameron (1973a, 1973b); Bonin (1977); Aage (1980); Israelsen (1980); Putterman (1980).

23. Bonin (1977), p. 78.

24. Israelsen (1980), p. 118.

25. Ibid.

26. Putterman (1980), pp. 147 ff.

27. Putterman (1983), p. 93.

28. Bonin (1977), p. 84. Indeed, the conclusion of the paper reads: 'Therefore, lessons learned from Soviet experience with the collective farm need not be reproduced in other agricultural environments.' Ibid., p. 94.

29. See Sen (1966); Putterman (1980). See also Berman (1977); Ireland and Law (1981).

30. Israelsen (1980), p. 103.

31. Ward (1958); Domar (1966); Oi and Clayton (1968). Subsequent contributions (cf. note 22 above) focus on the incentive aspect and thus relax the 'traditional' assumption of a constant labour input by the individual.

32. See above all Vanek (1970).

33. In Israelsen's formulation, the share of the individual member is: $y_i = (\ell_i/L)F(L)$, where L is total labour hours, ℓ_i is hours contributed by member i and F(L) is output as a function of labour alone. The incentive for the single member to perform an extra hour's work then becomes: $\delta y_i/\delta \ell_i = (\ell_i/L)F'(L) + F(L)(L - \ell_i)/L^2 = (\ell_i/L)F'(L) + (1 - (\ell_i/L))(1/L)F(L)$.

34. See further Cameron (1973a) for a discussion of the interdependence of behaviour between different kolkhozniks.

35. See further Hedlund (1984), pp. 160 ff.

36. Bonin (1977), p. 83.

37. Ibid., p. 93.

38. Aage (1980), p. 143.

39. The *magnum opus* on this period is Lewin (1968).

40. After the stagnation and collapse of the kommuna, the most rapidly growing form was the TOZ, which resembles our Mode C. See Lewin (1968), Ch. 5.

41. On the number of casualties in this process, Karcz (1971), p. 38, says: 'Several million households, up to a total of 10 million persons and more must have been deported, of whom a great many must have perished. . . . The total deaths due to the Great Famine of 1932–4 — a direct consequence of collectivisation — may never be precisely established, but a figure of some 5 million appears to fit well with demographic data.'

42. The exact pay for the individual was determined via a complicated system

based on an accounting unit called the 'work day' (*trudoden*). Wronski (1958).

43. It should be noted that collectivisation was not simply an element of agricultural policy. It had other important aims as well, above all political ones. See further Hedlund (1983).

44. Hedlund (1984), Ch. 3, *passim.*

45. Emelyanov (1979), p. 3, claims that 72 per cent of all Soviet agricultural investment undertaken between 1918 and 1977 took place after 1965.

46. Bradley (1971), p. 349.

47. Only 27 per cent of total household income derives from the plot. Kalinkin (1982), p. 63.

48. That this process was started early, is illustrated by the kolkhoz 'Gigant', which was formed in 1928 from 84 neighbouring kolkhozy, comprising together a total of 135,000 hectares of land. Davis (1980), p. 124.

49. It is typical that the above-mentioned Hutterian Brethren chose to split up and form a new settlement, rather than allow the membership to grow too large. Bennett (1977).

50. See Bradley & Clarke (1972) for a discussion of this problem.

51. See *inter alia* Hydén (1980).

52. See further Task Force (1982), p. 13.

53. Putterman (1980), p. 126.

54. Ibid. The same author also notes indications that the establishment of ujamaa villages based on full socialisation of labour would still remain a long-term policy goal. Ibid., p. 126, note 5.

55. Putterman (1983), p. 82.

56. See Hedlund and Lundahl (1984) and Lundahl (1979), Ch. 3, for such practices.

57. See further Mushi (1971), pp. 13 ff. for a distinction between these terms.

58. Putterman (1980), p. 128.

59. Statistical Abstracts of Israel, 1948/9 and 1981, Table II/9.

60. See Pospielovsky (1970), for the history of zveno proposals and Hedlund and Lundahl (1982), for a formal analysis of the possible impact of a wide scale application of this system.

61. See for example *Ekonomicheskaya Gazeta*, no. 42, 1982.

62. Pospielovsky (1970), p. 429.

63. Cf. Putterman's observation in footnote 2 above.

64. Putterman (1980), p. 126.

65. See Weintraub (1969).

66. Weintraub (1969), p. 30.

67. Putterman (1983), p. 80.

68. Stalin (1955), p. 120 f.

69. Wright (1979), p. 6.

70. Lenin's pamphlet was published in *Pravda* on May 26 and 27, 1923.

Bibliography

Aage, Hans, 'Labour Allocation in the Soviet Kolkhoz', *Economics of Planning*, vol. 16 (1980).

Bennett, John W. 'The Hutterian Colony: A Traditional Voluntary Agricultural Commune with Large Economic Scale', in Dorner (1977).

Berman, M.D. 'Short Run Efficiency in the Labour Managed Firm', *Journal of Comparative Economics*, vol. 1 (1977).

Bonin, John P. 'Work Incentives and Uncertainty on a Collective Farm', *Journal of*

Comparative Economics, vol. 1 (1977).

Bradley, Michael E. 'Incentives and Labour Supply on Soviet Collective Farms', *Canadian Journal of Economics*, vol. 4 (1971).

____ 'Incentives and Labour Supply on Soviet Collective Farms: Reply', *Canadian Journal of Economics*, vol. 6 (1973).

____, and Clarke, M.G. 'Supervision and Efficiency in Socialised Agriculture', *Soviet Studies*, vol. 23 (1972).

Cameron, Norman E. 'Incentives and Labour Supply in Collective Enterprises', *Canadian Journal of Economics*, vol. 6 (1973a).

____, 'Incentives and Labour Supply on Soviet Collective Farms: Rejoinder', *Canadian Journal of Economics*, vol. 6 (1973b).

Coulson, Andrew, *Tanzania. A Political Economy* (Oxford, 1982).

Davis, R.W. *The Industrialisation of Soviet Russia* (London, 1980).

Domar, Evsey, 'The Soviet Collective Farm as a Producer Cooperative', *American Economic Review*, vol. 56 (1966).

Dorner, Peter (ed.) *Cooperation and Commune* (Madison, Wisconsin, 1977).

Emelyanov, A.M. 'Problemy i perspektivy razvitiya selskogo khozyaistva SSSR v svete reshenii iyulskogo (1978) plenuma TsKKPSS', *Vestnik moskovskogo universiteta*, seriya ekonomika, January (1979).

Galeski, Boguslaw 'The Models of Collective Farming', in Dorner (1977).

Georgescu-Roegen, Nicolas, 'Economic Theory and Agrarian Economics', *Oxford Economic Papers*, vol. 12 (1960).

Hedlund, Hans and Lundahl, Mats, 'The Economic Role of Beer in Rural Zambia', *Human Organisation*, vol. 43 (1984).

Hedlund, Stefan, 'Stalin and the Peasantry: A Study in Red', *Scandia*, vol. 49 (1983).

____, *Crisis in Soviet Agriculture* (London, 1984).

____ and Lundahl, Mats, 'Linking Efforts and Rewards: The Zveno System of Collective Farming', *Economics of Planning*, vol. 18 (1982).

Hydén, Göran, *Beyond Ujamaa in Tanzania* (Stanford, 1980).

Ireland, N.J. and Law, P.J. 'Efficiency, Incentives and Individual Labour Supply in the Labour Managed Firm', *Journal of Comparative Economics*, vol. 5 (1981).

Israelsen, Dwight, 'Collectives, Communes and Incentives', *Journal of Comparative Economics*, vol. 4 (1980).

Kalinkin, A. 'Razvitie lichnogo podsobnogo khozyaistva', *Ekonomika selskogo khozyaistva*, no. 4 (1982).

Karcz, Jerzy, 'From Stalin to Brezhnev: Soviet Agricultural Policy in Historical Perspective', in Millar, James (ed.) *The Soviet Rural Community* (Urbana-Champaign, Illinois, 1971).

Lewin, Moshe, *Russian Peasants and Soviet Power* (London, 1968).

____, *Political Undercurrents in Soviet Economic Debates* (Princeton, NJ, 1974).

Lipton, Michael, 'Inter-Farm, Inter-regional and Farm-Non-Farm Income Distribution: The Impact of the New Cereal Varieties', *World Development*, no. 6 (1978).

Lundahl, Mats, *Peasants and Poverty: A Study of Haiti* (London, 1979).

Mushi, Samuel, 'Ujamaa: Modernisation by Traditionalisation', *Taamuli*, no. 1 (1971).

Nove, Alec, *The Economics of Feasible Socialism* (London, 1983).

Nyerere, Julius, *Ujamaa — Essays on Socialism* (Oxford, 1968).

Oi, Walter and Clayton, Elizabeth, 'A Peasant's View of a Soviet Collective Farm', *American Economic Review*, vol. 58 (1968).

Pospielovsky, Dimitry, 'The Link System in Soviet Agriculture', *Soviet Studies*, vol. 21 (1970).

Putterman, Louis, 'Voluntary Collectivisation: A Model of Producer's Institutional Choice', *Journal of Comparative Economics*, vol. 4 (1980).

____, 'A Modified Collective Agriculture in Rural Growth-with-Equity: Reconsidering the Private Unimodal Solution', *World Development*, vol. 11 (1983).

Raup, Philip M. 'French Experience with Group Farming: The GAEC', in Dorner (1977).

Sen, Amartya, 'Labour Allocation in Collective Enterprises', *Review of Economics and Statistics*, vol. 33 (1966).

Stalin, Joseph V.D. *Collected Works*, vol. 13 (Moscow, 1955).

Task Force on National Agricultural Policy, *The Tanzania National Agricultural Policy* (Dar es Salaam, 1982).

Vanek, Jaroslav, *The General Theory of Labour Managed Market Economies* (Ithaca, NY, 1970).

Ward, Benjamin, 'The Firm in Illyria: Market Syndicalism', *American Economic Review*, vol. 48 (1958).

Weintraub, Dov (*et. al.*). *Moshava, Kibbutz and Moshav* (London, 1969).

Wesson, Robert 'The Soviet Communes', *Soviet Studies*, vol. 13 (1962).

Wright, Arthur (ed.). *Jerzy F. Karcz. The Economics of Communist Agriculture. Selected Papers* (Bloomington, Indiana, 1979).

Wronski, Henri. 'Rémuneration et niveau de vie dans les kolkhoz. Le troudoden', *Ecole pratique des hautes études. Observation economique XIII* (Paris, 1957).

17 AGRICULTURAL SECTOR DEVELOPMENT IN TANZANIA 1961–82: PERFORMANCE AND MAJOR CONSTRAINTS*

Benno J. Ndulu and Lucian A. Msambichaka

1. Introduction

In this paper we will focus on the role and development of the agricultural sector in Tanzania. The first part discusses the expected role of the agricultural sector in the Tanzanian economy, policy-wise. It also briefly reviews the actual role played by the sector since independence against the expected role. The second part of the paper reviews and evaluates the performance of the sector over the same period. The third identifies the major constraints to the development of the sector.

2. The Role of the Agricultural Sector in Tanzania's Economic Development

2.1 Agricultural Policy and Its Evolution

The agricultural sector is dominant in the Tanzanian economy in many respects. Not only does it directly provide about 85 per cent of the population with incomes and employment, but it is also the largest contributor to gross national product and foreign exchange generation. Despite the relatively large imports of food, it still remains the main feeder of Tanzania's population. It is in the light of this dominant position of the sector that we look at both the expected and actual performance of the sector since independence.

In terms of both development philosophy and economic policy two major periods can be identified in the post-colonial Tanzania; namely the pre-1967 and the post-Arusha Declaration. The pre-1967 period was characterised basically by inertia from pre-independence development philosophy. There were only minor modifications to reflect some level of nationalistic consciousness. The driving force

* The research has been financed by a SAREC grant which is gratefully acknowledged.

behind agricultural development was to raise output through increased application of labour inputs and higher labour productivity. Consequently commercialisation of the agricultural economy would be intensified. During this period it was envisaged that apart from the reduction of subsistence production contribution to GDP from 38 per cent in 1960–2 to 14 per cent in 1980, favourable structural change would entail reduction of the primary sector's contribution to GDP (of which agriculture was 80 per cent) from 58 per cent in 1960–2 to 37 per cent in 1980. This was to be achieved through expected faster rates of industrial growth (14.3 per cent) in the productive sphere relative to the agricultural sector's growth rate of 4.8 per cent. The First Five Year Plan (1964–9) was largely drawn up on the basis of the 1961 World Bank Mission Report which drew experiences from other developing countries using conventional development philosophy.[1] Nevertheless it was recognised that the predominance of the agricultural sector was to continue for a long time to follow.

Agricultural growth during the 1964–9 period was to be achieved mainly through three organisational forms. For the indigenous smallholder peasant agriculture two approaches, 'improvement' and 'transformation' were to be followed. The 'improvement approach' involved the intensive use of agricultural extension and advice to improve husbandry among producers. Emphasis was to be given to relatively more developed areas with 'better' absorption possibilities and receptiveness to improved husbandry. The advantages of this approach were seen as meagre capital requirements and minimum disruption in social systems. The 'transformation' approach was to involve the development and opening up of new areas (lands) by using volunteer migrants (predominantly from high density/land pressure areas) to be provided with modern implements and improved economic and social infrastructure. The earmarked areas were basically the underdeveloped river basins. This approach was capital intensive and had a target of having 1 million people under settlement schemes by 1980. Private agricultural estates, contributing about 40 per cent of agricultural exports (1960–2), were encouraged to expand their acreage. Extra land and incentives to attract additional investments were provided.

The Arusha Declaration (1967) re-examined and clarified Tanzania's development strategy following the initial political independence consolidation, the pre-1967 experiences in plan implementations and changes in world economic conditions. The implementation failure in the transformation approach, due to massive capital requirements, inadequate detailed planning, and the non-appearance of anticipated investment provided a major input into the new policy and strategy consideration. As far as the agricultural sector is concerned the Declaration adopted a frontal approach in rural development. In developing this, efforts would focus on rural areas, so as not only to increase agricultural output but also to raise the standards of living. This meant that increasing the people's incomes was not enough. It was also imperative to develop a better way of life with increased productivity, better amenities of life and reduced drudgery of labour from improved farming techniques.

The main agricultural objectives and policies from the Arusha Declaration document on which all subsequent operational plans were founded can be summarised as follows:

1. Self-sufficiency in food production.
2. Earning of sufficient export earnings from agricultural exports to finance structural transformation of the economy towards a more inward-looking, independent and self-reliant economy.
3. Production of cash crops to be used as raw materials for the growing industrial sector (e.g. agro-industries, textiles etc).
4. Development of socialist rural production and socialist living and gradual extinction of exploitative forms of agricultural production.[2]
5. In meeting all the above targets, self-help and self-reliance was to be the main resource. Government help and external finance would be supportive in nature and *not* a substitute for own efforts.

The Second Five Year Plan (1969–74), the Third Five Year Plan (1976–81), the First Union Plan (1981–5) and the recently announced National Agricultural Policy (1983) are all designed towards meeting these major objectives. In all these documents agriculture was correctly given a dominant role to play in the economy and investment strategies, though directed towards structural transformation, seriously recognised the need for supportive infrastructural and social investment, even at the expense of directly productive investment in agriculture. A target of food self-sufficiency by 1981 was adopted. Communal farming was encouraged through government resource support, propaganda, villagisation campaigns

and the Villagisation Act (1975) Gradual and democratic transformation to this form was to be used. In the pronouncement of
Siasa ni Kilimo (Politics is Agriculture) in 1972, modernisation of
agriculture through improved crop husbandry and use of better
implements was stressed. Problems of land tenure, incentive
systems, production organisation, marketing, resource allocation
and production techniques were further reviewed and elaborated in
the National Agricultural Policy (1983) in the same light.

2.2 The Agricultural Sector's Contribution and Role in the Economy

The contribution of the agricultural sector to national income is
large relative to other sectors, although this contribution has been
declining over time. In real terms (at 1966 prices) the share of the
sector declined steadily, from an average of 59.9 per cent in the period
1961–3, to 43.8 per cent during the First Five Year Plan period
(1964–9), to 39.5 per cent during the Second Five Year Plan
period (1969–74) and finally to 37.7 per cent in the Third Five Year
Plan period (1976–81) (Table 17.1).

Table 17.1: Contribution of Agriculture to GDP at Constant
1966 Prices (%)

1962–3	1966	1970	1972	1974	1976	1978	1980	1981
59.9	45.3	41.7	40.1	46.3	37.0	39.4	37.6	36.1

Source: Central Statistical Bureau: Statistical Abstracts 1966, 1970 and Economic Survey 1981 (contains revised GDP figures since 1976).

This decline is partly explained by the deliberate efforts to effect
structural change in favour of non-agricultural sectors, particularly
industry and commerce. The decline is also explained by generally
lower growth rates of the sector from 5.5 per cent per annum in
1961–3 to 3.2 per cent (1975–81) in real terms due to various technical and organisational problems to be explained below. It is important to note though, that in nominal terms the agricultural sector's
contribution to GDP has increased to over 50 per cent in the last six
years due to relatively faster increases in agricultural producer prices
in official terms. The subsistence sector's share in agriculture has
remained constant at about 50 per cent.

In terms of the role of feeding the population and achieving food self-sufficiency, the sector has not performed well. Tanzania has grown to be a large food deficit nation as indicated by large food import volumes. Except for 1968 and 1969 Tanzania has been a net importer of food. Since the 1974 severe drought, food import volumes have increased with peaks in 1974, 1975 and 1980. Food production grew at about 3 per cent per annum between 1975 and 1981 against a population growth rate of 3.3 per cent over the same period. Nevertheless the agricultural sector has on average been providing more than 90 per cent of food consumption requirements in the country.[3]

The agricultural sector is the largest contributor to foreign exchange generation. The sector is a net foreign exchange generator in production and distribution. The largest export crop, coffee, uses about $20 of foreign exchange for $100 generated. For all the other crops foreign exchange use ranges between 12 and 60 per cent of earned value per unit. Although on average the sector contributed about 70 per cent of total foreign exchange earnings prior to 1976, with the drastic decline of industrial exports (which at the peak contributed about 19 per cent of export earnings) agriculture currently contributes over 80 per cent of the earnings (Table 17.2).

Table 17.2: Agricultural Exports Relative to Total Exports in %

1973	1974	1975	1976	1977	1978	1979	1980
76.4	78.3	79.5	83.9	87.6	86.8	82.0	83.1

Source: Marketing Development Bureau: Price Policy Recommendations for 1982–3, Summary.

Nevertheless the volume of imports paid for by agricultural export earnings declined to 35 per cent in 1982 from the peak of about 70 per cent in 1973. This decline is explained by a combination of several factors. On the one hand the volume of exports declined by about 34 per cent; on the other, worsening of terms of trade over the period in question accounted for 11 per cent of the decline in the contribution.[4] Secondly, over this period a rapid expansion of imports for industrialisation took place irrespective of the poor agricultural export performance, resulting in a heavy burden to be shouldered by agriculture and foreign capital inflow.

The total number of people seeking employment in the urban areas is increasing rapidly. Unfortunately employment opportunities in the industrial sector, commerce, service and other sectors of the economy are growing very slowly. Agriculture appears to be the only area where the rapidly growing labour force could easily be absorbed despite the current decline in agricultural wage employment. Agricultural wage employment contributed 51 per cent of total wage employment in 1961 and has since then almost systematically declined. It recorded 42 per cent in 1965; 29 per cent in 1970; 26 per cent in 1975 and 23 per cent in 1981. This decline was caused mainly by the persistent decline in wage employment on sisal estates. Despite this deterioration in agricultural wage employment the sector still employs about 80 per cent of the total economically active population in Tanzania.

3. Performance of the Agricultural Sector in Production

3.1 *Production Indices and Growth of the Agricultural Sector*

Indices of total agricultural production in Tanzania show a rising trend (Table 17.3).

Table 17.3: Agricultural Production Index in Tanzania (1969–71 = 100)

	1966	1970	1973	1976	1979	1981
Total Food Production	92	104	109	116	122	124
Total Agric. Production	96	103	107	113	116	120
Food Production *per capita*	103	104	100	97	93	89
Agric. Production *per capita*	107	103	98	95	89	86

Source: FAO, Production Yearbook, vol. 31, (1977), vol. 35, (1981), Rome.

Apart from a slight decline in the production index between 1971 and 1972, this trend maintained a continuous upward slope. Surprisingly the positive trend was also maintained during the drought years of 1973–4 and 1979–80. Table 17.3 on the other hand indicates that the country is facing a severe crisis in agricultural productivity. Total agricultural production *per capita* has shown a declining trend since 1966. Similar disappointments are observed in the food producing sector where, except for 1970, the trend of food production *per capita* has been consistently downward, reaching its lowest in 1981.

In terms of annual growth rates agriculture appears to have had a higher rate of growth during the period 1965–70 (Table 17.4).

Table 17.4:   Annual Rate of Growth of the Agricultural Sector at 1966 Prices

Year	Agriculture, Hunting Forestry and Fishing	Subsistence Agriculture	Monetary Agriculture	Total Economy
1965–80	3.3	4.8	1.2	4.4
1965–70	3.7	2.7	4.9	4.9
1970–5	1.9	1.9	0.2	3.7
1975–80	3.2	6.2	4.3	3.2
1980–1	–3.9	–6.1	0.5	–1.8

Source: Computed from: Tanzania, U.R.: The Economic Survey 1977–8; (Dar es Salaam, 1981).

The first half of the 1970s recorded a very poor growth rate. This reflects the impacts of droughts and the level of technologies used in production. It also explains why during this time and the latter part of the decade agriculture failed to keep pace with the demands of a population which was growing at 3.3 per cent.

3.2 *Volume of Crop Production and Explanation of Factors Behind Changing Volumes*

Smallholder production dominates food crop production. About 75–80 per cent of food output is consumed by the farm family households. This makes it difficult to determine accurately its annual production. However, the purchase of crops is to a large extent determined by the volume produced and the price of the crop on the unofficial market. It is assumed that data on NMC (National Milling Corporation)[5] purchases indicate the general production trend which is, however, not always the case because the NMC prices are not always favourable to farmers.

The low levels of marketed volumes in 1974/5 earmark the agrarian crisis which was a consequence of severe drought. A period of recovery followed thereafter registering a record production for most of the crops in 1977/8. Since then production of preferred cereals has persistently been on the decline. One of the reasons which supports the rapid increase of marketed volumes of food crops soon after the drought spell was the increase of the NMC purchase price for both preferred staples and drought resistant staples between 1975/6 and 1977/8. It is also assumed that some farmers abandoned the tedious and less paying crops and concentrated on producing food crops which could be sold easily and at a relatively higher price via unofficial channels. There is also evidence to believe that the 'Kufa na Kupona' (produce or perish) campaign, which was declared during the drought years, did contribute significantly to the rapid increase in NMC purchases.

The recent decline in food production is said to have been caused by the absolute lack of supportive services, inefficient marketing and input delivery systems.[6] To make the situation worse, the industrial sector has not been able to provide the rural sector with the most needed consumer goods. This failure has contributed to the destabilisation of the rural economy and placed agriculture in depression.

In the case of export crops, the situation is not much different (Table 17.5).

Table 17.5:   Export Crops Quantum Indices 1964–81 (1972 = 100)

Crop	1964	1966	1972	1976	1979	1981
Sisal Fibre	137.9	129.2	100	59.1	51.0	38.9
Cotton Lint	70	133.4	100	89.2	60.2	74.6
Coffee (Unroasted)	61.2	93.4	100	105.8	82.8	145.7
Tea	48.9	68.5	100	130.0	163.4	168.5
Tobacco (Unmanufactured)	22.8	32.4	110	222.5	98.8	166.2
Cashewnuts	50.2	64.0	100	58.8	33.5	26.7
Cloves (Unground)	–	–	100	61.0	44.9	51.7

Source: Computations based on MDB: Price Policy Recommendations (various years).

Marketed production of sisal has been on the decline since 1964. That of cotton and pyrethrum has been falling since 1966/7 and cashew production since 1973/4. The decline in sisal is largely explained by the drastic drop in the world market prices in the 1960s. From 1963 when the price of sisal was US$360.60 per tonne, the price dropped continuously to a low of US$146.00 per tonne in 1970.[7] The introduction of synthetic fibres in the world market also contributed to the displacement of sisal as Tanzania's leading export crop. Deficiency in soil nutrients appears to have affected cotton production. The fall in cashew production seems to have been affected by the low price and by the movement of people into new villages. Tobacco and tea production remained on the increase almost throughout, whereas coffee marketed production fluctuated around a constant level.

4. Major Constraints

Several resources are required for the development of the agricultural sector. The most important among these are land, labour, capital and technology. The increase in production capacity and efficiency of agriculture crucially depends on the quantity and quality of the resources deployed.

4.1 *Resource Allocation for Agricultural Development*

When one talks about investment in agriculture in the Tanzanian context, one basically is concerned with government development finance. Two main reasons can be raised for this. First, in view of the predominance of smallholder production and negligible rural savings out of disposable income, major investments are made through the government or its agencies. In terms of production capacity development, the rural sector itself contributes in the form of increasing the labour force (both human and animal stock). This occurs in the form of increasing the acreage under production with the techniques used remaining antiquated. Second, the bulk of agricultural surplus accrues in the form of tax revenues to the government. The allocation of these over various sectors is done through the budgetary process. Direct government investments for agricultural development include those into crop development, improvement in husbandry (crop and livestock) research, extension, pest control and seed production.

The agricultural sector has been starved of investible resources relative to its contribution to GNP and to foreign exchange generation. Although, in nominal terms, the sector has been receiving an increasing allocation for development, in real terms the allocation has decreased by 34 per cent over the last decade due to inflation. The share of total government development budget going to agriculture, after increasing from 10.5 per cent in 1972/3 to 29.1 per cent in 1975/6, dropped to 7.8 per cent by 1979/80, before increasing slightly to 8.9 per cent by 1981/2. As a proportion of total national capital formation this share declined from 7.5 per cent in 1976 to 4 per cent in 1980 in real terms. There emerges, therefore, a widening gap between verbal commitment to agriculture in terms of policy statements and the actual resource allocation pattern.

In terms of investment productivity, the agricultural sector has demonstrated higher returns per shilling of investment than industry.[8] Moreover there is no proven evidence as yet of lack of investment absorptive capacity in the agricultural sector. In terms of net foreign exchange generation productivity, the sector remains the most productive. Given the serious balance of payments situation in the country, relatively more investment in the sector would have gone a longer way towards reducing the deficits.

4.2 Technological Constraints

1. *Production Techniques in Use.* The hand hoe is the major farm implement used in Tanzania. About 80–85 per cent of the crop area is cultivated by hand; 10–15 per cent by oxen and only 5 per cent by tractor.[9] There is also a low level of mechanised irrigation and agricultural processing.

The substantial part of land cultivated by hand tools makes for difficulty in offering better soil tillage, and in meeting the demands of agronomy and modern farm inputs (fertilisers, pesticides, improved seeds etc.). Total cultivatable area is about 36 million hectares, out of which only 16 per cent is put under cultivation. The dominance of the hand hoe has made it difficult for farmers to expand crop areas rapidly and to practise intensive farming. In addition to the above, the non-availability of farm equipment compounded by the prohibitive unit prices are some of the reasons behind the slow adoption of modern agricultural technology which in turn has contributed to the slow progress in the agricultural modernisation process.

2. *Input Supply Constraints.* Here we refer to the availability of fertiliser, improved seeds and plant protection chemicals. There are two major problems which relate to input supplies. First, input volumes available are not adequate and are confined to only a few crops. Second, they are not timely delivered. For example between 1972/3 and 1975/6, more than 50 per cent of the fertiliser consumed in Tanzania went to cotton, coffee, tobacco and tea. Additionally, the average amount of fertiliser currently used per hectare is about 20 kg, which is a very small amount compared to more than 100 kg/ha used in developed countries.

The utilisation of improved seeds is also still very limited. In 1978 only about 9 per cent of the total crop seeds used in Tanzania were from the Tanzania Seed Company (TANSEED). In 1982, out of 8,029 tonnes of improved seeds produced by TANSEED, only 31.5 per cent was bought by farmers.

At the same time the use of Plant Protection Chemicals (PPCs) has not penetrated the smallholder market fully. Most of the PPCs are used in export crops and estate production. The average consumption stands at 320 g per hectare.[10] In summary it can be claimed that inputs in Tanzania have not occupied a central place in modern agriculture.

3. *Extension and Farm Management Problems.* Extension services are important in disseminating modern farm techniques to the farmers. Current figures indicate that there are 6,423 extension agents in the country. After deducting 2,900 for the regional headquarters, district and ward level, the effective number of extension staff is 3,515. This gives a ratio of about one extension agent per 1,300 farmers or one extension staff per two villages.

The FAO considers that one extension agent can effectively work with 500 to 1,000 farmers. However, this ratio assumes that most of the farmers are literate and that a good rural communication network exists. In Tanzania, besides the inadequate qualification of the extension personnel, poor rural transport is the main bottleneck which hinders the smooth running of the extension services.

The deficiency in extension services has had a negative impact on the farmer's organisational and operational decisions. The farmer thus failed to get adequate and proper guidance on what to grow, to produce or to use in production. He has also found it difficult to plan or to put his production plans into effect.

4.3 *Incentive-Related Constraints*

1. *Output Pricing.* The major incentive instruments used by the government to promote the development of the agricultural sector include pricing, input subsidies, and exhortation/campaigns (moral incentives).

Pricing policy as an incentive instrument began to be actively used in the post-1975 period.[11] The pre-1975 period was basically characterised by intensive use of campaigns and resource handouts to induce development. Thus one observed very stable prices over long periods with relative prices heavily in favour of export crops. The decline in food production in general and drastic drought crises in particular induced change in relative prices heavily in favour of food crops in the post-1975 period. This was further strengthened by the general falling trend of export crop prices in the world market in the absence of exchange rate adjustments. As far as absolute prices are concerned, food crops' nominal producer prices were actively increased in the post-1975 period to induce increased production and protect farmers' incomes in view of high inflation rates. However, for pure cash crops, the situation was different. World market prices for major export crops were declining over this period. This, coupled with increased costs of production and high inflation rates (over 30 per cent per annum in the post-1979 period), severely ate into producers' real income. The absence of exchange rate adjustments inflicted income losses not only on farmers but also on state marketing agencies as their margins grew smaller and smaller in the face of increasing operating and overhead costs. The drastic decline in export crop production in the post-1975 period is partially explained by this.

In real terms agricultural producer prices declined in the post-1975 period. Food crop prices declined by about 5.5 per cent over the period. The decline in the case of export crops was more drastic; it is estimated at 36.5 per cent. Low consumer prices (subsidised) placed a heavy burden on the government budget, thus limiting the government's ability to raise producer prices sufficiently to cover income losses from inflation. On the side of export crops, as pointed out above, non-adjustment of the exchange rate limited the ability of the government to raise producer prices in the face of falling world market prices. The impact of the decline has in general made non-agricultural activities (especially commerce) more attractive. Within the agricultural sector efforts have shifted more to food crops with relatively higher returns, especially horticultural crops which are sold in non-controlled markets.

2. *Input Subsidies.*   In an effort to induce farmers to adopt the use of more modern production techniques to increase productivity, the government instituted input subsidy programmes in the post-1973 period. The single most important subsidised input is fertiliser.

The subsidy is given in three forms for fertilisers. The government offers fertiliser at 50 per cent of ex-factory cost, the rest being paid for by the Treasury through agricultural export tax revenues. Secondly, the Treasury also pays for all transport costs from the factory to the village for smallholders. Thirdly, the main distribution of fertilisers to smallholder areas is not charged the retail margin on fertilisers delivered on credit by the Tanzanian Rural Development Bank.

Producers have not taken full advantage of this subsidy programme partly because of organisational problems. All inputs are sold to producers on credit arrangements. In the case of smallholders either the TRDB or crop authorities advance inputs to villages on credit and recovery is through levies on produce sales. Thus individual producers are not tied down to individual input uses. The result of this has been very poor recovery of debts. The penalty for non-creditworthiness of villages has been non-delivery of inputs for coming seasons. This has tended to penalise all individuals in a village irrespective of individual responsibilities. Moreover village-based input credits under the present arrangement have tended to lead to waste in the cases where most members were not willing to use the delivered inputs. The heavy input subsidies have also increased the budgetary burden on government without the realisation of expected increase in yield.

3. *Production Targets and Campaigns.*   In the annual production plans the party and the government set production targets at national, regional, district, village and individual household levels for specific crops. These targets have a legal binding nature in implementation. The government usually follows up with exhortation and campaigns for their implementation.

This has tended to generate the following impacts:

(1) Generally there have been overall overestimates in the targets relative to actual production capacity. This has led to pressure on producers and tendency for general negative feelings towards achieving them.

(2) The implied crop-mix from the targets has often openly come into conflict with the relative price signals from announced prices (in terms of expected income return). This has further made it difficult for producers to accept the targets and enhanced the alienation feeling from participatory decision making. Where implementation has been enforced in such cases, it has led to loss of producers' income. There are definite potential conflicts between national and individual interests in production decisions.

4. *Availability of Consumer Goods.*   The ultimate objective of the production process is consumption. For the agricultural producers, the earnings of each income have to be matched with availability of

commodities to buy; otherwise a disincentive towards earning cash income develops. Over the last five years a general shortage of both current and durable consumption goods has developed to a critical stage. Lack of adequate supply of raw materials and spares has led to drastic decline in industrial production. This situation has further been aggravated by inability to import the shortfall in consumer goods supply due to balance of payments crises. The result has been a general development towards producing less for cash and withdrawing more towards subsistence production.

4.4 *Organisational Problems*

1. *The Marketing System.* Looking through the last two decades of agricultural marketing in Tanzania, one sees a strong trend towards maintaining a single-channel marketing system. At various points in time centralisation and decentralisation as well as changes in agents handling crops rapidly occurred. Between 1963 and 1975 Cooperative Unions in conjunction with National Products Boards undertook agricultural marketing. Between 1976 and 1983, Crop Authorities (national) took over this function with the abolition of Cooperative Unions. From 1983/4 the functions will be carried out by Cooperative Unions at the regional level and authorities at the national level.

This rapid change has resulted in a high degree of instability in the marketing expectations of farmers, with its consequent disincentives in production. The fact that farmers have resorted increasingly to parallel markets bears testimony to this.

While marketing functions have been changing hands rapidly, no clear policy direction was adopted with respect to investment in marketing capacity. Thus the marketing system has remained plagued with problems of inadequate infrastructural facilities (transport, handling facilities and storage) and lack of skilled manpower for effective operation. Furthermore, failure by policy makers to separate marketing operations from production and processing activities within designated agencies, led to reduced effectiveness in marketing operations.

There has been no real incentive for agencies to keep costs low. Rather than economising, there are many instances in which the budget is fully spent even when the volume of crops to be handled falls drastically. The monopolistic nature of marketing activities has generally resulted in cost ineffectiveness and inefficiency in general High overhead costs have increased unit costs leading to reduction in the trade margins of the agencies and eventual heavy subsidies from the government budget.

The result of all this has been in some cases late payments to producers or even non-payment, inability to procure in time, haphazard accounts and physical losses of crops. This has contributed significantly to decline in those crops where producers have no alternatives except the official channels.

2. *The Planning of the Sector's Development.*   The problems related to planning of agricultural development are complex. However, recent observations reveal that though agriculture was expected to contribute substantially to the economy, no serious effort was made through development plan budgets to increase the production capacity of the sector. The planners have tended to focus their attention on production (output) targets without providing for the means to achieve them. The planning of the sector's development has always been seriously hampered by the scarcity of resources and the tight budget. At certain stages of the plan implementation, political pressures have disrupted the plan priorities, the approach to financing the projects as well as the method and means of plan implementation.

Agricultural planning has not been able to define the best combination and utilisation of major local resources (physical and financial) available in the country. Forward projections which use certain basic economic indicators such as population growth, urban incomes, production data, consumption data, financial statistics, trade statistics, improvement of living standards indices etc. have been lacking. In the absence of these projections the development trend of the sector has had no proper directional guidance.

5. Concluding Remarks

Looking back on the performance of the agricultural sector over the last two decades and its contribution to the general economic development in Tanzania, one tends to get a rather poor picture. Relative to the burden it was expected to shoulder, the performance has been poor. Productivity has in general declined, agricultural exports have severely declined, and the food self-sufficiency target is still far from being achieved. It is in recognition of this performance that policy makers decided to review the sector's performance and came up with the National Agricultural Policy in 1983 to help rehabilitate and boost the development of the sector. The potential for its rapid growth and development is definitely substantial.

It has been recognised that the sector in general received rhetorical emphasis without the resource support required to develop it. Thus agriculture has been starved of investible resources for development. As a result, to date, production techniques remain antiquated. Emphasis in investment was given to structural transformation (towards industrialisation) and the provision of social and economic infrastructure at the expense of the key producing sector.

Organisationally, the country has over the last two decades made several changes both in marketing and production leading to instability in expectations among producers. Lack of clarity in land tenure policy and late use of material incentive schemes have contributed to poor performance. High rates of inflation and slightly declining terms of trade in the absence of exchange rate adjustments have resulted in the fall in real producer prices creating disincentives to increased production.

The National Agricultural Policy critically looked at all the above problems and came up with several policy instruments towards alleviating them. Now the task is that of implementation, to get the sector back on its feet and moving forward. Primary emphasis in its implementation should be placed on increasing resources available to the development of the sector. Improvement in supportive infrastructure, removing bottlenecks related to marketing, raising producer prices substantially in real terms and increasing the availability of basic consumer goods constitute the immediate steps to be taken. In the medium to long term, gradual improvement in the production techniques to increase productivity should be undertaken.

Notes

1. Industrialisation was to provide the dominant dynamic base of both growth and structural change in the economy.

2. Communal agricultural production was to be introduced gradually and voluntarily as economic and social superiority of collective farming. As Nyerere remarked in his 1967 paper on 'Socialism and Rural Development': 'The people would keep their individual plots; the community farm would be an extra effort instead of each family trying to expand its own acreage . . . the final stage would come when the

people have confidence in a community farm, so that they are willing to invest all their effort in it, simply keeping their gardens around their houses for special vegetables, etc.' (Nyerere (1967) p. 19).

3. The food problem in Tanzania though, is partially a relative problem. Over time the non-agricultural population has adopted a consumption pattern which is heavily biased towards 'preferred cereals' (rice, maize and wheat) which are also heavily consumption subsidised. Thus while the country imports huge volumes of these cereals, one sees sizeable stocks of drought-resistant foodstuffs (millets, sorghum, cassava, peas) which the marketing authority finds difficult to sell, hence inflicting financial losses upon it. It is still questionable whether the volume of imports is justified. It is most likely the case that if subsidies on preferred staples were removed or reduced (average subsidy, 50 per cent), consumption and imports of these would decline in favour of the other staples. This will have to be combined, though, with better processing of the 'non-preferred' staples. In view of calorie supply shortfall (about 89 per cent of requirements are supplied) overall food production will have to be increased. See Ellis (1980); UNICEF (1982); Maletnlema (1982); Mudge *et al.* (1980).

4. World Bank (1981), pp. 53–4.

5. The sole official buyer of food crops in Tanzania.

6. National Agricultural Policy (1983).

7. Valentine (1981).

8. Ndulu (1983).

9. National Agricultural Policy (1983).

10. Khamis (1983); Msambichaka (1983).

11. Ellis (1982).

Bibliography

Ellis, Frank 'Agricultural Price Policy in Tanzania', *World Development*, vol. 10 (1982).
___ 'Agricultural Pricing Policy in Tanzania 1970–9: Implications on Agricultural Output, Rural Incomes and Crop Marketing Costs' ERB paper No. 80.3 (1980).
FAO Production Yearbooks, vol. 31 (1977) and vol. 35 (1981) Rome.
Hopkins, R.F. *Food Aid; The Political Economy of International Policy Formation* (Swathmore College, October, 1980).
Khamis, S. 'Address to the Ministerial Meeting on National Agriculture Policy, Arusha 28–31st March, 1983.
Maletnlema, T.N. *'Hunger Kills 150 a Day in Tanzania', A Wicked Distortion of Facts* TFNC (Mimeo).
Marketing Development Bureau, 'Price Policy Recommendations for 1980/1 and July, 1982.'
Msambichaka, L.A. 'Agricultural Development in Tanzania: Situation, Problems and Future Priorities', Paper presented to the Economic Policy Workshop on Tanzania Arusha, April 1983.
Mudge, J. Crosswell, M. and Kim, K. 'Tanzanian Development Performance and Implications for Development Assistance' (AID, Washington, D.C., November, 1980).
Ndulu, B.J. 'Investment Patterns and Impacts in the Post-Arusha Tanzania: 1970–80' Paper presented to the Economic Policy Workshop on Tanzania, Arusha, April 1983.
Nyerere, J.K. *The Arusha Declaration and TANU's Policy on Socialism and Self-Reliance* (Dar es Salaam, 1967).

Tanzania, U.R. *First Five Year Plan for Economic and Social Development 1964-9*, vol. 1 (Dar es Salaam, 1964).

_____ *First Five Year Union Plan for Economic Development and Social Development, 1981-6*, vol. 1 (Dar es Salaam, 1982 (in Kiswahili)).

_____ *The Agricultural Policy of Tanzania* (Dar es Salaam, March 1983).

_____ *The Economic Survey 1981* (Dar es Salaam, June 1982).

_____ *Third Five Year Plan for Economic and Social Development, 1976-81*, vol. 1 (Dar es Salaam, 1976).

_____ *Second Five Year Plan for Economic and Social Development, 1969-74*, vol. 1 (Dar es Salaam, 1969).

_____ *Statistical Abstracts 1966 and 1970* (Bureau of Statistics, Dar es Salaam).

UNICEF '1982 World's Children Data Sheet of Population Reference Bureau', Inc.

Valentine, T.R. 'Government Policy, Wage and Employment Trends, and Economic Instability in Tanzania Since Independence', E.R.B. paper 81.1 (1981).

World Bank, Economic Memorandum on Tanzania, January 1981.

18   AGRICULTURE IN THE TRANSITION TO SOCIALISM: THE CASE OF SOUTH VIETNAM

Melanie Beresford

Following the liberation of South Vietnam in April 1975, the new government of the country pursued two major economic goals: to achieve unification of North and South under a socialist regime similar to that already developing in North Vietnam and to build a modern economic system in Vietnam. These two processes, which are regarded as inseparable by the Vietnamese since they view socialist production as 'large scale socialist production',[1] are referred to as the processes of transformation and construction. As far as South Vietnam is concerned, the transformation aspect of this duality is aimed at bringing about uniform socialist relations of production. At the same time, the construction phase is intended to transform the region from a predominantly small-scale, backward economy, based on individual enterprise, into a modern, centrally planned production system in which the means of production are socially owned.

The first part of this essay aims to establish the importance of agricultural development both for the South Vietnamese economy and within the overall national development strategy. In the second part, the changes which took place in southern agriculture prior to liberation are reviewed and the implications of these for the process of transformation and construction are drawn out. The final section looks at the period since 1975, focusing on the way in which major problems were tackled by policy makers and the way in which the peculiar problems of the South have influenced Vietnamese thinking on the whole question of the socialist transformation of agriculture.

South Vietnam in the National Development Strategy

The southern Vietnamese economy inherited from the American-backed regime suffered from a number of severe structural problems brought about both by prolonged wartime conditions and by the system of social relations prevailing in the country since the end of the French colonial regime. In particular, it was heavily biased towards the non-productive services sector. This sector showed a real growth rate of 4.1 per cent per annum between 1960 and 1972, compared to a real growth rate of the economy as a whole of only 2.8 per cent (population growth rate is estimated at 2.7 per cent),[2] and its share in GDP rose to 52 per cent. The most rapidly expanding areas, understandably so during a period of warfare under a social system of predominantly private enterprise, were commerce, banking, administration and defence — the first two fuelled by a massive American-financed import programme. The productive sectors of the economy tended to stagnate and even decline during the war due to the inability or unwillingness of either foreign investors or South Vietnamese to undertake a substantial amount of investment in industry, agriculture or transport. Manufacturing, by the end of the war, contributed little more than 5 per cent of GDP and agriculture remained by far the most important of the productive sectors, providing 30–40 per cent of GDP.[3] Officially, one and a half million, or 20 per cent of the labour force, were unemployed towards the end of the war. However, labour force participation rates for the refugee-swollen urban areas of South Vietnam were, according to the official statistics of the southern regime, extraordinarily low, so that a more accurate reflection of the amount of surplus labour in the economy would give an overall unemployment figure of 2.7 million, or 30 per cent of the actual labour supply.[4] Urban unemployment under the new estimate would have been about 55 per cent compared to the official 25 per cent.

The most serious structural problems of the southern economy were brought about by its enormous dependence on United States' and other Western aid. South Vietnam's exports contributed virtually nothing to its balance of payments position. The two major exports of the French colonial period, rice and rubber, both suffered from war damage and lack of investment. Although rice production began to increase in the late 1960s, the changing social structure in the countryside meant that this did not have a corresponding effect on export income (this will be discussed further below). Whereas in 1960, exports had been able to cover as much as 38 per cent of import expenditures, by the 1970s the figure was reduced to 2–4 per cent.[5] At the same time, little effort was made to restrict the growth of imports: the constant inflow of consumer goods helped not only to stem the inflationary impact of wartime budget deficits, but to sustain the living standards of the urban wealthy and middle classes upon whom the regime depended for continued political support. There was also a high degree of reliance by both industry and agriculture on imported capital and raw materials inputs — in the major industries, 70–95 per cent of raw materials were imported.[6] Since the end of the war, determined efforts have been made to increase the output of such industrial crops as tobacco, rubber, tea, coffee, cotton, sugar, pineapples, groundnuts, as well as marine products in order to reduce this dependence. However, the agricultural sector itself had also become heavily dependent upon imported machinery and inputs, as a result of the Thieu government's efforts to implement a 'green revolution' in the peasant economy. Chemical fertiliser, insecticides, water pumps, tractors, etc., were very largely imported.[7]

An additional difficulty for the post-war economy of South Vietnam arose from the fact that the country was heavily reliant for all its imported goods on a handful of principal sources — chiefly the US and Japan.[8] This was largely due to a deliberate US policy of tying aid-financed imports and has made the imposition of the US-sponsored trade embargo against Vietnam in the post-1975 period considerably more effective, especially where goods are not readily substitutable (e.g., certain capital goods and spare parts).[9]

The huge South Vietnamese balance of trade deficit was almost entirely financed by American aid.[10] An alternative way of looking at the extent of the regime's dependence is to compare Gross Domestic Product with actual expenditure levels. From these figures we can see that public and private consumption expenditure, taken together, consistently amounted to more than GDP (averaging 104 per cent during 1960–72, the years for which data are available); gross capital formation, that is the item from which the increase in productive capacity of the economy must come, remained small at 10 per cent of GDP; total expenditure averaged 114 per cent of GDP, the difference being made up by US financing of the import programme.[11]

The situation was thus one in which the southern Vietnamese economy was consuming more than it produced and, at the same time, the rate of investment was barely sufficient to sustain a rate of growth of output equal to the population growth rate. These poor performance figures did not, however, indicate that the economy lacked potential for rapid development. There were extensive labour resources, including skilled labour. There were also certain elements of an economic infrastructure — roads, ports, airports — although others, particularly railways, waterways and electricity supply, remained inadequate or in need of major repairs. Most importantly, the Mekong River delta area was capable of producing a large agricultural surplus which could not only be used to supplement the output of traditional food-deficit areas of Central and North Vietnam, but could still provide a surplus for export and financing of capital accumulation. Great potential existed for developing other agricultural regions of the South for industrial crops as well. But if the economy was to become viable in the absence of the American aid prop, there would need to be some big changes in patterns of both consumption and investment.

The alternatives which faced the country's economic planners after liberation in 1975 were fairly strictly limited on account of the legacy of 30 years' war and successive French and American occupations. In the first place, there was no heavy industrial base. Even that which had been created in North Vietnam had been extensively damaged by American bombardments and was hardly in a position to increase dramatically the supply of capital goods for industrial development in the South. In the second place, the existence of artificially high consumption standards in South Vietnam and the possibility of rising political instability if these were reduced too far following the withdrawal of US aid, meant that it would not be advisable to base development strategy upon the traditional 'heavy industry priority' model which had been favoured by the Democratic Republic of Vietnam.[12] In view of the previous southern dependence on imported consumer goods, efforts would now have to focus on the development of agriculture and light industry in order to satisfy the basic consumer needs of the population. The large urban populations, in particular, had depended heavily on imported food during the war period (this applied to the North as well as the South) and it became imperative for the government, given the tremendous agricultural potential of the country, to achieve self-sufficiency in food in order to conserve valuable foreign exchange. Moreover, the agricultural sector could eventually supply raw materials to the industrial sector and, directly or indirectly, provide the basis for greatly increased export income.

A further important reason for a shift in the development strategy was the change, after 1975, in the nature and extent of external resources available to the country as a whole. During the war, North Vietnam, like the South, had been supported to a considerable extent by foreign aid injections, primarily from China and the Soviet Union. Following the end of the war in the South, aid from China began to be wound down (it ceased altogether in 1978) and economic assistance from the Soviet Union, which had previously been chiefly in the form of grants, was switched to loans. The grants and subsidies previously accorded to South Vietnam were, of course, almost completely eliminated. Vietnam was now faced with the prospect of having increasingly to find domestic sources of accumulation where in the past it had relied to a large extent on external ones. In view of the extensive wartime destruction of industry in the North and the heavy dependence of the tiny southern industrial sector upon external resources, the chief possibility for acquiring domestic surpluses for accumulation lay in agriculture, particularly in the Mekong delta which was a traditional surplus-producing area.

The 1976–80 national five year plan, therefore, represented a shift in emphasis of the economic strategy away from the priority previously given in the DRV to the development of an independent capital goods producing sector and towards a policy under which agricultural development was stressed *as a means* of achieving eventual industrialisation. This shift in emphasis is reflected in statements such as the one by Pham Hung (member of the Political Bureau) at the IVth Party Congress in December 1976[13] that:

the primary task of the second 5-year plan is to highly concentrate the forces of the entire country and all branches and echelons on developing all latent potentials concerning labour, land and material bases to bring about a giant leap forward in agricultural development, considering production of grain and food the main concern . . .

Similarly, an article in the Party journal *Tap Chi Cong San*, in September 1977, argued that in the past the leadership had failed to see the essential connection between industry and agriculture and had concentrated one-sidedly on developing industry;[14] instead industrial development should be made to serve the collectivisation movement in agriculture.[15]

One should not overestimate the importance of this shift in emphasis, however. The growing conflict with China and military involvement along the Cambodian border from 1975 onwards meant that Vietnamese leaders were anxious to push ahead with modernisation of the economy as rapidly as possible and this may help to explain the timidity of the initial move away from the more traditional policy. The share of investment in the national income remained high throughout the period 1976–80 at about 18–19 per cent, figures which are close to or even higher than those of the 3-year and first 5-year plans, and investment in heavy industry in fact rose as a share of national income between 1975 and 1979.[16] Moreover, the criticism of the second 5-year plan (1976–80), which emerged after its breakdown, suggested that too much stress was placed on grandiose schemes:[17] the third 5-year plan, 1981–5, ratified at the Vth Party Congress held in March 1982, was to focus instead on smaller and more practical projects in industry. The main emphases of the third plan were to be on agriculture, consumer goods industries (especially textiles and paper), oil and energy, exports and communications.[18] Since the collapse of the second 5-year plan and the introduction instead in 1979–80 of a number of reforms aimed at overcoming a crisis in the national economy, the change in direction of the development strategy, which began in a small and insufficient way in 1975–6, has been carried much further. In part these reforms were a response to a developing crisis in the transformation of agriculture in the North.[19] It will be argued below, however, that this change of direction was also based upon increasing recognition of the specific conditions existing in South Vietnamese agriculture and the effects these were having on the economy as a whole.

Southern Agriculture 1960–75

In the quest for food self-sufficiency, attention inevitably turned to the agricultural potential of South Vietnam, especially the Mekong River delta. A number of factors lay behind this, not least of which were the fairly high land–labour ratio in the delta area and the possibilities provided by areas of abandoned and previously uncultivated land.[20] Most of these uncultivated lands required considerable preparation before they could be brought into production — simply abandoned land had often reverted to jungle, while some lands held more serious obstacles to development: unexploded ordnance, chemical residues etc. Apart from the new areas which could be opened up for cultivation in the South, it appeared that output of a number of key agricultural products, which had suffered through war damage and lack of investment in the rural sector, could be rapidly increased.

Table 18.1 gives data on output of selected agricultural products in the period 1960–74.[21] The picture presented in this table differs according to crop, but for most it is a picture of expanding output during the early 1960s, followed by stagnation and/or decline through the late 1960s — the period of escalation of the war — and then recovery, sometimes dramatic, following the American troop withdrawal and signing of the Paris Peace Accords in early 1973. In the case of rubber, which is concentrated in areas which were heavily affected by the fighting and which requires substantial investment and long gestation periods, the decline in output was marked and continuous. In the case of rice, by far the most important crop, the recovery of output began slightly earlier than for other crops. This is probably due to two main factors: firstly, the land reform carried out by the National Liberation Front had affected the majority of farmers by 1968 (later it was ratified by the Thieu regime between 1970 and 1973, in effect recognising that the NLF had emerged victorious in the struggle over land tenure conditions in the country-side and attempting to defuse the issue by eliminating most remaining landlord claims to ownership); secondly, and relatedly, the spread of 'green revolution' techniques and inputs financed by American aid.[22] An alternative explanation is that government access to rural areas improved after 1968, as the war shifted from its guerrilla phase to more conventional warfare, and higher output statistics would in that case partly reflect better information.

As will be argued below, the issue of conditions of land tenure in South Vietnam was crucial to the success or otherwise of the policies adopted by the new socialist regime after 1975 and so it is worth taking some space to describe the changing situation during the years of the previous regime — especially as it bears on the question of surplus production and appropriation.

Southern Vietnam had, like the North, a long history of revolutionary activity prior to the French departure in 1954. Under direct French colonial rule from the 1860s (unlike the Centre and North which were protectorates), the peasants of Nam Bo (the former Cochinchina) experienced probably the most inequitable distribution of land in the whole country. In the Mekong delta, particularly its western part, French construction of irrigation and drainage works accelerated the opening up of land for cultivation and although in principle land could belong to those who first cultivated

Table 18.1: Agricultural Output and Yields 1960–74

Year	Paddy m.t.	Paddy t/ha	Rubber 000t	Rubber t/ha	Sweet Potato 000t	Cassava 000t	Maize 000t	Soy-bean 000t	Pea-nuts 000t	Tobacco 000t	Sugar Cane 000t
1960	4.9	2.14	77	.70	221	219	27	2.8	24	8.1	999
1961	4.6	2.10	78	.61	236	254	32	3.9	28	8.4	932
1962	5.2	2.10	78	.57	273	313	38	3.9	28	7.6	872
1963	5.3	2.10	76	.53	300	389	36	4.5	32	6.8	964
1964	5.2	2.03	74	.55	301	289	46	4.0	36	7.2	1055
1965	4.8	1.99	65	.50	278	236	44	4.3	32	7.6	1092
1966	4.3	1.89	49	.39	246	290	35	7.5	34	6.9	935
1967	4.7	2.04	42	.36	254	261	33	5.6	32	7.8	769
1968	4.4	1.82	34	.32	234	260	32	7.4	34	7.6	426
1969	5.1	2.10	28	.27	225	233	30	5.9	32	7.8	321
1970	5.7	2.27	33	.31	219	215	31	7.4	34	8.4	335
1971	6.3	2.41	37	.34	230	270	34	8.4	37	8.6	340
1972	6.3	2.35	20	.24	240	247	41	7.1	38	8.8	331
1973	7.0	2.48	19	.28	279	379	50	10.6	45	10.3	529
1974	7.1	2.48	21	.31	343	447	106	—	—	—	903

Source: Le Khoa *et al.*, (1979).

it, in practice a few wealthy French and Vietnamese were able to manipulate the legal and bureaucratic system to gain control of large estates.[23] A system of surplus appropriation through rent grew up and led to the Mekong delta becoming a large rice exporting region. The export of rice imposed a heavy burden upon the peasantry: there is some evidence to suggest that the *per capita* availability of rice for peasant consumption began to fall at about the time of World War I[24] while exports continued to rise.

The system of land tenure under the French played no small part in this relative immiserisation of the peasantry (by the Great Depression there is little doubt that this had become absolute immiserisation as *per capita* consumption fell below the subsistence minimum) since neither tenant nor landlord held any interest in raising productivity of the land through investment. Insecurity of tenure and lack of access to investible surpluses were the reasons in the case of the peasant cultivators, while the non-cultivating land-owner was concerned only with the distribution of the product, not with its production.

By the end of the First Indochina War, however, the Viet Minh (led by the Communist Party) controlled a substantial portion of the countryside and carried out a land reform, forcing most of the larger owners to flee to urban centres. Following American intervention to maintain President Ngo Dinh Diem in power and to prevent the reunification of the country scheduled for 1956 under the Geneva Agreement, the South Vietnamese government undertook its own land reform. Diem's programme, in effect, attempted to reverse the Viet Minh reform since it imposed a very high ceiling of 115 hectares on individual landholdings and there were many loopholes allowing landowners to maintain even larger holdings.[25]

The Viet Minh presence in the countryside, however, prevented any return to the pre-1946 situation and, after the formation of the National Liberation Front in 1960, more and more areas of the country fell out of government control. In the many regions in which the NLF had influence, land was either distributed to the cultivators or, in view of the Front's efforts to gain acquiescence of the smaller, 'patriotic' landlords, rents were maintained but reduced well below the government's legal maximum of 25 per cent. Sansom found that in the areas which were most securely controlled by the government, not only did large landowners retain control of their land, but rents were often well in excess of the legal maximum.[26]

Since the political support of the South Vietnamese regime lay in large measure with the class of landlords, the government and also the American advisers for the most part refused to recognise that land tenure was a factor in Communist successes. But after the Tet Offensive of 1968, which inflicted heavy blows on US and government morale, the Thieu regime began its attempt to defuse the whole issue by distributing 'Land to the Tillers'. This programme, which was eventually carried out between 1970 and 1973 distributed land to tenant cultivators free, up to a maximum of 3 hectares in the Mekong delta and 1 hectare in Central Vietnam where population pressure was much greater.

Title to the land given in various Viet Minh and NLF land distributions was finally recognised by the Thieu government. Landlords were compensated mainly from US funds. By this time, though, land ownership had become a relatively unprofitable source of income for most wealthy Vietnamese. As Gareth Porter points out, there had been a major shift in the concentration of wealth towards the commercial classes and corrupt officialdom.[27] Thieu's reform therefore encountered little resistance from the government's supporters, a reflection of the fundamental change in the balance of power already brought about by the revolution in the countryside. (It must be emphasised, however, that Thieu's reform did not have much effect in Central Vietnam where landownership remained in contention until the end of the war. The reasons for this have not yet been fully ascertained, but possible contributing factors are the more egalitarian distribution of land occupancy, the greater preponderance of small landlords whom the NLF was anxious not to antagonise (60 per cent of landlords were themselves full-time farmers) and the greater proportion of communal land together with lack of consensus about how it should be distributed and who should be compensated.[28])

In the longer run these changes in the rural balance of power did not necessarily work to the advantage of the revolution — at least as the Vietnamese leaders perceived the course of the revolution in the mid- to late-1970s. The land reform in North Vietnam had been followed fairly quickly by a movement towards collectivisation, ostensibly to prevent the emergence of capitalist agriculture and to take advantage of the productivity benefits of reorganisation of labour and specialisation. In the Mekong River delta area of South Vietnam, on the other hand, the distribution of land to individual families took place over a much longer period than in the North and in some cases was completed as long as 30 years before the ultimate military defeat of the anti-revolutionary forces. The consequences of this, both for the programme of socialist transformation after 1975 and for the development of production in agriculture were profound.

Figure 18.1 gives some indication of the extent to which the distribution of land ownership in the Mekong delta had changed. The picture of increased equality following the combined NLF and Thieu land reforms is reinforced by the fact that insecurity of tenure had been eliminated after 1975. Only 23 per cent of the population surveyed in 1978 fell into the category of farm labourer (which includes those owning insufficient land to maintain their families by farming alone).[29] Thus the redistribution of land before 1975 would appear, on the basis of the limited data available, to have produced a much more egalitarian distribution of land under which the majority of farmers in the delta have shifted into a 'middle' rather than 'poor' peasant category.

Alongside this shift in land distribution came a change in the methods of cultivation — use of mechanisation and modern inputs increased. The primary reasons for this are probably that: (a) the reductions in rent meant that for the first time some investible surpluses became available to the peasants themselves; (b) shortages of labour (both family and wage labour) were brought about by the disappearance of adult males into the armed forces of both sides or by population outflow to the urban areas;[30] (c) American aid programmes in agriculture were aimed at increasing the use of modern inputs such as high yielding varieties, chemical fertilisers and insecticides.

Mechanisation resulting from these combined pressures and inducements was not uniform. According to Sansom,[31] it was concentrated mainly in the upper delta where natural conditions allowed individual farmers more opportunities to make use of high yielding varieties (HYV) and multiple cropping techniques. Nevertheless, by 1972–3 about a third of the cultivated area had been sown to HYV rice, large numbers of tractors and other farm machines had been imported (those still in operation by 1978 were considered sufficient for basic soil preparation and irrigation requirements of the delta, provided they could be fully utilised and properly maintained[32]) and most farmers had become accustomed to using chemical fertilisers.[33] The extent of mechanisation is important because it is one of the chief areas of contrast between the Mekong delta in 1975 and North Vietnam in 1959 when collectivisation began there. Whereas in the latter

Figure 18.1: Lorenz Curves Showing Distribution of Land Ownership in the Mekong River Delta

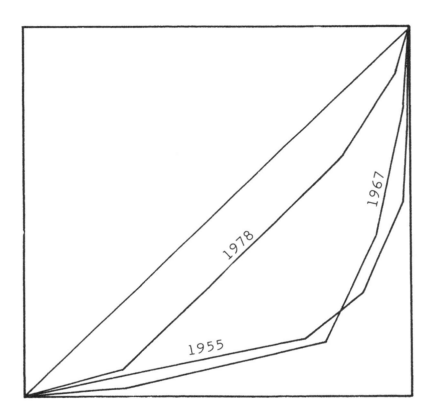

Note: Data for 1955 and 1967 are based on titles to land recognised by the Diem/Thieu governments and, especially those for 1967, do not reflect actual tenure conditions.
Source: Le Khoa *et al.*, (1979), pp. 124, 126–8; Tran Huu Quang (1982), p. 32.

case substantial improvements in yields had been made possible by the collective reorganisation of labour, in the Mekong delta peasants were already able to achieve yield increases via individually owned labour-*saving* devices. The immediate economic benefits of collectivisation would not have been so apparent to these peasants as they were to their much poorer, unmechanised colleagues in the North.

It has often been said that the land reforms carried out in places like Taiwan and South Korea and the relatively equal distribution of land in Japan formed the basis for the extraordinarily high productivity of peasant rice cultivation in those countries. It seems that a similar process was in the making in South Vietnam in the early 1970s. In contrast to the experience of the first three countries, however, the changed land tenure situation in Vietnam came about through revolutionary pressure, in the face of protracted resistance from landlords and their political allies. The paradox of this revolutionary development is that, in the Mekong delta at least, it has created the conditions for the development of a strong, privately based agricultural system. Therefore, the problem facing new Vietnamese policy makers in 1975 was not only one of how to continue to develop South Vietnamese agricultural *production* in the face of acute shortages of imported inputs, but also one of how to maintain the momentum of social and political change in order to achieve a further *transformation of social relations* in a socialist direction.

Southern Agriculture after 1975

Following the establishment of a socialist regime in the South, the key to agricultural development was seen, as in the North after 1955, to lie in the construction of large-scale collective and state farms. The main form of accumulation would come about via utilisation of large existing labour reserves to carry out major construction works of clearing and reclaiming land, irrigation systems, roads and other necessary infrastructure for the new agricultural areas. In the delta itself, the reorganisation of labour through collectivisation would release workers for the important task of rebuilding and repairing an extensive system of irrigation and transport canals. Because of the low-lying terrain of the delta (throughout its area is is rarely more than 2 metres above sea level) and the problem of saline water from the tides flowing up-river during the dry season, the scale of irrigation works required to make double cropping feasible in the lower delta area was, rightly, thought to require state or collective efforts and could not be left to individual farmers irrigating their own fields. Since irrigation was the pre-condition for further modernisation of agricultural techniques, the organisation of labour on a collective basis was seen as the only means whereby the foundation could be laid for the building of 'large scale socialist production' throughout the country.

The principle that collectivisation should be voluntary was in operation, however, and so the process of collectivisation was envisaged as a fairly long one, extending into the early 1980s. At this stage, it was assumed in official pronouncements that collective and state-owned agriculture would prove to be inherently superior in providing *economic* benefits as well as political benefits to the peasantry. The length of time required to complete the process of collectivisation was seen as merely a reflection of the extra-difficult conditions encountered in the South — the problems of reclaiming land, of sorting out conflicting claims to land brought about by the chaos of wartime, of the acute shortages of essential inputs and consumer goods engendered by the US withdrawal. Due recognition was given to the fact that the large number of relatively wealthy peasants in the delta would be unwilling to join collective units if it would put them at a disadvantage economically.

In the meantime, efforts were made to go ahead with the construction of state and collective farms in the New Economic Zones (NEZs). These included areas in the vicinity of Ho Chi Minh City which had been heavily bombed and defoliated during the war as well as more remote, mountainous and war-ravaged terrain along the Cambodian border and in the Central highlands. The NEZs were, for the most part, to be highly specialised units producing, for example, rice in the Mekong delta, cotton in the drier areas of Thuan Hai and Phu Khanh provinces, coffee and tea in the foothills of Song Be and Tay Ninh, sugar in Tay Ninh, etc.

By 1980, some 170–80[34] state farms had been established in the South. Rubber production, which was wholly concentrated in these farms, had increased to over 40,000 tonnes in 1978 and 1979[35] compared with the considerably lower outputs of the final years of the Thieu regime (see Table 18.1). However, the state farms experienced a number of problems similar to those experienced in North Vietnam, namely, a tendency to 'go for quantity and breadth rather than intensive cultivation'.[36] Crop and livestock yields tended to be low, reclaimed land was often wasted and reverted to scrub and the standard of living of state farm employees was regarded as 'not good'.[37]

Similar tales were told of the cooperative farms established under the NEZ programme. At first there was a high rate of return to urban areas by former residents who had emigrated to the NEZs.

For many, this would have entailed a return to acute economic insecurity which suggests that life, in some of the NEZs at least, must have been hard. Later, after the armed forces and 'youth brigades' were brought in to clear land and establish basic infrastructure, there was more success in holding people. But in the former free fire zone encircling Ho Chi Minh City, only a few had, by the end of 1979, achieved reasonably good income levels and most were beset with problems, including political problems.[38] Further away, in Tay Ninh and other provinces near the Cambodian border, many NEZs had to be abandoned during the war with Pol Pot.[39] Thus the overall record of the NEZs in achieving rapid expansion of output of food, import-substituting raw materials for industry or export crops is uncertain.[40]

Possibly a more serious *long-term* problem for the transformation of southern agriculture has been the apparent resistance of Mekong delta peasants to joining production collectives and agricultural cooperatives. While the collectivisation programme went ahead quite smoothly in the provinces of Central Vietnam, this was not the case in the provinces of the Mekong delta.[41] Part of the reason for this difference may be that, climatic conditions being much more uncertain in the Central provinces, peasants stood to gain more by being cushioned by the collective against the consequences of crop losses which could be economically disastrous for individual farmers.

A *Nhan Dan* article[42] of 27 June 1978 also suggested that the relatively poor peasantry of Trung Bo (Central provinces), in contrast to their wealthier compatriots of the Mekong delta, lacked machinery and draught animals and could benefit greatly from collectivised ownership of these means of production. There was also less differentiation of plot size in the Trung Bo provinces as well as a much higher proportion of wasteland and public land. The same article suggested that commodity production (i.e., production for the market) was much further advanced in Nam Bo and that not only did the predominant strata of middle to rich peasants own their own means of production (see above), but they had extensive links with commerce, industry, transport and communications (which they often ran as sideline operations, primarily for profit). While the article goes on to attribute the major problems experienced in collectivising Mekong delta agriculture to factors such as a lack of meticulous preparation or tight management, the clear implication is that the source of the difficulty lies much deeper in the type of *production relations* which had been developing in the delta zone over 30 years or more.

In other words, the initial advantages of collectivisation to Northern and Central Vietnamese peasants lay in their ability to mobilise a plentiful labour supply in an economy where both land and capital were extremely scarce and in a situation where even the wealthier peasants stood to gain more than they would lose in the redistribution of income and assets that the policy implied.[43] The greater mechanisation of Mekong delta farming and more abundant land, combined with the higher development of market relations outlined in the previous section meant that such advantages were absent. In fact the attempt to implement collectivisation in the South occurred simultaneously with the beginnings of an investigation in the North into the limitations of the collectivisation so far achieved and possible ways of improving the productivity of cooperative agriculture. In the context of these discussions, the difficulties being experienced in the Mekong area brought sharply into focus the importance of labour accumulation projects in the early phase of collectivisation, whereas under the different conditions of the South, such methods might not be the most appropriate. The experience of the Vietnamese leadership up to 1976 had been based essentially on northern conditions. A very high proportion of those Party members and administrators with extensive southern experience had been killed under the American Phoenix programme (which involved systematic assassination of collaborators with the NLF), and so it is not surprising that the leadership seriously underestimated the depth and importance of the social and economic changes which had taken place on the ground in the Mekong delta.

It was some time, therefore, before the difficulties of collectivisation in the Mekong delta were to lead to any new approach to the problem of agricultural production as a whole. In mid-1978 a crisis was developing in several areas of the economy, but particularly in agricultural production and distribution.[44] The response was to intensify the efforts to create a system of 'large-scale socialist production'. A movement was launched to attempt the completion of agricultural collectivisation in southern Vietnam by 1980; that is, in less than two years. Simultaneously, there was a clamp-down on the chiefly ethnic Chinese merchants, concentrated in Cholon (the Chinese quarter of Ho Chi Minh City). The aims of these measures were twofold: to achieve a large increase in agricultural output and, even more importantly, to break the system of production for the private market which was then a highly concentrated affair with a large number of village-based rice merchants locked into the commercial networks of several big Cholon companies. The campaign was construed quite frankly as one of increasing the ability of the state to mobilise agricultural surpluses (which were then being consumed at home or siphoned off by the merchants) in order to increase the sources of finance for accumulation. Vo Chi Cong, member of the Party Political Bureau in charge of southern agriculture, said in a speech in April 1979 that whereas tax collected on individual landholdings amounted to only 10 per cent of the harvest, with cooperativisation the share procured by the state could be raised to 30–40 per cent.[45] A great deal of urgency was given to the matter by the increasingly threatening international situation in 1978 and early 1979 — the escalation of the Cambodian conflict and the growing likelihood of a direct Chinese attack. The prospect of further prolonged military expenditures in a situation of reduced foreign aid availability provided the rationale and motivation for an attempt to increase sharply the rate of accumulation from domestic sources.

A discussion of the campaign can be found in the article by Nyland.[46] It is sufficient here to suggest that it was successful in driving out of business (and often out of the country) the major Mekong delta rice traders and their cohorts. However, it did not necessarily solve the twin problems then facing the government — how to increase the total volume of agricultural production and how to siphon off the marketed surplus in such a way that not only would there be enough to meet the requirements of the urban and export sectors, but there would be greater social (as opposed to private) control over this marketed surplus. Table 18.2 shows that 1978 was the worst year of all as far as rice production levels were concerned and, while these began to recover during 1979, the all-important procurement by the state continued to decline.

Table 18.3 illustrates the way in which declining yields occurred mainly in North Vietnam and the Central provinces of South Vietnam. This picture is consistent with the explanation that output was chiefly affected by poor climatic conditions — the Red River delta and the central coastal areas are both more susceptible to crop loss due to drought, typhoons and flooding than the more stable Mekong delta. But the figures also show that, in spite of strenuous efforts to open up new lands and reclaim abandoned and fallow lands in order more fully to utilise the labour resources of the South,

Table 18.2: Production of Foodgrains and Official Procurement, 1975–9

	All foodgrains (paddy equivalent) 000t	Rice 000t	Official Procurement 000t
1975	11,591.8	10,538.9	a
1976	13,510.0	11,866.0	a
1977	12,889.8	10,885.1	1,840.0
1978	12,902.9	10,040.4	1,590.0
1979	13,727.0	10,758.4	1,402.0

Note: 'a' not available.
Sources: So Lieu Thong Ke (1980), p. 55; IMF (1982), p. 13.

the area sown to paddy had increased by less than 100,000 hectares over the four-year period, of which a mere 7,000 hectares were in the Mekong delta.[47] By contrast, the North and Centre of the country, with their far greater pressures of population on land, were able to expand their paddy area much more. The collectivisation drive in the Mekong delta certainly did not have the expected short-term effects on either output or surplus appropriation. While it is impossible to separate the actual effects from those induced by independent variables such as the weather or war damage, the official criticism of rapid collectivisation which began to emerge in mid-1979 suggests that it might even have been counter-productive.[48]

Table 18.3: Paddy Production, Area and Yields by Region, 1976 and 1979

	Production 000 tonnes		Area Sown 000 ha		Yields per Crop tonnes/ha		Share of Total Output %	
	1976	1979	1976	1979	1976	1979	1976	1979
Total	11866	10758	5313	5484	2.23	1.96	100.0	100.0
North Vietnam	5058	4319	2245	2317	2.25	1.86	42.6	40.1
South Vietnam	6806	6439	3068	3166	2.22	2.03	57.3	59.8
of which:								
Nam Bo	4686	4369	2068	2075	2.27	2.10	39.5	40.6
Trung Bo[a]	2122	2070	1000	1091	2.12	1.90	17.9	19.2

Note: 'a' includes all of Binh Tri Thien province, part of which lies north of the 17th parallel.
Source: So Lieu Thong Ke (1980), pp. 58–9.

The crisis in agricultural production of 1977–80 was accompanied by declining output and availability of certain agricultural inputs and basic manufactured consumer goods. The causes of these shortages lay partly in the decline of agricultural output itself, partly in the increasing diversion of limited domestic and external resources to defence, partly in the coincidence of these with a number of cumulative problems in the management and planning of the economy. Of particular importance were the destruction of the North Vietnamese apatite plant by the Chinese in February 1979 and other war damage, as well as falls in coal and textile production caused by the exodus of ethnic Chinese workers. Hence one result of the failure of agriculture, and particularly southern agriculture, to achieve a big increase in output and surplus mobilisation was to threaten a cumulative process of declining production in the economy as a whole.

The Sixth Plenum of the Party Central Committee, meeting in August and September 1979, adopted new policies aimed at overcoming this economic crisis. As far as South Vietnamese agriculture was concerned, the effects of the changed direction began to be felt in 1980 with the effective abandonment of the collectivisation drive and with the implementation of new marketing arrangements aimed at increasing the supply of goods by using individual incentives and the market mechanism, at the same time attempting gradually to increase the state's surplus appropriation out of the enlarged flow of goods.

The reforms, as they affected the major portion of Mekong delta peasants, involved the introduction of direct contracting between individual farmers and the state in which the state undertook to supply inputs in return for a proportion of the harvest over and above obligatory quota sales. These above-quota sales can be made at a negotiated price which is closer to (but still below) the price obtainable on the free market. Agricultural taxes and obligatory sales (at state prices) were fixed for a five-year period. One of the major features of the reforms was a change in the price structure in mid- to late-1981, the purpose being to bring state prices closer to those prevailing in the free market, to bring prices in the North closer to the higher prices in the South and to offset the effects of a devaluation of the Dong.

There is insufficient data available at this stage, and the reforms have not been operating long enough, to be able to make any accurate assessment of their effects. Nor is it in any case easy to quantify the effects on output of such diverse factors as weather, relative peace (albeit highly mobilised for the possibility of war), economic reforms, etc. However, there have been substantial improvements in both output and state procurement since 1980 and the Vietnamese achieved self-sufficiency in food grains for the first time since before World War II in 1983.[49] Table 18.4 gives a summary of the situation before and after the reforms based on the data available so far. Vietnamese officials do regard the improved agricultural performance of the 1980s as a result of the new policies.[50] The use of individual incentives and market forces as economic levers is thus likely to be continued in the future — in spite of some extension of controls and political pressure to limit the scope of the reforms.

It should not be thought, however, that the extended role given to the market and slowing down of the collectivisation process necessarily represent a pulling back from the attempt to combine economic construction with the transformation of the social relations of production. On the contrary, the evidence of this paper seems to suggest that the conditions of agricultural development in South Vietnam were such that the effort to speed up the process of transformation (collectivisation) prematurely was at worst detrimental to and at best unhelpful to the process of economic construction. The 'liberalisation' of the economy, on the other hand, by allowing an improvement in agricultural output may have improved the *opportunities* for achieving an eventual socialist transformation. On the economic front this would be the result of increasing scope for the state to gain control over the agricultural surplus and on the political front it would be brought about by the elimination of a potentially destabilising situation of shortages of food and other consumer goods in which people would turn increasingly to the black market and social inequalities would be exacerbated. At the same time, it is likely that any tendencies for market forces to lead to increased social differentiation and private capital accumulation will be monitored carefully and severely restricted.[51]

The operation of the law of value (market forces) is not in itself an indication of a return to capitalism since it is the transformation of the relations of *production*, the extent of social ownership and control over the means of production, which is at issue.[52] In the case of South Vietnamese agriculture however, we have seen that private ownership and control of the means of production as well as the development of commodity relations were at a more advanced stage in 1975 than they were in North Vietnam in 1954. The problem for

Table 18.4: Foodgrain Production and Official Transactions 1975–83

	1975	1976	1977	1978	1979	1980	1981	1982	1983
1. Total foodgrain production (mill.t.)	11.6	13.6	12.9	12.9	13.7	14.4	15.0	16.6	16.7
2. Total domestic procurement (mill.t.)	1.69	2.03	1.84	1.59	1.40	2.01	2.50	2.90	3.75
of which:									
Agricultural tax			1.18	0.52	0.67	0.90	0.91	)	3.37
Quota sales			0.66	1.06	0.69	0.86	0.86	)	
Negotiated sales			0	0	0.04	0.24	0.73		0.38
2 as a share of 1 (%)	15	15	14	12	10	14	17	17	22

Sources: IMF (1982), p. 13; So Lieu Thong Ke (1979), p. 61; *Far Eastern Economic Review*, 10 February 1983, 2 February 1984.

the new regime, therefore, has been one of how to increase the socialisation of production relations in these very different conditions without jeopardising the transition towards an advanced agro-industrial economy. The solution which was adopted in the North, and which remained virtually unaltered for 20 years, was a rather rapid collectivisation of the means of production in agriculture, in emulation of the experience of most other socialist countries. This is not necessarily the only means of transforming social relations, however, and in view of the peasant resistance in the Mekong delta to the attempt to copy the northern example, it would also seem to be not necessarily the best. The policies adopted after 1979–80 were aimed at increasing the level of socialisation of production and distribution by creating a genuinely national economic system (breaking down the essential autarchy of peasant household production through increasing state control over investible surpluses, supplies of necessary inputs and consumer goods, creation of specialised economic zones and building up of district and provincial, as opposed to smaller village-based, industrial complexes). Ultimately, as the economy becomes increasingly sophisticated, cooperative production relations should be expanded and the relative importance of the individual economy should then diminish.

It is not possible to discuss the merits of this view in any depth here, but it is certainly a very different conception of how a socialist economy should be created to that expounded, for example, by Le Duan in 1974[53] in which he argued that collectivisation was a precondition for the construction of large-scale socialist production in agriculture. The alternative position, which would appear to have gained ascendancy since 1979, is that cooperatives cannot be consolidated in the absence of industrialisation, with an advanced division of labour. At the present stage, 'the peasant has not yet been bound firmly to collective production by an economic power such that apart from the collective he could not exist'[54] — put another way, the level of technology prevailing in Vietnam is not such that an industrial division of labour which necessarily socialises production is possible. In this essay I have tried to show that the very strength of individual peasant production in the Mekong delta and the overall importance of that region to the process of economic construction in Vietnam has been one of the key factors in bringing about this changed conception of the socialist transformation process.

Notes

1. See, for example, Le Vinh (1977).
2. Le Khoa *et al.* (1979), pp. 116–18, 215.
3. Ibid., pp. 116–18.
4. Calculated from data in ibid., p. 113.
5. Ibid., p. 33.
6. Moody (1975), pp. 100–1.
7. One estimate from the 1970s put the annual value of imported agricultural inputs at 156 million dollars, of which 100 m. consisted of fertiliser (IBRD (1974), p. iii).
8. National Bank of Vietnam (1972).
9. In May 1975 Vietnam was added to country Group Z in the US export control classification which imposes a general trade embargo. The embargo was strengthened after the 1979 Vietnamese invasion of Cambodia which the US used as a pretext to pressure its allies (e.g., Australia's conservative government) to halt economic aid to Vietnam (at the same time apparently abhorring the Pol Pot regime which nevertheless continued to received aid, through western aid agencies in Thailand). The US have also made fairly successful efforts to prevent multilateral aid agencies lending to Vietnam — see *Far Eastern Economic Review* (1980, 1981).
10. Amounting on average to 30 per cent of GNP (Asian Development Bank, (1971), pp. 617–18.).
11. Calculated from data in Chi Do Pham (1976), p. 29.
12. See White (1982).
13. JPRS, 68992, p. 134.
14. JPRS, 70036, p. 10.
15. White (1982), p. 10, gives the example of the Thai Nguyen steel complex, built with Chinese aid, which imported nearly all its raw materials and exported its output to China, as a case of the type of industrial development on a scale which meant that it could have few short-term backward and forward linkages to the Vietnamese economy.
16. So Lieu Thong Ke (1979), p. 37; (1980), p. 41. See also Nguyen Tien Hung (1977), p. 108.
17. These are now described as 'subjectivist errors'. White (1982), p. 11, attributes this type of approach to the existence of 'Maoist' elements of influence on Vietnamese thinking about development strategy, but there are plenty of precedents in Soviet history also. The uniqueness of Maoism lies not in its investment policies or reliance on 'moral incentives', but in its attitude towards the peasantry *vis-à-vis* other revolutionary classes.
18. *Far Eastern Economic Review*, 29 January 1982.
19. See White (1982); Le Thu Y (1975).
20. The Stanford Research Institute (1968), Summary volume, p. 33, estimated the undeveloped arable area in 1965 as 20.2 per cent of the total land area, or nearly 3.5 million hectares (compared with the 1968 cultivated area of 2.3 m.ha.). Nguyen Ngoc Triu, Minister for Agriculture of the SRV, estimated in 1980 that half a million hectares in the South had been abandoned and left untilled, sometimes for a dozen years; JPRS, 76196, p. 56.
21. This data should be treated with even more caution than is usual for statistics from Third World countries on account of the war conditions prevailing in rural areas and the fact that government access to certain areas was uncertain. Government access to rural areas was at its lowest in the mid-1960s.
22. Callison (1974) found a significant increase in investment among recipients of Land-to-the-Tiller titles.

23. This history is documented in, among others, Ngo Vinh Long (1973) and Popkin (1979).

24. Norlund (1983).

25. Race (1972).

26. Sansom (1970), pp. 57, 69.

27. Porter (1976).

28. Burr (1976), pp. 131, 225 et seq.

29. Tran Huu Quang (1982), p. 32.

30. Sansom (1970), pp. 124–5. Shortages of animal draught power also developed during the war. Whether this was a cause or consequence of the adoption of mechanised draught power is unclear, but Trullinger (1980) cites cases of US troops deliberately shooting buffaloes in a village which was thought to be sympathetic to the NLF (p. 117).

31. Sansom (1970), p. 215.

32. Le Nhat Quang (1980), pp. 29, 32.

33. Imported fertilisers rose from an annual average of 96,000 tonnes per annum in 1955–62 to 207,000 tonnes p.a. in 1963–7 and 323,000 tonnes p.a. in 1968–73 (Le Khoa *et al.* (1979), p. 189). For data on the area sown to HYV rice, see Burr (1976), p. 177. The increase was from only 500 ha. in 1967–8 to 835,000 ha. in 1972–3.

34. The lack of precision is in the sources. *Nhan Dan* in January 1980 gives the number as 174, in April 1980 as 181 and in October 1980 as 176. The fluctuations are possibly due to new areas being opened up at the same time as others were abandoned — see JPRS, 75301, 75637, 76867.

35. So Lieu Thong Ke (1980), p. 68.

36. JPRS, 75301, p. 59.

37. JPRS, 76867, p. 38; also JPRS, 75858, pp. 46–7, where, for example, rice yields in NEZ farms were put at under one tonne per hectare.

38. Author's trip notes, December 1979.

39. An estimated three-quarters of a million refugees, about one-half of them from Cambodia itself, added to the economic and social problems in the border areas.

40. Five years after the end of the war, about three quarters of a million people had left Ho Chi Minh City for the rural areas — either to the NEZs or to their villages of origin. This was considered to be well below the government's target rate of departure (author's trip notes).

41. See, for example, *Nhan Dan*, 27 June 1978 (JPRS, 71776, p. 43) and 29 April 1980 (JPRS, 75723, p. 11).

42. JPRS, 71776.

43. Note that most of the conflict in North Vietnam arose over the initial Land Reform in which large landlords and rich peasants had their land expropriated, and *not* over the collectivisation policy.

44. Real GDP growth rate was falling below population growth rate in 1977–8 and agricultural production fell by 5 per cent in 1977 and did not grow in 1978 (IMF (1982), p. iv).

45. Cited in White (1982), p. 19.

46. Nyland (1981).

47. One of the referees of this paper suggested that the greater decline in yields for the North and Centre might simply be due to the greater degree of collectivisation and lack of efficiency of this type of farming. This is, however, hard to reconcile with the fact that (a) North Vietnam had been collectivised for some 16 years prior to 1976; (b) the crop yield of 2.25 tonnes/ha in 1976 is not very close to that of the mainly privately farmed Nam Bo region, but was achieved in more adverse climatic conditions and is the average for the whole area of the former DRV and not just the high-yielding regions; (c) per hectare per *year* yields would be much higher for both

North and Centre because, under the collective system, double cropping is far more widely practised.

48. In a fairly gloomy picture of agricultural development from 1976-9, there were, however, some important gains in secondary food and industrial crop production in the South. In particular there were fairly consistent increases in output of maize, cassava, soybeans and tobacco.

49. *Far Eastern Economic Review*, 10 February 1983.

50. Ibid.

51. See, for example, the introduction of tax reform and renewed clampdown on private 'speculators' in 1983.

52. This is extensively discussed in relation to Vietnam in Nyland (1981). See also Phan Le Phuong (1977).

53. In Le Duan and Pham Van Dong (1975), pp. 32-3.

54. Le Thu Y (1975), p. 19.

Bibliography

Burr, J.M. 'Land-To-The-Tiller: Land Redistribution in South Vietnam 1970-3', PhD thesis, University of Oregon (1976).

Callison, C. Stuart, 'The Land-To-The-Tiller Program and Rural Resource Mobilisation in the Mekong Delta of South Vietnam', Papers in International Studies, Southeast Asia Series No. 34, Ohio University (1974).

Chi Do Pham, 'Inflationary Finance in Wartime South Vietnam, 1960-72' PhD thesis, University of Pennsylvania (1976).

Far Eastern Economic Review, 9 May, 19 September 1980; 1 May, 10 July 1981; 29 January 1982, 10 February 1983.

IBRD 'Current Economic Position and Prospects of the Republic of Vietnam' January 1974.

IMF 'Socialist Republic of Vietnam — Recent Economic Developments', May 1982.

JPRS 68992, Translations on Vietnam No. 1916;
    70036,   "   "   "   No. 1983;
    71776,   "   "   "   No. 2058;
    75301, Vietnam Report No. 2177;
    75637,   "   " No. 2187;
    75723,   "   " No. 2189;
    75858,   "   " No. 2193;
    76196,   "   " No. 2205;
    76867,   "   " No. 2230.

Le Duan and Pham Van Dong, *Towards Large-Scale Socialist Agricultural Production* (Hanoi, 1975).

Le Khoa *et al. Tinh Hinh Kinh Te Mien Nam 1955-75* (Economic Situation in Southern Vietnam 1955-75) (Ho Chi Minh City, 1979).

Le Nhat Quang, 'Mechanisation of Crop Growing in the Mekong River Delta' *Nghien Cuu Kinh Te* (1980) translated in JPRS, 76711, Vietnam Report No. 2222.

Le Thu Y 'Improve Planning in Agricultural Co-ops', *Nghien Cuu Kinh Te* (1975) translated in JPRS, 66638, Translations on Vietnam No. 1759.

Le Vinh, 'Grasp the Line of the Party and Advance to Building Large-Scale Socialist Production in Our Country', *Nghien Cuu Kinh Te* (1977) translated in JPRS, 69071, Translations on Vietnam.

Moody, Dale L. 'The Manufacturing Sector in the Republic of Vietnam', PhD thesis, University of Florida (1975).

National Bank of Vietnam, *Bulletin Economique*, no. 9-10, Saigon (1972).

Ngo Vinh Long, *Before the Revolution* (Cambridge, Mass., 1973).

Nguyen Tien Hung, G. *Economic Development of Socialist Vietnam 1955–80* (New York, 1977).

Nørlund, Irene, 'Rice Production in Colonial Vietnam 1900–1930', unpublished, Copenhagen (1983).

Nyland, Chris, 'Vietnam, the Plan/Market Contradiction and the Transition to Socialism', *Journal of Contemporary Asia*, vol. 11 (1981).

Phan Le Phuong, 'Several Thoughts Concerning the Application of Market Relations in Planning', *So Tay Giang Vien* (1977) translated in JPRS, 70675, Translations on Vietnam No. 2013.

Popkin, Samuel L. *The Rational Peasant* (Berkeley, Calif., 1979).

Porter, Gareth, 'Imperialism and Social Structure in Twentieth Century Vietnam', PhD thesis, Cornell University (1976).

Race, Jeffrey, *War Comes to Long An* (Berkeley, Calif., 1972).

Sansom, Robert L. *The Economics of Insurgency in the Mekong Delta of Vietnam* (Cambridge, Mass., 1970).

So Lieu Thong Ke (Statistical Data), Hanoi (1979).

So Lieu Thong Ke, (Statistical Data), Hanoi (1980).

Stanford Research Institute, *Land Reform in Vietnam* (Menlo Park, Calif., 1968).

Tran Huu Quang, 'Nhan dien co cau giai cap o nong thon dong bang song Cuu Long' (Identifying Class Structure in the Rural Areas of the Mekong Delta), *Nghien Cuu Kinh Te*, 1982.

Trullinger, James W. *Village At War* (New York and London, 1980).

White, Christine Pelzer, 'Debates in Vietnamese Development Policy', IDS Discussion Paper, University of Sussex (1982).

LIST OF CONTRIBUTORS

Alia Ahmad is Research Fellow at the Department of Economics, University of Lund, Sweden. She is the author of *Agricultural Stagnation under Population Pressure*. At present she is involved in research on the status of women and the population problem in Bangladesh.

Tom Alberts is a Swedish consultant in development planning. He has written *Agrarian Reform and Rural Poverty — A Case Study of Peru*.

Melanie Beresford was formerly Tutor in Politics at the University of Adelaide, South Australia, and is now studying for a PhD in Economics at the University of Cambridge, England. She has published articles on the politics of Australian economic policy, on Marxist economic theory and on Vietnam and is on the editorial board of *Journal of Contemporary Asia*.

Arne Bigsten is Associate Professor of Economics at the University of Gothenburg, Sweden. He is specialising in development economics and his publications include *Regional Inequality and Development. A Case Study of Kenya*; *Income Distribution and Development. Theory, Evidence and Policy*; and *Education and Income Determination in Kenya*.

Ester Boserup is an author and consultant on economic development problems. Her publications include *The Conditions of Agricultural Growth*, *Woman's Role in Economic Development*, and *Population and Technology*.

Steven Englander did his PhD thesis at Yale University (1981) on the role of agriculture research and technology transfer in agricultural development. He is now Chief of the Business Conditions Division of the Federal Reserve Bank of New York.

Ronald Findlay is Professor of Economics at Columbia University. He is the author of *Trade and Specialization*, *International Trade and Development Theory*, and of numerous journal articles, dealing mainly with problems of international trade and economic development.

Christer Gunnarsson is Lecturer in Economic History at the University of Lund, Sweden. He has specialised on studies on Third World economic history, with emphasis on West Africa and South East Asia.

Stefan Hedlund is Research Fellow of Economics at the University of Lund. He specialises in development economics and Soviet studies. He has recently published *Crisis in Soviet Agriculture*.

Edward Horesh is a Senior Lecturer in Economics and Director of Postgraduate Development Studies at the University of Bath. Recent publications have been on 'British Aid, Performance and Policy' and 'High Level Technical Assistance'.

Susan Joekes, formerly of the University of Bath, is a Research Fellow at the Institute of Development Studies at the University of Sussex, England. Her special interests are trade and employment in developing countries; most recently her work has been on the use of female labour in industrial development, with special reference to North Africa and East Asia.

Frank Kirwan is Industrial Economist, Scottish Development Agency, Glasgow. His publications include *Irish Economic Statistics* and a number of articles on migration.

Mats Lundahl is Associate Professor of Economics at the University of Lund. He has published *Peasants and Poverty: A Study of Haiti*; *Haiti: Man, Land and Markets*; *Migration and Change in Rural Zambia*; *Unequal Treatment: A Study in the Neoclassical Theory of Discrimination*, as well as journal articles on economic development and discrimination.

Per Lundborg is a Senior Research Fellow at the Department of Economics, University of Gothenburg, Sweden. His research deals mainly with agricultural trade relations between rich and poor countries.

Markos Mamalakis is Professor of Economics at The University of Wisconsin-Milwaukee. He is the author of *The Theory of Sectoral Clashes and Coalitions*, *The Minerals Theory of Growth* and of seven books and more than fifty articles dealing with economic development.

Lucian A. Msambichaka is Associate Professor and Director, Economic Research Bureau, University of Dar es Salaam, Tanzania. He specialises in agricultural development, public sector economics and food policy.

Benno J. Ndulu is Associate Professor of Economics, University of Dar es Salaam, Tanzania. He specialises in transport economics, economic policy and development.

Michael Roemer is Institute Fellow in the Harvard (University) Institute for International Development. A former Executive Director of the Institute, he is currently the resident Senior Economic Advisor to the Ministry of Finance and Planning in Nairobi, Kenya. His publications include *Economics of Development*; *The Appraisal of Development Projects*; *The Republic of Korea, 1945-1975: Growth and Structural Transformation*, and *Fishing for Growth: Export-led Development in Peru, 1950-1967*, as well as numerous articles on trade, industrialisation, planning, and development.

Ian Simpson is Senior Fellow in Agricultural Economics at the University of Leeds, UK. He has specialised in agricultural planning and policy in developing countries and undertaken assignments in a number of such countries as well as supervising doctoral theses in this field. He has a particular knowledge of the Sudan. He is the author of various papers on problems of agricultural development.

Bo Södersten is Professor of International Economics at the University of Lund. He has published *A Study of Economic Growth and International Trade* and *International Economics*, various books in Swedish and articles in professional journals. He is also a Member of Parliament.

INDEX

Aage, H. 339, 348
Adams, F.G. 36
Addo, N.O. 203
Adelman, I. 133, 150
Africa
  development in primary sector 6-8,
    56-65; obstacles to 58-62; per-
    spectives for 62-5
  Dutch disease in 234-5, 240, 242-3,
    245, 247-9
  see also Ghana; Kenya; Namibia;
    Tanzania
agricultural-industrial model 43-4, 49
agricultural-industrial-services model
  43-7
agriculture
  development, research and training
    27-9, 309-25
  Jordan 265-7
  Namibia 214-15
  see also Bangladesh; Brazil; Chile;
    cooperation; Ghana, cocoa;
    intervention; Kenya; land;
    Malaysia; Peru; Tanzania
Ahmad, A. 9-10, 35, 87, 103, 396
Ahulwalia, M.S. 54
aid
  food, Africa 60-2
  retarded growth and 237
  see also foreign
Alamgir, M. 103
Alberts, T. 26, 35, 291, 296, 307, 396
Allende, President 48, 211
Amin, S. 176, 203
Anderson 288
'Anglo-Italian' equation 226
Apeldoorn, G.J. van 287
Arab world, industrialisation 64
  see also Middle East
Arusha Declaration 352-4
Asia
  Dutch disease in 234-8; 240-3
  industrialisation 64
  migration from 253, 256
  population density 59

  see also Bangladesh; India; Indo-
    nesia; Korea; Malaysia; South
    Vietnam
Askhari, H. 278, 287
Asombang, W.W. 212, 216
Aulakh, H.S. 212, 216

Bacha, E.L. 149
Backman, B. 203
Baer, W. 134, 150
Bairoch, P. 36
Balassa, B. 251
Baldwin, R.E. 36, 181, 203, 219, 232
Ballesteros, M.A. 107, 115, 127-8
Bangladesh 10-11
  Dutch disease in 237
  migration from 253
  population growth and peasant
    economy 87-104; Boserup's
    theory 88-91; change in agricul-
    tural practices 93-5; demo-
    graphic responses 92-5; Mal-
    thusian theory 87-8; non-rural
    sector, role of 99-101; popula-
    tion growth, negative effect of
    95-9
Baran, P. 176
Barlow, C. 176-7
Barnum, H. 83, 278, 287
Barro, R.J. 269
Bauer, A. 119, 128
Bauer, P.T. 163, 176
Behrman, J.R. 36
Beinart, W. 288
Bennett, J.W. 347, 349
Beresford, M. 33, 370, 396
Bergsman, J. 134, 150
Berman, M.D. 348
Berry, S. 176, 203
Bertram, G. 297, 307
Bhagwati, J.N. 36, 269
Bigman, D. 288
Bigsten, A. 8-9, 66, 83, 396
Binswanger, H.P. 324
Birks, J.S. 255, 268-9

birth control 88, 92
Blomström, M. 36
Bolivia
    agriculture 304
    Dutch disease in 235-6
Bonin, J: 336-7, 339, 348
booming commodities *see* Dutch disease
Borde, J. 119, 128
Boserup, E. 6-7, 9, 35, 56, 65, 396
    population theory 88-93, 102-3
Bradley, M. 340, 348-9
Brazil 280, 320
    Dutch disease in 234-6
    income distribution and government policies 13-14, 131-52;
    agriculture-non-agriculture distribution 135-7; Computable General Equilibrium model 137-49
Brecher, R.A. 269
Brezhnev, L. 340
'broadest primary sector' 45-6
Brundenius 295
Bruton, H. 251
Bukharin, N. 333
'Bulldozer theory' 51
bureaucracy, rise of 118, 280-1
Burgstaller, A. 228
Burr, J.M. 393
Byres, T.J. 35

Callison, C.S. 392
Cameron, N.E. 348
capital
    accumulation 52-3, 95, 98-9
    'circulation' 224
    see also credit
Capstick, C.W. 278, 287
Cardoso, E.A. 132, 150
Caribbean
    see Dominican Republic; Jamaica
Carr, E.H. 277, 287
Casarosa, C. 219, 232
cash crops *see* agriculture
Caves, R.E. 36, 219, 232
cereals
    breeding 309-18
    see also rice
Chayanov, A.V. 156, 176
Chi Do Pham 392
Chile
    agricultural stagnation (1930-55) 11-13, 105-30, 282, 336

factor market imperfections: agricultural productivity and 123-7; credit market 119-23; labour market 113-19; land concentration 109-13; role of 108-9
    output and productivity 106-8
China 374
    migration from 164-5, 167, 175, 253
Clark, C. 1-2, 35, 44-5, 54, 279, 287
Clarke, M.G. 349
Clausen, A.W. 288
Clayton, E. 348
Cobb-Douglas production functions 137-8
cocoa farming, Ghana 182-3, 191-7
    employment categories 193-5
    government and 189, 195-7
    labour organisation 191-2
    peasant enclave 191
    remittances 195
collectives 331, 335-44
    in South Vietnam 379, 382-5, 391
Colombia, Dutch disease in 235, 245, 248
colonialism
    Malaysia 154-6, 162, 167
    South Vietnam 371, 373, 376
communes 331-5
comparative cost approach 158
composition and functions of primary sector 3-6, 43-55
    capital accumulation 52-3
    income distribution 49-52
    production 44-9
Computable General Equilibrium model, global, simulations for Brazil 137-49
construction sector, Middle East 257, 264-5
consumption linkages 197
cooperation, agricultural, and socialisation of labour 30-1, 329-51
    association 331, 344-6
    collectives 331, 335-44, 379, 382-5, 391
    communes 331-5
Corbridge, S. 35
Corden, W.M. 20-1, 36, 222, 232, 237, 239, 241, 244-5, 247, 251
Cotterill, R.W. 276, 287
Coulson, A. 348
credit
    agricultural 274
    market, Chile 119-26

markets and population growth;
Bangladesh 98-9
see also capital
crop breeding 309-18
Crosson, P.R. 127-8
Crotty, R. 177
Cummings, J.T. 278, 287
customs union, South African 213,
216

Dalrymple, D.D. 324
Davidson, B. 203
Davies, R.W. 277, 287
Davis, J.M. 248, 251
Davis, R.W. 350
Davis, T.E. 107, 115, 128
de Melo, M.H. 133, 150
decentralisation of government ser-
vices 47-8
demographic responses, Bangladesh
92-5
dependency approach, Malaysia 155-7
Dessouki, A.E.H. 268-9
Dias, G.M. 287
Dick, H. 245, 248, 251
direct production linkages 200
diversification in rubber smallholdings
153
Domar, E. 339, 348
domestic
policies effect on Brazil 131-49
research 311-19
Dominican Republic, Dutch disease in
234-5
Dorner, P. 36, 303
Dos Santos, T. 204
Drabble, J.H. 164-5, 176
Drobny, A. 150
D' Silva, B.C.D. 287
Duarte, J.C. 149
Dumont, R. 65
Dutch disease in developing countries
19-22, 232, 234-52
diagnosis of 236-9
treatment, reasons for 246-7

Ecevit, Z.H. 268
education in Brazil 132
Egypt
Dutch disease and 237
migration from 256, 265-6
Ellis, F. 368
Ellis, G.M. 112
Emelyanov, A.M. 349

Emmanuel 228
employment categories, Ghana 193-5
see also labour
Englander, A.S. 27-8, 309, 325, 396
equilibrium theory 159
Eriksen, T.L. 216
Etienne 287
Euler's theorem 224
European Economic Community
agricultural policies 276-8
effect on Brazil 131, 134, 140-4
Evenson, R.E. 324-5
exchange rate protection 247-9
expenditure family, Brazil 138
exports
agricultural 234-5, 245; Brazil 135;
Peru 292-3, 297, 305; Tanzania
356, 358
Dutch disease and 234-52
mining 234-5, 237-8, 241-2, 245-7;
Namibia 206
of primary products: Africa 56-7,
61, 63-4; neglected in Chile
107; *see also* Ghana
petroleum 234-5, 237-8, 241-2, 247
primary models of 18-19, 218-33;
Hansen 219-23; industrialisation and 228-32; Ricardian
223-8
'extended primary sector' 45-6
extensive margin, Bangladesh 93-4

factor market imperfections *see* Chile
family size and income 79, 81
farm size
Chile 109-13, 125
Ghana 191
income and 81
Malaysia 153-4, 163, 171-2, 174-5
see also land tenure
Fechter, A. 268-9
Feder, E. 35, 120, 127-8
Fei, J.C.H. 44-5, 49, 54, 279, 287
fertility rate, Bangladesh 92
Fields, G.S. 149
Figart, D.M. 176
Findlay, R. 18-19, 36, 176, 218-19,
232-3, 246, 396
Finkler, K. 288
fiscal linkages 182-3
see also taxation
Fisher, A.G.B. 1, 35
Fishblow, A. 132-3, 144, 149-50
food availability, Chile 108;

see also self-sufficiency; subsistence agriculture
foreign
  aid 80-2, 237
  investment: Ghana 195, 198-9; South Vietnam 371-4
  ownership: Africa 57-8; Brazil 138; Malaysia 154-6, 162, 167
  remittances and incomes, Ghana 185-8, 190
Fryer, D.W. 164, 176

Galeski, B. 347
Ganguli, B. 103
Georgescu-Roegen, N. 330, 347
Ghana
  Dutch disease in 235-7; *1956-69* 16-17, 181-205; cocoa farming 182-3, 191-7; linkages and leakages in mining and cocoa 197-202; mining 182-90
Ghatak, S. 35
Gillis, M. 36
Golabian, H. 282, 288
Góngora, M. 119, 128
Gordon, S. 203-4
Goreux, L.M. 269
government support and policy 90-1
  Bangladesh, need for 94, 100, 102
  Brazil *see* international *below*
  Chile 105, 107, 118
  Dutch disease and 239, 247-50
  Ghana 189, 190, 195-7
  international and domestic; effect on Brazil 131-49
  Malaysia 167-8, 173-4
  Namibia 212-14
  Peru 297-302
  Tanzania 352-5
  training and research 320-4
  see also intervention
'Green Revolution' 309, 319
  Malaysia 153, 170
  South Vietnam 372
Griffin, K. 30, 35-6, 123, 128
Grigg, D.B. 35, 90, 93, 102-3
gross domestic product
  agricultural 279; South Vietnam 371; Tanzania 355
  booming commodities and 234
  Jordan 261
  Kenya 68
  Namibia 206, 215
  Peru 292-5

Grossman, H. 269
growth
  retarded by export booms 236-8, 242-3
  stagnation and, *see* Malaysia
Guggisberg, Governor 201
Gumbel, E.J. 324
Gunnarson, C. 14-15, 152, 176-7, 397
Gupta, S. 251

Hansen, B. 18-19, 36, 219, 232
  model 219-24
Harberger, A.C. 241-2, 245, 251
Harris, J.S. 44, 49, 54, 83
Hartwell, R.M. 3, 35
Haugerud, A. 83
Heckscher-Ohn in theory 159, 218, 258-61
Hedlund, H. 349
Hedlund, S. 30-1, 329, 347-9, 397
Helleiner, G.K. 176
Herrick, B.H. 128
Hettne, B. 36
Hicks 224
Hill, P. 191, 203, 275
hired labour
  Bangladesh 97
  Chile 113
  Ghana 192-3
  Kenya, agriculture 80
  see also labour
Hirschman, A. 16, 36, 181, 198, 202-3, 251
Hoffman, R. 149
Hopkins, A.G. 183, 185, 203
Horesh, E. 16-17, 181, 397
Hossain, M. 103
households
  agricultural, Brazil 138, 140
  income of, Kenya 69-79, 81
Howard, R. 203
Hurtado Ruíz-Tagle, C. 128
Hydén, G. 349
Hymer, S. 203

imports
  Brazil 131, 135
  food, Africa 60-2
  Ghana 197, 200
  South Vietnam 372
incentives
  income distribution 50-1
  modelling of 80
  price Bangladesh 100

income
distribution 49-52; Brazil 13-14,
131-52; Kenya, comparisons
69-79, 81; Malaysia 171-2;
Namibia 209-11; Peru 300-1,
307; reform and incentives
50-1; services, catalytic role
51-2
Ghana 185-7, 189, 193-5, 197
mining: Ghana 185-8, 190; Namibia 208-11
stagnation *see* Bangladesh
see also leakages
India
agriculture 275, 310
migration to Malaysia 161
indirect linkages 201-2
Indonesia, Dutch disease in 234-5, 238,
240-3
industrialisation 49, 64, 90
Africa 56, 59, 63
Peru 297, 299
resource-based 228-32
industry
Brazil 133, 136-7, 139
Chile 105, 107, 114-15, 117
models of primary exports 221-2,
225, 227-8
Namibia 211-12, 214-15
see also mining
infrastructure
improvement, Ghana 201
rural, poor: Africa 59-63; Bangladesh 94
Ingersent, K. 35
Ingham, B. 203
Innis, H.A. 219
input
subsidies, Tanzania 363-4
supply constraints Tanzania 361-2
institutional longevity, excessive 276-7
intensive margin, Bangladesh 94-5
'intermediate primary sector labour
surplus' 45
international policies, effect on Brazil
131-49
intervention, agricultural 25-6, 273-90
hazards of 275-7
limitations of 277-82
regulatory policies for stability
282-6
scope of 274-5
see also government
investment

agricultural 90, 275; Peru 298-9;
Tanzania 360
Brazil 139
government project 281
Ireland, N.J. 348
irrigation
Middle East 267, 283
Peru 297
South Vietnam 382
Sudan 276, 283
Israel, agriculture, cooperation in
331-2, 333-5, 343-6
Israelsen, D. 336, 338, 348
Ivory Coast, Dutch disease in 235,
245, 248

Jabbar, M.A. 103
Jaber, K. 268
Jackson, J.C. 164, 176
Jamaica, Dutch disease in 235-6
Jamieson, B. 325
Japan 382
Joekes, S. 16-17, 181, 397
Johnson, A.L.H. 127-8
Johnson, C.W. 324
Johnson, H.G. 36
Johnston, B.F. 35
Jones, R.W. 223, 232
Jordan, migration and remittances
22-3, 253-70
Jorgenson, D. 44, 54
Just 288

Kalinkin, A. 349
Karcz, J. 348
Kenen, P.B. 269
Kennedy, J. 291, 298
Kenya 320, 323
Dutch disease in 234, 236, 245, 248
smallholders 8-9, 66-83; agriculture
67-9; households, modelling 80;
income comparisons 69-79, 81
Khamis, S. 368
Kiguel, M. 228
Killick, T. 187, 203
Kinsey, B.H. 287
Kirwan, F. 22-3, 253, 255, 268, 397
Kislev, Y. 324
Knowles, L. 176
Knudsen, O. 36
Korea 133-4, 382
Dutch disease in 241
migration from 253
Kotey, R.A. 203

Krassowski, A. 203
Kraus, J. 203-4
Krauss, M.B. 269
Krueger, A.O. 36
Kuznets, S. 35

Labour
  market: Bangladesh 97-8; Chile 113-19, 124
  mining: Ghana 185; Namibia 210
  organisation, Ghana 191-2
  socialisation of *see* cooperation
  surplus: and types of primary sector 45-6; pool 239-40
  unlimited supply model 223
  utilisation and land in Malaysia 160-1
  see also employment; hired labour
Ladd, G.W. 324
land
  concentration, Chile 109-13
  labour utilisation and, Malaysia 160-1
  /man ratios 95, 101, 125
  markets 283-4; and population growth, Bangladesh 96-7
  resettlement and expansion, Malaysia 168-73
  tenure and reform 50-1, 90, 274; Bangladesh 96-7; Chile 108-13, 124-6; Kenya 64, 74, 79; Peru 291-3, 296-7, 301-6; South Vietnam 376-82
  unlimited supply model 223
  see also agriculture; farm size
landowners
  Brazil 140
  Chile 109-19
  Malaysia 156
  Peru 293, 303-4
  South Vietnam 379
Langoni, C.G. 132, 144, 149-50
Latin America
  Dutch disease in 234-6, 238, 241-3, 245, 247-9
  industrialisation 64
  population density 59
  see also Bolivia; Brazil; Chile; Peru
Law, P.J. 348
Le Duan 391, 393
Le Khoa 377, 381, 392-3
Le Nhat Quang 393
Le Thu Y 392-3
Le Vinh 392

leakages in mining and cocoa, Ghana 181-3, 199-200
  see also income
Lee, E. 177
Lee, G. 176
Leff 134, 150
Leibenstein, H. 102
Leland 285
Lenin, V.I. 347, 349
Levin, J. 210, 216
Lewin, M. 347-8
Lewis, W.A. 36, 43, 45, 49, 54, 103, 163, 176, 223, 232, 244, 248, 251
linkages in mining and cocoa, Ghana 181-3, 197-9, 200-2
Lipton, M. 4, 35, 330, 347
Little, I. 36
Livingstone, I. 35
Lobdell, R.A. 268
Loveman, B.E. 110, 114, 127-8
Lundborg, P. 13-14, 131, 133, 135, 140, 150, 397
Lundgren, N.G. 176
Lundahl, M. 1, 11-12, 35, 105, 127, 349, 397

MacBean, A.I. 36
Macedo, R.B.M. 133, 150
MacLaren, D. 276, 287
Malaysia 232
  Dutch disease in 234, 236, 241
  rubber smallholders, growth and stagnation 14-15, 152-78, 278; Chinese settlers 164-5, 167, 175; dependency approach 155-7; expansion, early 152, 154-5; growth, effects on smallholdings 169-74; growth, limits to 165-6; growth, mechanisms of 162-4; poverty, expansion of 166-9; statistical picture 153-4; structural change, need for 174-6; vent for surplus theory 157-61, 164
Maletnlema, T.N. 368
Mali, agriculture 276
Malthus, T. 9-10
  population theory 87-8, 92, 101-2
Mamalakis, M. 3-4, 8, 35-6, 43, 54, 107-8, 206, 216, 398
man/land ratio 95, 101, 125
Maneschi, A.Z. 219, 232
Manu, J.E.A. 203
market

credit, Chile 124-6
imperfections *see* Chile
incentives, need for 50
labour, Chile 124
land 283-4
marketing, Tanzania 365-6
Matos Mar, J. 48, 54, 307
Mayer, T. 251
McBride, G.M. 127
McHale, T. 163, 176
McKinnon, R.I. 36
Meesok, A. 133, 150
Meier, G.M. 35
Mejía, J.M. 48, 54, 307
Mellor, J.W. 35
Melton, B. 324
Mexico agriculture 276, 280-1, 283,
    304, 319
Dutch disease in 234-5, 238, 241-3
Middle East, migration and remit-
    tances 22-3, 253-70
economic welfare and 258-61
macroeconomic impact of 261-7
migration
    Africa 63, 66, 81
    Brazil 136-7, 143
    Chile 115
    Middle East 22-3, 240, 253-70
    to Malaysia 161, 164-5, 167, 175
Mill, J.S. 157
mining
    Africa 58, 64
    Chile 114-15, 117
    exports 234-5, 237-8, 241-2, 245-7
    Ghana 182-90; employment and
        labour 185; foreigners, income
        and remittances 185-7; govern-
        ment, payments to 190; income
        distribution 187-8, 190; mining
        companies, profits and remit-
        tances 186, 188, 190
    Jordan 255
    see also Namibia
Miracle, M.P. 203
monopoly in Chile
    land-ownership 109-13, 126
    moneylenders 121-3
monopsony power in labour market,
    Chile 113-19
Moody, D.L. 392
Moris, J.R. 74, 83
Morley, S.A. 132, 149-50
Mottin, M.F. 65
Msambichaka, L.A. 31-3, 352, 368,
    398

Mudge, J. 368
multinationals 58
multiple cropping 91
    Bangladesh, rice 93, 102
Mushi, S. 349
Myint, H. 36, 157, 176, 203, 219,
    232

Namibia, political economy 17-18,
    206-17
    development and trade policy 212-14
    industrial and agricultural pro-
        motion 214-15
    rents, mining: capturing 206-9;
        income distribution and devel-
        opment 209-11; norms and
        industrial strategies 211-12
Ndulu, B. 31-3, 352, 368, 398
Neary, P. 20-1, 36, 251
Netherlands *see* Dutch disease
Newbery, D.G. 36
Ngo Dinh Diem 378
Ngo Vinh Long 393
Nguyen Tien Hung 392
Nigeria, Dutch disease in 235-6, 238,
    240, 242-3
Nisbet, C. 121, 123, 125, 128
non-agriculture
    Brazil 133, 136-7, 139
    see also industry
non-rural sector
    Bangladesh 40, 99-102
Nørlund, I. 393
'North-South' models of trade and
    growth 228
Nove, A. 335, 348
Nurkse, R. 16, 36, 53-4
Nyerere, J. 332-3, 341-3, 346-7, 367-8

Oberai, A.S. 268-9
Oi, W. 348
Ojala, E.M. 273, 286
Okali, C. 194, 203
OPEC countries 253
    see also Middle East
output
    agricultural 357-9; Brazil 135-6;
        Chile 105-8, 123-7; Malaysia
        152, 154-62, 169-74; Peru
        292-3, 306; South Vietnam
        376-8, 387-9; input model,
        Brazil 132
    population growth and 88-9;
        Bangladesh 92, 95

pricing 362-3
stagnation *see* Chile
technological change and 88-9, 91
see also production

Pakistan, migration from 253, 256
Parnes, A. 36
Pasinetti, L. 219, 232
Paterson, D.B. 83
Peacock, F. 176
peasant
    enclave in Ghana 191
    'mode of production' 156
Peru, agriculture reform 26-7, 291-308
    income distribution 300-1
    poverty, rural 301-6
    problem, agrarian 292-3
    stagnation: causes of 293-8; reform
        and 299-300
petroleum exports 234-5, 237-8, 241-2,
    247
Petty, W. 2
Pfefferman, G.P. 134
Pham Van Dong 393
Philippines, Dutch disease in 236, 241
Pinstrup-Anderson, P. 36
policies *see* government
population
    density 90; Africa 59, 63; Asia 59;
        Latin America 59
    growth: Africa 63; Bangladesh,
        negative effects of 95-9; Malay-
        sia 166-7, 171, 175; and output
        88-9, 92, 95, 105; Peru 292
Porter, G. 379, 393
Pospielovsky, D. 349
poverty
    Brazil 133-4
    Malaysia 166-9
    Peru 301-6
Prebifch, R. 36, 228
prices
    agricultural 276-9, 285, 305
    booming commodities 235
    incentives, Bangladesh 100
    intervention 277-9
    minerals 208
    oil 234-5, 253
    output 362-3
    policies, Bangladesh 90
    primary exports 228, 230
    reform 50-1
    rubber 173
    stabilisation 285

production and primary sector 44-9
    concepts of 44-5, 53
    labour surplus 45-6
    revolutions 47-9
production functions 137-8
productivity *see* output
public support *see* government
Putterman, L. 330, 336, 342-3, 346-9

Race, J. 393
Radwan, S. 288
Ranis, G. 44-5, 49, 54, 279, 287
Raup, P.M. 347
Raza, M.R. 287
reform, income distribution 50-1
    see also land tenure and reform
refugees 254
regression, time series 278-9
remittances
    Ghana 185-8, 190, 195
    Kenya 78
    Middle East 22-3, 253-70
Rempell, H. 268
rents, mining *see* Namibia
research, agriculture 280
resources
    allocation for agricultural develop-
        ment, Tanzania 360-1
    base preservation 285-61
    base industrialisation 228-32
    mineral, Namibia 206-7, 215
    movement effect of booming sector
        237-8
    Peru 292
    revolutions in primary sector 47-9
Reynolds, C.W. 127
Rhoades, R. 269
Ricardian concepts 18, 208-9, 218, 222
    model 223-8
    theories rent 208-9, 215
rice (wet cultivation) 90-1
    Bangladesh 92, 94-5, 101
    South Vietnam 387
Rivera-Batiz, F. 36, 258, 269
Robertson, A.F. 203
Robinson, J. 226
Robinson, S. 133, 150
Robinson, W. 102-3
Roemer, M. 20-1, 36, 229, 233-4, 398
Rourke, B.E. 203
rubber smallholders *see* Malaysia
Rudner, M. 177
rural revolution 47
rural urban model 44, 49

migration *see* migration
resource flow, Bangladesh 100
Ruttan, V.W. 325

Saadat, O. 287
Saavedra-Rivano, N. 228
Sako, B. 276, 287
Sakyi-Gyinae, S.K. 203
Sanders, T.G. 287
Sandmo 285
Sansom, R.L. 378, 380, 393
savings 52-3
  Brazil 139
  Ghana 185, 197
Schultz, T.W. 36, 43, 54, 324
Schutjer, W. 102-3
Schwartz, A. 269
Scitovsky, T. 36
Scott, M. 36
self-sufficiency, food in South Viet-
    nam 375, 389-90
Sen, A. 348
Serageldin, I. 269
services 43-7
  catalytic role of 51-2
  Chile 117
  revolution 48-9, 51
sex distribution of agricultural work
    60, 97
share cropping 113-15, 283
Shaw, R.P. 269
Simon, J.L. 35, 103
Simpson, I. 25, 273, 287, 398
simulations of effects of
  international and domestic policies
    on Brazil 131-49
Sinclair, C.A. 255, 268-9
Singer, H.W. 36, 228
Singh, H.K.M. 268-9
Smith, A. 43, 157-8
Socknat, J.A. 268-9
Södersten, B. 17-18, 206, 216-17, 398
South Vietnam: agriculture in transi-
    tion to socialism 33-4, 370-95
  National Development Strategy
    370-5
  1960-75 375-82
  after *1975* 382-91
Soviet Union 278, 331-3, 336-7, 339-
    41, 344, 346, 374
specialisation *see* vent for surplus
'specific factors' model of primary
    exports 222-3
spending effect of booming sector 237

Spraos, J. 36
Squire, L. 83, 278, 287
stagnation
  agricultural *see* Chile; Peru;
    Malaysia
  income *see* Bangladesh
Stalin, J. 336-7, 340, 346, 349
'staple theory' of primary exports 219
Stavenhagen, R. 35
Stiglitz, J.E. 36
subsidies, agricultural, Africa 61
subsistence agriculture
  Africa 56, 59-61
  Kenya 73-4
  Ghana 192
  Malaysia 155-9
  primary exports of cash crops and
    219-22, 224, 227
'subsistence equilibrium level' 87
Sudan irrigation 276, 283
Swanson, J.C. 267, 269
Swift, J. 129
Swynnerton plan, Kenya 66, 74
Szal, R. 150
Szereszewski, R. 191, 203-4

Tabah, L. 65
Tanzania 236
  agriculture cooperation in 331-3,
    336, 341-3, 345-6
  agricultural development (*1961-82*)
    31-3, 352-69; constraints 360-6;
    performance of 357-9; role in
    economic development 352-7
Tavares, M.C. 149
taxation
  agricultural 90, 274
  Ghana 182-3, 190, 198-9
  see also fiscal
Taylor, L. 133, 140, 149-50
technology
  agricultural: Tanzania 361-2; South
    Vietnam 380
  change output and 88-9, 91
  transfer 309-18
Thailand 232
  Dutch disease in 234, 236, 241
Thieu regime 372, 376, 379
Thoburn, J. 176, 203
Thomas, V. 36, 287
Thorp, R. 297, 307
Timmer, C.P. 241-2, 245, 251
Todaro, M.P. 44, 49, 54, 83
Tolley, G.S. 36, 287

trade, international
  Malaysian output and 157-9
  Namibia 212-14, 216
  Tran Huu Chang 381, 393
  transfers, income, Kenya 69, 73, 76-7
transport 201
  improvement: Africa 57-60, 62-3;
    need for 49, 60, 62-3

ul Haque, I. 244, 251
unions, rural, Chile 115-16, 118
United Kingdom, agriculture 279
United States 237
  agriculture 277, 279; policies effect
    on Brazil 131, 140-4
  in South Vietnam 371-2, 380
  urban-rural model *see* rural-urban

Valentine, T.R. 368
Van Gigh, F. 287
Van Wijnbergen, S. 246-7, 251
Vanek, J. 348
Veiga, A. 134, 150
Venezuela, Dutch disease in 235-6,
  238, 242-3, 247, 249
vent for surplus theory 157-61, 164
  219
Vincent, D. 251

Viner-Ricardo model 222
Vo Chi Cong 386
von Doellinger, C. 134, 150
Voom Phin Keong 177
Vylder, S. de 216

Wade 287
wages incomes, Kenya 69, 72-3, 75-7
Wallace, T. 287
Wallerstein, I. 204
Ward, B. 339, 348
Watkins, M.H. 36
Webb, R. 134
Weintraub, D. 347, 349
Weisskoff, R. 182, 203
Wells, J. 149-50
Wesson, R. 347
White, C.P. 392-3
Williamson, J.G. 132, 149-50
Wolff, E. 182, 203
Wong, C.M. 36, 287
Wooton, I. 228
Worsley, P. 282, 288
Wright, A. 346, 349
Wronski, H. 349

Yates, P.L. 288

Zambia, Dutch disease in 237, 249